TREES IN THE SNOW

Trees in the Snow

by

Eva Smiller

With Michael Lehrman

Colonnade

Copyright © 2019 by Michael Lehrman
All rights reserved. No part of this book may be reproduced, scanned,
or distributed in any printed or electronic form without permission.

First Edition, October 2019
ISBN 978-1-7334572-1-7

Published by Colonnade, New York
Direct inquiries to:
contact@colonnade.online

Library of Congress Control Number: 2019913282

The epigraph on the next page has been excerpted under the Creative Commons license from Barry Mitchell's translation of Schubert/Müller's *Winterreise;* "*Schubert's Wanderers*" by Barry Mitchell, Theory of Music, London 2014

Picture credits further in the book constitute an extension of the copyright page.

As a stranger I arrived
As a stranger I shall leave
I remember a perfect day in May
How bright the flowers
How cool the breeze

CONTENTS

ACKNOWLEDGMENTS ... i

PREFACE ... iii

BOOK I   1

HOUSE ON THE HILL   3

1. Father's Return ... 3
2. The Famine ... 5
3. High Holidays ... 7
4. Bookstore Inventory ... 10
5. Letter to Molotov ... 12
6. Komsomol Affair ... 14
7. Dental School ... 16

THE CONQUEST   19

1. German Butter ... 19
2. Work Brigades ... 21
3. Liquidation ... 23
4. Dr. Lebow and Manya ... 25
5. Kitchen Garden ... 27
6. Uncle's Address ... 29

    7. Undesirables 32

    8. Father's Death 35

    9. Birth Certificate 38

TOWN AND COUNTRY   43

    1. Cover Story 43

    2. Multicolored Shawl 45

    3. Frostbites 51

    4. Doctor's Appointment 55

    5. Honey Cake 59

    6. Trees in the Snow 63

    7. Sviatoshyno Misfortune 66

    8. Cold Spell 68

    9. Captured (1943) 74

    10. Breakout 78

KITCHEN HELPER   83

    1. Job Fair 83

    2. The Wardrobe 87

    3. Zum Dortmunder 90

    4. Escape from Berlin 94

    5. Dormitory Trip 98

    6. Back to Business 100

    7. Red General 103

    8. The Fall of the Town 105

THE RUSSIAN ZONE   107

   1. New Career 107

   2. Special Assignment 110

   3. Car Accident 113

   4. Proposal 115

   5. Homecoming 118

ILLUSTRATIONS   121

BOOK II   129

PREAMBLE   131

DAY AFTER DAY   137

   1. The Courtyard 137

   2. Sanatorium Lermontovsky 142

   3. Apartment Exchange 146

   4. Uncle Zachary and Aunt Rose 150

   5. Boarding School 158

   6. Summer Time 163

   7. Security Clearance 167

   8. Postgraduate Distribution 175

   9. Moscow Vacations 183

THE BOARDING SCHOOL   185

   1. Primer 185

   2. First Impressions 187

 3. Keeping Promises 190

 4. Teacher's Chair 194

 5. Parking Space 198

 6. Full Board 201

 7. General's Daughter 205

 8. The Pitcher 208

 9. Pickle Factory 211

THE OTHER SIDE   213

 1. Provenance 213

 2. Family Photograph 217

 3. Old Watch 223

 4. Lucky Break 228

RETURN TO CHUDNOV   233

 1. Personal Salary 233

 2. Kidney Stone 236

 3. Bed and Breakfast 241

 4. Ranger's Farm 244

 5. Tall Grass 250

 6. Disclosure 253

 7. Nadja's Letter 256

THE RUPTURE   257

 1. Tectonic Shift 257

 2. Prince of Order 259

   3. Political Education 265

   4. Physical Exam 272

   5. Exchange Rate 277

   6. The Parting 281

EN ROUTE   285

   1. Across the Barricade 285

   2. Vienna Connection 288

   3. Champagne and Caviar 291

   4. Briefness of Stay 297

   5. Road to Rome 298

   6. Anna's Inn 301

   7. Engineers 303

   8. Rental Blues 305

   9. Balcony Apartment 308

   10. Sharing Arrangements 312

   11. Flea Market 315

   12. Political Divide 319

   13. Arrivederci Roma 322

THE NEW WORLD   329

   1. Long Day 329

   2. Hotel Lucerne 332

   3. Cityscape 338

   4. Furniture Store 342

5. Classified Ad	348
6. Wedding Anniversary	353

FULL CIRCLE 359

1. Associate in Arts	359
2. Baby Bird	370
3. Transit Strike	373
4. Corporate Lounge	376
5. People's Court	380
6. Medical History	383
7. Co-op	387
8. The House on the Hill	389

KADDISH 393

ILLUSTRATIONS 397

ACKNOWLEDGMENTS

My special thanks to Jerome Rosenstock for reading the first draft and for his advice and encouragement. I also want to thank Boris Feldblyum, Michael Foygel, Nadya Frid, Michael Gerenrot, Alexander Gofen, Dimitri Leshchenko, Claire Plager, and Lauren Rosenstock for their suggestions and additional materials.

– Michael Lehrman –

PREFACE

In the "Preamble" section of the second book of this title (which consists of two books), I describe the title's writing history in more detail, but here, I will briefly introduce the authors and explain the organization of the entire work.

Eva Smiller is my mother (by her birth name). She was fifteen years old and living in a small town in the Ukrainian northwest (then a part of the Soviet Union) when the area was overrun by Hitler's armies. In the following few months, the town's Jewish population of fifteen hundred people was executed, including my mother's family, but she survived the carnage. For the next two years, she wandered under an assumed name over the occupied Ukrainian territory, starved, almost froze to death, got arrested as a suspected Jew, and eventually ended up in Nazi Germany's Berlin, where she worked in a restaurant and lived with the family of its owners until the arrival of the Soviets. After the war's end, she remained in Germany for two more years, working as a translator for the Soviet military administration, then returned to the USSR. Her own account of that journey is presented in the first book.

The second book brings the storyline towards more recent times and is written by me, except for the first ("Day after Day") chapter, which also contains my mother's text. She continued her chronicle into the post-German period but did not progress very far; hence, I included that segment in the first (joint) chapter of the second book. There, her writing is interspersed with mine, laying the groundwork for the succeeding sections. Throughout these two volumes, a separate font is used for each narration—my mother's and mine—and in the second book's joint chapter, my mother's text is boxed over a shaded background to further differentiate between her and my lines. The joint chapter starts and ends with my mother's words. After that, I felt it was appropriate to pause—and wrote the next chapter ("The Boarding School") as an interlude. It is an organic part of the reading experience, yet does not advance the plot. The momentum returns in the following sections, driving the story to its conclusion.

– Michael Lehrman –

BOOK I

Trees in the Snow

by Eva Smiller

Translated, edited, and annotated
by Michael Lehrman

Chapter 1

HOUSE ON THE HILL

1. Father's Return

My aware life began when I was five years old. I remember myself as a child living with my mother and twin sisters in one room of a house in the little town of Chudnov of the Vinnitsa oblast (province) in Ukraine (later, Chudnov became a part of Zhitomir Oblast). The house belonged to my paternal grandmother. It stood on a hill between the main road and a narrow street. The street led to the farmers' market in one direction and to the Teterev River in another. The river separated the old and the new sections of the town. We lived in the old section.

Grandmother's house was old, too, and in need of repairs, which were never done. A hallway with a clay floor divided the house into two parts; each part had two rooms, and one part had a kitchen. My family lived in the part without a kitchen, in a larger of two rooms. In a smaller room, lived my grandmother. The dividing hallway had a Russian stove[1] with a small table next to it. The other part of the house was occupied by my father's sister, Aunt Baila, with her husband and three sons.

I did not remember my father and only heard from the adults that he was alive and serving a five-year prison sentence in the far north of the Soviet Union. Occasionally, I was told that a letter from my father had arrived; however, in my mind as a child, my father's absence did not sit well. I could not understand what prison was and why my father lived there and not with us. What I did understand: my mother's life was very difficult. Sometimes, when waking up at night, I saw her cooking, doing laundry, or cleaning the house. During the day, she worked at a produce

---

[1] A cube-shaped brick stove fired by coal and wood. Kind of a masonry heater.

warehouse, sorting vegetables. She had to leave early in the morning; the warehouse was far away, and she walked there for over an hour. She returned late at night and started the home chores. Not much time was left for her to sleep.

As I grew a little older, my mother told me about her family. Her mother died young, leaving behind a husband, two daughters, and four sons. My mother was the oldest daughter, and all the homemaker's responsibilities fell on her shoulders. In the early nineteen-twenties, her father, with the rest of the family, emigrated to the United States. By then, my mother was married and expecting a child[2]. She could not go with her father and siblings. It was decided she would join them in America after giving birth, with her husband and the newborn. Sadly, the reunion did not happen: the Bolshevik government sealed the border, parting my mother and her family for the rest of their lives. My mother took the separation hard. She cried often, especially missed her father, whom she adored.

And so we lived with the grandmother in two rooms, waiting for my father's release. I was two years old, and my sisters were just born when my father was arrested and put in jail. What was his crime? My father loved horses and was an expert in that field. He frequently traveled to Poland, bought horses from breeders there, took the animals back to Zhitomir, and sold them to local farmers. He knew all the crossings and the countryside and continued his trade even after the Soviets shut the border. Someone reported my father's activities to the police; he got arrested, tried for contraband (a political crime in those times), and was sentenced to five years of hard labor. He was sent to the "famous" Solovki prison above the Arctic Circle, with the consequent ban on living in Chudnov.

I was already seven years old and slept in the grandmother's room one night when my mother woke me up and took me to the larger room. The larger room was full of people. My mother brought me in front of a thin, light-haired, balding man and said, "This is your father." The man hugged and kissed me; he sat me on his lap and handed me a present: a small leather wallet. The smell of new leather unpleasantly struck my senses; I threw the wallet on the table, ran out of the room, and began to cry. I did not want this man, a complete stranger, to be my father and live with us in the same room. But soon, he became the dearest, the most important person in my life.

---

[2] The child did not survive.

2. The Famine

Before my father's release, I attended kindergarten. I was a shy, quiet girl, well-liked by the teachers and the staff. After kindergarten, I entered the first grade of a Jewish school. Such schools still existed in the Soviet Union then, but in my second grade, the authorities closed the Jewish school and transferred its students to a Russian one. I was very nervous. At home, we spoke Yiddish; I was afraid I would not be able to answer in Russian if asked something by a teacher. I couldn't sleep at night because of those fears, and every school trip was a trial… The situation at home was also bad. My father was summoned to the local police station and ordered to leave Chudnov immediately. "Go wherever you want. Your family? Not our concern." My father said, "All right," and walked out of the police station, but did not leave the town and went into hiding. Now, we were worried he might get arrested and sent back to prison. All those troubles made me reticent and jumpy. There was nobody to speak with, to ask for advice. But then I had a dream that I remembered all my life. In that dream, I spoke Russian fluently and with joy. The next morning, I went to school for the first time in a good mood and had no issues there since. I did well in the Russian language and other subjects, becoming the first student in my class and a favorite of our class teacher[3], a young, amicable man who had come to our school right after college.

Despite my successes in school, the atmosphere in our house affected me badly. I did not want to go home after classes and would rather be somewhere else. My mother cried all the time. My father was hiding in his friends' homes during the day, sneaking in to see his family at night. He risked being arrested and jailed for violating his residency ban as police informants watched our house. My sisters and I were afraid to go to bed at night, trembling with fear when we heard a knock on the door.

The year 1933 brought famine. The economy was at its lowest; people were dying of starvation and disease. Everything was rationed, and there were long lines to buy bread and everything else that appeared on store shelves. One was lucky to reach the front of the line and not get ejected by the angry, belligerent mob. The line formed in the evening, and people waited all night for the store to open in the morning.

In Chudnov, opened a *Torgsin*[4] store, where food and clothing could be purchased for foreign currency (dollars, pounds, marks) and gold. My mother's father died in America in 1931, but her siblings continued to

---

[3] The teacher in charge of the class.

[4] A contraction of the Russian "Trade with Foreigners."

help us. They were sending parcels with Boston fabric, cocoa cans, and other items. The blue Boston was in high demand and could be sold on the flea market for good money. Besides the parcels, every letter from America included a few dollar bills. The dollars could be exchanged for roubles at the bank or used to buy directly from Torgsin. Without that help, it would have been difficult for us to survive those hard times… One day, after receiving a letter from America, my mother gave me an envelope to play with. I was sick with chickenpox and very restless. The envelope was colorful and pretty, with stamps and postage marks. I took scissors and started cutting the envelope, trying to make a fringe on its edges. I will never forget my mother's desperation and uncontrollable sobs when she discovered that, with the envelope, I had shredded a few dollar bills accidentally left inside.

My mother bought mainly food in Torgsin. Clothing was expensive there, so we wore clothes that were old, used, or sent to us by American relatives. One day, I learned that our local store had received a shipment of viscose fabric and decided to contribute to the family's struggle. My mother gave me the money, and I went to the store to join the forming line. The limit was two dress lengths per head. It was illegal to assemble at night, so the police tried to disperse the crowd, but as soon as the policemen left, the line reassembled again. I spent all night hiding from the police, together with other shoppers, who were mostly women. Men did not stand in a line—they would come at the store's opening and try to force their way inside… In the morning, the store opened, and the tussle began. I was pushed, shoved, and squeezed between enormous bodies, yet fought with my entire child's strength to remain in the line. Despite my efforts, I was ejected. I cried, begged to let me back in the line, but nobody paid attention to the crying girl. I returned home empty-handed, tired, and deeply hurt. I went to bed and slept all day and the following night. My mother did not console me, and I felt rejected and lonely. I remembered that feeling all my life.

The famine and cold winter took many lives in Chudnov and across the country, but in our family, nobody died. Moreover, thanks to the help of her brothers in America, my mother was able to give some food to the children of our relatives and neighbors.

3. High Holidays

The grandmother was a religious woman, and everyone in her house adhered to the rules of the Jewish faith. My mother maintained a kosher kitchen. Every Friday, she got up at two in the morning and baked *halla, kishleki, kashneki,* and other dishes for the coming Sabbath. When my sisters and I woke up before school, we were treated to our favorite meal: freshly baked *popoliki*[5] with chicken fat and sweet tea. It was the most delicious breakfast.

Before the Sabbath, a samovar was polished to a high shine, and the house was thoroughly cleaned. On Saturday, nobody did any work. In the morning, grandmother headed for a synagogue; my mother sometimes accompanied her. Passover, we celebrated with great festivity. A beautiful china set was brought from the attic. Matzos were prepared in advance. I remember my mother making matzos by hand, but later, the authorities allowed the town's bakery to make matzos from clients' flour a couple of days per week, beginning a few months before Passover. On those days, the line formed in the evening, and people waited all night to have their matzos baked.

The first and second Seders were conducted with proper decorum. Sitting high on the pillows at the head of the table, my father said a prayer. The specially prepared food was very tasty. As difficult as our life was, holidays were observed with great devotion and joy. It was possible to some degree because of the help from our American relatives, who remembered their left-behind sister, particularly during the high holidays. Right before Passover, my sisters and I received new dresses and shoes. My grandmother and mother attended holiday services in the synagogue, where they reserved seats in advance. As for my father, he never showed up there for fear of being arrested.

Beyond holidays, the circumstances and mood at home were bad. My mother sorted vegetables at the warehouse all day, starting a new "shift" upon coming home. My father settled in a nearby village, bought a horse with a cart, and worked for the local farmers, earning very little. He was coming to see us secretly, after dark, once or twice a week. We lived mainly on my mother's salary and the aid of American relatives. I helped my mother as much as I could—washing dishes, sweeping the floors, and doing other chores. Once a week, I would go to the river to polish the samovar. In winter, I polished it inside the house.

---

[5] Kind of bread buns.

The grandmother did not do any work. She sat all day in her room, reading the Torah. My mother cleaned the grandmother's room and did her laundry while my sisters and I served her food, cleaned the table, and washed the dishes after she ate. As grandmother's eyesight weakened, it became my responsibility to read her the Torah as well as letters from her brother in Kishinev[6] (which was a part of Romania at the time). She also dictated to me replies to those letters. To improve my Yiddish grammar so I could better satisfy the grandmother's writing needs, the family hired a woman tutor who studied with me once a week. My mother paid for the lessons out of her meager salary.

Grandmother was a healthy woman (only later did she develop poor eyesight), yet she would not lift a finger to help my mother. She believed that as long as the daughter-in-law and the grandchildren lived in her house, they had to cater to her every whim. She did not demand similar subservience from her own daughter, who lived on the other side of the house, or from three other daughters who lived nearby. She was utterly indifferent to the plight of her son and his family, which made me very angry. I hated her guts, but was not allowed to say a word. Once, I lost it and talked back. "Because I want it so," I told the grandmother when she requested to explain my disobedience. She promptly complained to my mother, who beat me so badly that bloodied my nose. I lay on the floor for almost an hour, but nobody came to comfort me. I got up and walked out of the house. I went to the river and sat there all day, returning home by nightfall. Nobody noticed my absence or showed any concern.

I did not receive much encouragement and love from my mother; on the contrary, she stifled my every endeavor. When I tried to show my affection, she turned me away, saying it was improper. She forever killed in me the desire to sing. My mother had a good singing voice and sang a lot, but when I once tried to sing in her presence, she laughed and said that my voice was better suited to cutting wood. I never sang again.

My mother loved my sisters very much, maybe because they were younger and not in good health. Ita and Gita (or Itochka and Gitochka[7]) were their names. Itochka was crosseyed, and Gitochka suffered from tuberculosis of the bone in her ankle. A few times, my mother took her to Odessa to the Black Sea, seeking a cure from mud applications, seawater,

---

[6] Throughout these volumes, geographical locations in the Soviet Union are mentioned by their Russian names habitually used in the described period. For example, Zhytomyr, Kyiv, and Chisinau, as they are officially called today, are referred to as Zhitomir, Kiev, and Kishinev.

[7] Affectionate forms of those names.

and the sun. Sadly, there was no improvement. Gitochka continued to feel pain and developed a limp... I loved and pitied my little sisters, and they were attached to me. They followed me everywhere. Sometimes, I would become annoyed and slap them gently or try to sneak out of the house unnoticed so that they wouldn't see me and tag along. They were average students, although they studied hard. I helped them as much as I could. My own grades were straight As, and I always received plaudits from the school's principal. My mother enjoyed attending the parents' meetings and hearing the praises the teachers bestowed on my grades and behavior, but she never praised me herself.

4. Bookstore Inventory

I attended the Russian school for four years, then got transferred to a Ukrainian school, the only middle school in the town. In elementary school, all the subjects were taught by the same teacher, but in middle school, different teachers taught different subjects, and one of the subject teachers (a class teacher) was in charge of the class. Subject and class teachers changed when the class advanced to the next grade. In middle school, I became a "young pioneer[8]" and, later, a "pioneer leader." The responsibilities of a pioneer leader included teaching lower-graders to be good "Leninists," helping laggards with homework, organizing meetings, school theatre programs, and so on.

In school, I studied hard, but troubles at home distracted me. Once in a while, when called to the blackboard, I was consumed by sad thoughts, couldn't concentrate, and felt my answers were not good enough; still, I received top grades. I often suspected I was getting some of those grades unfairly and felt guilty before the rest of the class, but the teachers liked me and probably overlooked some wrong answers. I was a pretty, neat girl—polite and well-behaved. I had dark eyes, rosy cheeks, and light wavy hair (the hair turned dark as I grew older). During one of those self-deprecating moments, I complained to our Russian literature teacher (who was the school's head teacher). His name was Nikolai Nikolaevich Khomenko. He was a short, middle-aged man with a bald head and dark, piercing eyes. I started telling him that I had received an A unfairly, but he interrupted me. "You are too modest," he said, "You've got what you deserved." Of course, some students reacted to the teachers' partiality toward me—girls envied me while boys teased me, calling me a "face-painting favorite" (the teasers referred to my rosy cheeks, implying that I wore makeup). That nickname stuck with me until the end of my school days. Such treatment by classmates upset me, but I kept it to myself and never complained, neither in school nor at home.

I did not have many friends in school. Among the few I had was a girl named Genya Zack. Her father died in an accident, and her mother had to work long hours to support the family. Genya spent a lot of time helping her mother at home and babysitting the children of her older sister, who also worked. Genya's family situation was somewhat similar to mine, so we became friends. Because of her circumstances, Genya had little time for homework and even less time for me. I always did my homework, and she sometimes asked me to let her copy it. I loathed cheating and felt

---

[8] A member of the "Pioneers" youth organization in the USSR.

uneasy about those requests, but couldn't say no because I pitied the girl. Still, my conscience bothered me, so I began to come to Genya's home less frequently. I also sensed that her mother was not happy with my visits, maybe because she thought I distracted Genya from her household duties. In a little while, Genya stopped coming to my house, too, and we saw each other only in school. During breaks, she copied my homework.

One time, Genya's mother offered me a chance to make some money by working a couple of nights with her daughter at a bookstore run by their acquaintance. Our job was to inventory the books, and Genya's mother promised to pay for it. The pay was minimal, yet I was thrilled by the opportunity to earn my own money and happily agreed to the terms. I spent two evenings cataloging those books while attending school and doing homework until late at night. I'm not sure about Genya, but I never received the promised pay. I waited and waited, afraid to ask, not to offend anybody, but to no avail. Alas, someone else got my money, and I suspected it was my friend's mother. I said nothing, but my friendship with Genya was over.

Meanwhile, the situation at home was getting no better. My mother toiled around the clock. My father worked in a nearby village, coming to see us once a week under the cover of darkness. One night, when he was in the house and everyone was asleep, came the police. My sisters began to cry. The policemen announced that they were arresting my father for violating the ban on staying in Chudnov. They told the rest of us to go back to sleep and took my father away. Of course, nobody in the house slept for the remainder of the night. In the morning, I didn't go to school; I went to the police station to see the police chief. The chief received me in his office. He spoke in a friendly, fatherly manner and promised to look into the matter. Two days later, my father was released, but he had to sign a pledge that he wouldn't break the "law" in the future. Of course, he continued to see us, but less frequently.

Whenever my father appeared at our door, I was happy and worried at the same time. I loved him very much. He was always kind to me. He brought me my favorite toffee sweets—we called them "irises," and my father bought boxes of them. He bought me clothes, gave me the money to go to the movies, and supplied pocket change. He was proud of my achievements at school and excited to hear teachers praising me. He dreamed of my glamorous future. He believed that his daughter was the smartest, most beautiful girl in the world. That aggravated my relations with my mother, who probably thought that my father paid less attention to her and the twins because of me, as if it were my fault.

5. Letter to Molotov

Came the year 1937, the high mark of Stalin's purges. The secret police conducted mass arrests of so-called enemies of the people. That period came to be known as Yezhovshchina, after Nikolai Yezhov, the head of the NKVD[9] at the time. Those who escaped the repressions still had many relatives, friends, and coworkers arrested on false charges and sent to labor camps or executed. The arrests were mostly conducted at night when everyone was asleep. When darkness fell, people became fearful, unsure of where they would find themselves the next morning: at home or in a prison cell.

One night, when everybody was asleep, the secret police came to arrest my uncle, Aunt Baila's husband, whose family lived on the other side of the house. My uncle was born and grew up in Poland, came to Chudnov as a young man, worked, married, and even became a member of the Communist Party. During the purges, he was labeled a spy, like many other Polish natives. Such people were frequently targeted for persecution because they had lived abroad. But my uncle outsmarted his pursuers. He anticipated the arrest and built a hideout in a storage shed outside the house. The shed contained firewood logs arranged in large cubes. My uncle cut a niche in one of the cubes, where he slept at night. He would crawl into the niche, and his wife would cover the opening with a lid made of log cuts. The lid masked the niche perfectly, so no one could tell there was a space inside. When the police came to arrest my uncle, he was in the niche, and they couldn't find him despite turning everything upside down, including our part of the house. In the morning after the police raid, my uncle disguised himself as a woman and sneaked out to his relatives' house. In a few days, he left Chudnov and settled in the city of Kerch in Crimea. In Kerch, he found a job, and two years later, when the purges eased a little, Aunt Baila, with the children, joined him. They lived in Kerch until the beginning of the Great Patriotic War. When the war started, my uncle and his oldest son were drafted into the Soviet army, and both were killed in combat. After the Germans occupied Kerch, Aunt Baila and her other two sons were captured as Jews and executed.

Meanwhile, the arrests in the Soviet Union continued unabated. My father stopped visiting us altogether. He was hiding in the village where he worked. One day, the police showed up at our house, looking for him. It happened right before dawn when we were asleep. The sound of the

---

[9] The People's Commissariat of Internal Affairs.

doorbell awakened everybody. The twins began to cry, and I was shaking uncontrollably. A few men in civilian clothes walked into the house and demanded that my mother tell them where her husband was. They threatened to put her in jail unless she revealed his whereabouts. Now, we were all crying and screaming. The policemen left, taking my mother with them. They held her overnight, but she told them nothing. In the morning, they let her go. It was a nightmare. They kept coming again and again. We lived in constant fear that someone might betray my father's hiding place—the police and NKVD had many informers scouting out fugitives. I woke up every morning with a terrible feeling and worried even more when going to bed at night. I was afraid the policemen would find my father and imprison or kill him.

By the year 1939, the arrests began to subside, and I wrote a letter to Vyacheslav Molotov, the Soviet Premier and Stalin's close associate. In that letter, I asked the premier to allow my father to reside and work in Chudnov, where his family lived. I received a reply from the Molotov office, informing me that my request was under review and I would be notified of their decision. I never heard from them again.

6. Komsomol Affair

My father moved to Zhitomir, where he found employment at a local manufacturing plant. After several attempts, he was granted temporary permission to reside on the outskirts of the city. In Chudnov, my mother worked hard at home and in her job; I studied diligently while helping her around the house and my sisters with their schoolwork. All the time, I had a heavy heart as I worried about my father. In school, I was afraid the teachers and classmates would find out that my father was a former political prisoner, a matter of great public shame. I never talked about my family, not to reveal those "shameful" details. I shut myself in. There was not a single person I could confide in. Even at home, nobody cared about my issues. I dreamed of leaving Chudnov, getting into medical school, becoming a doctor, and not coming back.

In my eighth grade, the time came for me to become a member of the Komsomol[10] organization. The membership was not mandatory (as it was considered an honor); still, all high-school students were encouraged to join, especially those with better grades, since being a Komsomol member was essential for college admission and an early work career. I was pressured from every side to apply; however, the prospect of being asked at the interview about my father terrified me. Questions about parents were a part of the "vetting" process, and nothing could be hidden from the interviewers. The Soviet Constitution stated that children were not responsible for their parents' deeds, but if that was the case, why ask about parents at all? I delayed my application for almost a year and finally submitted it to the school's Komsomol committee. I was accepted immediately, but the next step was approval by the regional Komsomol office. I will never forget the day I came for an interview. I trembled with fear, waiting for my turn. Finally, they called me in. I briefly told my biographical data, and the questions began. I answered them one by one. In the end, one of the committee members asked, "What was the reason for your father's arrest and conviction?" I threw my papers on the floor and ran out of the room. I came home crying, on the verge of a nervous breakdown, telling myself I would never apply to Komsomol again. However, they decided without my presence—in a couple of days, I received a letter from the regional office instructing me to come and pick up my membership card.

---

[10] "Young Communists Union," a government-sponsored political organization for young people of high school age and older.

One could imagine what transpired in my father's heart and mind. He hated the Bolsheviks and the system that had caused him and his family so much suffering. By the time of my Komsomol admission, he had lost all hope of having his Chudnov ban lifted and now wanted to bring his wife and children to Zhitomir, where he worked. He talked to his mother and siblings, and they decided to sell our half of the house, or all of it (the other half was rented out after Aunt Baila and her family moved to Kerch), and buy a place in Zhitomir or nearby. The house was registered in my grandmother's name, so her other children needed to approve the sale or sign a waiver for their part of the inheritance. My father had three sisters in Chudnov, and they all signed the required papers, but at the last moment, the grandmother changed her mind and refused to sell. I recall a heated argument between her and my father. I did not understand how she could undercut her own son, knowing what he and his family were going through.

After a row with his mother, my father left Zhitomir and went to Moldova, where he got a job at a collective farm near Kishinev. Kishinev was much further away from Chudnov than Zhitomir, so my father saw us even less often, maybe once every couple of months. Occasionally, my mother traveled to Kishinev to visit him. On one such trip, she took me along. My father was delighted to see me—he bought me gifts and showed me around the town. I liked the city very much and had a great time. I was going back home in a happy mood, full of impressions. The home greeted me with the same depressing atmosphere, and I hated the grandmother even more.

Among the people most dear to me, I want to mention my mother's aunt, Tsylia. A Chudnov native, she lived in Leningrad and was coming to her hometown twice a year to see my sisters and me, and to help my mother. Aunt Tsylia's specialty was quilted comforters, which she sewed by hand. Her work was renowned in Chudnov, and people placed orders through my mother in advance. Upon arrival in the town, Aunt Tsylia fulfilled those orders and shared the proceeds with my mother. For me, her visits were eagerly anticipated events. She was my best friend, with whom I felt completely at ease. We often had long, candid conversations where I shared my most private thoughts with her. The war claimed her, too. She died during the Siege of Leningrad. She had a daughter and three sons. I tried to locate them after the war but found no trace of their existence. They must have also perished in the besieged city—died of starvation or in a bomb explosion.

7. Dental School

I read romantic novels and dreamed of big, pure love. The first man I had a crush on never learned about it. He was an army officer stationed in Chudnov. I met him every morning on the way to school—he walked to his job. He was young (albeit much older than me), of average height, with blue eyes and brown hair. He always looked at me, but I was afraid to look back, although it felt good to be noticed. He probably saw me as a cute child. I wished I could talk to him, get to know him better. Soon, the war broke out, and I never saw him again… Boys of my age did not interest me. My difficult childhood made me reticent and somber like an adult, and I regarded those boys as featherbrained teens. Many showed interest in me, but I ignored them, and they thought I was haughty. Only after the war did I learn about some of my classmates' feelings toward me. I missed out on those naïve teenage relationships most girls of my age had. I was attracted to older, serious men and dreamed of a strong, happy family. I told myself that I would be a good mother, a true friend to my children, and would avoid the mistakes my mother made toward my sisters and me.

My father continued to work in Kishinev, far away from home. He was renting a room in a private house. Loneliness and separation from the family badly affected his morale, but bringing the wife and children to Kishinev was beyond his means. So he came back to Zhitomir and got a job in the village where he had worked before. Lately, the police eased up on chasing him. Maybe they grew tired or had more pressing matters to attend to, but the policemen stopped showing up at our house. Still, my father was afraid to visit Chudnov more often. He saw us every two weeks, at night, as he did not risk coming in daylight. In summer, when my sisters and I had recess in school, we often traveled with my mother to the village where he worked. He lived in the attic, and we stayed with him there, sleeping in the hay.

I was about to finish the ninth grade when I decided to speak to my parents about my future. I told them I wanted to go to medical school after tenth grade. I intended to apply to a medical college in Kyiv or Lviv and study for four years. My plan included receiving a stipend and living in a dormitory. However, the stipend alone was not enough to live on, so I wanted to know if my parents could help me. My parents discussed the matter between themselves and got back to me with the answer: they did not have the resources to support me for five years (one more year in school and four years in college). The response disappointed but did not surprise me, as I had known all along that my parents could not afford it.

Thus, when someone mentioned a two-year dental school in Zhitomir that accepted students after the ninth grade, I decided to apply there. I hoped that after finishing dental school, I would work as a dentist and study at a medical college at the same time.

Suddenly, the grandmother fell gravely ill. She went to visit her oldest daughter, who lived nearby, and, while there, suffered a stroke. She fell to the floor and lost her speech and the use of her right side. In those times, ambulances did not transport people with a stroke to a hospital since it was considered unsafe. The paramedics put the grandmother in bed and stopped at our house on the way to inform my mother about the incident. My mother took my sisters and me and rushed to see her mother-in-law. The grandmother did not recognize anybody. In a couple of days, she improved a little and regained her speech. She then asked my mother to care for her, as with her own daughter, my grandmother did not get along. Hence, my mother quit her job and started coming to her sister-in-law's house every day to look after the grandmother. She fed the sick woman, washed her body, changed her bed sheets. She neglected her own home and spent most of her time with her mother-in-law. That put an even greater strain on me. In school, began the graduate exams. I had to study while taking care of my sisters, cooking meals, and cleaning the house. As a result, I received two Bs and, for the first time in my life, did not make the straight-A list.

I finished the ninth grade in the summer of 1941 and went to Zhitomir to apply to dental school. I submitted my application on June 21. The school's secretary informed me that I would receive a notification in the mail if I were admitted to the entrance exams. I stayed with my father's relatives and decided to spend a few days in the city—go to the movies, see a play, walk the streets. The next day, I returned to the train station to buy an advance ticket to Chudnov. As I entered the station, the voice on the radio announced that Soviet Premier Vyacheslav Molotov would address the people of the Soviet Union. It was six in the evening. The station became silent—the grave tone of the announcer suggested that something terrible had happened. Then Molotov spoke, "The German armies have treacherously invaded the Soviet territory...." It was a declaration of war. Within seconds, panic began. People rushed toward the platforms and ticket booths. I ran to my place of stay, picked up my belongings, and returned to the train station. The station was in complete chaos, packed with people who pushed and shoved each other, trying to board the trains. All tickets were sold out. For a few hours, I could not even get near the platforms. It was already late at night when I got on a cargo train, which arrived in Chudnov the following morning.

In those years, Chudnov had no buses or taxicabs; transportation was provided via horse carts. By the time my train stopped at the Chudnov station, panic had already spread in the town, and no horse carts were available. I walked home for over an hour. When I reached our house, my mother greeted me with the news: the grandmother had passed away the previous morning and was buried the same day. It was the day of the beginning of the war. My grandmother was so fortunate—she died in her own bed, unaware of the coming catastrophe and escaping horrors that so many soon would go through on the way to their final hour.

Chapter 2

THE CONQUEST

1. German Butter

My father returned to Chudnov for the first time without fear of getting arrested. Nobody cared about his residency status anymore. The Germans were approaching with blazing speed. On Chudnov's streets appeared refugees from Poland[1], who were running from the German troops like deer from a forest fire. The refugees recounted stories about Jews being robbed, raped, and killed under the Nazi-established regimes.

The Soviet authorities announced an evacuation. The first to evacuate were employees of large industrial plants. All passenger and cargo trains were consigned to carry the families of those workers; others had to fight for a few remaining seats. Children's cries were heard all over the town. My parents did not work in the heavy industry, so the only way we could leave Chudnov was by horse-cart. Many families were looking for such transportation. My father had a horse cart, but he refused to go. After decades of persecution by the Bolsheviks, he could not imagine anything worse and dismissed the rumors about the cruel treatment of Jews by the Nazis as Soviet propaganda.

Despite his harsh life, my father was an energetic and sociable person. While working in Chudnov and the surrounding villages, he made many friends among local Ukrainians and particularly among German farmers. The Germans lived in Ukraine for centuries. They settled in separate communities, maintaining their original language and customs. In our area, German farmers specialized in dairy foods. Their butter and cheese

---

[1] Germany and the Soviet Union carved up Poland in 1939; however, people in Ukraine still referred to the former Polish territories as "Poland."

were in high demand. We had a farmers' market a few minutes walk from our house. The market was open once a week on Sundays. People got up early to buy German butter there, as it was selling fast.

My father's German friends, who were coming to Chudnov to sell their produce, stayed in our house. In the large room, they cut butter, weighing it in pounds. The butter looked and smelled wonderful. After the market, the German guests returned to our house to eat and have a few drinks before heading home. My mother cooked dinner for them. The Germans were very cordial and always brought gifts to my sisters and me. My father held his German friends in high esteem, praising their honesty, work ethic, and sense of duty. And now, with German troops nearing Chudnov, he expected better times ahead. He was glad to see the regime that had ruined his life go away, while he still remembered the previous war[2] when the advancing German armies halted the persecution of Jews in the conquered territories. Hence, when told about the Nazi atrocities, my father replied that it could not be true. "I know Germans," he said. This time, however, those were not the Germans he knew.

The number of Polish refugees continued to increase. They confirmed the rumors of savageness against Jews. The panic among the Chudnov Jewish population reached its peak. Meanwhile, the Soviet authorities began destroying the Party archives. I was summoned to the regional Komsomol office to help. We burned documents all night. The next day, the first German airplanes appeared in the sky, and bombs started falling on Chudnov. We were hiding from the airstrikes in the basement of our house. During one such raid, my mother got wounded. She did not make it to the basement fast enough, and a bomb fragment lodged in her leg. Luckily, it was a flesh wound. In the morning, my father took her to the hospital, where the doctor removed the fragment.

I begged my father to leave Chudnov, but he did not listen. It was too late, anyway. The word spread around that German airplanes bombed the refugees on the roads. Many were killed in such attacks while trying to escape from Chudnov. Those who evacuated early had reached the safety of the eastern parts of the Soviet Union. My family, together with most Chudnov Jews, ended up in a hopeless situation. The enemy was already in the town. We sat in the house near the window and watched in despair the last columns of the Soviet Army pulling out, and then the German troops marching in[3].

---

[2] World War I.

[3] The Germans entered Chudnov two weeks after invading the USSR.

2. Work Brigades

As the first order of business, the occupiers established a police force assembled from local volunteers. Then, opened a chapter of OUN. The new authorities posted signs all over the town. The posters denounced Soviet Russia and called for an independent Ukrainian state. They also called for the elimination of communists and Jews. To my surprise, many locals enthusiastically responded to those appeals, taking an active part in the persecution. I did not understand how people with whom we had grown up, gone to school, exchanged visits, shared meals—whom we considered friends could overnight become our enemies: betray, pillage, and murder. I was shocked. My father had many Ukrainian friends and business associates. One of my best friends in school was a Ukrainian girl named Galina. Her father used to be a high-ranking government bureaucrat under the Soviets. I often visited their home and even stayed overnight. Galina's parents were pleased by their daughter's friendship with me and always encouraged it. After the Germans captured Chudnov, Galina's father was offered a prominent post in the new administration, which he accepted. I passed Galina a letter through our mutual friend, asking her for help, but did not receive a reply. They no longer cared or were too afraid to do anything.

The Germans, together with the local police, began to organize work brigades made up of Chudnov's Jewish males, including teenage boys. Those brigades performed hard labor tasks around the town and nearby. Shouting "Dirty Jews," the guards beat the workers for minor infractions or no reason at all. The workers received no pay, but they were given a meal once a day—usually a bowl of light vegetable soup and a piece of bread. Their families starved or lived off stockpiled supplies. Under the communist regime, with its constant shortages, people stocked up on flour, bread, potatoes, and similar items, and many still had those Soviet purchases in their homes when the Germans occupied Chudnov. Some residents owned livestock, such as cows and pigs. They slaughtered the animals, sold some meat and lard on the market, and used the rest to feed themselves.

My father was assigned to the railway station to repair tracks. He was coming home tired and anxious. He worried about his family, as German soldiers were breaking into Jewish homes, raping women, robbing and assaulting those inside. One night, soldiers broke into the house of Aunt Sonia, my father's older sister. They shot Aunt Sonia's husband, who tried to defend his family, and raped her daughter Chaya. The girl was only fifteen. After that incident, Chaya fell ill and never recovered. She died two months later... I did not fully comprehend the meaning of rape at the time. I was also fifteen and knew about sex mainly from girls in school. My mother never spoke about such matters at home. In her younger years, physical relations between the sexes were not discussed before marriage, and she believed it was improper for children. I read many novels about love, but they mainly described its emotional side. Yet, I understood that what had happened to my cousin was horrible and irreversible. Almost every morning, I heard another story about this or that woman raped by the Germans. A sense of fear and a premonition of imminent disaster stayed with me all the time. At night, we locked all doors and windows and remained fully dressed, ready to escape through the backyard if soldiers started to break in.

A sickening smell appeared in the house, a smell of death. When I was in the fifth grade, a girl in my class died from typhus. She had been sick for a long time from complications of the disease, and I visited her at their home. During one of those visits, I sensed that smell and later felt it at the cemetery during the girl's funeral. And now, a few years after my classmate's death, I smelled that dreadful scent again—in our house. I said nothing to my parents and didn't know if they had sensed it, too, but the smell followed me there until I left my home, never to return.

3. Liquidation

One night, we heard a knock on our door, but it wasn't the Germans. The visitor was Stepan, son of one of my father's Ukrainian friends. Stepan's family lived in the Yagodinka village of the Zhitomir oblast, where my father used to work before the war. Stepan's father was a forest ranger. In summer, my father took us to the ranger's house for strawberry season. The hosts had a large strawberry field. We picked strawberries, ate them, and my mother made delicious strawberry jam. Stepan's parents were always hospitable and pleasant. The ranger's farm lay a few kilometers away from the village, surrounded by fields and woods. The air in that place was particularly fresh and aromatic. Stepan took us to the river and deep forest, where we picked berries and mushrooms... At the beginning of the war, Stepan was nineteen years old. He had studied in college in Kiev and came back home when the fighting began. After the Germans occupied Chudnov, he was offered a policeman's job but turned it down.

Stepan came to tell us that the Germans had received an order from their high command to liquidate all Jews in Chudnov. The operation was to be conducted in two phases: men would be killed first, followed by women and children. Many of Stepan's boyhood friends now worked as policemen, and he freely walked in and out of the police building. While there, he spoke with his former buddies, listened to conversations, and was well-informed. Stepan instructed us to remain in the house and not respond to any public announcements. He brought with him some food we badly needed. Stepan said that he would come again and bring more. He would be coming after dark, not to be seen by passersby, and keep us up to date... My parents were surprised and touched by Stepan's action. If the Germans and the police discovered that Stepan was helping us, he could be arrested and shot. We always knew him as a good, honest young man, but taking such risks? It was unusual and brave.

Stepan's information was correct. Soon came an official proclamation instructing all able Jewish men to assemble in the movie theater, from where they would be transported to a new place of residence and work. The announcement provided the date and time of the gathering but not the destination of the trip. The instructions suggested that the travelers take with them extra clothes, money, and valuables. They were promised their families would soon join them at the new site.

On the announced day, my father did not go. Some others also sensed a trap and stayed home. A few hours after the stated gathering time, we heard remote machine-gun series and multiple single shots. The shooting continued for half an hour. The next day, Stepan came to our house and told us that the Germans, together with the local policemen, had executed the assembled men. The executioners collected the victims' belongings, forced the latter to dig their graves, and started shooting. The massacre took place in the park near the old army barracks on the outskirts of the town. Stepan warned us that the police would search for the remaining Jews after finishing those who had come voluntarily.

The execution of the Jewish men was kept in strict secret. A few days later came another announcement commanding the victims' families to assemble at the same location, also with belongings, money, and jewelry. Most respondents did not realize what had happened to their husbands, fathers, brothers, and sons, expecting to see them soon… On the day of the new gathering, early in the morning, the march of the condemned began. The elderly, the women, and the children walked unknowingly to join their loved ones in still-open graves. My family was hiding in the woodshed next to our house. The woodshed had a small window facing the street. Through that window, we saw a moving line of the ill-fated stooped under the weight of bags and suitcases. Babies in mothers' hands cried unstoppably as if sensing their fate. The old and the frail tried to keep up with the rest. It is hard to describe the sadness and desperation that overcame us at the sight of that procession. We knew they walked to their death and were certain the same destiny awaited us.

None of us in the shed said a word. After Stepan's warning about the police's plans to search Jewish homes, we knew that we could no longer remain in our house. We had to find another place to hide or get out of Chudnov. Stepan came the following day late at night. He told us that the families who had passed our shed the day before were also executed. They got to the movie theater, left the belongings there, and were taken to the park near the army barracks, where their male relatives had been killed a few days earlier. The executioners divided the new victims into groups: older men, women, and children. The shooting was done with a machine gun. Those wounded or missed by the bullets were finished off with rifles and pistols. Both German soldiers and Ukrainian policemen took part in that slaughter.

4. Dr. Lebow and Manya

Among the victims of the Chudnov massacre was Dr. Lebow, the town's oldest physician, who was eighty years old at the time. When Dr. Lebow started his practice many years ago, he was the only physician in the area. He did all sorts of medical procedures—delivered babies, treated illnesses, performed routine surgeries. He was a kind and amicable man who never refused service to anyone, often treating the poor without charge. He was loved and appreciated by everybody, young and old, and especially by the local women whose many children he brought to this world and treated for illnesses. Later, a new hospital and clinic were built in Chudnov, and several doctors of different specialties came to practice in the town. Still, Dr. Lebow continued to work day and night, receiving patients in his office and making house calls. My mother used him exclusively, and he would always visit our home when somebody among the children got sick. He had many patients and sometimes showed up at midnight or the following morning. He lived in his own house with a maid who cared for him. His wife died young, and he never remarried. He had a son and a daughter, also physicians, who lived in Kiev.

When the news about the executions of Jews spread around, a group of Ukrainian women circulated a petition asking the authorities to spare Dr. Lebow's life. The petition described Dr. Lebow's age, his skills, and how much he had done for the area's residents. Hundreds of women from Chudnov and nearby villages signed it. In the police headquarters, where the petitioners brought their letter, they were assured that Dr. Lebow would not be harmed.

Dr. Lebow did not react to the first "relocation" announcement, as it applied to physically able men. After the second massacre, policemen, like bloodhounds, began to rummage through the houses, looking for remaining Jews. Those captured were brought to the police station, taken to the park near the army barracks in small groups, and executed. With one of those groups, they dragged sick old Dr. Lebow. The executioners ordered him to take off his clothes and mockingly inquired if he had anything to say. Standing with great effort on his feet, Dr. Lebow made a speech. He spoke about his years of dedicated service, about the many people he had helped. "I love my country, and I am not afraid to die," he concluded, "but you, traitors, will not escape justice, and neither will your masters, Nazi murderers. Long live the Soviet Union!" A machine-gun series, fired across the victim row, killed him instantly. All those details told us Stepan, who had learned them from eyewitnesses living near the park (shortly before leaving the USSR, I visited Chudnov and met with my school friend Galina, who confirmed the Dr. Lebow story).

People also talked about the death of a girl named Manya. I remember her well. She was a few years older than me, with long blond hair and big blue eyes. Slender and well-built, she dazzled everybody with her beauty. She was among the last Jews executed. The shooting was done by a German soldier with a pistol. When Manya's turn came, he refused to shoot. The officer in charge of the execution ordered another soldier to fire, but that soldier also refused. Finally, a local policeman pulled a gun and shot the girl. The Germans turned away. The executioner pushed Manya's body into the ditch, where other victims already lay dead.

5. Kitchen Garden

After Aunt Baila with her children moved to Kerch, the other side of our house was rented by a family of four. The renters were husband and wife, their fourteen-year-old daughter Ellochka[4], and the wife's mother. The wife's mother was insane. She had spent years in a mental institution until the family decided to take her home. They kept her locked inside while the parents were at work and Ellochka was in school. All day long, the madwoman paced around her half of the house, yelling, hitting walls, and banging on the kitchen window that faced the common hallway. I was terrified of her, especially when home alone. I was afraid she might break the glass and wriggle through the window onto our side. Many times, I asked my mother to secure the window, but she did not take my fears seriously.

A few days after the killing of Aunt Sonia's husband and the rape of her daughter, German soldiers broke into the other side of our house. Perhaps the mad woman's cries attracted their attention. The soldiers raped Ellochka in the presence of her parents and grandmother. At that horrible moment, a mind returned to the insane woman—she understood what had happened and wept with the rest of her family. The next day, when Ellochka and her parents briefly left home, the madwoman took a rope, went to the woodshed, and hanged herself. That tragedy crushed our neighbors' spirit; they remained in the house and did not attempt to find a safer place. Following the first two rounds of mass executions, the policemen began to scour Chudnov, looking for survivors; they found Ellochka and her parents in their home, took them to the park, and shot.

My family did not stay in the house. During the day, we hid in the woodshed. I suffocated from the "death smell" when I sneaked into the house to get something. At night, we would go to the kitchen garden of our neighbors and lie down among the plants. Holding our breath, we remained there until dawn. Next to us sprawled the kitchen garden's owners. Shivering from cold and fear, we listened to every rustle, every sound of a voice. The police searched our houses every night. In the morning, we would quietly move back to the woodshed. That continued for several weeks. Stepan kept bringing us food: bread, sausages, onions, apples, and melted sugar that looked like chocolate. He melted sugar in his home. With each delivery, he also brought a few bottles of water. Chudnov did not have running water; the water was taken from wells. The wells were under police surveillance, so nobody among us dared to

---

[4] Affectionate of Ella.

go there, even at night, as it meant almost certain capture. Cooking was out of the question—we did not have enough water to wash our hands. The food brought by Stepan we shared between my family and the family of our neighbors. The neighbors were a middle-aged couple, their son Fima (my classmate), and a one-year-old son of their daughter. The daughter lived in Kiev; she left the little boy with her parents right before the German invasion.

Every day, we heard distant gunshots. They were coming from the park where the police executed captured Jews. Stepan begged us to leave the shed and find a more secure place or go to the woods. The neighbors in whose kitchen garden we were hiding at night had a large basement, which they had finished shortly before the war. They invited us to move there with them. The entry to the basement was through a trapdoor in the house's storage room. Using the wooden planks stockpiled there, we masked the trapdoor by building a booth above it. To get to the basement, one had to enter the storage room, walk inside the booth, lift the trapdoor, and then descend the stairs. Now, Stepan was leaving the provisions in the booth, and at night, one of the adults in the basement would come up the stairs and bring the food down.

The basement was cold and damp. The owners brought blankets and warm clothes. My family contributed warmers from our house. Many things had been looted by the locals there, but none of us cared about the stolen items—we were totally focused on saving our lives and the lives of our loved ones.

6. Uncle's Address

Following her husband's murder by the German soldiers and her older daughter's rape and consequent death, Aunt Sonya was in an incoherent state. She and her younger daughter, Zhenya[5], were hiding in their house. My mother worried about their safety, so we decided to take them to the basement with us. The next night, risking his life, my father went to Aunt Sonya's house and brought her and Zhenya to our hiding place. They stayed only for a couple of days. Aunt Sonya said she would go back home with Zhenya to take a bath and change clothes. She had some water left in her house and did not want to waste it. She said they would return soon. We tried to dissuade her, telling her that it was dangerous to go outside, but Aunt Sonya insisted. They left at nightfall and did not come back. We realized they had been captured by a patrol, on the streets or in their home, and executed.

The neighbors' one-year-old grandson cried all the time. Maybe he caught a cold from the basement chill, yet we didn't know how to help him. We held and rocked the child, played with him, but he would not stop crying. It was scary. German patrols and local policemen constantly searched the house; sometimes, we heard their footsteps in the storage room above us… One evening, Stepan came down to the basement and told us that the child's cries could be heard outside, especially at night, when it was very quiet. Stepan was worried those sounds might betray our hideout. But what were we supposed to do? Nobody could suggest a solution. Finally, the basement owners offered to smother their grandson. I was horrified—how was it possible to kill a child? Thank goodness, neither the grandparents nor anyone else in the basement could do such a thing. At the same time, we understood that our days in the basement were numbered. Sooner or later, we would be discovered, and waiting for it to happen was not an option.

I suddenly felt an urge to get out of the basement, late at night or before dawn, and try to escape from Chudnov. I talked to my parents, who agreed that it would be better to separate. But where would I go? I offered our neighbors' son, my classmate Fima, to join me. Maybe we could reach a place not occupied by the Germans or go deep into the forest to find the resistance fighters. However, my classmate refused. He lacked the courage to part with his family. So, I decided to talk to Stepan to hear his opinion. The next time he brought food, my parents and I went upstairs to see him. Stepan urged us to leave the basement as soon

---

[5] Diminutive of Yevgenia (Eugenia).

as possible. He said there were almost no Jews left in Chudnov—all had been killed. Every day, the police ferreted out a few more, took them to the park, and shot them. Stepan proposed to hide my father and me in his parents' house in Yagodinka. My mother and sisters would move to the attic of an empty house across the street, from where they would be retrieved by another of my father's friends, Ivan Chernenko. Stepan had already spoken to Chernenko, who agreed to help us. He only asked for money, claiming he needed it to cover the expenses. We had no cash, so my parents decided to give him their jewelry: two rings, a small gold watch, two gold chains, and a bracelet. Stepan offered our neighbors to arrange something for them, but they wanted to remain in their house.

The first phase of Stepan's plan was to transport my father and me to Yagodinka. After nightfall, Stepan would bring a horse cart, load it with our belongings, and wait outside. Shortly before dawn, my father and I would come out of the basement, and Stepan would ride us to his home. The riskiest part was getting out of Chudnov, as the town was heavily patrolled by German soldiers and local policemen.

My farewell with my mother and little sisters was glum—we had a premonition we would not be together again. From a secret pocket inside her dress, my mother pulled out a small piece of paper. Written on it was the address of her brother in America. She handed the paper to me and said, "If you survive, get in touch with your uncle. He will substitute for your parents." Then, my mother gave me things I liked: an American wristwatch, a length of English Boston fabric, also from America, and a large, brightly colored shawl my father had bought for me in Kishinev. She told my father to take their chrome-plated bed, an album of family photos, and a few other items rescued from our house. She asked Stepan to keep it in his home for those who might survive. Stepan loaded all that stuff into his cart, where he slept overnight, and at dawn, my father and I came out of the basement to join him. My father lay on top of our belongings in the cart; Stepan covered him with canvas, leaving a small opening to breathe. I fastened a white scarf on my head, climbed in the driving seat next to Stepan, and we set off for Yagodinka.

We got out of Chudnov with no problems, but toward the village, we encountered Ukrainian policemen traveling in the opposite direction, also on a horse cart. It was daylight already. "Hey!" yelled the policemen (some of whom must have known Stepan) jokingly, "What is in the cart? Hiding Jews?" "Taking my sister home," Stepan replied, pointing at me. The policemen did not stop and rode past us. I was shaking with fear; Stepan was edgy, too. He decided to get off the road and go through the woods. A descendant of a line of rangers, he knew the forest very well.

It was raining. The ground was covered with tree leaves mixed with water. The horse could barely move through that mush. We had been riding all day, and it was dusk already. The rain became heavier. Stepan got off the cart and walked in high rubber boots next to the horse, holding the reins. The forest became thicker and completely dark. My father and I also alighted from the cart to ease the horse's load. We were cold and wet. I wore rubber boots, and my father had high boots, too, but the water was up to our knees. We walked like that all night, reaching Stepan's house in the morning.

7. Undesirables

Stepan's parents met us with an icy welcome. They took their son aside and started to admonish him for risking his life and the lives of his family members. My father and I had no idea that Stepan had brought us to his parents' home without telling them first. They were very unhappy and visibly afraid. Their fears were justified, as the authorities posted signs everywhere, warning residents not to help Jews. "Death awaits those who hide Jews," the signs read. I suddenly had a sinking feeling: the promised sanctuary of the ranger's house now appeared a death trap.

The ranger, my father's old friend, did not say hello or invite us to the house, but Stepan unloaded the cart and asked my father and me to come inside. We were drenched to the skin and quivering from the cold. Stepan gave me his sister's dry clothes and some of his to my father. He then told his mother to bring us hot tea with milk and something to eat. Looking aside, she complied. My father and I swallowed the food and lay on top of the Russian stove.

I woke up and did not remember how long I had slept—it seemed like days. My father was not in the room. Stepan told me they had put my father in the barn, next to the horses and cows, while I had to remain on the Russian stove behind the curtain, out of sight of strangers. And so I stayed in the house, getting off the stove only to go to the toilet when it was dark outside (the toilet was the forest itself, where the ranger's family satisfied their natural needs). Stepan was bringing me meals to the Russian stove. Next to me slept Stepan's sisters, Olga and Nadja. Olga was two years older than I, while Nadja was my age. During the day, I lay on the stove alone as the girls helped their mother at the farm. They did not go to school because it was too far away.

Late at night, when everybody was in bed, from my place behind the curtain, I could hear Stepan and his parents quarreling in hushed voices. Stepan's parents chastised Stepan for bringing my father and me to their home, for putting their lives in danger. Using a derogatory form of the word "Jew," which I had never heard from them before, they promised to report us to the police. I did not believe my ears. How could my father's close friends of yesterday become our nemeses so fast? Had they better told us to leave? I only wondered why Stepan was so eager to save my father and me, as to defy his kin.

The arguments between Stepan and his parents continued every night, and one night, I heard the following words from Stepan's mother: "What do you need this Jewess for? What did you find in her? Why can't you choose a girl among our people, our nationality, and marry her? Whom are you risking your and our lives for?" To which Stepan replied, "I love her and will do everything to save her life, even if it costs me my own. I do not plan to marry her now—she is only fifteen and knows nothing about my feelings—but I will do all I can to help her and her family…" I was stunned. The revelation was a complete surprise to me. I never suspected Stepan of a romantic interest, even when he looked at me with adoring eyes. I was accustomed to such looks from the adults. I was a pretty girl with long, wavy hair, dark eyes, and rosy cheeks. Many people complimented me on my appearance, but I was far from any emotional involvement. I could hardly imagine anyone being in love with me, especially in those awful times. I thought about my family's survival, and before the war, I wanted to study, get a profession, and have a family of my own. Stepan's admission confused me. I did not know what to do. Talk to him and explain that I did not share his feelings? Tell him the truth or remain mum, pretending I didn't know about his affection? I decided to say nothing but to wait and see.

Believing I was asleep and didn't hear them, Stepan's parents scolded their son night after night. Now, they were saying they could not risk it anymore and would no longer put up with "those Jews" in their home. Stepan spoke in an angry tone of voice. "How can you even think of betraying your friends? If you do it, and they get executed, I will kill you and myself. I am warning you!" I was appalled. I feared Stepan's parents would bring the police… One day, when Stepan was out of the house, his mother started a conversation with me. She asked about my plans, noting that I could not stay in their home forever. She advised me to leave their house and go east toward the Soviet-held territory or find the resistance fighters. She promised to give me money if I told Stepan nothing and left in secret. I asked her what would happen to my father. She replied that he would remain in their house. I did not trust her and decided to talk to my father myself.

My father and I had been at the ranger's farm for two months already. Stepan brought us there in the fall, and now it was winter, snowy and cold. My father continued to hide in the barn while I spent most of the time on the stove in the house. We met rarely to avoid being seen or heard by the farm's visitors. Stepan told his sisters to keep mum about our presence. The girls worshipped their brother and did as he said.

When I came to the barn, my father already knew that Stepan was in love with me. Stepan had told him that he, Stepan, would do all possible to save my life and asked for my father's blessing in case my father did not survive. "Do what you must to stay alive," said my father to me, "I will happily go to my grave, knowing that you may live." Then, he told me terrible news—Stepan had brought it to him a month ago, but they decided to say nothing to me at the time. My mother and twin sisters had been captured and executed. My father's former friend, Ivan Chernenko, who had taken our jewelry (Stepan had given it to him as they agreed), did not keep his promise and left my mother and sisters in the house across the street. Whether the police found them during a random search or Chernenko reported their whereabouts, nobody knew. Everybody knew, however, that Chernenko had become a policeman. Stepan did not meet with him to find out more, as no longer trusted the renegade and was afraid that such a meeting might further jeopardize my father's and my lives. My father said that our neighbors had also been executed. They remained in the basement, and one night, a passing patrol heard the child's cries. "I know I will be killed, too," said my father, "I used to be afraid to die, but after what happened to my wife and daughters, I am not afraid anymore. My only desire is for you to survive…" I was devastated by the news of my mother and sisters' deaths. I went back to the house and lay down on the stove. I cried all evening and all night.

8. Father's Death

Stepan's mother insisted that he ask my father and me to leave. "They will not leave," Stepan replied, "or I will leave with them, and you will never see me again." Everything in me was turning upside down—I wished I had never set foot in that place... One night, the argument between Stepan and his mother was interrupted by the barking of a dog and loud voices outside. Stepan ran out of the house and soon returned. He came to the stove, told me to put a scarf over my head, and ordered his sisters to lie beside me. "The policemen have surrounded the house," Stepan said, "They demand to hand over Jews." Then he turned toward his parents. He said he suspected they had something to do with the raid, and he would never forgive them if they revealed to the police those hiding at the farm. Stepan's father went outside. A few minutes later, I heard a heavy stomping around the barn, followed by a short scuffle and several gunshots. I realized something terrible had happened: perhaps my father had been killed.

The house's door opened, and several policemen walked in. They were followed by the ranger. "Where are the other Jews?" asked one of the policemen. By the sound of his voice, I recognized Vassili, another former friend of my father, who sometimes visited our home before the war. After the Germans occupied Chudnov, Vassili went to work for the police and was promoted to some senior post. He took an active part in hunting down and killing Jews... Stepan intensely stared at his mother. She opened her mouth and stumbled. "We have nobody here," she said. Vassili stepped toward the stove. "And who is that?" he asked, pointing at the girls and me. "These are my sisters," replied Stepan. All three of us lay covered with one blanket, wearing white headscarves, and it was difficult to see our faces in a dimly lit room. "Get rid of the body," said Vassili, "and come tomorrow to the police station." I suddenly felt that I was going into shock, but clenched my teeth and remained quiet. Stepan followed the policemen out of the house. He returned a minute later and uttered something to his parents in a low voice. Then he walked to me and said: "Your father has been killed. When the police began to search the barn, he jumped out of the window and ran toward the woods. The policemen saw him and started shooting. He was killed by a bullet from Vassili's gun. Put on your coat. We will bury your father, and you must leave this place right away before the policemen return."

Years later, I visited Yagodinka with my son and met the village's residents who knew of my father and told me more about his death. The policemen and the ranger went to the barn together. My father hid in a stack of hay. The policemen yelled for him to come out. The barn was large and dark, so they couldn't pinpoint his location. The ranger took a pitchfork and began to comb the hay. The pitchfork's tines punctured my father's leg; he screamed and jumped out of the barn's window. Weak in his feet and suffering from the pitchfork wound, he ran across the field toward the forest. The policemen opened fire, and Vassili's shot killed my father. All those details Vassili told in court himself when, after the Soviets' return, he was tried and convicted of treason and murder.

Stepan pulled a bed sheet out of the closet, helped me put on my snow boots and coat, and led me outside. It was an awful night, bitterly cold with deep snow. The strong wind wailed between the trees, accompanied by the howling of dogs. I could not cry or speak, feeling like my entire body was made of stone. Stepan walked through the snow, treading a path, and I trailed behind. Finally, we reached what, from afar, looked like a dark patch in the snow. There, in the middle of the field, lay face down in a frozen pool of blood the dearest person in my life—my father.

The snow on the ground illuminated the nightly forest like giant candlelight. Stepan covered my father's body with the sheet, lifted it on his back, and walked toward the woods. I followed him, holding a shovel in my hands. Stepan got deeper into the forest, set his load down, and began digging a grave. While he was doing it, I bid the final farewell to my father, hugging his lifeless body and kissing his ice-covered face. Stepan finished digging, wrapped the body in the sheet, and lowered it into the pit. "Throw in some soil," he said to me. Each of us threw a dash of soil into the open grave, and Stepan put the earth back in. He made a small mound, on top of which he inserted a tree branch. We said our last goodbye to my father and slowly walked toward the farm. Stepan kept saying we had to leave Yagodinka immediately because his parents, who had been ordered to come to the police station in the morning, might tell about me. I did not answer. Something buzzed and cracked in my head, and a strange voice repeated, "Jews, damned Jews!"

We stood in front of the ranger's house for a couple of minutes; Stepan tried to calm me down, to cheer me up. Then we walked inside. The ranger's family was at the table, having a council. Stepan told his mother to bring my belongings. Without a word, she complied. I took the blue Boston, the wristwatch, and the multicolored shawl, put them in my bag, and returned the rest to her. "Food for two," ordered Stepan, "I am going with her." When Stepan's mother heard his last words, she went berserk. "You are not leaving with this Jewess," she screamed, "Over my dead body!" The girls began to cry while the ranger silently stared at the floor. "You did not betray just them; you betrayed me, too," shouted

Stepan at his parents, "You will never see me again!" Stepan's mother threw herself onto the ground across the doorway and started banging her head on the floor. "Over my dead body, over my dead body," she yelled. I started toward the door. Paying no attention to his mother's cries, Stepan put the food in the bag, kissed his sisters, and followed me. As I reached the door, Stepan's mother moved aside to let me pass, then lay across the doorway again. Stepan stepped over her, took my hand, and we walked toward the forest.

9. Birth Certificate

The snow was deep and falling, making it difficult to walk. I was in a comatose-like state and had not spoken since my father's death. Stepan was quiet, too; he looked upset. The dawn was breaking on a new day. With the first ray of daylight, I regained my reactions and spoke first. I asked Stepan where we were going and how long it would take to get there. I was very tired and felt weak in my knees. We saw a fallen tree covered with snow. I wanted to sit down, but Stepan did not let me. "We cannot waste a minute," he said, "We must keep going. I do not trust my parents; in the morning, they may tell the police that I left with you. They will do everything to bring me back." He seemed anxious. He worried about me, but also about his parents. "They can get shot," he added. I sensed a struggle inside him. "Get me to the main road," I told Stepan, "and go home. I will continue on my own." Stepan replied that he would take me to Zhitomir, where his relatives lived.

We walked through the woods for a while, avoiding roads, as we were afraid of pursuit. It was full daylight when we heard the buzz of an engine and saw a moving truck behind the trees. It was the road to Zhitomir. Only a person like Stepan, who knew the forest so well, could find his way in such conditions without getting lost… We were about to come out to the road when Stepan became emotional. He started saying that he loved me and would do everything to save me. He did not know what might happen to him, so he wanted to tell me about his feelings. He was not asking for an answer now, as I was still young and naïve. He wanted to marry me after the war and was ready to forego his family.

Stepan's confession struck me as grossly inappropriate. Yes, I was young and naïve. I had just buried my father and was crushed by the loss of the entire family. How could anyone in such a moment talk to me about some silly "love"? "Why are you telling me this?" I replied to Stepan angrily, "Are you looking for a clue about what to do next? I am not in love with you. I do not know what will happen after the war or if I live long enough to find out. If you need to decide whether to stay with me or return home, go home. It will be better for both of us, as your parents will stop looking for you and for me. Otherwise, the police will catch us, you will be sent back to Yagodinka, and I will get shot. Thank you for everything you have done for me and my family. I will walk this road to Zhitomir, then go to Kiev. I will ask people for a place to sleep, sell my things, and have money to buy food. If such is my fate, I will survive; otherwise, I will go where my parents and little sisters went…" For many years after, I regretted saying those words. After all, Stepan's affection was no news to me, and I doubt he would have revealed it had he not been under severe emotional stress. I should have kept quiet or said that I hadn't yet sorted out my feelings. I feel ashamed recalling that moment even today.

Stepan was dazed and disappointed by my response, but he quickly regained his self-control. As if nothing had happened, he said we would stay with his relatives in Zhitomir for a few days, then decide what to do next. We walked along the road. Stepan kept turning around, and when the next truck approached us, he raised his hand. The truck slowed down and stopped. Stepan asked the driver to take us to the nearest village, saying that we were tired and it was difficult to walk in the deep snow. The driver agreed to give us a lift. Stepan and I climbed in the back. Our food supply was already gone. We were exhausted and needed a place to spend the coming night—to rest and, if the policemen were chasing us, let them pass… At the first sight of a village, the driver halted the truck, and Stepan and I disembarked.

We got to the nearest house and knocked on its door. A young woman came out to the porch. Stepan told her we were going to Zhitomir and were tired and hungry. The woman invited us inside. She served us a meal and made sleeping arrangements on the floor in the living room. It was only late afternoon, but Stepan and I were so drained physically and emotionally that we collapsed, fully dressed, on the improvised "beds" and slept until the next day's late morning. When we woke up, the host was already waiting for us with breakfast. We ate, thanked her for the hospitality, and continued our journey.

Many people roamed the German-occupied territories during the war. Some got stranded far from their homes; others' homes were destroyed. Farmers headed for the city to sell their produce and buy goods on the market, while city dwellers went to the village to barter their personal belongings for food. There were many former Red Army soldiers who had been captured and released by the Germans or deserted after the collapse of the Soviet defense at the beginning of the war. All tried to get to their destination any way they could. The majority traveled on foot or in a horse cart; the rest attempted to hitch a ride in a truck. Even during wartime, country folk were very accommodating. They seldom refused to give a lift (usually on a horse cart, as passenger cars were few and most roads unpaved). Many homeowners allowed travelers to stay overnight and occasionally offered the guests something to eat. Former Red Army soldiers often remained with local farmers for longer periods, working on farms in exchange for food and shelter. Some soldiers even started new families and never went back to their old ones.

Stepan and I walked along the road, hiding behind the trees, as we were still afraid of the pursuers. The day was ending, and we decided to hitch another ride. A couple of drivers stopped, but they were not going to Zhitomir. Finally, one truck picked us up. With his friendly manner and pronounced Slavic features, Stepan raised no suspicions while I wore a headscarf, presenting myself as his sister, which made it easier for us to obtain shelter or a lift.

On his route, the driver dropped us off at the nearest point to Stepan's relatives' house, and we walked a couple of blocks. I could not recognize Zhitomir. Before the war, it was a charming city with neat painted-white houses, tree-lined streets, and flowerbeds. Now, the place was in ruins: the bombing and shelling destroyed it. Stepan became agitated, thinking perhaps his relatives had not survived the destruction or had left the city. He sighed with relief when he saw that the house was intact. The owners were inside, a middle-aged couple (I do not remember their exact relation to Stepan) who lived in the house alone. They greeted us warmly and asked us to come inside. Stepan spoke with them in another room, so I didn't hear how he explained our visit, but the owners invited us to stay for a couple of days, served us dinner, and arranged a place to sleep on the floor.

Stepan looked distracted and anxious. Maybe he was worried about the pursuit, but more likely, he was afraid something bad had happened to his parents. Once more, I tried to convince him to go home, but he did not know what to do. He was torn between concern for his family and the desire to help me. Finally, he decided to confide in his relatives, tell them who I really was (something he didn't do in the beginning), and ask for their advice. Stepan was correct in trusting our hosts. Without hesitation, they suggested I stay with them while Stepan goes back to Yagodinka. He would check on his family and return to Zhitomir. I would wait for him for a couple of days, and if he did not return in time, I would leave and go to Kiev.

However daunting the prospect of being alone—in constant danger, with no money, shelter, or close friends—seemed to me, I felt relieved that Stepan was leaving. He would check on his family, and the police would stop looking for him and for me. The trip home would let him examine his feelings, his willingness to risk his life to save mine, possibly for someone else. I wished that everything would turn out well for him and he would not come back. Perhaps those were ungrateful thoughts toward a man who had done so much for me, but that was how I felt. I didn't want to stand between Stepan and his parents, did not want his sacrifice—to always feel his unrequited love, to sense his affection every moment, and not be able to respond in kind. I felt deep gratitude to him and wished for no more.

Stepan pulled a piece of paper from his pocket and handed it to me. It was his younger sister's birth certificate. "Take this," he said, "From now on, you are Momot, Nadezhda Pavlovna, a Ukrainian born in Yagodinka village of the Chudnov district in Vinnitsa Oblast. Forget your old name and origins. This document may save your life. Wait for me for three days. If I do not come back, then leave." He hugged and kissed me and walked out the door.

Three days had passed; Stepan did not show up. His relatives invited me to stay for a few more nights, but it was too dangerous to remain in Zhitomir—I had to hurry up, reach Kiev, blend into the crowd, and do everything in my power to survive… I warmly thanked my hosts, picked up my bag, and, without a penny in my pockets, in cold, snowy winter, set out on a long and perilous journey.

Chapter 3

TOWN AND COUNTRY

1. Cover Story

To get on the road to Kiev, I crossed the entire city of Zhitomir. I asked passersby for directions, but cautiously so as not to raise suspicions and to avoid police informers and policemen in civilian clothes. Why I chose to go to Kiev, I didn't know. I was attracted to a big city where nobody would recognize me, and one could disappear among the busy streets and crowded markets. Yes, nobody knew me in Kiev, but where would I live, and how would I support myself? I had no answer to those questions. I walked into the unknown with only one goal—to survive. I decided to fight for my life until my last breath.

The road to Kiev had many villages and towns on the way. At first, I wanted to hitch an automobile ride but gave up the idea, fearing that the driver might suspect me as a Jew and deliver me straight to the police. Nobody could be trusted. So, I decided to travel on foot: walk during the day and ask for shelter in people's homes at night. It might be necessary to explain who I was, where I was from, and my reason for coming to Kiev, so I thought up a cover story.

There were good, kindhearted individuals among the locals. The war caused great hardship. Multitudes perished during bombardments; others died from hunger and disease. People starved in the city, and many traveled to the country to exchange their possessions, such as clothes and jewelry, for food. They went from house to house, looking for a better deal. Farmers headed to the city to sell their produce (mainly lard and potatoes) at farmer's markets. During the day, the roads were packed with travelers, but by dusk, the area became deserted and scary. Those caught by the darkness and cold looked for a place to spend the night.

Despite the hard times, the old tradition of giving asylum to strangers was still alive. One could knock on many doors and get rejected, but in the end, meet friendly hosts who would offer a place to sleep and even something to eat, like a bowl of soup or a piece of bread with hot tea.

My cover story was as follows: the war caught me in Lvov; I was heading to Kiev, where my mother lived; I was traveling on foot because I had no money… I did not know if people believed that, but it mattered little as long as they let me stay. I was happy to get inside a warm house and, without taking off my coat, drop onto a bench, lie down on the floor, or, when especially lucky, settle on the top of a Russian stove.

The winter in north-western Ukraine (where Chudnov, Zhitomir, and Kiev are situated) was harsh: brutally cold, with frequent snowstorms. I wore a wool dress sewn from American fabric, a dark green winter coat my father had bought for me in Birobijan, padded with sheet wadding and topped with a synthetic fur collar. I also wore quilted felt boots (valenki) with rubber galoshes, a warm mohair headscarf, and mittens. A bag behind my back with the multicolored shawl and a blue Boston inside, an American watch on my wrist—I walked into the cold and snow and total uncertainty.

2. Multicolored Shawl

The first stop after Zhitomir was Korostyshev, a small regional center. I asked for a night's stay in several houses but was turned away. I did not know what to do. It was getting dark, and I began to worry I might end up on the street on that freezing, snowy night. Finally, at the edge of the town, a young woman invited me into her house. She seemed a little intoxicated. I walked inside and saw a group of German soldiers behind the dinner table, together with several local women. They drank home-brewed vodka, taking it with bread, pickles, and roasted meat. The girl who answered the door (she was the house's owner) introduced me to the party. I suddenly felt ghastly—what had I stepped into? The Germans picked up their ears: who I was and where I had come from. One girl in the company spoke some German. She translated my answers to the soldiers as I pretended not to understand the language[1].

The Germans asked me to join them and filled a glass of vodka. I sat down but didn't drink and, when nobody was watching, emptied the glass under the table. The soldiers started groping and tried to kiss me, but soon they got so drunk they fell asleep, snoring on the table and the floor. I gathered all my strength and sat without motion, like a statue, waiting to escape the unwanted company with the first ray of daylight. I was afraid the Germans would sober up in the morning and take my presence more seriously. I did not close my eyes the entire night and, as soon as the dawn arrived, sneaked out of the room and rushed toward the main road—away from that place, away from danger. I was groggy after a sleepless night, but had the entire day ahead of me before I could start looking for shelter again and possibly get some sleep... It was bitterly cold. I walked like under a spell, like a robot, occasionally asking people for directions. The darkness had set in when I reached the next village. In a slight reversal of fortune, the owners of the first house I asked to stay at did not refuse my plea, and I rejoiced when they brought me a bowl of hot soup and made a bed on top of a Russian stove.

In my wandering years, whenever I had a place to sleep, I wished the night continued on and on and possibly never ended. Most days, I had nothing to eat, and only by night, when looking for shelter, I began to hope I would be offered a meal. Frequently, there was no such offer, and I went to sleep hungry. I also suffered from a lack of personal hygiene, which was impossible to maintain in the countryside. Even to wash my

---

[1] Many Jews understood German because of its common roots with Yiddish, so showing such aptitude could raise suspicion, especially among the natives.

hands, I had to ask the owners' permission, since water in the villages came from wells and was used sparingly. I couldn't wait to get to the city, sell some of my belongings, and buy a ticket to the public baths. Other than that, I felt nothing except drowsiness and exhaustion. I was a bundle of nerves wrapped in chains on a padlock... Despite my wishes for the opposite, the dawn had arrived. I got up early, pretending to be in a hurry to meet my relatives in Kiev. I thanked the hosts and was on my way—road again, another night, another door to knock on.

By today's measure, the distance between Zhitomir and Kiev is rather short[2], but in times of war, in cold winter, deep snow, and with primitive transportation, it was a very long way. I had been walking for over a week, covering as much distance as possible during the day and staying in people's houses at night. Fortunately, the weather was not very cold, and settlements along the way were smaller villages with residents more willing to take in strangers. Of course, being a woman who posed no threat also played in my favor... I was already close to Kiev when I walked into a larger town. I saw rail tracks and multifamily homes, while people on the streets looked like city folks. I learned from a passerby it was the town of Irpen, a regional center. The town had a flea market that opened twice a week, so I decided to pause to sell my English Boston. I wanted to keep the multicolored shawl—the last memory of my poor, dear parents and the home that was no more.

I had missed the midweek market, and the next one was on Sunday. I found a place to stay with a family of cultured and educated people. The head of the family used to be a college professor, but he lost his job after the Germans occupied the town. His wife was a schoolteacher. They had two children, also college graduates. The son was in the Red Army, and the family had no information about him, while the daughter lived with the parents. My hosts hated the occupiers and locals who collaborated with the Nazis. The Professor was a member of the Communist Party, which put him in a precarious position. He quickly guessed I wasn't who I claimed to be and got a little nervous, albeit he said nothing, and the family continued to share with me all they had. They lived quietly, trying not to attract much attention. I remained in their home for two days, and every time someone knocked on the door, they would rush me to another room before answering the knock. They were afraid of the Germans and the police and, at any moment, could become a target of persecution. I realized it was dangerous to remain there and started looking for another place. I walked from apartment to apartment, house to house, until one

---

[2] Approximately 140 km, or 85 miles.

woman took me in. She lived alone in a large flat and offered me a separate room without asking for anything in return. Her name was Svetlana. She told me her husband had served in the Red Army and was missing in action. Later, she noticed I had no money and began inviting me to eat with her.

I do not remember the price I set for the English Boston, but before taking it to the marketplace, I consulted with my hostess. She fetched her neighbor, who owned a fur shop and was considered an expert in such matters. The furrier examined the fabric, felt it in his fingers, and told me the price I was supposed to ask. As I was opening my bag, he saw the multicolored shawl and wanted to take a closer look. I pulled the shawl out of the bag. The furrier became very excited and offered me a large sum for it, but I replied that the shawl was a gift from my parents and not for sale. The furrier left a little disappointed, and I forgot that episode.

Sunday had arrived—the day of the big market. I took my English Boston and went to the marketplace. It was a riot. People came from all over the town and the surrounding areas. There were many sellers but not so many buyers. I laid out the fabric, and a small crowd gathered around me. The fabric was pretty—deep blue with English stamps, shimmering in the morning sunlight. The stamps made it particularly attractive, as English Boston was highly valued for its quality. The people in the crowd admired my fabric but did not rush to buy. They touched the material, tried to read the stamps, talked to each other, and had a good time. It continued for a while until the group was joined by a German officer. He asked how much I wanted for my Boston, paid the price, and left with the fabric. I was happy. Now, I had a decent sum of money, which, if spent thriftily to buy perhaps one meal a day, could last me a long while.

With the money in my pocket and a place to stay, I decided to spend a few more days in Irpen—rest a little and plan my next move. In the evening, the furrier came to Svetlana's apartment and tried again to talk me into selling the shawl. Once more, I refused. For whatever reason, Svetlana was especially friendly to me that night. She asked me to stay with her a little longer, saying she was lonely and enjoyed my company. However, my hostess was not as lonely as she claimed to be. Every other night, she partied in her apartment with suspicious individuals: men and women. On such nights, I tried to go to bed early, not to see those orgies or be seen by their participants. I was getting restless in Svetlana's place and decided to leave, but it was too late. The following night, when I was already in bed, someone banged on the outside door. Svetlana rushed to my room. She told me to go to the kitchen, lie on the Russian stove, and cover myself with blankets. She suspected it was the police. And sure it was. A few men in police uniforms barged into Svetlana's apartment and accused her of hiding Jews. She denied the accusation. The policemen went straight to my room and started ransacking it. One of them turned out to be Svetlana's acquaintance, probably a guest at her gatherings. After the introduction, Svetlana offered the intruders vodka and some food. They interrupted the search, got to the dining table, and began to party. Holding my breath, I lay on the stove—my stomach was churning, and I felt nauseous. I heard the drunken policemen depart, leaving behind my hostess' friend, who promptly got with her on the floor next to the darkened kitchen. I pulled the blanket over my head, not to hear their moans.

In the morning, Svetlana woke her companion; he put on his uniform and left. Then Svetlana came to the stove. She told me that her neighbor, the furrier, had figured out I was a Jew. According to him, those were mostly Jews who owned such English Boston fabric, which they received from their relatives in America before the war. The policeman my hostess slept with told her that the furrier had reported me to the police. "He wanted to get rid of you to have your shawl," Svetlana said. I replied that I was not Jewish and had a paper confirming my Ukrainian nationality. Svetlana invited me to have breakfast. As soon as we sat down, there was a knock on the door, and another policeman, this time of a higher rank, stepped into the room. He was accompanied by the furrier. "This is she!" exclaimed the furrier, pointing at me. Svetlana got up from the chair and hatefully looked at her neighbor. "She is not a Jew!" she shouted at the intruders, "Why are you harassing her? Leave her alone; she is just a child." "We'll find out who she is," replied the policeman, "in the police station." "Take your belongings and go with me," he addressed me. "She doesn't have any belongings!" screamed Svetlana, who had prudently hidden my bag with the shawl after the first police raid. She then blasted the furrier, calling him a traitor and a scumbag. "You wanted the shawl, but she would not sell it to you, so you ratted her out. You will never get the shawl; it is not here!"

I put on my coat and followed the policeman outside. On the way to the police station, he kept saying I was a "Jew" and would not escape the retribution. I would be shot that day, together with the "other Jews" who had been captured earlier. I did not answer. I walked silently toward my life's end, realizing that it was useless to plead with those murderers and traitors. We reached the police station. My captor led me into a room where, behind a wooden desk, sat a red-haired, middle-aged man in a police uniform. He was the police chief. The deputy announced he had caught "another Jew," whom he wanted to get shot together with a group of Jews scheduled for execution that day. The chief replied it was too late since that group had already been escorted out of the building. "Take this girl," he waved in my direction, "to another room and let her wait there. I want to talk to her." "What do you want to talk to her about?" cried my captor, "She is a Jew and must be shot! Let me take her outside and do it myself so there would be no Jewish stench in this building." "No," replied the chief, "do as I say."

The deputy took me to an adjacent room and placed me next to a wall. Suddenly, we heard multiple shots coming from the courtyard. "Do you hear this?" exclaimed the deputy thrillingly, "These are your people getting shot. You are a little late, but do not worry, you will catch up with them in hell," and he laughed. At that moment, the chief called the deputy into the office. Through the wall, I could hear their conversation and understood that the police chief was resigning from his post and turning the affairs over to my captor, who would become the new chief tomorrow. I stood near the wall, biting my nails. My headscarf was tied on the back, covering the hair completely. I wore that scarf at all times because my hair was slightly wavy, which was considered a Jewish trait by the locals… In a few hours, the deputy returned and tore the scarf off my head. "Hiding your curly, Jewish hair?" he yelled, "It is better this way; you will die beautiful. Why are you biting your nails? Nervous?" I did not answer. My fingers were bleeding. I had little sleep the night before, and my legs and back were like on fire. I asked the deputy for a chair, but he giggled in my face. I fell on the floor. The deputy lifted and put me against the wall. I fell again, and he raised me once more. That was repeated several times to my tormentor's sadistic enjoyment.

Finally, the chief called me in. I could hardly walk, and the deputy hurried me up by kicking me from behind. We entered the chief's room. The chief asked the deputy to step outside and offered me a chair. I sat across that man, my hair flowing over my shoulders, my cheeks blushing from anxiety and exhaustion. I was young and good-looking despite the stress and suffering of the past months. "Who are you?" asked the chief. I showed him Stepan's sister's birth certificate and told my usual tale. The chief asked a few more questions and paused. Of course, he could have checked my story. He could have requested information from Kiev to see if it was my mother who lived at the address I had given him. Or, he could have contacted someone in Yagodinka, where the real Nadezhda Momot lived. Or, he could have kept me overnight, passing my fate to his deputy, who was to become the new chief in the morning and who would have killed me for sure. But the chief did none of those things. Maybe he felt pity for me, or it was fatherly instinct that spoke in him, or he had a guilty conscience and did not want to burden it further by taking another innocent life. He sat quietly for a moment, then called the deputy. "Today, I am still your boss," the chief said to his subordinate, "and I can order you. But I am not ordering—I am asking: do me the last favor, let this girl go." The deputy almost screeched, "How can you do this? She is a Jew!" but the chief insistently repeated his request. "Very well," said the deputy, "I will release her, but she must promise not to leave Irpen until I have contacted her place of birth and her mother's residence in Kiev." "Agreed," replied the chief and, all of a sudden, winked at me conspiratorially as if suggesting not to take my promise seriously.

    I could not believe my eyes and ears. Once again, I had escaped the claws of death. It was a miracle! I quickly signed the form, stating that I would not leave the town, and ran out of the police station. I do not know where I found the courage to go back to Svetlana's apartment to pick up my bag with the unfortunate shawl—it was a huge risk to come near that scoundrel-furrier, who could see me leaving with the bag and alert the authorities. Svetlana was not home, but I knew where she kept her spare key. I quietly opened the door, got inside, and started looking for my bag. At that moment, Svetlana walked in. I told her that I was leaving. She went to the other room and returned with the bag. She then asked me where I was going. I answered that I had to find another place to live since I was afraid of her neighbor. She hugged and kissed me and wished me the best of luck.

3. Frostbites

I rushed away from Irpen as if I had wings. My feet were weak from exhaustion and stress. Constantly turning around, I was running like possessed. I was afraid the Irpen police would discover my absence and start a pursuit. I raced that way for almost an hour until I got to a wide thoroughfare—the road to Kiev.

It was too risky to walk on the open road where the pursuers could easily spot me, so I decided to stop a car or a truck and ask for a ride. I raised my hand. The vehicles kept passing at high speed until one car slowed down and stopped. I approached it and, to my dismay, saw four German officers inside—two in the front and two in the back. It was too late to beat a retreat, so I plucked up my courage and asked the Germans to take me to Kiev. They looked at each other, perhaps surprised to hear a local girl speaking German, then ordered me to the back seat between its two occupants. The officer in the front passenger seat, who seemed to be of a senior rank, inquired where I was heading and who my parents were, and the car moved. For a few minutes, everybody was quiet. Then, one of my neighbors began to fondle me, attempting to reach under my coat. I pushed him away, but he kept charging. The officer in front noticed the scuffle, turned around, and yelled at my attacker to leave me alone. The groper made a gesture of comical frustration and complied.

The car was going very fast. I sat like on thorns. At first, I wanted to ride straight to Sviatoshyno[3], but because of an uneasy company, decided to get off sooner. It was fairly far from Irpen and close to my destination so I could continue on foot. I asked the Germans to stop the car, got out, and walked along the road, looking for passersby who would direct me to Sviatoshyno.

I walked for a long time but did not encounter a single person, on foot or in a horse cart. I got off the main road, hoping to meet someone there. It was getting dark. The weather was terrible—bitterly cold, with strong wind and heavy snow. My hands and feet started to freeze. I felt an urge to relieve my bladder, but could not unbutton the coat with numb fingers. The urge was getting stronger. I could no longer hold it; my pantaloons became wet and froze to my skin. I continued walking. Suddenly, a horse cart appeared from behind the snow curtain next to me. A young man in the driving seat said he was headed for Sviatoshyno, which was not far away. I asked him to give me a ride. He agreed, and in half an hour, we reached the borough.

---

[3] The westernmost borough of Kiev.

It was already dark when I got off the cart. I didn't know where to go. My legs barely carried me, and the frozen underpants made walking even harder. I suddenly felt nauseous and dizzy and realized that I was about to faint. Passing out on the dark, desolate street in bitterly cold weather, almost certainly meant to be found in the morning, frozen to death. The nearest houses were yards away. I gathered all my strength and staggered toward them.

I reached the first house and knocked on its door. A young woman appeared in the window. She saw me and rushed to the entrance. As soon as she opened the door, I slumped to the ground—my eyes rolled up, and my speech was slurring. The woman called someone in the house. An older man came out, and together, they pulled me inside. They laid me on the floor and started removing my clothes. My briefs and pantaloons froze to the skin, and the woman poured warm water over them to melt the ice. When everything came off, I saw lesions on my legs, especially at the top. Those were frostbites. The older man brought a large pan with more water and placed it on a kerosene burner. When the water heated up, the woman washed my body with a sponge and dried it with a towel. Then she gave me a robe to put on and made me hot tea with raspberry preserves and a few teaspoons of alcohol to stave off hypothermia. After that, the hosts put me on a sofa in another room. I fell asleep right away and slept for two days.

I woke up and did not know where I was or what had happened to me. Behind the wall cried a child. A young woman entered the room, and I recognized her as the one who had opened the front door for me. Then, I remembered the rest. The woman introduced herself. Her name was Masha[4]. She lived in the house with a two-year-old son. Her husband served in the Red Army, and she had not heard from him since the war began. The older man who had helped Masha defrost me was her father. He happened to be in Masha's house by chance—came to visit her and the grandson. He and his wife, Masha's mother, lived in their own house, also in Sviatoshyno.

The next two days, I spent at Masha's home. She did not ask me who I was, yet must have guessed it. We quickly developed a rapport. Masha was a little jumpy and hot-tempered, but a sincere and warmhearted woman. Her mother was Jewish and converted to Christianity before the Bolshevik coup to marry Masha's father, who was Russian. Masha's father was a shoemaker, a kind and gentle man. Before the war, he used to make custom shoes mainly for women, but since the occupation, lived

---

[4] Diminutive of Maria.

off occasional repair work. Masha had a brother who, like her husband, was in the Red Army and whose whereabouts were also unknown. Masha got out of the house infrequently and did not want others to see me, either. Being half-Jewish, she felt insecure, as many neighbors stopped acknowledging her after the Germans took over. As for Masha's mother, she was too scared to step outside of her house, even for a little while; Masha's father did all the shopping and other external chores.

Masha did not want me to leave. I was still weak, and she worried I might get sick or freeze to death on the streets. Her house was in a busy section of the borough, while her parents lived in a more secluded area, so they all decided to move me there. The following evening, when it became dark outside, Masha took me to her parents' house. It was a small summer bungalow in a pretty area near the woods. It had one large room, an open kitchen, and a shower stall. The house looked a little cramped in winter, but it was beautiful in summer and appeared far more spacious because of a large, forest-facing deck, where Masha's mother spent most of her time.

When I came to their home that harsh, cold winter, Masha's parents welcomed me with open arms. They gave me food to eat and a place to sleep on the bed of their son, Masha's brother. The name of Masha's mother was Yelena[5], and the father's name was Stepan. I called them aunt and uncle. After introducing me to her mother (Masha's father I had already met), Masha went back home, and I began settling in the new place. My head and entire body itched terribly, so I asked for permission to take a shower. Aunt Yelena looked at my hair and became horrified—it swarmed with lice. She took a comb and started combing the bugs out. I was shaking from embarrassment and fatigue. Seeing my anguish, Aunt Yelena began to cry. Meanwhile, Uncle Stepan heated several pots of water and filled the shower tank. The hosts seldom took showers, saving water, but they were happy to arrange one for me. Aunt Yelena got in the shower with me and washed my body with a brush and soap (which, in those times, was almost as valuable as gold). After the shower, she gave me a clean nightgown, washed my underwear, and hung it in the kitchen to dry. For the first time in several months, I felt clean. I went to bed and slept through the night and the following day. My hosts did not disturb me. When I woke up, Aunt Yelena was sitting next to my bed. She was looking at me, and tears rolled down her face. Nobody asked me any questions. They understood everything.

---

[5] Russian equivalent of "Helen."

Aunt Yelena and Uncle Stepan insisted that I remain with them a few more days. The frostbite on my legs bothered me, but I didn't mention it, not to inconvenience the hosts even more. I realized I would be leaving soon. They worried about me, but also about themselves. Aunt Yelena implored me to stay inside, not to be seen by the neighbors. She, herself, got out of the house as seldom as possible. I understood her well. Having married outside her faith, when such marriages were unwelcome and rare, she got hung in limbo. The Jewish relatives disavowed her, while the new family and friends could not entirely fill the void. After the Bolshevik revolution, mixed marriages became more common, but now, under the Nazi regime, the past divisions grew deeper and more deadly for the Jews than when they were based on religious beliefs. Aunt Yelena was unsure and scared of what the Germans and the police might do if they discovered her origins. Uncle Stepan loved his wife and worried about her safety. He tried to bring everything into the house so that Aunt Yelena wouldn't have to go outside and remind the neighbors of her existence.

When I told Aunt Yelena that I was leaving, she cried again and urged me to be careful. She said I could visit them anytime, take a shower, and stay overnight. She only asked to come after dark so the neighbors would not see me… The next morning, I put on my coat, kissed Aunt Yelena, Uncle Stepan, and Masha (who came over to wish me good luck), and thanked them for helping me in a critical moment, for saving my life. Once more, they asked me to come and take care of myself. In a few short days of living with those kind people, I got attached to them, and it was difficult for me to say goodbye.

4. Doctor's Appointment

I walked toward Kiev, not knowing whom I would meet on the way and where I would sleep the approaching night. It was very cold; the snow began to fall. The frostbites on my legs were like on fire, but I tried not to think about them. I walked slowly. The roads were filled with people going to the city and coming from it. There were many German soldiers and officers on foot and in moving vehicles. The Germans were armed.

By dusk, I was in Kiev-proper, knocking on doors and asking for a place to sleep. I modified my story, adding a part where I did not find my parents at their address (maybe they got killed or had left Kiev) and was now going back to Lvov… Compared to the countryside, the city had many more places to ask for a night's stay, but not as welcoming a public. Some did not have enough space; others were afraid to let strangers in. Finally, I found lodging in a two-family house. A middle-aged woman who invited me inside warned that the premises had no heat, and I would have to sleep under my coat and other warmers the hosts might provide. It was still better than spending the night on the street, so I gladly agreed. The apartment had two rooms and a kitchen, accommodating a family of five. After hearing my story, the hosts invited me to join them for dinner. They noted the meal was particularly delicious that night. Earlier in the day, they found bovine guts in a refuse bin near a meat factory where the Germans slaughtered livestock to feed the army. My hosts stuffed those guts with other meat refuse from the same bin and made soup and a main course. Everybody sat down at the table. In those days, hunger was my constant companion, and that soup with stuffed guts, made from refuse, tasted so good that I savor its memory even today.

We finished dinner and prepared for the night's sleep, as it was too chilly in the apartment to do anything else. The hosts showed me to my bed and brought me a blanket. My hands and feet were numb from the cold, and the frostbites ached and burned. I lay down, covered myself with the owners' blanket, and added my coat on top, but couldn't sleep because of the chill and pain. I endured the entire night. In the morning, I said goodbye to my hosts, thanked them for the delicious supper, and headed for the Volynski Market to buy myself something to eat.

I calculated that eating one small meal a day would stretch my Boston fabric money until spring. At the Volynski Market, farmers sold portions of yellow pig fat (salo) with slices of cornbread. One small salo cube and a thin slice of bread cost ten roubles. It was a lot of money, but there was nothing cheaper—everything was very expensive. I would buy one such portion and eat it slowly, in small bites, to prolong the pleasure and better satisfy my appetite. An hour later, I was hungry again and remained so until the next morning, when I would buy the same meal and quench the hunger a little. Such a ration ought to sustain me through the winter. As soon as the weather became warmer, I could go to the countryside, where it was easier to obtain food. The farmers had bread, milk, and potatoes. If they let me stay overnight, they might also offer me something to eat.

Meanwhile, I remained in Kiev, going from apartment to apartment, from house to house, asking for a place to sleep. I alternated between different parts of the city, not to become a familiar face, as I kept telling everybody I was passing by. It was easier to find accommodations in the city outskirts in private houses, where owners were more hospitable. One night, I had been searching for shelter unusually long. It was midnight already, but nobody let me in. I did not know what to do. The weather was cold but tolerable, as the deep freeze of the past few weeks yielded to a thaw. I was afraid to walk Kiev's streets at night because of drunks, thieves, and other nefarious characters, so I hid in a latrine booth in the courtyard of one of the buildings. I locked the booth's door inside and spent all night suffocating from the stench and trying not to fall asleep. At dawn, I left my hideout and wandered the streets.

During the day, I usually went to the nearest marketplace and walked between the aisles as if looking for something to buy. When the weather was warmer, I would go to a city park, sit on a bench near some older, decent-looking folk, and try to strike up a conversation. I always carried my bag, so the bench neighbors occasionally asked me who I was and where I was heading. I told them my usual cover story and often evoked a sympathetic response, at which point I asked for a place to sleep. Many agreed to provide accommodations, although only for one night. But for me, even one night was bliss: I would stretch on a cot or a floor and drop off in seconds. It seemed I had just closed my eyes, but the morning was already there—time to get up and be on my way.

A few more months had passed; spring was around the corner. All that time, I did not bathe or take off my clothes. The frostbite pain was almost unbearable; I was afraid to even look at my legs. Clearly, the problem would not go away on its own, so one day, I inspected the sores. What I saw frightened me: deep, festered wounds almost to the bone. I realized I needed medical attention. Seeing a doctor was too risky since it involved filling out a questionnaire and giving out personal information that might raise suspicions. So, I decided to go back to Sviatoshyno to see Aunt Yelena and ask for their help. I started to Sviatoshyno on foot, but my legs were weak, wounds ablaze, and I had no strength to walk. I raised my hand to stop a car. Nobody reacted to my gestures for a while until one truck halted, and the driver took me straight to Aunt Yelena's house. As I got out of the truck, Uncle Stepan saw me through the window and ran outside. He and Aunt Yelena kept hugging and kissing me like their daughter. Aunt Yelena couldn't hold back tears looking at my haggard, anguished face. She began sobbing uncontrollably when I showed her my legs. Uncle Stepan stood silently, his head hanging in sorrow. He then put on a coat and went out to bring Masha while Aunt Yelena undressed me, combed my hair, and started the shower. Like the last time, she gave me her nightgown and washed my clothes. Then, she gave me something to eat. The food was scanty, but they had little of it in the house, even for themselves.

Masha and Uncle Stepan arrived, and we began discussing how to arrange my visit to a doctor. Sviatoshyno had a clinic where physicians of various specialties treated patients for a modest fee. The fee was paid at the time of registration for the visit. We decided Masha would make an appointment for herself, and I would go to the doctor in her place. The clinic was always busy, and appointments were made days in advance, so it was unlikely anyone would notice the switch. In the meantime, my hosts made me a bed; I lay down and, as usual, dropped off in seconds... The next morning, Masha went to the clinic to set up an appointment with a surgeon. I wanted to give her the fee money, but she categorically refused it and paid out of her own pocket. Of course, Aunt Yelena and Uncle Stepan did not let me leave, so I remained in their house, waiting for the day of the doctor's visit.

The trees and grass had already turned green. It was getting too warm for my winter boots, but I had nothing else to wear. Uncle Stepan found a pair of old Masha's shoes, fixed them, and gave them to me. Now, my stay became even more pleasant. Days I spent in the nearby forest, where I sneaked early in the morning via a path from Aunt Yelena's house. The forest was peaceful and cheery. The budding vegetation filled the air with lovely smells under the high dome of birdsongs. Nature celebrated new life, oblivious to the death and destruction inhabiting its realm. I returned to the house at dusk, hoping my hosts had finished dinner. I felt uneasy eating their scant food, but they insisted I join them. In the beginning, they asked me where I had lived and what I had been doing over the past few months. I told them little. I did not want to lie, but could not tell the truth either. They understood it and asked no more.

On the day of the appointment, I went to the clinic alone. The surgeon was appalled when he saw my sores. He started to admonish me for neglecting the wounds. He could not understand why I asked for medical help only now. I was silent. He looked at me suspiciously. "You could have gotten an infection of the entire body and died," he said. I felt indifferent and showed no reaction to his warnings. The doctor cleaned my wounds, put on bandages, made an injection, and told me to come back in a couple of days. On a given date, I went to see him again. He changed the bandages, applied ointment to the sores, and made another injection. "It is healing well," he said, "Come see me in two weeks to make sure everything is alright." I thanked him and went back to Aunt Yelena's place.

After the second doctor's visit, I felt much better and was ready to move on. I saw my hosts' concern for me and was grateful to them from the bottom of my heart. Although the doctor told me to come in two weeks, I could no longer stay with those people, eat their paltry food, and sense their fear for me and themselves. And so I left, having promised Aunt Yelena to visit them soon. Once again, to roam the streets and markets of Kiev and not know what the next day would bring.

5. Honey Cake

I returned to Kiev and resumed my "normal" life—roaming the streets during the day and searching for a place to sleep at night. One morning, I went to the formerly known as "Jewish" market to buy myself something to eat. It was the largest market in Kiev, always crowded, especially on Sundays. As I walked through the aisles, the smell of freshly made pastry pleasantly struck my senses. The smell was coming from a stand where a middle-aged woman was selling honey cake. I bought one piece for ten roubles. The cake turned out to be very tasty and filling. For the same money, it was a far better meal than my daily menu of yellow salo with cornbread, so I decided to switch. I started coming to the Jewish Market to buy that woman's cake. She noticed my regular appearances and asked why I was buying a piece of cake every day. I told her my story, which I altered, replacing the going-back-to-Lvov part with where I remained in Kiev, waiting for my parents to find me. The woman reacted with great empathy and invited me to her home. The following day, I waited until she had sold the cake and went with her.

The woman's name was Maria Ilyinichna[6]. She was a widow, living with her daughter, Olga, in a semi-basement studio in a large apartment building. The entrance to their apartment was through the building's courtyard. Maria Ilyinichna was a cultured person. She was an excellent seamstress but had few customers in those desperate years. She baked the honey cake at home. Olga worked as an accountant's assistant. Both mother and daughter were warm, lovely people. Having learned that I had nobody in Kiev, they invited me to stay with them for several days. Maria Ilyinichna said that her late husband's relatives, who lived in the same building, occasionally visited her apartment, and they'd better not see me. She was especially afraid of the son of her sister-in-law, a young man named Zhora[7], whom she suspected of being a Gestapo informer. He was the main reason Maria Ilyinichna asked me not to walk through the courtyard and use the apartment's window facing the street instead.. She seemed not to have entirely bought my story, but it did not stop her from taking me in.

I was thrilled by so generous a sanctuary offer. Maria Ilyinichna slept on a bed in the living room while Olga on a sofa there, and they gave me a cot to sleep in the kitchen. Olen'ka (as people affectionately called Olga) was a beautiful young woman. A slender brunette, she attracted

---

[6] First name + patronymic.

[7] Diminutive of Georgy (George).

everyone's attention with her good looks. She dressed in style in clothes tailored for her by Maria Ilyinichna. Olen'ka had an engaging personality and, like her mother, was educated and refined. She was the only child whom Maria Ilyinichna gave the best rearing she could afford. Having met Olen'ka once, people remembered her for a long time. She used to attend a medical school and was about to start the third year when the war interrupted her studies. The two women were close; Olen'ka revered her mother and kept no secrets from her.

Olen'ka was courted by a young man named Zhenia[8]. He followed her everywhere, partly at the behest of Maria Ilyinichna, who was afraid of Olen'ka's good looks attracting the attention of the Germans. Zhenia was a polite and quiet person, if not particularly handsome. He walked Olen'ka to work in the morning and waited for her outside when she was leaving the office at night. Before the war, Zhenia studied in college but did not graduate. Maria Ilyinichna loved Zhenia like her own son, yet Olen'ka was lukewarm about him. Zhenia's parents adored Olen'ka and dreamed of their son marrying her. They were well-to-do, and it was Zhenia's father who had helped Olen'ka with the job. He was a scientist, a full professor in one of Kiev's colleges. After the city's capture by the Nazis, he worked with his German colleagues on research projects and had connections in the new administration.

I lived in the home of Maria Ilyinichna and Olen'ka for two weeks. Maria Ilyinichna had a bad heart, so I helped her carry the cake. Early in the morning, when the neighbors were still asleep, Maria Ilyinichna and I would go to the market together. Our stand's size was just enough to hold a single loaf. I stood behind Maria Ilyinichna, and when she finished one loaf, I passed her another so that the selling could continue uninterrupted. The cake was selling fast, as it was very tasty. Maria Ilyinichna did not make much money off it, but that income helped them get by. Coming from the market, we would separate: Maria Ilyinichna would go through the courtyard, open the window, and I would crawl into the apartment from the street. A couple of times, her husband's relatives came for a visit. Upon the knock on the door, I would get under the bed and lie there quietly, like a mouse, for a few hours until the visitors left.

During my stay with Maria Ilyinichna and Olen'ka, I visited public baths twice. What a pleasure those trips brought me! The first time I went there, Olen'ka gave me her clean nightgown, bra, and panties so I could wash my underwear. Like most homes in Kiev at the time, Maria Ilyinichna's apartment had no running water—the water had to be carried

---

[8] Diminutive of Yevgeny (Eugene).

from the courtyard, where the building's only functioning faucet was located, operating for a few hours a day. Olen'ka and sometimes Maria Ilyinichna hauled the buckets of water into the apartment. I couldn't help them without showing my face in the courtyard, so I tried to use as little water as possible. I washed my underwear in a shower stall at the public baths. I dried it up at home and returned to Olen'ka her things.

Maria Ilyinichna and Olen'ka were artistic individuals with excellent taste. Olen'ka sometimes combed my hair like a stylist or made me try her high-heeled shoes and evening gowns. I looked good in them. Alas, fate planned for me not the life of a young woman, full of happiness and love, but years of distress and need to hide all signs of femininity and beauty. A headscarf down to the eyebrows concealed my lush hair, and when talking to others, I looked down and made a forced smile: not to attract attention, to remain in the shadow. I was afraid of everybody and everything. And still, behind that meek appearance, a strong voice in me kept saying: "Do not give up. Fight. You must survive."

I saw that Maria Ilyinichna and Olen'ka felt sorry for me. They never asked about my family and past life, but must have realized who I was and what had happened to me. They likely figured I was Jewish—a tiny fragment of a smashed vessel that had escaped the sweeper's blade—and wanted to help as much as they could. Of course, they were afraid of punishment for sheltering a Jew, yet tried not to show their fears.

While in Maria Ilyinichna's home, I caught a cold and coughed a lot. Maria Ilyinichna made me warm milk with baking soda, but the cough would not go away. All that time, I evaded Zhora, Maria Ilyinichna's nephew, whom she had warned me about, but eventually, he spotted me. I was getting into the apartment through the window when he walked to the street from around the corner and saw me. In the evening, he paid a visit to Maria Ilyinichna. I hid behind the cupboard. Suddenly, an urge to cough overwhelmed me. I tried to suppress it by swallowing, but the urge was getting stronger. There were a few pillows behind the cupboard; I sank my face into them, trying to hold the cough. Sweat was running down my face, and I began to choke, but managed to remain silent until Zhora left. When Maria Ilyinichna saw me—disheveled, red-faced, and gasping for air—she started to cry and developed chest pain. Olen'ka got scared and confused: she didn't know whom to help first, her mother or me. She gave Maria Ilyinichna nitroglycerine, put her in bed, and sat nearby, gently stroking her mother's hand. I was sitting on the floor, exhausted and upset, with a terrible sense of guilt before my hosts. In an hour, Maria Ilyinichna recovered. Olen'ka got up, hugged and kissed me, and started setting up my cot for the night... The next morning, I decided to leave. After the encounter with Zhora, I no longer felt safe in that place, nor did I want to cause my hosts more trouble. Maria Ilyinichna and Olen'ka did not stop me. They said they would be happy to see me again, and I could always count on them when I needed a place to stay.

6. Trees in the Snow

The day I left Maria Ilyinichna and Olen'ka, the people who became so dear to me, I went to the countryside. The spring was in full bloom, and I needed a lighter headscarf. My winter scarf was too warm, but I was still afraid to take it off... The money from the English Boston had run out. I went to the marketplace and sold my beloved multicolored shawl. I was no longer sorry to part with it—the passage of time and experience of the past months had set my priorities straight, making survival my conscious, most important goal.

With a part of the shawl money, I bought a light headscarf to replace the one I had been wearing since Yagodinka. I put the old scarf in the bag and set out for the country. The frostbites on my legs ached a little, but they were healing fast, and the pain would soon go away... I got to the nearest highway and joined the stream of city dwellers heading for the village. I was lucky to have owned the English Boston and the shawl, which sold quickly for a good price, but most pilgrims had nothing for sale at the flea market, so they roamed the countryside, trying to barter their possessions for bread and potatoes. I did not have anything to trade either, but walked with the rest, blending in. From early morning to late night, I was on the road, occasionally resting on a rock or a fallen tree. I traveled ten to fifteen kilometers a day. My legs were tired, my head ached, and my stomach cramped, but I walked and walked, looking for a place to spend the coming night. Frequently, nobody let me in, or the night caught me on the way. When that happened, I would walk into the forest, lie under a tree or a bush, and sleep there until dawn. It was not a sound sleep; I was afraid of wild animals and even more of people. I yearned for a little room with nothing but a bed—a place to sleep, safe and quiet, far away from everybody and everything. At daybreak, I got up and walked again.

In Kiev and its surroundings, there were many German soldiers and officers; however, I was not afraid of them. They could not tell Ukrainian Jews from non-Jews—to Germans, all natives looked the same. I feared more my compatriots, who had a keener sense of local ethnic differences and could recognize me as a Jew. Former Soviet prisoners of war and deserters who roamed the area often worked for the farmers in exchange for food and shelter. I thought of getting a similar job (crop picking or housework) but gave up the idea, afraid to stay in the same home, and even the same village, for more than a few days.

Things started to look up with the arrival of summer. I no longer had to search for shelter every night and slept in the forest or at the roadside.

It became easier to walk; I could get near a lake or a river and rest. There were days when I did not eat at all. When that happened, I would go to a local market the next morning and buy some food or, if there was no marketplace nearby, knock on someone's door and ask the owners to sell me a piece of bread and a glass of milk. Many sold it for little money; others refused the payment and gave the food out of the goodness of their heart. That summer, I did not return to Kiev but drifted between villages in the Kiev Oblast. Autumn came, and my life became more complicated. Strong winds and frequent rainfalls made it harder to travel. I often asked farmers' permission to hide from the rain in a storage room or under an overhang near the house. Some invited me inside, where they offered me a hot meal and a place to sleep. What happy moments those were!

The money from the multicolored shawl also ran out, and I decided to return to Kiev to sell my American watch. I was far from the city, albeit within the Kiev Oblast, which spanned a vast territory. Again, I walked toward Kiev, asking for a night's stay. A few years into the war, people were less welcoming to strangers, and after several attempts to secure a roof over my head, I often ended up on the street. In those cases, I slept in the forest on the village outskirts—took my winter coat and headscarf out of the bag and put them on, as nights were already chilly. That fall, I did not reach Kiev; I got a babysitting job in one of the villages. The pay was room and board. The child's mother had surgery in the town and was expected to remain in the hospital for a month. The owners seemed like nice people, so I took a chance on a longer stay.

The winter had arrived, snowy and cold. The babysitting job ended, and I resumed my route. One day at sundown, I wandered into a small village and started knocking on doors, asking for a place to spend the night. Nobody let me in. People on the street told me the next village was not far away. They pointed me in that village's direction, and I walked there, following the footprints in the snow. The old village had already vanished from sight when, all of a sudden, heavy snow began to fall, accompanied by a strong wind. The beaten path quickly disappeared, and I lost my way. I stood in the back of beyond, surrounded by darkness, and did not know where to go. Suddenly, far ahead, I saw what looked like a cluster of black patches on a boundless white blanket covering the ground. I thought the patches were a settlement and walked toward them, struggling with the wind and wiping snow that plastered my face. When I reached the dark objects, they turned out to be several trees with nothing nearby. I realized I had strayed. Wild gusts of wind made it difficult to stand. I began to worry that I might not endure until morning, when it would be possible to see around and look for help. I sat down on a snow-covered tree stump. An urge to empty my bladder rose in me, but I could not change my position and went into my pants, which froze right away. I sat immovable, fighting drowsiness, as I knew I would turn into an icicle and never wake up if I succumbed to sleep. "This is where death caught up with me," I thought, and summoned all my willpower to stay awake. Whenever slumber descended upon me, a mental alarm rang in my head, and I woke up.

Incredibly, I managed to remain awake until dawn. At the first gleam of daylight, I saw a sleigh pulled by a pair of horses and realized I was close to the road. I waved my hand, trying to attract the people in the sleigh's attention. They noticed me, got off the sled, and walked toward me. The last thing I recalled was two figures approaching me through the snow, and then everything went blank… A couple of days later, when I regained consciousness, my rescuers (they were husband and wife) told me how they had carried me to the sleigh and brought me to their house in the village. They checked my pulse to see if I was still alive, undressed me, and began to rub my body to restore circulation. When I showed signs of life, they poured a glass of vodka into my throat and put me on the top of a Russian stove, where I slept for two days and two nights. In two days, they woke me up to give me something to eat. That I already remembered, hazily, like in a dream—the hosts fed me chicken soup with a spoon. I felt weak and slipped back into slumber. The sleeping spell continued for five more days. Then, I woke up with a terrible headache and muscle pain. I was running a high fever. My hosts figured I had the flu or pneumonia. There was no doctor in the village, and no medications were in the house, so the owners treated me with herbs and other natural remedies.

I don't know how I pulled through, but in about a week, I suddenly felt better and was able to get off the stove and walk around the house. My hosts asked me who I was and what I had been doing in the open field where they found me. I told them my story about the parents I had been looking for since the beginning of the war. The hosts invited me to stay with them as long as I needed, but in a few days, when the neighbors became curious about my persona and the freeze eased slightly, I thanked my rescuers and continued toward Kiev.

7. Sviatoshyno Misfortune

I reached Kiev, exhausted from the long walk and weak from the recent illness. I had no strength to go between homes looking for a night's stay, and went straight to Maria Ilyinichna. It was already dark outside when I came near her window. Behind the closed shutters, I saw the light in the room and gently tapped on the glass. Olen'ka appeared behind the pane. She saw me and called her mother. Maria Ilyinichna opened the window; I looked around to make sure nobody was watching and crawled inside.

Maria Ilyinichna and Olen'ka were delighted to see me. They were already worried, not having heard from me for an extended time. Maria Ilyinichna started preparing dinner while Olen'ka brought a few buckets of water, heated them on a kerosene burner, and made me a "bath." She poured the water over my head, and I washed my hair, which had not seen such a treatment for quite a while. Then, I washed my body and feet in a large basin. Olen'ka brought more water, and I washed my clothes, wearing Maria Ilyinichna's robe. We hung the clothes near the stove to dry. I was so grateful to my dear friends. Once more, I felt like a human being and not a dirty animal. Maria Ilyinichna and Olen'ka did not ask me anything. They guessed from my appearance that I had been through a lot and were glad to see me alive. They made me a bed in the kitchen, like before. Maria Ilyinichna invited me to stay for a few days; she asked me to be cautious and remain inside, as her nephew Zhora had already inquired about me. He could be watching their apartment. The rumors were that he was a Gestapo agent. I told Maria Ilyinichna I had come to Kiev to sell my watch. I would wait until the Sunday market, go there early in the morning, and not come back, thus escaping Zhora's sight.

The following three days, I spent in Maria Ilyinichna's home. In the morning, Olen'ka would leave for work, Maria Ilyinichna would go to the Jewish Market with the cake, and I remained in the apartment alone, waiting for their return. When someone knocked on the door, I did not answer, and if my hosts had visitors in the evening, I would crawl under the bed and lie there until the guests left. Maria Ilyinichna seemed more anxious lately; her heart condition had worsened, and I felt guilty causing her trouble. She had a lot on her mind, although not all of it was bad. The better part was that Olen'ka and Zhenia were getting married. Maria Ilyinichna always wanted that marriage; however, Olen'ka did not hurry. She didn't love Zhenia, but must have decided that such a marriage was advantageous in those times. She would enter a well-to-do, privileged home, where Zhenia was the only child, and the two women would find safety and comfort. Olen'ka said that she wanted me at the wedding, but realized I might be risking too much.

On Sunday, Maria Ilyinichna woke me up early, and I left my usual way—through the apartment's window. Our farewell was heartfelt. The hosts asked me to come again. Three days in their home had given me much-needed rest, helping me recover from the deadly ordeal in the frozen steppe... Despite the early hours, the market was full of people. I sold the watch quickly, albeit not for a lot of money, as there were many watches for sale that day. Still, I was happy with the money I got. After the market, I decided to go to Sviatoshyno to visit Aunt Yelena and Uncle Stepan, whom I had not seen in a while. The shoes Uncle Stepan gave me during my last stay there had fallen apart, so fixing them was a good excuse to drop by.

I reached Aunt Yelena's house at dusk and knocked on the door. An unfamiliar woman came to the porch. Surprised, I asked for Aunt Yelena and Uncle Stepan. The woman replied that they no longer lived there. Aunt Yelena and her daughter with the little boy had been detained by the Gestapo as Jews. What happened to them, the woman didn't know. After his family's arrest, Uncle Stepan lost his mind, and where he was, or still alive, she did not know, either.

I was shocked by the horrible news, but afraid to ask more questions. I turned around and quickly walked away, trying not to raise suspicions, as I sensed the woman's joy over the previous owners' misfortune. How sorry I was for those kind and generous people. All my life, I carried love and gratitude toward them. Years later, when visiting Kiev for the first time after the war, I went to Babi Yar[9] and laid flowers at the mass grave of Nazi victims in sacred memory of Aunt Yelena, Uncle Stepan, and Masha with her little boy—my beautiful friends, whose true resting place remains unknown to me.

---

[9] A place of mass executions of Jews, marked by a postwar memorial.

8. Cold Spell

I did not walk but ran away from Aunt Yelena's house. I was crushed and saddened by the dreadful news, but also afraid. The emotional stress had stirred in me all kinds of fear. What if the neighbors recognized me as someone who had stayed in Aunt Yelena's house? They might report their suspicions to the police, which would start looking for me... I got on the Brest-Litovsk highway and walked toward Kiev. Night caught me on the way, and except for the forest, there was no place to sleep. I kept walking. Occasionally, I sat down on a mound or a tree stump, but when I started to feel drowsy, I got up and walked again.

I reached Kiev by dawn, gloomy, tired, and hungry. I went to the Vladimirsky Market, bought a small piece of bread with stale butter, and devoured it. What's next? The weather was freezing, and I felt slightly feverish but was afraid to go to Maria Ilyinichna because of Zhora. I walked in a random direction, still shaken by the tragedy that had struck Aunt Yelena's family, and in some while, found myself in Demeevka, the city's outer section of mainly one-story houses. I made several attempts to find shelter for the night, but without success. It was still daytime, so I went to the local market and meandered there until dusk. After the market closed, I resumed my shelter search, where I knocked on the door of a small house not far from the marketplace. A middle-aged woman opened the door. She asked who I was and invited me in. After hearing my story, she said I could stay for a couple of weeks until I was ready to continue looking for my parents. The woman's name was Christina; she was the house's owner. Christina lived alone. Her husband died before the war, and they had no children. She was employed at a pastry factory, often working night shifts. Christina said I could sleep on a cot in the kitchen and use her bed when she worked overnight.

Christina owned half of the house, which, like many similar houses in the city, had a second apartment on the other side. Christina's apartment comprised a living room and a kitchen. In the evenings, it would become a meeting place for her friends, a group of young men and women. They listened to music, discussed the situation on the battlefront, sometimes had drinks. They were coming even when the hostess was away, and often stayed overnight, sleeping all over the premises. It was dangerous to walk Kiev's streets late at night, as there were many robberies, rapes, and even murders.

Staying at the same address for an extended time was less risky in the city than in the country. In a small village, where everybody knew each other, a new face aroused great curiosity, while city people encountered unfamiliar faces all the time. Thus, lodging with Christina for a couple of weeks was a stroke of luck, especially during one of the winter's coldest stretches. Still, the enduring sense of danger kept me on alert. I tried to limit human interactions to a minimum. I would leave Cristina's house in the morning, pretending to have some business in the city, and wander through the streets and marketplaces. I ate once a day, buying food with the money from the American watch. Cristina's friends often invited me to join them, but I shunned their company. In the evenings, when they assembled in the apartment, I would go to the backyard and sit in a small gazebo, but eventually, I had to go back to the house. When it was too cold to stay in the gazebo, I would take a book and pretend to read while listening to the conversations around me. I didn't know if those meetings had an agenda, but I frequently heard discussions about the underground and events on the battlefield. The way they talked, it was hard to tell on whose side those young people were—everything was roundabout—but they would not be masking their thoughts if they sympathized with the occupiers.

Two weeks had passed. The freeze continued, and Christina invited me to stay for a few more weeks until it got a little warmer outside. I was very happy about that invitation. The money from the American watch had already run out, and I had nothing else to sell. Christina sometimes treated me to pancakes and boiled potatoes; however, I remained hungry. When she was out at work, I could be tempted by the food in the house, but never thought of touching it. That would have meant betraying my hostess' trust, becoming a thief, and it was not how my parents brought my sisters and me up. We were taught to be always honest. On the days when Christina was home, I often told her I was going to a cafeteria, but walked the streets instead and returned at sundown, pretending to be full.

One day, I noticed that a young man who was a regular at the nightly gatherings developed an interest in me. His name was Vadim. He was about twenty years of age, tall, handsome, with blond hair and blue eyes. He was a little overweight but stood out with his good looks. I liked men with light hair and blue or grey eyes; however, in those times of danger and turmoil, such fancies were deeply buried inside me. I was terrified to have become an object of Vadim's attention, but couldn't leave, as the frigid weather had trapped me in Christina's home. Vadim started to bring me chocolates and pastries. At first, I refused to accept them, but Christina assured me that Vadim was a highly ethical person and I ought not to doubt his intentions. She told me that he was from an upscale, well-to-do family. His father had died, and his mother was obsessed with her son. Vadim had attended medical school before the war, but since the occupation, did various odd jobs. His mother pampered him; she worried that he might marry someone undeserving of their status… I asked my host why Vadim stayed in her apartment overnight and how his mother allowed it. Christina explained that Vadim's mother was glad that he had a place to stay after dark because of the street crime, even if she might not entirely approve of his company.

I liked Vadim. He was of fine stock, had excellent manners, and was warm, attentive, and generous. Still, I ought not to entertain romantic thoughts. Stress, grief, and fear for my life suppressed in me every desire. I felt like a trapped animal looking for an escape route. I could not show the slightest interest in Vadim, as doing so might raise questions about me. "Maybe he suspects that I am Jewish," I thought, "What would he do if he knew for sure? And what about his mother? Would she report me to the police, like Stepan's parents once threatened to do, to stop her son from marrying a Jew?" I hoped that my lukewarm response would discourage Vadim, but his affection grew. The nights I slept in Christina's bed and Vadim stayed overnight with the others, he would often ask me to move over and lie down next to me. We all slept fully dressed. At first, I could not close my eyes, afraid he might start making advances, but he never touched me. In the morning, he would get up, wash his face, and leave, only to show up in the evening with more presents. When I was in the gazebo, he would go to the backyard, looking for me. He would sit next to me and try to start a conversation, sometimes asking about my past, but I would change the subject and suggest we go back to the house. He obediently followed me inside, where his friends had been waiting for him already.

Vadim's gentlemanly behavior, his correctitude, drew me to him. I often fantasized about such a friend in life. He seemed to be the man of every woman's dreams. Still, deeply inside, my guiding spirit whispered to me: "Do not let your emotions get the best of you. Run away, or you will perish." And I decided to leave—secretly, without telling anyone. Of course, it might have been ungrateful to my hostess, a kind woman who helped me in a difficult moment, but I could not risk being deterred by her. It was still freezing outside, so I postponed my escape for another week…

The following night, Vadim did not come with the others. His friends informed the group that he had the flu. In those days, even a simple cold presented a serious health risk, and I would have felt awful if I had left without knowing Vadim was all right. Thus, I decided to wait until he got better and reappeared at Christina's house.

BK1.CH3 — TOWN AND COUNTRY

A few days passed; Vadim did not show up. One of his friends told me that Vadim had developed pneumonia. Vadim's friend gave me a note from Vadim asking me to visit him. The note provided the address. The next day, I went to see Vadim. I could have never imagined that he lived in such a large, beautiful house. An attractive, young-looking woman opened the door. She was Vadim's mother. The woman politely asked me to come in, but her eyes expressed some caution. I walked inside and was astonished by the opulence of the interior—large rooms, shiny parquet floors covered with Persian rugs, mahogany furniture, and paintings on the walls. Fine crystal, antique china, and various trinkets were scattered throughout the house. I had never been to a place like that in my entire life... Vadim's mother invited me to take off my coat and sit in the hall. She then went upstairs to tell Vadim I had arrived. By her demeanor, I understood she had expected me. I took off the overcoat, exposing the dress I had worn since Chudnov, and removed the headscarf not to look like a farm girl amidst that luxury. I wore a scarf even inside Christina's apartment. Perhaps she and her guests found it odd, but nobody said anything.

Vadim's mother returned. I saw she was surprised by my look with long, flowing hair. My cheeks blushed as I was nervous, even more so under her visual inspection. She said Vadim was waiting for me in his room. We got to the second floor; she pointed me to Vadim's bedroom and went downstairs. I knocked on the door. Vadim half-sat on a pillow in the bed, dressed in blue silk pajamas. His eyes lit up when he saw me. He looked very sick. A severe cough suffocated him, and he had a fever. I came closer. Vadim took my hand and said: "How beautiful you are. Your hair, I have never seen you so beautiful. I asked you to come because I wanted to tell you that I love you. I am very ill right now, but if I recover, I will marry you and go with you to Earth's end. My mother knows everything. I told her that nothing would separate you and me. You have just come in, and I am already feeling better." I stood quietly. He kissed my hand. I sat on the chair next to his bed and tried to comfort him, saying that he was strong enough to overcome the disease and would be all right. Vadim calmed down a little and continued in a more composed manner. He told me that his family was of Polish descent. His father used to be a prominent architect but died early. Vadim's father worshipped his wife and might have spoiled her; still, she was a good mother who loved Vadim very much. Of course, no woman in the world was worthy of her son, but she would have to accept his choice or risk losing him forever... I saw that it was difficult for him to talk. I got up to leave, but he asked me to stay a little longer. I promised to come again. Vadim was happy to hear it. At that moment, his mother walked into the room. She saw me leaving, thanked me for stopping by, and escorted me to the outside door.

I walked back to Christina's apartment, seeing nothing before me but Vadim's ecstatic face. A strong desire to confide in him, to tell him about myself, arose in me, but that feeling yielded to my usual wariness. "No," I thought, "I cannot take a risk. I must vanish, disappear from his life. I will wait a few days, and as soon as he gets better, I will leave and never see him again. As time passes, he will forget about me, find another love, and be happy." I wished him happiness with all my heart. "As for me, danger and suffering are my lot. Future struggles will fade my feelings toward Vadim. If I survive, I will remember him as a beam of light in my dark existence." So I mused on the way to Christina's place. Christina was home. She noticed that I was upset and asked what had happened. I replied that I was saddened by Vadim's condition. A couple of days later, Vadim's friends brought a message from him—he felt better and wanted me to come again. I went there once more.

Vadim's mother opened the door and impassively let me inside. I walked up the stairs to Vadim's room. Vadim was pacing across it, his eyes glowing with love and joy. He smiled and kissed my hands. He was pale but very handsome—the blue pajamas accentuated his good looks. I smiled back and asked how he was. "Very well," said Vadim, "After your first visit, I felt much better and have been improving since." Then, he asked me to visit him every day until he fully recovered. His mother was informed of his wishes and did not mind my coming. I replied that I had to leave Kiev for a week to attend to some personal matters, but would see him as soon as I came back. "Of course, you should go if you must," Vadim answered, "I will be waiting for your return. And then we will be together, and nothing will set us apart." It is hard to describe what I felt at that moment; I thought I would faint, but contained myself, smiled, and kissed Vadim on the cheek on the way out. I knew it was our last encounter, but he did not suspect anything and was happy.

The next morning, I collected my belongings and told Christina I was leaving Kiev. I asked her to keep it a secret and tell everybody I would be back in a week. Christina became upset and tried to make me stay, saying that Vadim was a wonderful person, a rare breed, and that he loved me very much. It turned out she had visited him a few days earlier, and he confided in her. Christina added that Vadim's mother was somewhat apprehensive, as she knew nothing about me, albeit she thought I was pretty. Christina was sure Vadim would persuade his mother to accept his choice. "No," I replied, "I have made up my mind. I am not his match. I wish him happiness, and I am sure he will find it. Time pales memories;

he will forget about me." Once more, Christina pleaded with me to think it over and come back to claim my fortune. She promised not to tell anybody that I would not return and asked me to visit her if I happened to be in the city. I tenderly hugged and kissed her, thanked her for the kindness and shelter, and walked out the door.

9. Captured (1943)

Where to go? No money and nothing to sell. The cold weather retreated a bit, and the smell of spring was in the air; however, it was too early to go to the country, which was impassable after the long winter. I got an idea to sell my coat's lining. Such items were in demand among resellers, who purchased them for pennies and sold to seamstresses. The spring was coming, and the coat's shell with the wadding ought to be enough to keep me warm… It was still early in the day. I went to the Demeevka Market, took off my coat, and removed the lining, but the offers were low and few. So, I went to the Jewish Market, which was much bigger and had many more buyers. The distance from Demeevka to the Jewish Market was long, and by the time I reached the latter, it was closed. I needed to find a place to spend the night. Maria Ilyinichna's home was not far away, but I was still afraid to go there.

I walked into a small park and sat down on a bench. A middle-aged man approached my bench and sat next to me. He had a weird look: unshaven, with long hair. I got up to leave, but the man spoke to me. He asked if I was afraid of him, adding that he meant no harm. I sat down again. The man told me that he had worked as a civil engineer before the war but was now unemployed. He lived nearby, sharing an apartment with his two sisters. He asked where I lived. I replied that I was looking for a place to sleep, as I had just arrived in Kiev, hoping to find my relatives, whose exact address I did not know. The man invited me to spend a night in his apartment. He said I might stay for a couple of days. Unfortunately, he could not offer me anything to eat, as they did not have enough food, even for themselves.

My new acquaintance escorted me to a large apartment building a few blocks from the park. The elevator was out of order, and we walked up the stairs to the sixth floor. My companion opened his apartment's door, and I saw large, stately rooms with high ceilings, dingy and poorly kept. There was almost no furniture. The man introduced me to two women, his sisters, who were about his age. He told them I would be staying for a few days. Then he left, and the women started whispering in each other's ears, looking at me with an unnerving mix of curiosity and suspicion. During the entire evening, they did not speak to me once. I understood that my presence was not welcome, but had nowhere to go as it was already dark outside. I asked the sisters for a place to sleep; they showed me to a small room with an old couch, which had numerous holes in it. I lay down, fully dressed, and closed my eyes. I heard my host return and argue with his sisters behind the closed door in an agitated, angry voice. I realized I had to leave as soon as possible.

In the morning, I woke up very early, tiptoed toward the apartment's front door, and locked it behind me. I went to the Jewish Market to sell the lining and buy myself something to eat. I had not eaten for two days and felt dizzy and nauseous. The lining sold quickly, purchased by a woman reseller for a paltry sum. As soon as I got the money, I bought a piece of cornbread with jam and ate it with great pleasure. Drinks I never bought. Sometimes, my overnight hosts offered me tea, which, in those moments, tasted like nectar, but most of the time, I drank water from courtyard faucets in the city or wells and brooks in the countryside. And despite such a diet, I never had diarrhea or even stomach pain.

Meanwhile, posted on every corner were signs in German, Ukrainian, and Russian, calling on young people to go to Germany to work. The posters asked for volunteers, promising good pay and a great life in the heart of the Third Reich. It occurred to me that by posing as a volunteer, I could leave Ukraine, go to Germany with other workers, and escape the searchlight of Jewish persecution. Some fellow volunteers might suspect me of being a Jew, yet they wouldn't be able to prove it, especially in Germany. But how would I accomplish all that? It would be necessary to come to a recruitment center and express my desire to go to Germany. They would verify my story, including my home address, and discover it was fake. Or the policemen might suspect me from the start. It was too risky. I had no courage to go through such a trial. So, I abandoned the volunteer idea and continued wandering the city streets.

The spring was in full bloom. The money from the coat lining ended; however, there remained the wadding. I decided to sell it, too. I ate only once a day, trying to save those coupons, but they were so few and disappearing quickly. I went to the Jewish Market and sold the wadding, realizing that the proceeds would not last long. What would I do when the wadding money also ran out? The synthetic fur collar still adorned what was left of my coat, but how much longer could I endure in the city if I sold the collar, too? So, I decided to go to the country. This time, I went in a different direction, not to show up in the same place again.

For the next few months, I roamed between villages. It became easier to walk, as the summer sun had dried the ground, but I needed to take a bath and wash my clothes—an impossible task in the country. Farmers bathed once a week in large wooden basins filled with well water. It was some bathing. So, I decided to return to Kiev, sell the collar, go to the baths, and visit Maria Ilyinichna and Olen'ka. I wanted to see them and also wash my clothes. After that, I planned to go back to the countryside and spend the rest of the summer and early fall there.

The first thing I noticed upon returning to Kiev was the scarcity of young people on the streets. I asked a few passersby what was going on, and one woman explained that many had left for Germany to work while others were hiding from the authorities. It became known that the earlier volunteers received no pay for their work and lived in dismal conditions, almost like prisoners. All promises of a happy life in Germany turned out to be lies. So, people stopped coming to recruitment centers voluntarily and ignored summonses in the mail. The Germans, with the help of local policemen and building superintendents, raided homes, forcibly removed younger residents, put them in cattle cars, and transported the detained to Germany. The police also conducted roundups in public places, such as markets and movie theaters.

I went straight to Maria Ilyinichna. When approaching her building, I ran into Zhora, who gave me such a stare that I felt weak in my knees. Since he had already seen me, I did not use the window and walked through the courtyard. Maria Ilyinichna welcomed me affably, seated me at the table, and began preparing a meal, but when she learned that I had met her nephew, she became nervous and implored me to avoid him at all costs... Maria Ilyinichna confirmed that the Germans were hunting for laborers. She said there were almost no young people left in Kiev. The authorities grabbed everybody in sight. Olen'ka got married and moved in with her husband's family. When they lived together, Maria Ilyinichna worried her daughter might be forced to go to Germany, but now Olen'ka was safe—she was Zhenia's wife, and his parents had connections in the German administration. Maria Ilyinichna suggested that I leave Kiev to avoid getting captured on the streets. Of course, I could stay in her place and wash my clothes.

I spent the night in Maria Ilyinichna's home, washed my clothes, and at dawn, left through the window for the Jewish Market. I sold the collar for a measly sum and went to the "Vladimirski" farmers' market to buy something to eat. The earlier encounter with Zhora still worried me, so I decided not to return to Maria Ilyinichna but to go straight to the country. I got on the former Red Army Street and walked toward the highway. Suddenly, I sensed that someone was following me. I was too scared to turn around to see who it was and walked faster. The steps behind me picked up the pace, too. I ran into the nearest courtyard, locked myself inside a latrine, and waited there, hoping to outstay the tracker. But how long could one remain in a latrine? In half an hour, I left my hideout and got back to the street. Right away, my pursuer arose before me. It was

Zhora. He had tailed me since I left Maria Ilyinichna, and must have watched her windows before. "No use to hide," uttered Zhora, "You are under arrest." "What did I do?" I replied. "What did you do?" Zhora mimicked me, "You did nothing; I know you are a Jew and must be dealt with like the rest of your kind. I am taking you to the Gestapo." My heart stopped. "This is the end," I thought, and followed my captor.

We reached the Gestapo building. Who didn't know that address in Kiev? People took detours several blocks long to avoid coming near that scary structure. The word had it that those brought there never saw the light of day again… Zhora showed the guard at the door an identification of a Gestapo agent and took me to the lobby, where he told me to sit down and wait. He then walked upstairs and vanished.

10. Breakout

I sat in the lobby of the Gestapo building. Beneath me was a basement where the Germans kept their prisoners. Through the concrete floor, I could hear the blood-curdling screams of tortured inmates. Fear and desperation overwhelmed me. What unspeakable horrors ought I to go through before meeting my death? Would I have been better off dying in Chudnov with my parents and little sisters? Had the years of misery and struggle been in vain? "No," I answered to myself, "I will not give up. I will fight for my life to the last breath. I must show no fear or confusion but remain calm and never change my story…" So I mulled for a couple of hours when a middle-aged man in a Gestapo uniform appeared in front of me and, in a pure Ukrainian tongue, asked my name. He then ordered me to follow him. We walked up to the second floor and entered a room where two German officers behind the office desk had been waiting to question me. My escort turned out to be a translator, a local man working for the Gestapo. He joined the officers at the desk while I stood in front of them, frozen with fright. Nobody offered me a chair—apparently, the arrested were not supposed to sit.

The interrogation began through a translator. The translator's German was far from perfect, but the officers understood him, and so did I. My answer to the initial question—who I was—he, on purpose, translated incorrectly. I took out Stepan's sister's birth certificate and handed it to him. I said that I lived with my ailing mother in Sviatoshyno and gave a fictional address. "Why aren't you going to Germany to work?" asked one of the officers. I replied that I could not leave my sickly mother. To the question of whether I was Jewish, I answered no and cited the birth certificate as proof.

Not knowing I could understand him, the translator tried to convince his German bosses that I was not telling the truth. He kept saying I was a Jew and insisted on checking the Sviatoshyno address. My answer that I could not go to Germany because of my mother's illness, he translated as I *did not want* to go. I saw the displeasure of the Germans at such a reply and realized I had to speak out. I apologized for the interruption and told the officers that the translator had mistranslated my answers. "Where did you learn to speak German?" asked one officer with surprise. I replied that I had studied the language in school. The Germans then blasted the translator, accusing him of deception and threatening to fire him if he tried to mislead them again. The translator turned almost blue and gave me such a look that my hair curled. The officers then commanded him to take me to another room and come back. That room was empty, with no furniture. I could barely stand on my feet and sat down on the floor. An hour later, the translator returned. "Get up, you filthy Jew!" he yelled, "You will not get out of here alive." I did not answer and followed him back to the interrogation room.

The Germans started asking the same questions again, but this time, the interpreter translated correctly. I stuck to my story and denied being Jewish. "You'd better tell us the truth," said one of the officers, "or we'll torture you and get a confession anyway." The threat of torture chilled me to the bone, but I did not give in. Several times, the interrogators sent me to the other room, talked among themselves or handled other matters, and called me back. That continued until the late afternoon. Finally, they called me for the last time. The officers spoke to me directly. "We have made our decision," one of them said, "You are going to Germany to work. You know the language; it will come in handy there. Good luck…" I was dumbstruck. Having lost all hope of surviving the Gestapo ordeal, I fought the interrogators out of sheer defiance, but it paid off. I still do not understand what motivated those Germans and why they decided to close the case without sending the translator (who had already volunteered for such an assignment) to Sviatoshyno to check my story.

The officers ordered the translator to take me to the transition camp on Lvov Street, not far from the Gestapo building. We started toward the door. "Hold on!" one officer halted the translator, "We do not trust you. Bring back the receipt you have delivered her in one piece." I will never forget the expression of hatred and menace on the translator's face as we walked toward the camp. He kept grabbing the revolver on his waist as if attempting to draw it. "What a pleasure would it be for me to shoot you," he said, "You did not fool me; I know you are a Jew. You are lucky those Germans spared your life and asked for a receipt, or I would have put you against that wall," and he pointed at a nearby building, "and blown your brains out. But you will not escape punishment. You will meet your death in Germany or on the way there." I did not answer. I was drained physically and emotionally, and just dragged my feet, trying not to fall.

We reached the transition camp, a large parcel of land behind a high barbed-wire fence with guarded gates and several buildings within the perimeter. The translator took me to the camp's main office. He handed my birth certificate to the receptionist, got the receipt, and faded into the doorway. The next thing I remembered was waking up in the doctor's room. The nurse told me that, as soon as the translator left, I had passed out. The guards carried me to the medical station, where I was brought to life. I felt thirsty and asked for something to drink. The nurse gave me a glass of water. In a few hours, I felt stronger. The guard then instructed me to go to the cafeteria, eat something, and proceed to the barracks. In the morning, I would be called to the main office to receive my papers.

The barracks were packed with men, women, and children. Those with families were mainly Asian people from the eastern parts of the Soviet Union, waiting for the train to Germany[10]. There were no bunks; everybody slept on the floor. The air was dirty and stuffy, saturated with the vapors of sweat. The windows with metal guards did not open. My years of roaming the country, sleeping in the forest, and suffering from hunger and cold had one benefit—plenty of fresh air—which I came to appreciate in those barracks... I found a spot near the entrance, hunkered down, and spent the entire night in that position, suffocating from the stench and wondering if I would endure until morning. But I survived that one, too. In the morning, the laborers rushed to the cafeteria, where everybody received a small piece of bread and a cup of sweetened tea. As soon as I finished eating, the camp's radio called my name, directing me to come to the central gate. A German soldier was already waiting for me there. He escorted me to the office, where I received an identification card—my entry paper to Germany.

From the inside, the camp looked like a prison. Surrounded by a tall fence, it was guarded by armed soldiers. The weather was very warm. During the day, the transients spent most of their time in the camp's yard. One could breathe fresh air there, but the area swarmed with suspicious individuals, probably Gestapo agents like Zhora. They snooped around the yard, striking up conversations and asking questions. I tried to evade them by hiding behind people's backs or returning to the barracks. At lunchtime, a large wooden cask with the broth was wheeled to the yard, and the laborers formed a line to get their rations. In the evening, there was another piece of bread and a cup of tea in the cafeteria. It was a scant diet, but I did not complain, as I had not eaten three meals a day in a long while. The food was not my primary concern, however. I was afraid that someone might suspect me as a Jew, but my greatest fear was that the Gestapo translator might have persuaded his German bosses to check my story. I shuddered from every radio announcement, expecting to be called to the office and taken back to the Gestapo. I could not wait to get on the train and leave those fears behind.

Two days had passed; nobody bothered me. Then, in the middle of the night, the camp was awakened by a siren. The voice on the radio ordered

---

[10] I am unsure who those people were—perhaps natives of the easternmost occupied Soviet territories, who had some German connections or were selected for special work that required resettlement.

all workers who did not have families to come out with their belongings to the yard. Almost immediately, the trucks began to arrive. Each truck had two armed guards in the back. The workers mounted the vehicles, the gates opened, and the motorcade rolled into the darkness... In half an hour, the trucks arrived at a railway station in the woods outside the city. A freight train was waiting on the tracks. The boxcars' doors were open; the floors were covered with hay. Shouting *"Schnell,"* the soldiers herded the workers into the cars, pushing the people on each other. The boarding proceeded very fast and was finished in minutes. Each car was rounded off with two German soldiers (guards) carrying sub-machine guns, the locomotive sounded a siren, and the train moved.

The passengers began to settle on the floor. I suddenly felt great relief and, for the first time since Chudnov's occupation, let loose the hope I might survive the war. The train was gaining speed, carrying me away from almost certain death and leaving behind, farther and farther, the saddest chapter of my life.

Chapter 4

KITCHEN HELPER

1. Job Fair

"Who can speak German?" shouted the guard into the settling crowd. I raised my hand. Nobody else in the car knew the language. I did not speak it very well, either, but understood almost everything. The guards asked me to translate their message, and all future announcements they would be making through me.

When the train approached the Polish border, we were told that the guerrilla groups active in the area might attack the convoy, attempting to release the workers. We had been traveling with the boxcar's sliding doors half-open, but near the border, the doors got shut, and the guards clung to small holes in the walls, staring intensely into the passing forest. Suddenly, someone in front of the convoy yelled, "Partisans." The train stopped, and the shooting broke out. However, it did not last long. The guerrillas lacked the firepower to overtake the convoy's defense; they retreated into the woods, and all became quiet. The train resumed its movement, and shortly, we entered the Polish side.

As soon as the train crossed the border, I took off my headscarf and combed my long, flowing hair. People in the railcar began to notice my presence; however, I was no longer afraid. I heard some workers talking about the "Jewishness" of my hair, but it did not bother me because the gossipers could not speak German, and the guards treated me well. They frequently asked me to sit next to them, telling me about their life back in Germany. Both were friendly people, especially one by the name of Kurt. Kurt told me he had two daughters, one of whom was about my age. He said I reminded him of her.

On the way, the train made brief stops where the laborers would get off to attend to their natural needs and receive food and water. We were given mess kits to eat inside the cars. At one stop, while out for a meal, I was spotted by the convoy commander—a stocky, middle-aged German officer. He rode with his staff in two passenger cars in front of the train and, during the pause, stood outside observing the proceedings. I saw him summon Kurt and the other guard from my car and speak to them, glancing in my direction. I sensed they were talking about me.

After the conversation with his superior, Kurt returned visibly upset. He took me aside and said that the convoy commander had ordered them to bring me to the first car. The commander told the guards he wanted to interview me for a maid's job at his house. "You must do everything to avoid going there," said Kurt, "This old lecher, I know him well. He is not interested in having you as a maid. He will rape you and throw you away like an empty bottle." My heart halted. "But what should I do?" I asked Kurt. "Lie down on the floor," he replied, "and cover yourself with a coat. Start complaining of fever, headache, and stomachache. I am going to tell him you are sick, and it looks like typhus." The Germans were panicky about typhus, so Kurt's plan might work.

I lay down as instructed by Kurt while he walked to the front of the train to deliver the "bad news." He returned with medications—a bunch of white tablets, courtesy of the convoy commander. On the way, I kept throwing them out stealthily, one by one, so that nobody noticed and suspected me of faking illness. The next day, the convoy commander came to our car to inquire about my condition. I lay on the floor under the coat and faintly groaned from time to time. Kurt dutifully reported I was very ill, and the commander went back empty-handed... I lay like that for the rest of the trip. Kurt was bringing me food doled out at the train stops. During those stops, when the workers were getting out to relieve themselves, the girls in the car would help me go outside, as I pretended I could hardly walk. Everybody thought I was very sick. The convoy commander did not return, but Kurt remained on his toes—as long as I was on the train, the commander could snatch me even at the last moment.

When the train approached its destination, Kurt came to me with the rest of the escape plan. I was to remain in my place, waiting for all the workers to get off the train, then, at Kurt's signal, spring out of the car and vanish among the disembarked... At four in the morning, the train arrived at a brightly lit station surrounded by trees. The guards' duties included clearing the cars of the passengers, and Kurt made sure I was the last inside. There was another guard, but he was Kurt's friend and had to be informed of the scheme. When everybody left, Kurt told me to get ready, then leaned out the door, looking for the convoy commander. "Go!" Kurt said. I thanked him heartily, jumped out of the car, and darted into the mass of workers, which was already moving away.

It was still predawn when we reached a large encampment not far from the train station—the place where the arriving laborers from the East were processed. There, in the open air under the trees, stood long, wooden tables with attached benches. We were told to sit down and wait. In a couple of hours, the soldiers brought breakfast: margarine and jam sandwiches, along with containers of tea. Having not eaten since the previous day, the workers were starving and lunged at the food like a pack of wild animals. When the dust settled, all that was left to me was one tiny sandwich, but I had been accustomed to small portions and enjoyed it all the same.

After the meal, the arrivals were split into two groups—women and men—and escorted to the showers, where everybody received a towel and a small soap bar. What a pleasure that showering was. The grating sense of uncleanness and sickening body odors that had pursued me since the Kiev transition camp were finally gone. The next step was a physical exam. One by one, we were called to the doctor's office. There was a Russian translator inside. The doctor asked routine questions about past illnesses and present complaints. The questioning was followed by chest X-rays in the radiology room. The last part was fingerprinting and taking pictures with an identification number in front.

The processing ended in the late afternoon, and "employers" began to arrive. They were farmers, factory managers, and owners of restaurants, stores, and similar establishments. Hitler kept his promise to the German people: twenty years of free labor from the conquered lands. The laborers were brought to a big, darkened hall, where they stood in a row, waiting for their future bosses. The latter entered a few at a time, escorted by the processing camp's official, and chose their employees.

The camp's official inquired who among the workers spoke German. A couple of newcomers, including me, stepped forward. A middle-aged, grey-haired man, who had arrived with the latest group of employers, walked between the responders and pointed at me. "I am taking this girl," he said. He then led me to the main office, where I received an official German identification paper, an *Arbeitskarte*[1]. After the paperwork was complete, we headed back to the station to take a train to Berlin, where my new master lived. On the way, he told me he was the owner of the

---

[1] Work Paper.

"Zum Dortmunder" restaurant located on Alt-Moabit Street in Berlin, near the jail that housed prominent German communist Ernst Thälmann. Perhaps my new boss mentioned Thälmann because, knowing I was from a communist country, he wanted me to feel more welcome.

We waited for the Berlin train to arrive, then got in. I sat next to the window. The sun came down and followed the train—a hazy red ball rolling along the horizon line. Soon, the first Berlin houses and industrial structures emerged. It was getting dark, and as we rode further into the city, more windows lit up, twinkling merrily at a distance and flashing glimpses of a new life along the train's path. I saw pictures on the walls, cabinets, flower pots—hallmarks of a safe, peaceful home, perhaps like one I soon would call my own. What awaited me in that German home, I didn't know. I knew, though, I might hope to survive, walk the streets without fear, ease up a little. But Germany was an unfamiliar place with a different way of life. How would I adapt to the new habitat? Still, I was fortunate to escape my country, my homeland, where all that awaited me was almost certain death. I also realized I had to work hard to keep that job at the restaurant, as it was a far safer place than a factory or a farm. Here, I would be removed from my compatriots who otherwise might suspect me as a Jew and report to the authorities or start causing trouble on their own. I did not trust people, especially those I had grown up with. I knew of many cases where husbands gave away wives, wives betrayed their husbands, and friends became enemies, as had happened to my father.

It was already dark outside when we approached a big apartment building on Alt-Moabit Street. The entrance was through the courtyard. We took an elevator to my employer's residence on the fourth floor. It was a large, luxurious apartment with two bedrooms, a dining room, a kitchen, a bathroom, and a tiny room for a maid. The maid's room had a bed and nothing else. The room was so small, almost like a closet, that one could only walk inside and lie on the bed. It probably used to be a walk-in closet, which the owners converted into a living space. There was not enough room even for a chair, and the clothes had to be hung over the bed's footboard. However, I could not dream of anything better: I would have a place to sleep, a roof over my head, some privacy, and no longer be afraid to open my eyes in the morning.

2. The Wardrobe

My master's name was Hans Hunke. Upon entering the apartment, we were greeted by a very obese woman about forty-five years of age, who introduced herself as Irma Hunke, Hans' wife. She smiled and said that they would treat me well if I worked well. "The most important quality is honesty," she added. Then she invited me to unpack my bag and put my things in the closet. I took out my winter headscarf and what was left of my coat. "Is this all you have?" exclaimed Frau Hunke incredulously. I replied that it was. "Tomorrow morning, we have an appointment with a hairdresser, but after lunch, Herr Hunke will take you to a warehouse where workers from the East receive their clothes. Poor girl," cried out my new mistress, "Take a bath and go to bed." And she showed me to my minuscule quarters. She and her husband lived in the apartment alone, using the second bedroom as an office or a guest room. I went to take a bath. The bathroom was cozy and clean, with aromatic soaps and soft towels, but I was too tired to enjoy that luxury. After the bath, I returned to my room, fell onto the bed, and within seconds was in a deep sleep...

I woke up from the sound of my mistress' voice. It seemed I had just gone to bed; however, it was late morning already. Frau Hunke decided to awaken me, as I could sleep all day. Herr Hunke had long gone to his restaurant, and I was greeted by the breakfast he had prepared before leaving: four thin slices of bread with margarine, jam, and cheese spread. The cheese smelled terrible, but I later learned that the worse the cheese smelled, the better the cheese it was. I swallowed that food in an instant, washed it down with coffee, and felt like I could have a main course, yet pretended to be full and thanked my hostess for a delicious meal.

After breakfast, Frau Hunke and I went to a hair salon, which was just around the corner. The hairdressers met us with great curiosity. Frau Hunke explained to them who I was, adding that they did not have to be squeamish as I was very clean. I got into a chair. The woman coiffeur cut my hair short, laid it out, and fastened it with a pin in a style very popular in those times. In the mirror, I saw a face I did not recognize. The stylists gathered around me, admiring my new look. "How pretty she is," said my mistress. "Yes," replied the stylist who had worked on my hair, "a completely different person." She then asked me to come again whenever I needed my hair done. I thanked her and followed my mistress back to the apartment.

We waited for the "chef" (as Frau Hunke referred to her husband) to take me to the clothes warehouse. He showed up after lunch. He and I left right away, took a bus, and, in half an hour, arrived at the warehouse building. The entrance led to a large hall with many rows of tall wooden shelves filled with merchandise. The attendant took us to the section that stocked garments for forced laborers. Those were hideous clothes: men's suits and women's dresses made of rough canvas with stripes, the same outfits prisoners in concentration camps wore. I saw that Herr Hunke was flabbergasted. He did not expect such a collection and wanted nothing like it in his home. "Will you wear this?" he asked me hesitatingly. I replied that I would not. I was angry and upset. Not only did laborers work without pay, but they also had to suffer the humiliation of wearing such garbs. Still, not to waste the trip entirely, I took a pair of synthetic leather shoes on a wooden platform, as my old shoes had fallen apart. The attendant handed me a yellow armband with the letters "OST" on it[2], which I was supposed to wear outside (but never did), and my boss and I headed back to Alt-Moabit.

As soon as we came home, Herr Hunke spoke to his wife, and she began calling her friends, asking them for clothes they didn't need. Frau Hunke could not offer me anything of hers, as she was extra-large, while I was skinny at the time. The next day, one of her lady friends came and brought a couple of dresses, a shirt, and two skirts. My mistress called me into the room to try them on and say dankeschön to her friend. The clothes were used but in excellent condition and looked brand new. I did not believe I could retire my old dress, which had numerous holes in it, and put on something nice and clean. After we finished with the clothes, Frau Hunke opened the closet and showed her companion the remains of my coat. "Such are the coats people wear in Russia," she said, and they began to laugh. I interrupted their laughter, saying that coats in Russia were normal, but I had to sell the lining, wadding, and collar of mine, not to starve to death. "How awful!" exclaimed my mistress' friend, and I saw that both women were embarrassed.

My mistress' friend, who brought me those first German clothes, merits a special mention. Her name was Ruth, and she was the wife of a Wehrmacht officer serving in the occupied Soviet territory. Ruth was a classy woman—warm, open, and charming. She was curious about life and customs in Russia, but in the beginning, my German was not good enough to satisfy her curiosity. We soon became friends, and as my language improved, I told her more. She was very fond of me, and I liked her, too. Despite our differences in age and upbringing, we enjoyed each other's company and often had heartfelt conversations, sometimes of an intimate nature. Ruth's tactfulness made it easier for me to loosen up, and

---

[2] "EAST," an armband identifying laborers from the East.

even my secret was not a hurdle during those chats. Somehow, she avoided subjects that might have put me in a precarious position… She was close to my mistress and a regular in the Berlin apartment. Later on, when our building was destroyed in an air raid and my masters and I moved to the suburbs, Ruth would often come from Berlin for a visit and bring something for me, usually items from her vast wardrobe. I didn't care for those things, but appreciated her attention and desire to see me happy. She made me try on those clothes and was delighted that I looked good in them. "I never knew there were such pretty girls in Russia," she once said, "I was told women there were fat, man-like, and Mongolian type." She, herself, was very good-looking—slender and noble.

3. Zum Dortmunder

I had been living in my masters' home for two days already. I dressed up, put myself to rights a little, and Herr Hunke announced it was time to go to work. He took me to his restaurant, a few blocks from home, where he explained my responsibilities. Every day except Sunday, I had to get up at four in the morning and walk with him to the restaurant to prepare for the opening. Firstly, I ought to set the tables, dust the furniture, wax the floors, and clean the toilet; then, wipe the bar, buff it to a high shine, wash the china, and put it on display. Meanwhile, Herr Hunke would be cooking the day's menu. After he finished, I had to polish pots, pans, and other utensils, then wash the windows and the ceramic floor near the entrance. At that point, my restaurant shift ended, and I would go back to the apartment to clean it, too. My other duties included washing clothes, although not bed linens, which were handled by a professional laundry service. A laundry truck picked up the linens on specific dates, bringing them back the next day, washed and pressed, in special bins with the owners' name tags attached. I had never seen so clean, snow-white bed linens before. Such neatness was highly valued in Germany. Everywhere in the city, trams and buses carried big signs reading, "Clean and snow-white linens are the pride of a German woman." In Germany, I became familiar with powder detergents. We washed laundry in Ukraine with lye soap bars and an alkaline bleaching solution. The soap did not lather well, while the bleach was caustic, removed stains poorly, and produced an unpleasant odor. It was much easier to wash laundry in Germany, albeit it was still done by hand.

And so my job began. I worked like a horse, from dawn until late at night. At four in the morning, when, with great effort, I opened my eyes, the first chore awaiting me was to shine my masters' shoes. Later, they allowed me to do it in the evening before bed, which gave me a few extra minutes of sleep. I did my duties in the restaurant, swept and waxed the apartment floors, dusted furniture, cleaned the windows, and washed the dishes. By the day's end, I was so exhausted I could only crawl into bed, close my eyes, and the next reality to reach me was the sound of an alarm clock at four in the morning. At first, before I became accustomed to such a routine, I thought I wouldn't make it on that job. There was not a moment of rest.

Like other laborers from the East, I was not paid money for my work but received free room and board. The meals in my masters' home were frugal. Breakfast was the customary four skinny sandwiches made by the chef himself. Dinner we ate after the restaurant's lunch hours. It typically included a small piece of game meat, a side dish with gravy, and pudding for dessert. There was no bread. The supper consisted of a cup of coffee and a piece of cake or a little sandwich. Such a diet, combined with hard work, kept me constantly hungry. I was surrounded by food, but never asked for anything or took it on my own. I knew I would forever lose my masters' trust if they discovered that I had helped myself without their consent. My masters' menu was similar to mine; however, they sustained full body weight, perhaps because they drank a lot of beer, which was excellent in Germany, both regular and women's brands. For my part, I drank water, tea, and coffee. I particularly liked the coffee, which was very tasty mixed with chicory.

Sunday was my holiday. The restaurant was closed, but there was usually work in the apartment. My boss and his wife often had guests on Sundays, and I would serve the meals and wash the dishes. The main course was prepared by the chef himself—it was simple and required little effort. After a few months, my masters started asking me to join them and their guests at the table; however, I tried to come up with some excuse to decline those invitations. I would have lain down and had a nap instead, but never said a word and kept toiling. One time, my masters took me to the opera with them. Throughout the performance, I tried not to fall asleep, and the only thing I could think about was the peaceful solitude of my tiny room in the Alt-Moabit apartment.

On Sundays, when they didn't have guests, my masters frequently ate out at a fancy restaurant in Berlin's center or in the suburbs. Sometimes, they invited me to go with them. I was delighted with those invitations—we traveled by tram or bus, and from a window seat, I saw streets, parks, and buildings of Berlin. It was a beautiful city, but most importantly, I could admire it freely, undistracted by fear and pain. I wore secondhand clothes donated by my mistress' friends and felt like a human being. I was young and good-looking, and those clothes complemented me well. Despite hard work and a moderate diet, I had blossomed in my masters' service. On their part, they grew attached to me and valued my effort and duty. Occasionally, the dreadful memories made me sad and depressed. Seeing that, my masters asked if anything was wrong. I answered that I missed my mother, and they empathized with me.

Happier times arrived when Herr Hunke started taking me with him to buy provisions for the restaurant's kitchen. We visited different parts of the city, walked the streets, and I enjoyed the surroundings and sense of freedom. Sometimes, we ran into my boss's acquaintances, who asked him if I was his daughter. My boss answered yes, later saying he would be fortunate to have a daughter like me. I did not react, thinking of my uncertain future. How long would such procurement trips and occasional Sunday outings remain my only window into the world? Was it meant for me to spend my best years toiling under an assumed name, shut out of life's pleasures and the appeals of a young age? Would my boss still want me as his daughter if he knew who I really was? On various occasions, especially in the beginning, I eagerly listened to conversations between my boss and his wife, trying to catch references to Jews, perhaps hateful, derogatory remarks, but heard nothing of the kind. They did not touch that subject, at least in my presence.

Meanwhile, Herr Hunke trusted me more and more, which made my workload even bigger. He worked very hard, too. He was a waiter, a cook, and a busboy. He did the accounting, ordered supplies, and often delivered them himself. I mopped the floors, washed the dishes, polished the bar and the display. There were no other helpers in the restaurant. Frau Hunke did not do any physical work because of her obesity and poor health. As his confidence in me grew, my boss started asking me to clear tables and later wait on customers. Now, I was spending more time in the restaurant's dining room, including some of its busiest hours. Herr Hunke had many patrons, some of whom inquired about me: who I was and where I was from. One of those patrons was a former Wehrmacht officer named Willi. He had spent a few years on the Eastern Front, lost one arm, and was now a fixture at *Zum Dortmunder*. He often looked at me with a long, probing stare and occasionally started a conversation. I do not know what his military duties used to be, but he knew Russia and Ukraine very well.

One evening, Herr Hunke came home very amused. Frau Hunke was also in the room. "You know, Nadia, what Willi said to me today?" my boss addressed me jollily, "He said you don't look like a Ukrainian; you look like a Jew." My stomach turned upside down, and blood rushed through my veins. Death suddenly swung its scythe again. "Why does he think so?" I asked in a fainting voice. "He claims Russian and Ukrainian women are different, while your type is more common among Jews there," replied my boss. "But I am not a Jew," I almost screamed, "My papers state I am a Ukrainian. You know that!" Perhaps my response was too spirited for what had started as an innocent chat, but the crushing topic came so unexpectedly that I could barely contain myself. Herr Hunke was not the most perceptive of all people; however, very little escaped his wife. She could not have missed the excessiveness of my reaction, but said nothing. The conversation withered; I went to my room and fell onto the bed, still trembling from fear and shock. A minute later, I heard a knock on my door, and a large figure shadowed the opening. It was Frau Hunke. "Do not get upset," she said calmly, "We don't care who you are. We love you, anyway." She closed the door, and that topic never surfaced again.

4. Escape from Berlin

The war had reached the very heart of Germany; Allied warplanes began to bomb Berlin. It was relatively calm in the daytime, but at night, the sirens filled the sky over the city. The residents had readied emergency bags with necessities, which they carried to bomb shelters during the attacks. After each raid, more buildings turned into smoking rubble, and more people remained without possessions and a place to live. Panic was growing among Berliners, who were scared to go to bed at night.

At the sound of a siren, my masters ran to the restaurant's basement, which was designated and equipped as a bomb shelter. I seldom went there. My emergency bag was in the kitchen, where I worked nights. As my boss and Frau Hunke were leaving for the shelter, they would call me to follow them, but I did not go. I felt no fear for my life, maybe because I was too tired from hard work and disheartened by dark thoughts about my future. I listened to official radio broadcasts announcing the glorious victories of the Wehrmacht and the Red Army's crushing defeats. What would happen to me if the Nazis won the war? And if they did so well on the battlefield, why were all those bombs falling on their capital city?

One night, the sirens started up, and everyone rushed to the shelter. I was in the apartment's kitchen alone, washing dishes. Herr Hunke ran into the kitchen, grabbed my hand, and forcibly dragged me outside. As soon as we reached the restaurant's basement, bombs began to fall on our apartment building, and one of them exploded in the kitchen where I had stood before the attack. The building was destroyed, and we remained in the restaurant, which did not open for business the following day.

My masters were unfazed by the loss of business and possessions. They kept telling everybody of my miraculous escape and Herr Hunke's role in it, but I felt no excitement or joy. As fiercely as I had struggled for my life before, I was now indifferent. The immediate danger had passed, and apathy followed—a reaction to the years of fear and angst.

We stayed in the restaurant for the next two days. Berlin was steadily destroyed by the airstrikes. Many residents tried to escape the battered city. Herr Hunke was also looking for a place for us to live in the suburbs or in the country. At the end of the second day, he came to the restaurant and told Frau Hunke and me to pack (which was easy, as most of our belongings were buried under the rubble); we were leaving Berlin. The next morning, all three of us went to the train station, boarded a train, and in an hour, arrived at a large country hotel not far from the train stop. The hotel was packed with Berliners. There were no rooms available, and we settled in the lobby. All the couches and chairs were taken there. It was difficult for Frau Hunke to stand. My boss brought a chair from somewhere, and Frau Hunke sat in it; I hunkered beside her. The hall was crammed with people. Adults looked scared and distraught; children were crying. It reminded me of the beginning of the war back in Ukraine. Chickens came home to roost. Hitler had promised the German people to conquer the world for them, and now they were learning the plight of those conquered.

As we remained in the hotel's lobby, the area's property owners kept coming in, offering apartments and houses for rent. Despite his age[3] and poor health, Herr Hunke was an energetic and efficient man. He quickly struck a deal with one of the landlords, and by nightfall, we moved to a new home in Weissensee, a pretty village with winding, narrow streets and neat houses. Our residence was a summer cottage near the lake. The cottage had two rooms, a kitchen, a bathroom, and a patio. It stood on a big lot, which also contained a pool, a garden, and a vegetable patch—all surrounded by a tall fence. My boss had rented the place fully furnished, complete with furniture, tableware, and even bed sheets.

It was early spring[4]; the weather was still chilly. My masters took a larger room and gave a smaller one to me. Without a restaurant, there was not much for me to do, so I wondered whether my employers might keep me. If they let me go, I would likely be reassigned to a factory or a farm—not an attractive proposition, but there was little I could do other than force the issue. "Do you need me now?" I asked my masters when we assembled in the kitchen for breakfast the following day. "We always need you," replied Frau Hunke, "We are not going to stay here long. The chef will start another business, and we will move there. When the war is over, we will go back to Berlin, and you will go with us. You are our family now." "Our family," I thought, "What would you say if you knew who I really was?" My secret burdened me. Sometimes, I felt an urge to confide to my masters, to tell them the truth, but understood it would be imprudent, at least at the moment. By then, I was certain they did not espouse hatred toward Jews. I never heard them discuss Jewish matters, neither among themselves nor in the company of their friends who often visited our old apartment in Berlin and now saw us at Weissensee. Frau Hunke was an intelligent woman who could not have overlooked many holes in my story, but she was only too glad to ignore her suspicions. She and her husband asked very few questions about my past. By revealing

---

[3] Hans Hunke ought to be around fifty years old, but it was considered a fairly advanced age in those days.

[4] The spring of 1944.

my identity, I could put in danger not only myself but them, too, as they would be knowingly harboring a Jew. Therefore, I decided to say nothing but wait and see.

Life in Weissensee was peaceful and quiet. Chef traveled to Berlin almost daily, "on business," he explained, but nobody knew where he went and what he did there. Frau Hunke made the breakfast sandwiches herself. The dinner was prepared by the chef upon his return from the city. I did the housework: cleaned the rooms, washed and ironed laundry, took care of the backyard, and tended the kitchen garden.

Unlike Berlin, Weissensee did not have a professional laundry service to take care of bed linens, so I washed them at my neighbors' house. Our house did not have a laundry room, and the neighbors offered to let me use theirs. I met those neighbors the day after we moved in. They were friendly, unassuming people: a middle-aged couple, their adult daughter, and the daughter's child, a five-year-old girl. The daughter had divorced her husband, left the child with the parents, and lived in Berlin, coming to Weissensee from time to time. I felt at ease in that home and often visited it to chat with the owners and play with the little girl. My masters weren't close with those neighbors, regarding them as a lower class ("simple farmers"), yet would not mind me going there. The laundry room was in the house's basement, and I enjoyed working in it. It was the first time I saw such a spacious, well-equipped laundry room with a big iron tank for boiling linens. The owners taught me how to operate the equipment, and I was turning out sheets that looked as if they had come from a professional service. I dried them in the neighbors' backyard, which had amenities for that, too. Frau Hunke was ecstatic about my work, showing the linens to her friends from Berlin. Seeing that, Herr Hunke, who had been ironing his shirts himself, now entrusted that job to me after explaining how to do it right. By and large, I received excellent housekeeping training in my masters' service. Germans were particular about such matters. Girls were introduced to homemaking at an early age, as schools and gymnasiums taught tailoring, embroidery, knitting, and similar crafts.

The summer had arrived. Every morning, I got up early and headed for the lake. The water was clear, the air fresh and aromatic. I swam in the lake and returned home before my masters woke up. After that, my working day began. Of course, I had less work than in Berlin—there was time to visit neighbors and to sit in the garden listening to my mistress' stories about her childhood and youth. She was from a wealthy, upper-class family. Her parents died early, leaving her a large estate. She grew up in Königsberg[5] in the house of her aunt. My mistress loved her aunt and always spoke about the latter with great affection. When she was a teenager, my mistress became afflicted with some metabolic disorder and developed severe obesity. She wed a simple lad from Dortmund, my boss, who married her for her money. He was not a faithful husband; my mistress knew it, but tolerated his behavior to preserve the family. She never had children, also because of the illness. I felt sorry for her; she was a wise and understanding woman.

Occasionally, my mistress would go for a stroll and take me along. There was an old cemetery nearby that she liked to visit. We walked the cemetery's alleys, stopping at headstones and reading the epitaphs. "And where are the graves of my mother and little sisters?" I thought, and my heart filled with grief, "There will be no epitaph over my father's resting place in the Ukrainian forest." Then, and later, my family's fate weighed heavily on me. I convinced myself that I could not enjoy life when my closest kin lay in the ground, stricken by violent death long before their time. Today, I realize that I should not have denied myself many simple pleasures, but then, I felt differently and carried that feeling all my life.

---

[5] Currently, the city of Kaliningrad, a part of Russia.

5. Dormitory Trip

On the train to Germany, I befriended a few girls who rode with me in the same car. Upon arrival, they were sent to a factory, and I had not heard from them since. I wanted to know how they were. Herr Hunke found out for me the address of the dormitory where those girls lived. The dormitory was outside Berlin; to reach it, I had to go to the city and take another train there. Our house in Weissensee was several kilometers from the train station, so going there on foot would have taken too much time out of the entire trip to make it practical. People in the village used bicycles to get to the station, but I did not have one and would not have known how to ride it, anyway.

Besides the next-door neighbors with a laundry, I befriended another family who lived a few minutes walk from our house. They were a middle-aged couple—husband and wife, Dietrich and Elma—and I often visited their home. During one such visit, I mentioned my transportation problem. The hosts offered me a bicycle of their daughter, who lived in Dresden, but I still needed riding lessons. Dietrich suggested that I come to their house in the evenings when the traffic was light, and he would teach me on the main road. I told my masters about Dietrich's offer, and they agreed to excuse me for a few nights.

Dietrich hated the Nazis and everything about their rule. He was well-educated and articulate. Maybe because I was a forced laborer from the East, he felt safe to vent his anger in my presence. I remember some of his tirades: "Hitler is a madman, completely insane. Just look at him and listen to his speeches. He should be in an asylum, but he is our Führer instead, and the German people follow him as if under a spell. What has happened to us?" "Jews did not do us any harm. We have lived together for centuries. They were our friends, Germans like us, and we had many intermarriages. Banks, factories, and stores were owned by Jews. They greatly contributed to the German culture." "Time will come when we recognize the great injustice Germany has done to other nations and feel ashamed before our grandchildren and the entire world." I listened, sometimes asking questions, but did not engage in the conversation. My experience taught me to be cautious; I did not want to take unnecessary risks. I never talked politics with my masters either—just worked hard and followed their directives.

Dietrich taught me to ride a bicycle in a couple of days. Now, I could go anywhere my masters wished to send me, and they started regularly sending me to Berlin. The shops that had supplied Zum Dortmunder continued to attend to the personal needs of the restaurant's owners; it was only necessary to pick up the food at the stores' locations. I went to Berlin every week to make those purchases. Sometimes, my boss would go with me. We would ride our bicycles to the train station, leave them in a designated parking area, and board the train. Upon returning from the city, we would load the packets onto the bicycles and pedal back to the house. I enjoyed those trips. They brought variety to my life, and I liked Berlin very much. Although the city was partly destroyed by the air raids, it still beguiled me with its timeless beauty.

With the newly acquired mobility, I set about making a long-planned trip to see my Ukrainian friends. Frau Hunke gave me a little money and asked me to come back before dusk. The dormitory was in the barracks, several that housed laborers from the East. An armed soldier stood at the entrance. I explained the purpose of my visit, and he let me inside. The conditions in the barracks shocked me. The floors, window sills, and scanty furniture were covered with thick dirt. The laborers sprawled on the wooden bunks, fully dressed in work clothes, with their boots on. I do not know whether they had separate male and female accommodations, but both men and women were in the barracks when I walked in. The windows, secured by steel guards, did not open, and the air was stuffy and smelly. There were strong odors of alcohol and cigarette smoke. Food leftovers lay on the floor, caked with cockroaches. It was like the transition camp in Kiev, only worse.

From the porch, I called out the names of the girls I had come to see. There was a short silence, and then the people in the barracks responded with thunderous laughter. Nobody uttered a word. The reaction was so sudden and so bizarre that it scared me. I ran out the door like a scalded cat and rushed to the train station. All the way home, I felt nauseous, and the barracks scene stood before my eyes. "How lucky I am," I thought, "I did not end up in a place like this. I should be grateful to my masters and never complain. I will work day and night, thanking God for sparing me such a dreadful existence in the barracks."

I returned to Weissensee earlier than expected. Frau Hunke noticed right away that I was in a bad mood. "What happened?" she said, "You look upset." I described what I had seen. My masters were silent. What could they possibly say? I went to my room and never mentioned the dormitory or my Ukrainian friends again.

6. Back to Business

One quiet afternoon, my boss came back from Berlin and announced that he had rented a hotel-restaurant in Mittenwalde, a small town not far from Weissensee. We were moving there. I felt sorry to part with our little house on the lake, my friends Dietrich and the little girl next door, their families, and other people I had met in the past few months. During our stay in Weissensee, I fell in love with that village, its tranquil life and beautiful surroundings. I understood it was a short respite before future upheavals, a lull in the hurricane's eye, but tried to enjoy that moment for as long as I could… Not far from our house was a dormitory where construction workers from Italy lived. They built homes for the German owners during the day, and assembled in the evening in front of their dwelling to sing Neapolitan songs. There were truly gifted singers among them. I remembered those enchanting nights all my life.

Mittenwalde made a good impression on me. Like every town in the German countryside, it was picturesque and calm, with clean, narrow streets and friendly residents. The hotel-restaurant the chef had rented was a two-story building with a restaurant on the ground floor and several guest rooms on the floor above. My masters did not plan to stay in Mittenwalde for too long and wanted to go back to Berlin at the first opportunity, so instead of renting a separate place to live, they took one guest room for themselves and put a bed in an empty storage room on the ground floor for me. The storage room was damp with no heat, but I did not complain, as it was better than a forest or a latrine booth. When the weather turned colder, the room would become too chilly to remain there during the daytime, and at night, I slept under several blankets. The worst part was getting out of bed in the morning. Shivering from the cold, I quickly dressed and ran to the kitchen, where it was a little warmer. I started working and warmed up with physical activity. Why couldn't I sleep in the kitchen or in the restaurant's dining room? All I needed was a cot. But nobody suggested it, and I was afraid to ask. My masters saw me suffer yet did nothing.

With the guest rooms upstairs, my workload became bigger, as I now had to clean the second floor, too. The rooms were occupied mainly by SS and Wehrmacht officers. Every morning, I would bring a jar of fresh water to each room, where half-dressed guests reacted to my appearance with bawdy looks and lewd remarks that made me very uncomfortable. One time, I complained to Frau Hunke, but she politely replied that I had to be patient and follow the chef's instructions until the war ended and we returned to Berlin. Like her husband, she did not doubt that Germany would end the war on favorable terms, and they would resume their normal, comfortable existence. However, things did not go well for the German military. As the year 1944 was coming to an end, the Red Army divisions had freed Ukraine and Poland and were pushing into German territory. But the German people were not told the truth. The radio and newspapers lied about the Wehrmacht's successes, predicting the war's imminent and triumphant finale. Hitler screamed on the radio, calling on the German population to disregard the rumors of defeat and promising all earthly riches after victory.

Despite long hours in the hotel-restaurant, I made new friends among the Mittenwalde residents. One of those friends was a young, charming woman I met in a food store while shopping for my masters. The woman turned out to be the wife of the town's *Bürgermeister*[6]. She invited me to her house, a beautiful place with a cozy atmosphere. The *Bürgermeister* was a fairly young man, energetic and good-natured. The couple had two lovely children—a boy and a girl—between the ages of four and seven. I became a frequent guest in the *Bürgermeister's* house. The children grew attached to me, and I liked them, too. We frequently had coffee together at their home or a sidewalk café, or strolled through the magnificent old part of town with its massive church and castle. The *Bürgermeister* and his wife told me about the town's history and its famous residents, dating back to medieval times. They were curious about the Soviet Union and asked me many questions, trying to understand the country Germany was at war with. Both husband and wife were always courteous to me and each other, and I felt very comfortable in their company.

My masters were flattered and surprised by my friendship with the *Bürgermeister* family, telling everybody about it. As for myself, I did not know why the *Bürgermeister* and his wife treated me so kindly. Maybe they sensed that I had suffered a lot, and tried to atone for the sins of their countrymen. They may not have been big fans of the regime, yet they never talked politics in my presence. I also became friendly with another German family, who, unlike the *Bürgermeisters*, were poor and lived in a small basement apartment. They struggled to make ends meet but always welcomed me with heartfelt hospitality, bringing to the dinner table everything they had in the house. They were fiercely anti-Nazi and wished for Germany's defeat in the war. At night, they listened to the German-language radio broadcasts from London and Moscow, what was

---

[6] A mayor. In Russia (USSR), a mayor of a German town was commonly referred to by a German title (or sounding very similar). In the original Russian text, the author used such a reference, which has been preserved in this translation.

prohibited by the Nazi regime. It was from them that I learned what was happening on the battlefield. They told me of the opening of the Second Front and that the Soviets would soon be in Berlin.

Herr Hunke was an NSDAP[7] member and wore a Nazi button on the lapel of his jacket. He was not political, though, and I am sure his Party affiliation was mainly a business maneuver. The membership gave him some advantages, allowing, for example, to choose free help among the workers from Ukraine. Many of his regular customers were army officers and government officials. While talking to them, he must have heard about Nazi atrocities, especially toward Jews. Still, like many others, he conveniently ignored that information and minded his own business, entrusting higher matters of the state to the Führer and his gang. I rarely heard him discuss politics at home. He was not a bad man, and deep inside, his conscience bothered him. I remember one of our journeys to Berlin. We were walking down the street when we saw two male figures in long black coats with yellow stars in front. The men trotted in the middle of the road, constantly turning around to dodge the passing cars. I was struck by the look of those ill-fated—the memories from occupied Chudnov arose in my mind. "Who are those people, and why aren't they going on a sidewalk like everybody else?" I asked my boss, playing ignorance. "They are Jews," he replied, "They are forbidden to use the sidewalk and enter stores. Hitler expelled Jews from our country, but some were kept because of their value to the Reich. They live in barracks in a special area, and their talents benefit the German people." "And what will happen to them after the war?" I asked. "I don't know," replied my boss, "I think there will be no Jews left in Germany." "In Kiev," I continued, "I heard about mass executions of Jews by the German authorities…." Herr Hunke's face became red. "This is not true!" he exclaimed fervently, "This is misinformation spread by our enemies. We, the Germans, are the most talented, industrious, and cultured people in the world. Others envy us and plot our downfall. Jews are also smart and good businessmen. They are our competitors. Führer banished them from Germany and Europe, but they were resettled in the East. Nobody got killed." I did not argue. Herr Hunke's outburst echoed my own reaction back in the Berlin apartment when he repeated patron Willi's comment about the Jewishness of my appearance. My mention to Herr Hunke of the killings also touched a nerve, but if my past denial meant to convince others, my boss was now trying to persuade himself.

---

[7] The Nazi Party.

7. Red General

The war situation in Germany continued to deteriorate; the authorities began conscripting the old and the sick. My boss was drafted, too. He had a bad heart and high blood pressure. He also claimed a problem with one leg and was limping. They put him in a uniform, and his mere look in that outfit spoke volumes of Germany's military successes. In a couple of weeks, he ended up in a hospital, and I was on my way to see him, carrying a package from Frau Hunke. She could not go herself—she had to take care of the business, and it was difficult for her to walk.

The hospital was outside Berlin, so I had to go to the city and switch trains there. In Berlin, I would meet my boss' sister, Gerta, who was to join me on the trip. Gerta lived in Berlin with her husband. She was a pretty, young woman, much younger than my boss. She was close with her brother and, before marriage, lived with him and Frau Hunke in their Berlin apartment. She married a baker who owned a shop in the city's center. They and my masters frequently exchanged visits, but I got to see Gerta's home and place of business only after we moved to Weissensee while accompanying my boss to Berlin. It was my first time at a typical, family-owned German bakery-café, where the wife stood at the counter and the husband, with two helpers, made pastries in the basement. Gerta and her husband lived in a small, ground-floor flat. "This is how you start," explained to me my boss, "so later you can have a good business and a nicer apartment or a house."

Gerta met me at the station. We took a connecting train and, in half an hour, arrived at the hospital's gate. It was a military medical facility set in a pretty location in the woods. The guards let us through. Herr Hunke was sitting outside and did not look sick at all. I do not know what put him in the doctors' care, but he might have exaggerated his condition to get out of the army. He was happy to see Gerta and me and gave us a tour of the park and the hospital's building. While inside, my boss announced that he had a surprise for me. There was a former Soviet general among the patients, who had switched sides at the beginning of the war and whom Herr Hunke wanted me to meet. We went to the general's room. The general sat behind the desk; next to him stood his wife. They must have expected us, for the general greeted me in Russian as I entered the room. He offered me a chair. I sat down. The general started asking me who I was, which parts of the Soviet Union I came from, and how I ended up in Germany. My boss settled nearby, listening to the sounds of an unfamiliar language. I kept answering the questions, but could not wait for the meeting to be over. I worried I might betray myself by a slip of the tongue. I also felt repulsed talking to a renegade who served Hitler. The conversation paused; I apologized for not staying longer, as I could miss my train, and started toward the exit. My boss followed me. Gerta was waiting for us in the hallway. "Wasn't it good to talk to a compatriot in your language?" asked my boss. "It was good, thank you," I replied, but thought differently. "How is the situation on the battlefront?" I asked him in turn. "Not so great at the moment," he answered, "but it does not matter. We will win the war. Hitler promised us, and he will keep his word." I saw that my boss was getting tired. Gerta and I said goodbye to him and headed for the train station. "I think Hitler is lying," Gerta said to me as we got outside, "We are losing the war. Do you sense the mood in Berlin? People are in a panic." "You may be correct," I replied and changed the subject.

Gerta and I returned to Berlin in the late afternoon. Gerta invited me to her home for tea, but I wanted to spend some time in the city alone. It was a beautiful autumn day, clear and crisp, long-shadowed and tranquil. I immersed myself in the maze of cobblestone streets, park alleys, little cafes, and store windows, coming back to the train station hours later when it was already dark outside.

Except for air raids later in the war, it was completely safe to walk in Berlin at night. I never heard of anybody being mugged or assaulted on the streets or homes burglarized, and not just in the city but anywhere in the country. Apartments and houses had simple locks, which were frequently left open. Bicycles parked in public areas were unchained, and nobody touched them. Despite shortages, especially by the war's end, felonies were practically nonexistent. Laborers from the East were under strict control and, beyond work, seldom left their barracks. When they did go outside, mandatory armbands made them instantly recognizable. I admired German honesty, in part because I grew up in a country where people feared ruffians and thieves. I am sure there was street crime in Germany, but too little to be noticeable. I appreciated the diligence of the German people, their cleanliness, sense of responsibility, and the way they treated their families and friends. Unfortunately, some of those same qualities were partly responsible for the blanket obedience to the Nazi regime, even if many disagreed with its actions.

I came home late at night. Frau Hunke was already worried, as she had expected me earlier. I went straight to bed, full of impressions from a rendezvous with the enchanting city. Soothing images of buildings and leafless trees floated before my eyes, circling in a silent lullaby until I fell asleep, peaceful and content.

8. The Fall of the Town

By the end of 1944, everybody knew that Germany had lost the war. The Nazi propaganda broadcasts claimed that the retreat was temporary—a tactical maneuver to lure the enemy deeper into the German territory before the final, victorious offensive—but nobody believed those tales anymore. Panic was growing among German civilians, and many tried to escape from the front lines. Frau Hunke decided to evacuate, too. She called me to her room and said, "I am planning to leave. The Russians will be in Mittenwalde any day now. If you wish to go back to the Soviet Union, stay here and wait for your countrymen, but if you want to be our daughter and heir, go with me…" I forgot, for a moment, that it was my countrymen, Nazi collaborators, who had betrayed and murdered my family, my countrymen, the Bolsheviks, who persecuted my father most of his adult life. It seemed the Soviet victory was the answer to my hopes, and everything would be different from now on. I could not wait to see the first Russian soldier on the street, the first shiny red star on an army hat. "Thank you for your kind offer," I replied to my mistress, "but I decided to return to my homeland." Frau Hunke embraced me and cried. I did not doubt her sincerity. For the next few days, I helped her pack. As for Herr Hunke, we did not know where he was.

The Soviet troops were at Mittenwalde's outer reaches—we could hear distant gunfire. Stories were told about Russian soldiers robbing houses, raping women, and killing men. Civilians trembled with fear. The Russians were seen as barbarians set upon Germany's destruction. Frau Hunke had packed her bags and waited for the transportation to arrive in the morning, but it was not about to happen. That night, the Red Army entered Mittenwalde.

Chapter 5

THE RUSSIAN ZONE

1. New Career

Frau Hunke, I, and a few women neighbors with their children hid in the basement of the hotel-restaurant's building. Heard from the outside were numerous rifle shots and machine gun series. Russian troops combed the town, firing at scattered German soldiers, who shot at the Russians. It was dawn already. I got upstairs to the restaurant's hall and peeked through the closed shutters out of the window. The gruesome reality hit me like a punch in the face. I saw Red Army soldiers with madly twisted features, leaning their backs against the walls and firing at anything that moved; others breaking into homes and getting out with piles of the owners' possessions. I heard screams and calls for help from women being violated. That ghastly scene filled me with sorrow and shame about those I so eagerly had waited for. I returned to the basement and described what I had seen. The women and children burst into tears. "Do not go out," implored me Frau Hunke, "Those animals will rape or kill you!" And so I remained in the basement all day.

By dusk, the shooting had abated, and I decided to step outside. As soon as I got to the street, a Soviet soldier with a submachine gun rose in front of me. I spoke to him in Russian, trying to explain who I was, but he did not listen. Pointing the gun at my chest and cursing with terrible words, he threatened to shoot me. Suddenly, I heard the buzz of an engine, and a Soviet military truck rolled from around the corner. The truck stopped. A man in a Red Army captain's uniform jumped out of the cabin. He ran toward the soldier and me, grabbed my hand, and ordered the soldier to lower the weapon. The soldier hesitated. The captain repeated the order, warning of a court-martial if not obeyed at once. The mention of a court-martial cooled the soldier like a splash of cold water. He turned his gun away, saluted the officer, and trotted down the street, glancing around, till he passed from sight.

My savior turned out to be a deputy commandant (deputy chief) of the Soviet military administration, which was setting up a regional office (*Kommandatura*) in Mittenwalde. The deputy commandant was surprised to hear me speak Russian—he thought I was a German girl when he saw me standing under the soldier's gun. The deputy then asked me to follow him to the *Kommandatura*, where the truck was heading. I got in the cabin. The *Kommandatura's* building was not far away. The captain (his name was Simeon Voronoy) took me to an empty room, gave me a chair, and brought another for himself. We sat down. "Tell me about yourself," the captain said... For the first time since leaving Zhitomir, I was telling someone what happened to me—the death of my family, Stepan's sister's birth certificate, surviving on the streets of Kiev and in the Ukrainian countryside, and working as a domestic in Germany. The captain listened with great interest, sometimes asking questions. I saw he was moved. After I finished, he sat quietly and then spoke. "Normally, we would send you to a repatriation camp, like other displaced persons from the Soviet Union," the captain said, "but the commandant's office needs a German translator. I am offering this job to you. You will have a room in this building, where you will live, and free use of the cafeteria. Let me know if you agree, and I will take care of the formalities." Of course, I agreed. A brief scare in front of the hotel-restaurant was a blessing in disguise, as only an hour later, I had a place to live, food to eat, and a job that was easier and more rewarding than in the restaurant. And although I did not know it then, I was fortunate to escape the repatriation camp, where many were accused of collaborating with the Nazis and repatriated straight to Siberia. And even if such an outcome were unlikely in my case, there would have been interrogations by the secret police, let alone filth and overcrowding of the internment.

Captain Voronoy showed me to my room and suggested that I stay inside the Kommandatura building for a couple of days until the anarchy on the streets died out. I told him I needed my things left in the hotel-restaurant. I also wanted to check on Frau Hunke and her neighbors to make sure they were alright. The captain said he would go with me. It was late at night already. We walked through the deserted streets to the hotel-restaurant. I unlocked the front door with my key. The basement was empty, and we went upstairs. Frau Hunke was in her room. She was crying. She probably thought I had been shot or violated; she rejoiced when she saw me. I introduced Captain Voronoy and explained what had happened. Frau Hunke said that the neighbors who had been hiding with us in the basement sneaked back to their homes after dark. Then, she started begging the captain to help her leave Mittenwalde. The captain replied that it was not a good idea to travel amid the fighting and chaos and that Frau Hunke ought to wait it out. "Tell her," the captain said to me as I was doing my first translation for the new employer, "it will take us a couple of days to restore order, and until then, she should lock the doors and windows and remain inside…" The captain's unruffled tone and polite manners calmed Frau Hunke down, reassured her. I promised to visit her when I had a chance, took my belongings, and followed the captain back to the Kommandatura.

It is hard to describe the mayhem that Red Army soldiers and even some officers unleashed on the German civilian population. They robbed, raped, and murdered. There was little the commanders could do to stop the savageries in the first days after the town seizures; however, upon gaining control, the administration and the army command came down hard on the violators. Rapists, robbers, and murderers were arrested, tried by court-martial, and sentenced to long prison terms or even executions by a firing squad. It was sad to see the soldiers who had survived such a long and bloody war only to be shot by their comrades for the crimes committed in a frenzy of drunkenness and hatred.

For the next couple of days, I remained inside the *Kommandatura* building. I became acquainted with many officers and members of the commandant's staff. They learned my story and treated me with empathy and respect. Captain Voronoy took care of my employment papers. We soon became friends. Before the war, he worked as a civil engineer and was called to duty when Germany invaded the USSR. I also met his wife, Julia, who came to visit him in Mittenwalde. She was a physician, an army surgeon also stationed in Germany, and, like her husband, a kind and charming person. Simeon worked in the military administration until the first wave of demobilization, when he and Julia returned to the Soviet Union. They got back to their civilian professions and had a son. We stayed in touch for many years after that.

2. Special Assignment

I had been working in the *Kommandatura* for several months when we received the news of Germany's surrender. The war was over. I felt joyous but also sorry—sorry for the soldiers who did not live to see the victory, sorry for the women, children, and men who had perished in ghettos and concentration camps, sorry for the countless civilians who became victims of violence and starvation. It was then that I started to feel guilty because I had survived while my parents and sisters died. That feeling I carried all my life; when others celebrated, I grieved and often had nightmares, reliving the horrors of the past. An invisible wall stood between others and me. I felt lonely and isolated; there was nobody, even among the closest of friends, in whom I could confide.

Shortly after the war's end, *Kommandatura* moved to Luckenwalde[1], and I followed with the rest of the staff. In Luckenwalde, I met my future husband. His name was Yefim. He was a counterintelligence officer who occasionally worked with the commandant's staff. As a translator, I was sometimes assigned to interrogations of suspected Nazi conspirators, or "spies," as they were called. I hated those assignments and tried to avoid them, but it was not always possible. The interrogators shouted at the suspects and beat them up, trying to wrest an admission of guilt. I felt sorry for those Germans, even if some did turn out to be Nazi activists, but the majority were completely innocent. The Soviet secret police applied its old methods in the new setting. I do not believe there was any organized resistance from the defeated enemy; still, the interrogators invented conspiracies and beat out confessions to receive promotions and other rewards.

One day, I was sent to translate at such an interrogation. The officer in charge was unknown to me. He was in his forties, thin, of average height, with brown hair and grey eyes. The quizzing began. I do not remember the details of the case, but the way it was conducted surprised me. There was no yelling or violence; all questions were asked in a calm voice, with a clear purpose of determining the truth. In the end, the arrested person was let go... The officer was Yefim. He thanked me for the assistance and asked if I could translate for him in the future. I gladly agreed.

Yefim held a senior post and questioned suspects mainly in higher-profile cases. One such case involved the wife of a top-ranking German military officer, an admiral, I believe. The admiral was in a Nuremberg prison, awaiting trial, while his wife lived in their house in Luckenwalde.

---

[1] German town about fifty kilometers from Mittenwalde.

Someone discovered the woman's identity; she was arrested as a spy and brought to the Kommandatura. Yefim was called to question her, and I did the translation. Standing before us was a scared, confused woman, suddenly removed from the life of privilege and comfort. It was hard to imagine she had plotted anything. Yefim realized at first glance that the charges were absurd. He offered the woman a chair, asked her a few questions, and then called the arresting men waiting outside. "I have determined that this woman is not a spy," Yefim said, "Take her home…" Yefim was Jewish and fully aware, at the time, of the destruction that befell the Jewish people at the hands of the Nazis, yet he never let personal feelings affect his judgment. During interrogations, I remember him raising his voice only once when questioning an unrepentant Nazi, but he never hit anybody or directed others to do so.

The story of the admiral's wife did not end with her release. A few days later, she appeared in the Kommandatura, looking for Yefim. He received her in his office and called me in to translate. The woman explained that she had come to thank Yefim for letting her go. She pulled out a small jewelry box from her purse and opened it. From the dark felt, sparkled several diamonds. The woman placed the box on Yefim's desk and asked him to accept it as a gesture of gratitude. Yefim refused. She persisted, pushing the box toward him. He pushed it back, and the box fell to the floor. The woman picked it up. "Herr Captain," she exclaimed almost desperately, "if you do not want these stones for yourself, take them for the Soviet Army!" "It is not my job to collect donations for the army," Yefim replied. He then saw the woman to the door, and she left with the diamonds.

Yefim could have taken those stones without anybody making a squeak. His was a position where the spoils of war were readily available to him. Others did not need a special invitation to possess themselves of things no longer claimed by the previous owners. Yefim's commander, a high-ranking army officer, dispatched an entire boxcar with valuables to his home in the USSR and "entrusted" the shipping arrangements to Yefim, who spent all day directing the loaders and doing the paperwork. Of course, Yefim acted on his commanding officer's orders, but when left to his own devices, he did nothing to enrich himself. He was a man of principle to whom such deeds seemed like plunder. A few "trophies" bestowed on him by his superiors quickly disappeared in the postwar Soviet existence, which turned out to be a real struggle, but he never voiced any regrets.

Yefim was twenty years older than me, a divorcee with a former wife and two sons living in Tashkent[2], where he had served before the war. My difficult childhood with practically no father and little motherly love, followed by the horrors of the war, made me reticent and somber, too much for my age. I needed care, tenderness, and love. Many younger officers wooed me, but I was not attracted to them. Yefim's kindness, self-control, honesty, and culture won my heart, and I fell in love to the point that I couldn't imagine my life without him. I did not think about our age difference, his family, or my future with a man from a different walk of life. My friends at the commandant's office were saying that I was too young for Yefim, that it could affect our relations later on, but I ignored those warnings. I felt good with him. We talked for hours, and my fears disappeared. On weekends, we traveled to Berlin, Leipzig, and other places. Yefim had an official, chauffeured car and another for personal use. He was an excellent driver and, even in an official capacity, often dismissed the chauffeur, getting behind the wheel himself. I was nervous when driven by other officers, who usually lacked experience and were under the influence of alcohol, but I felt safe with Yefim in the driver's seat. He did not drink and was all attention and responsibility. When Yefim was busy or away, I traveled alone by train. Germany and Berlin were divided into four occupation zones at the time: American, British, French, and Soviet. The Soviet personnel were not allowed to leave their zone without permission, but I disregarded that rule and often crossed zone boundaries pretending to be a local[3]. Nobody suspected I wasn't German.

---

[2] The capital city of Uzbekistan in Central Asia.

[3] For a few years after the war, before Germany was divided into East and West German states, the native German population could travel freely between zones.

3. Car Accident

My fear of being chauffeured by drivers other than Yefim was prescient, as one such ride resulted in an accident that caused me a serious injury. It happened on some Soviet holiday. The military had a banquet and invited the Kommandatura staff. I do not remember how we got there, but on the way back, a group of army officers offered me a ride in their car. The officers didn't appear too drunk, so I agreed to go with them. It was already dark outside. The driver did not know the road well; he drove the car into a ditch, and the car's door crushed my foot. I underwent surgery in a military hospital and spent several months in a cast. After the cast came off, the injured foot developed a painful sore on the bottom, which did not heal. The doctors tried everything—covered the wound with an antibacterial substance, changed bandages—but nothing helped. I didn't know what to do and decided to see a German doctor. It was uncommon for a member of the Soviet occupying force to seek medical help from a local practitioner. Shortly after the hostilities, there was some lingering distrust between the former enemies, plus seeking help from the losing side did not look good for the victors. Still, having lived among Germans for over two years, I felt in many ways like them and even made some local acquaintances in Luckenwalde. For his part, Yefim welcomed the idea. He realized that German medicine was better than the Soviet, and that my health was a priority. So I asked around my German contacts, who recommended a doctor in Berlin. He was a professor of medicine, a scientist of international acclaim (later, in the Soviet Union, I mentioned his name to several doctors, and some were familiar with his work, having studied it in medical school). I was told that appointments with him were made months in advance. I conveyed my findings to Yefim, and the following morning, he drove me to Berlin.

When informed of the unusual visitors, the professor received us right away. He invited Yefim and me to his office, opened my bandages, and looked at the wound. "This is easy," he said, "My assistant will do the operation." I am certain the doctor mentioned the assistant only to show that my wound was a simple matter and there was nothing to worry about. He didn't recognize that such a response could be seen as a refusal to provide service, an act of defiance and disrespect, and that was how Yefim interpreted it. His face flushed with anger. He didn't travel all that distance to see the famed healer, so someone else would take care of me. Perhaps the German ought to be reminded of who had won the war. Yefim stepped forward and put his hand on the holster at his waist. "I am sorry, Herr Professor," he uttered menacingly, "but your assistant will not do this operation. This operation will be done by you." In his wrath, Yefim did not ask for my translation and spoke Yiddish, but the doctor understood. The latter had already realized his mistake. "Please, follow me," he said to me, and headed to the operating room. Yefim remained in the office. In the operating room, the doctor cleaned my wound, made a few fresh incisions around it with a scalpel, applied some ointment, and put new bandages. The entire procedure took less than thirty minutes. During the operation, the doctor was cordial, asking me about myself and where I had learned to speak German so well. He seemed impressed and touched by my story. Then he told me of another Russian patient whom, as a young physician, he had treated many years ago. That patient was Vladimir Lenin, the future founder of the USSR, who was living in exile in Germany at the time.

The doctor took me back to his office, where Yefim had been waiting for my return, and told us to come in two weeks. The next day after the operation, the pain became weaker, and I felt much better. The army surgeons, who had treated me before and some of whom had heard of the Berlin professor, were surprised by his method of freshening the wound; they were curious about the results. Two weeks later, Yefim and I went to Berlin for a follow-up. The doctor removed the bandages, and the wound was gone—healed completely. Yefim was delighted and later sent the doctor a box with cognac, caviar, and other sought-after delicacies.

4. Proposal

Life in Germany was getting on a normal track. Started opening stores and restaurants. In Berlin, opened a supermarket "Moscow," serving the Soviet military command and administration. The supermarket carried caviar, smoked fish, sausages, and other items. After years of starvation, all that food was readily available to me, and I put on some weight.

My involvement with Yefim was getting deeper. He knew of some of my friends' disapproving opinions and had his own doubts. The time came for his vacation, and he went to the Soviet Union for two weeks. He wanted to see his father, change the atmosphere, and reflect on our relationship. On the train, he shared a compartment with several army officers, also traveling home on leave. As the conversations became more open, Yefim confided to his new friends about me and his dilemma. The advice was unanimous: "Don't be a fool. Who knows what the future holds? You ought to understand it better than most, having come out of the war where death trailed your every step. Follow the counsel of your heart and waste no time."

Yefim returned to Luckenwalde one week sooner and made me a proposal, which I joyfully accepted. My happiness had no bounds. God sent me a man—kind, intelligent, and honest. I could not wait to return to the Soviet Union and start a family. However, it was not so easy. An officer in Yefim's line of service could not just marry anybody. He had to report his intent to the personnel department, fill out a questionnaire on the prospective wife, and receive approval. Such approval, Yefim did not get. The official reason for the denial was that I had lived in German-occupied Soviet territory and later in Nazi Germany. "If she is Jewish," they told him, "why wasn't she killed?" Yefim tried to explain what had happened to me—how I wandered under an assumed name, miraculously survived, and was transported to Germany against my will—but the officials did not listen. So, Yefim and I decided to live together without a marriage license until his demobilization and our return to the Soviet Union, where no such permission to marry would be necessary. But Yefim's superiors did not like that arrangement, either. They decided to transfer him to the Soviet Union and keep me in Germany, promoting me to a senior interpreter. The transfer process took time, so to separate us immediately, the higher-ups moved Yefim to Potsdam while I was sent to another town near Berlin. Working for the military, I could not choose where to live—I received orders and had to obey them. Neither could I quit my job without coming under the jurisdiction of the repatriation authorities. The only option was for me to get pregnant and state it as a reason for asking to return to the USSR.

The decision to transfer Yefim to the Soviet Union had been made, but he remained in Potsdam, waiting for his papers. I became pregnant and submitted a request for relocation to the USSR, directly or through the repatriation program. The administration officials tried to change my mind. I was called to the headquarters in Berlin, where I was offered a job in the city and another promotion with a pay increase (we started to receive a small salary in German marks by then). The officials promised me generous benefits, including a nanny for the baby, but I insisted on going home.

Shortly after the Berlin meeting, I received my transfer papers in the mail, permitting me to settle anywhere in the Soviet Union. I chose the city of Odessa, where my father's sister and her husband lived. I found them through the Red Cross. The aunt was my only close relative who had survived World War II. She and her husband lived in Odessa before the war; they had a son who died as a child. When the war started, they evacuated to Siberia and returned to their old apartment in Odessa after the Soviet victory. I sent my aunt a letter from Germany, and she replied with an invitation to come and live with them. "All that we have is yours," she wrote, "We are eagerly awaiting your arrival." Yefim did not object. He hoped that being next to relatives would help me cope with the loss of my family; plus, he had lived in Odessa during his youth.

Yefim's paperwork was taking a long time. He was being transferred to Tashkent, where his former wife and their children lived. Such a destination showed the true motive behind his transfer: punishment for disobedience… My pregnancy was difficult. I often felt nauseous and threw up after meals, but continued seeing Yefim regularly. We were free on weekends; still, he had to remain in Potsdam for emergencies. Hence, on Saturday morning, I would take the train and travel for two hours to Potsdam. Yefim would meet me at the station, and we would spend the weekend together. Sunday night, he would put me on the return train or, if it was too late, drive me home in his car. Monday morning, we had to be at work: he in one place, I in another. And despite all that hassle, I was happy. I always considered myself fortunate to have experienced such a strong feeling of love.

The day of my going back to the old country had arrived. Yefim drove me to Frankfurt, where I would take a train through Poland to the Soviet border town of Brest-Litovsk, an entry point to the USSR. In Brest-Litovsk, I would go through customs and take another train, to Odessa. I had very little luggage since most of our belongings had been shipped to my aunt's address... The parting with my beloved husband was sad, but we hoped to reunite soon. "I will do everything for you and the child," Yefim said. I got inside the railcar and came to the aisle window facing the platform. The locomotive moved. Yefim followed the train, waving me goodbye until the speeding engine left him behind. I was going to where it all started. The train made a slight turn, flashing the platform at a distance. I saw Yefim's lone figure gazing after the receding railcar chain, and then he vanished in the morning mist.

5. Homecoming

My aunt and uncle met me at the Odessa train station. I was twelve years old when I last saw them during a trip to Odessa with my mother and sisters, yet I now recognized my relatives at once, and they recognized me. I suddenly sensed a bad vibe, but the aunt and uncle greeted me jollily, and the disturbing feeling disappeared. I had left my suitcase at customs for inspection to pick it up the next day, so we went straight to my relatives' home. As we walked in the door, I recalled their little flat: a living room, a small kitchen, and a toilet. The toilet was so small that it fit only one person. The apartment was very cramped, and I wondered how my relatives had invited me to a place that didn't have enough room even for one family. "How will we live here when the baby is born?" I asked. "We will exchange this apartment for a larger one—only have to pay extra," my aunt replied. "But where will I get the money?" I thought. We had no savings. Yefim sent all his earnings to his children in Tashkent and his widowed sister, while I did not work, expecting a child.

I realized life in Odessa would be difficult, but waited for a message from Yefim with the date of his return to the Soviet Union. He did not want me to go to Tashkent, as he had no intention of staying there. I felt gloomy. I knew it would be hard for Yefim to arrange his transfer to Odessa. I asked him in my letters not to make waves and to remain in Tashkent until we found a better solution. One month later, Yefim wrote me that he had received his papers and was ready to leave Germany. Upon arrival in Tashkent, he sent me another letter. Despite his dislike for writing, he wrote to me every week. The letters were full of love for me and the child. Having had two sons, he wanted a daughter who would look like me in my childhood photograph: in a short dress with a bow in her hair. I wanted a girl, too, maybe because I missed my sisters.

A few months passed, and I received a letter from Yefim that he had submitted a transfer request to Ukraine. That request was denied. Yefim reacted to the denial by resigning from the military and forfeiting his pension. He had just over a year left to become eligible for the benefits, but could not accept the unfair verdict, and he worried about me. He did not ask for my advice and would not have listened to it anyway.

I waited for Yefim impatiently, even though I understood that our life would be difficult, at least in the beginning. On the day of his arrival, I went to the train station to meet him. Our joy had no bounds, but when we came home and sat at the dinner table with my relatives, Yefim and I felt like strangers. At bedtime, we started to divide the room by hanging bedsheets across it. Yefim and I slept on one side of the divider, while my relatives slept on the other. In the morning, we resumed the discussion of the apartment exchange. Yefim suggested selling things from Germany to raise the money, but when we opened the parcels, the most valuable items were missing. My aunt denied seeing those packages; however, years later, her sister-in-law told us that my aunt did receive those parcels and sold them at the flea market. I do not know if that was true, as the sisters-in-law loathed each other, but my aunt seemed unhappy with the presents Yefim and I had brought her. She probably expected jewelry and furs, but we did not have those things.

Later, I discovered my aunt and uncle were quite well-off. They had money in the bank, owned gold and jewelry that they hid inside furniture. But my aunt wanted more. That was why she invited me to Odessa—she hoped Yefim and I would bring her expensive gifts. She had no kindred feelings toward me and had disliked my husband since the day they met. Despite their wealth, my aunt and uncle lived like paupers. The furniture in the apartment was old and cheap; the clothes were drab. They never went to any places and did not enjoy the good things in life. Whom were they saving money for? They had no children, and most of their relatives perished during the war. I was the only surviving relative on my aunt's side, and her husband had a sister my aunt hated. The sister's family was very poor; however, my aunt did not want to hear about them. My uncle sometimes helped his sister, secretly so his wife would not know, but that help was not nearly enough.

Anguish and sorrow filled my heart—what would I do when the baby was born? My relatives did not hurry with the apartment exchange. The fall was approaching, and I grew desperate. Yefim did not work. A career military, he had no civilian profession. He kept coming to the *Voenkomat* (Military Registration and Enlistment Office), where, as a war veteran, he was supposed to get help with a job, but the *Voenkomat* officials were in no rush to assist him. We sold more things from Germany to buy food. The provisions were costly, as they had to be purchased at the farmers' market. The government food stores were empty, and when something edible appeared there, the line stretched several blocks long.

In the summer, I gave birth to a son. We named him Michael after my father (Yefim's father was still alive then). Yefim arrived at the hospital carrying flowers, but when informed he had a boy, became so upset that he neglected to give the flowers to me and realized it only upon returning home with the entire bouquet still in his hands. Although disappointed at first, we quickly came to love our son and forgot we had wanted a girl.

ILLUSTRATIONS

Pictures #11, #13, & #17. Courtesy Boris Feldblyum Collection; http://www.bfcollection.net

Picture #15. TUBS / CC BY-SA (https://creativecommons.org/licenses/by-sa/3.0); desaturated; https://commons.wikimedia.org/wiki/File:Kiev_(oblast)_in_Ukraine_(claims_hatched).svg

Other pictures in this section are owned by the author or in the public domain.

1. Eva with her mother, Chaya, and twin sisters.

2. Eva at an early age.

3. Moshe Smiller, Eva's father.

4. Eva's maternal grandfather, Jacob, with his children (Sam, Morris, and Rose) in the US.

5. Stepan.

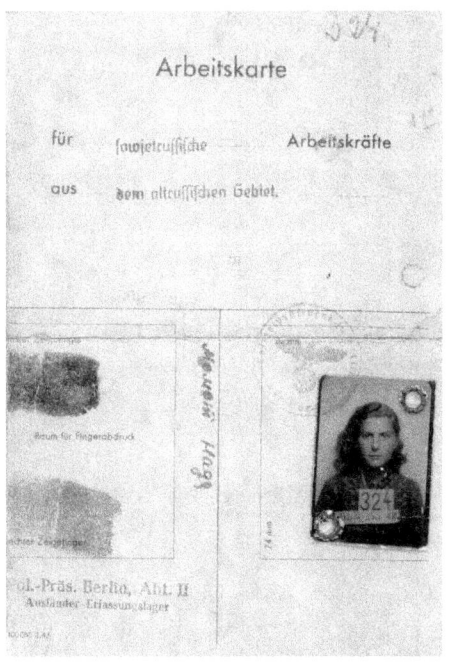

6. Eva's German work paper (*Arbeitskarte*).

7. Yefim (postwar Germany).

8. Eva in Germany after the war.

9. Polish church in Chudnov. Watercolor by Napoleon Orda, 1874.

10. Kishinev; Choral Synagogue.   11. Zhitomir in the early 20th century.

12. Kiev; The Jewish Market and surroundings.

13. Kiev; Red Army (Velyka Vasylkivska) Street.

14. Two-karbovanets bill, 1942.

15. Kiev Oblast on Ukraine map.

16. Exhibition Palace; Moabit, Berlin.

17. Berlin; Landwehr Canal.

Моя сознательная жизнь началась, примерно, в 5 лет. Я помню себя ребенком, живущим вместе со своей матерью и 2 сестричками близнецами в одной комнате. В провинциальном городке Чуднове, Винницкой обл. (затем Житомирской области). на Украине Мы жили в доме бабушки по отцу, который находился на горе между бульваром и узкой улочкой, которая вела к крестьянскому базару с одной стороны и к речке "Тетерев" с другой стороны. Эта речка разделяла старый город и новый. ~~новый~~ Мы жили в старом городе. Дом моей бабушки был очень стар, нуждался в хорошем ремонте, но никогда не ремонтировался. Дом разделялся на две части коридором (глиняным). Каждая половина имела по 2 комнаты и одну кухню. Мы жили в половине без кухни. Русская печь была сделана в коридоре и рядом стол, стульк кухонный. Как я уже говорила, мы жили в одной комнате, а в другой маленькой комнатке жила моя бабушка. Во второй же половине жила моя тетя, сестра моего отца, с её мужем и 3-мя сыновьями.

Своего отца я не знала, только слышала, что он жив и отбывает ссылку

18. The first page of Eva's manuscript.

End of Book 1

BOOK II

The Offshoots

by Michael Lehrman

(with Eva Smiller)

PREAMBLE

My parents' desire to have a daughter rather than a son cast a few clouds over my otherwise untroubled early years: the bow and long hair from my mother's childhood photograph ended up on my head, causing a reaction of resentment and vehement protests. I was almost four years old when, after a nasty courtyard fight with little bullies who had called me a "girl," I threw such a tantrum before my parents that they promptly retired the bow and asked the nearest barber to remove the rest of the "disguise." It was the last time I showed those pygmies in the courtyard that looks could be deceiving, and since then, my life assumed a fairly normal route—growing up in Odessa, school, work, emigration…

Of course, I knew of my mother's adventures during the war, as she told me many stories about it. Those stories made a deep impression on my young mind, but so did other events that were far more numerous and recent. Perhaps the daily routine affected my mother's perception of the past, too, as she did not record her war experiences while in the USSR. It was only in America that she decided to commit her memories to pen. I participated little in that endeavor but was informed of its progress. Occasionally, when visiting my mother's apartment, I saw her teary-eyed behind the dining table, writing. "I have completed the war years," she said to me one day. I replied that it might be time to share her story with the world, but she wanted to continue writing. She did not discriminate between different phases of her life; they were all equally important. But how is it possible to self-describe the entire lifespan? Such a story has no happy ending, and when coming to that point, the person is no longer there to tell it, anyway. One might choose some uplifting moment and make it a finale; yet, the closer the tale approaches the present, the sparser such moments become—and that's what happened to my mother's work: disappointments and poor health had dampened her enthusiasm, and she stopped writing… A few more years passed, and my mother's interest reawakened. She started talking about the details left out of her earlier text and was eager to fill in the gaps. I was pleased by that development, encouraging my mother to proceed, but then her condition turned for the worse.

My mother died in New York in the winter of 2004. Among the few things she left behind was a cardboard portfolio with laces on its side neatly tied in a bow. Inside that portfolio were three hundred pages of handwritten text. It was the manuscript. Despite being the first and only draft, the document had few corrections—only occasional inserts and annotations in the margins. Like in life, my mother, in her writing, had little doubt about the choices she made… I began to read and, from the first lines, was transported to another world, so different and remote yet indelibly connected to mine, like being its forgotten part. Now that the person who straddled those worlds was gone forever, that connection became even stronger, filling the void left by her departure and guiding my imagination through the written words. The scenes passed before my eyes as if viewed from a moving train, essential and concise, shaping, frame by frame, a story intensely personal, achingly tragic, and strikingly unique.

Unlike the subjects of most Holocaust accounts, my mother spent no time in a confined environment, side-by-side with other victims, except for the first few months of Chudnov's occupation. Hers was an escapade with the course of events undetermined, where every day could be her last. Her survival might be attributed to several factors—Stepan's help, the English Boston, unlikely benevolence of the police and Gestapo officials, encounters with Aunt Yelena and Maria Ilyinichna—however, the more I thought about those seemingly unrelated events, the more I sensed a connection between them: some propitious force that guided my mother on her journey, rising in critical moments to her defense. That force manifested itself in the strength of my mother's character, the correctness of her instincts, and an overwhelming urge to act upon them. It was no accident that my Chudnov grandmother gave the Blue Boston and American address to my mother, whom she viewed as the family's likeliest survivor. And my grandfather's sad words in the ranger's barn in Yagodinka shortly before his death showed a similar understanding. He also knew who his beloved daughter was.

I wondered why the Irpen police chief let my mother go. After all, he had sent many Jews to their deaths, the last ones right before her capture. He may not have been an eager participant in those murders—perhaps a Ukrainian nationalist whose dream of an independent state and hatred for the Bolsheviks had prompted him to accept a position in the new government, which he later regretted—but what difference would one more nameless victim have made to him? I am sure that he shared his deputy's opinion about the captured girl being Jewish, as he didn't claim the opposite as the reason for her release and, nonetheless, went out of his way to save her. When faced with a choice between my mother and his deputy, the chief decidedly took my mother's side.

A similar scenario took place in the Kiev Gestapo. Like in Irpen, there was a villain, the translator, who sought to have my mother shot, and his superiors, the Germans, who overruled him. Perhaps the very zeal of the Irpen deputy and Gestapo translator worked against them. Most people, when put in a position to decide others' fate, would render the decision impassively, following some established protocol to lessen doubt and remorse, and any emotional interference makes them uncomfortable. Besides, the translator's attempt to mislead his Gestapo bosses gave the latter an incentive not to please him. And yet, those were not pivotal factors in the above verdicts. After all, if verifying my mother's identity might take days or even weeks in Irpen, the Kiev Gestapo could have accomplished it within hours by contacting a Sviatoshyno outpost and checking the address my mother had given them. That the Germans did not do it shows they made up their minds early, perhaps without even realizing it. And so did the Irpen police chief when he mentioned he wanted to talk to the captured girl, although he had a better idea of how that conversation would end.

From my mother's account of the Irpen police and Kiev Gestapo episodes, one might conclude that she attributed their happy outcome to her good looks. She certainly possessed those qualities, but judging from her wartime photograph on the *Arbeitskarte,* they were not so obvious, at the time, to make a difference. The photograph shows a young woman, gaunt and dark, with sadness and suffering in her eyes. In truth, from a casual glance, I might not have recognized my mother at all. However, looking closer at the face in the picture, one senses the willpower and determination that helped her endure such odds. It was those qualities, I believe, that had a crucial effect on my mother's captors to the degree they went the extra mile to ensure her survival.

As I pondered my mother's ordeal, it occurred to me that she was not the type of survivor who employed their circumstances to excuse moral lapses. She was more troubled by eating scarce food in Aunt Yelena's home than by starving on the streets, more concerned about Maria Ilyinichna's sudden heart condition than of having almost suffocated behind the cupboard minutes earlier. She was always ready to move on, into the darkness and cold, not to inconvenience her hosts or use much of their hospitality. And she got the smallest sandwich at the welcome breakfast upon arrival in Germany from Ukraine. How many among us, when facing mortal danger, would reprimand a person whom their life depended on, as my mother scolded Stepan on their way to Zhitomir? But she did not think of the consequences and later regretted being, not imprudent, but too harsh on her guide. And even if she felt ungrateful to Stepan, her desire to travel alone was a correct impulse, which might have saved her life. Such integrity and directness evoked a sympathetic response from the people she met on the way, making up for her lack of effrontery and connivance.

The first pages of the manuscript introduced me to my grandparents, whom, of course, I did not know and imagined rather vaguely from occasional mentions at home, but here, within a continuous narrative, a few lines of text sufficed to vividly portray them in my mind. My mother complains in her notes about the lack of love and understanding from her own mother. I recognize my mother's sentiment, yet must speak in my grandmother's defense. For one, her life was very difficult, but the main reason for that "neglect" was, oddly, her nature as an equalizer—a supporter of the luckless and the weak. She had a broader sense of justness, which extended beyond her immediate family and demanded giving more attention to the younger daughters, who were not as gifted as the oldest one, helping neighbors' children during the famine, taking care of the mother-in-law who had become immobile after a stroke, and perhaps doing many more things of the kind. As for my mother, she was good-looking, smart, and strong, and did not need greater notice than she was already getting.

In contrast to my grandmother, my grandfather's life centered around his family, and especially his eldest daughter, whom he adored. What a cruel joke fate had played on him by separating from his loved ones for many years, only to reunite them at the end, for a few short months, on their path to destruction. He suffered the injustices of incarceration and exile, yet remained an honest and a proud man. Both my grandparents were decent, hardworking people, and the twins were frail, innocent girls. It is heart-rending that they died so early and such a terrible death. I cannot even start to imagine what they felt in their final moments.

I was moved by my mother's childhood reminiscences, shattered by the Chudnov carnage, awed by the escapes through occupied Ukraine, and enthralled by her German experience. The childhood part was brief but did not suggest that anything was missing. My mother's candor and sense of narrative allowed her to choose the most relevant episodes and present them with utter sincerity. Before starting to work on her notes, I had limited literary exposure, and while gaining it, I kept returning to the earlier sections to revise the text. The childhood part required the fewest of revisions, despite being drafted first.

I wished the Chudnov occupation section were shorter. It wasn't very long, but the gruesomeness of the described events did not beg for more. It ought to be hard for my mother to relive those memories, which she was likely doing when she cried over the manuscript. Her description of the harrowing episodes was plain, almost matter-of-fact, yet even more compelling because of that. The mood of helplessness and doom is heart-wrenching there, from the Red Army's retreat to the moment my mother left Yagodinka—the family's sole survivor—to begin her travels.

The following year and a half was an unrelenting flight. There were two places my mother kept returning to—the homes of Aunt Yelena and Maria Ilyinichna—and the first one was destroyed by her pursuers, as going back to the second resulted in my mother's arrest. An attempt to relax after selling the English Boston almost got her killed. Thus, her urge to change places was the right instinct. Such constant movement yielded a plethora of characters and events, which, except for episode reshuffling, required little effort on my part to knit the story. The notion one gets after reading this segment is that the described period extended over a much longer time than it actually did.

As I read about my mother's encounters, I noticed that she little analyzed the people she dealt with. She might describe what they did and said, but wouldn't speculate about their motives and thoughts. Perhaps such a visceral approach was pivotal in making critical decisions fast, but it also curtailed generalizations that sometimes take unpleasant forms. I rarely heard her speak of "Ukrainians," or "Germans," or similar categories. She judged people individually, and even if I disagreed with her assessments, such consistency drew my acclaim. She never dismissed anybody because of their group characteristics and was not impressed by pumped-up credentials and phony attitudes. Just one day after starting at Zum Dortmunder, she showed displeasure with the warehouse clothes and rebuked her German benefactresses for making fun of her coat. Such conduct seemed reckless, but for my mother, it was a natural reaction to other humans, her peers. She was on equally peer terms with the humble Weissensee neighbors, whom her masters looked down upon, and the Mittenwalde *Bürgermeister*, whom they looked up to. The Nazis' role in her family's destruction had little bearing on my mother's relations with her German friends, and years later, when telling me stories about Zum Dortmunder's owners, she always mentioned them with respect.

Reminiscing on her odyssey, my mother seldom spoke of Chudnov's occupation and her wanderings over Ukraine, but often talked about her German experience, especially its postwar part. That oral account came in handy in putting these tomes together, as my mother's writing became sketchy at that point. The story about her foot surgery in Berlin, which she had told me many times and based on which I bragged to other kids that my mother and Lenin had gone to the same doctor, was missing from her text, as were other episodes I remembered. Perhaps those were the events she had in mind when later remarking on the manuscript's omissions, so I incorporated them into her narrative.

My mother's notes did not mention Frau Hunke beyond the author's return to the hotel-restaurant with Captain Voronoy on the day of the town's seizure by the Soviets. That day drastically changed my mother's circumstances, so the above omission from the first and only draft is understandable; however, I remember her telling me that Frau Hunke followed the captain's advice to remain inside and was unharmed. My mother visited her at the hotel-restaurant a couple of times, and one time, Frau Hunke was no longer there. The neighbors told my mother that her former employer had left the town for an unknown destination. I hope the latter did not go to her native Königsberg, as she had planned, because the city soon became part of Soviet territory. My mother never heard from the Zum Dortmunder's proprietors again.

The storyline became even patchier as it entered the Odessa period, but I was already there and now can expand on the described events. To preserve the narrative's flow, I injected my perspective early, interlacing it with my mother's text (of which too little remained to sustain the momentum) and taking over as her voice faded away. And as soon as her notes proved my existence, I launched the second book… The following sections are less dramatic than the previous ones and often mention my mother only in passing, but they complement her account, depicting the time she lived in and the people she was surrounded by. Whether she recognized it or not, my mother's postwar existence was greatly affected by her wartime experience, and I will bear this in mind while trying to paint the detailed background of a remarkable story.

Chapter 1

DAY AFTER DAY

1. The Courtyard

While in the hospital with a newborn son, I did not receive proper nutrition. There was nobody to cook chicken soup or other fresh meals for me. My aunt did not come for a visit. Yefim brought me dry foods he was buying in the stores and at the farmers' market, but I needed liquids. I did not have enough breast milk—the baby was hungry and cried day and night. My aunt did not even congratulate me. One can imagine how I felt during the first days of motherhood. The situation with breast milk was not improving while baby food was unavailable, so I started giving the child regular food early; he did not like it and cried all the time. That bothered my relatives, especially at night. They demanded that I rock the child; the boy got used to it, and I lost the last moments of peace… Yefim and I realized we had become a burden to my relatives, and they were no longer interested in a bigger apartment for all of us. One day, looking them straight in the eyes, Yefim asked my aunt and uncle if they were still planning the apartment exchange. "No," replied my aunt, "we like it here." So, Yefim and I decided to buy one room in a communal apartment[1]; as for anything better, we had no money. After more than

---

[1] An apartment shared by several families. People in the Soviet Union could own houses; however, apartment buildings belonged to the government, which sort of leased the units to their occupants. The "lease" had no expiration date and was akin to ownership, except that the tenants could not officially buy or sell their units. The apartments and rooms could be exchanged, though, within the same city or between geographical regions. The state recognized such exchanges regardless of their particulars, so if a family needed more space and had the means, they could trade their quarters for larger ones and pay an agreed-upon sum to the other party. Sometimes, those trades were quite complicated, involved several parties, and resulted in net room sales.

twenty years in the military, Yefim, a decorated war veteran, could not get an apartment from the government and had to spend his life savings on a place to live.

Meanwhile, my aunt was getting rid of us. The weather was already cold. The apartment was heated by a wood- and coal-fired furnace. The coal and wood were kept in a storage room in the building's basement. Every morning, my aunt disappeared, taking the storage room's key with her and leaving the child and me without heat. The baby peed from the cold every few minutes, his diapers were wet, and I sat there and cried with the child, waiting for my aunt to come home and turn the heat on. There were no disposable diapers then—all diapers were made of cotton. I boiled and washed the diapers on a kerosene burner every day, then dried and ironed them.

In November[2], we "bought" a room in a communal apartment for ten thousand roubles, a substantial sum at the time. The room was small and partly occupied by a large Russian stove. When fired, the stove produced puffs of black smoke, which settled on the furniture and walls. The walls had bugs we were trying to exterminate. The apartment had no kitchen. There was no toilet, either; we used a latrine in the building's courtyard for those needs. The baby went in a bucket, which we emptied inside the latrine. We bought a sofa bed, a crib for a child, a cupboard, and a table with a couple of chairs. The furniture took up the remaining space, so one could only walk into the room and sit down. Still, we were happy: there were no relatives to watch our every step, and the child was warm and dry. We purchased coal and firewood to last us through the winter and stored it in the common hallway, as neither our apartment nor the building had storage space. Our neighbors in the commune (a single family) stacked their coal and wood next to ours.

Yefim found a position with the administration of a public school, but the pay was low, so he got another job, then another, trying to increase his income. It was difficult for us to live on his salary. One by one were sold items from Germany to buy necessities such as food and clothing for a child. At the age of one, Micka (the nickname we gave our son) was a cute boy with blond hair and blue eyes. People paid attention when I walked him on the street. Occasionally, my aunt and uncle would come for a visit. Micka was growing up and getting funny. He called my relatives "Baba" and "Deda" ("Grandma" and "Grandpa"). They became attached to him and began to talk again about exchanging our rooms to live together. Yefim was ready to accept their proposal—he understood it

---

[2] of 1947.

was difficult for me to do the housework and care for the child. I did not like the exchange idea, expecting little help from my relatives. My uncle worked all day, while my aunt disliked house chores. And even if she did something for me, I would be constantly reminded of it later. I quickly figured that woman out. She did not wish me well and would rather see me desperate, begging her for favors.

In the building where we lived, I befriended a family of neighbors: a divorced mother with two teenage daughters. The daughters became fond of my son and enjoyed spending time with him. Micka liked them, too, and did not complain when left in their company. It was a big help for me, especially when I had to go shopping, as now I could leave Micka with the girls. The girls' father lived in the Soviet Far East, occasionally coming to Odessa to see his children. He suggested that my family move to the Far East, where it would be easier to find a better-paying job, and the housing situation was better, too. However, Yefim did not like the idea. I begged him to reconsider, arguing that we could stay in the Far East for a few years, make some money, come back, and exchange our room for a larger place, but to no avail. What happened to his willingness to go anyplace and do everything to provide for his family? He lost his spirit. Having served in the military for most of his adult life, he expected the government to provide him with a good job, a place to live, and financial security. But the officials in *Voenkomat* and *Gorispolcom*[3] did not listen to him. Key positions in those places were held by younger apparatchiks, who felt no gratitude or sympathy toward war veterans. Living well were cheats, bribe-takers, and other unsavory characters. Yefim was a scrupulously honest person, and life was hard for people like him, especially in the post-war Soviet Union. Having made the big mistake of quitting the army without a pension, he could not adjust to the new environment and fell into despair. It was necessary to look for solutions, change the scene, learn a profession, but he gave up and lost everything in my eyes.

My own recollections go back to when I was very young. I remember myself at the age of two or even earlier. The first memory permanently etched in my mind was a view through the crib's guarding rails of my mother sitting next to a pan with water and scaling a fish. The fish stared at me with one eye, but I was not afraid of the beast—just curious. The room did not seem small to me, and I recall a big Russian stove near the window. The window faced the street on the second floor of a two-story sandstone building. The building's entrance tube (passage), connecting

---

[3] Military Registration Office and City Government Office, respectively.

the street with the courtyard, had a side door, behind which began a staircase to our apartment. Curiously, there were no portals around the staircase on the ground floor, and no symmetrical opening existed on the tube's other side. The entry to the apartment led into a narrow hallway with two doors on the right: first, to our room; second, to the room of our neighbors. It was probably once a private apartment where our room served as a kitchen. I believe this to be the case because of the enormous Russian stove, and there was no sign of a kitchen otherwise.

The neighbors in the apartment were also a family of three: Uncle Simeon, Aunt Dora (as I called them), and Marik, their son, who was a few months older than me. Uncle Simeon worked as a barber while Aunt Dora stayed home with the child. Our families were on good terms and remained in touch for many years until my mother and I emigrated from the Soviet Union. The neighbors' room was bigger than ours and had a foyer they used as an extra room. The foyer was tiny, about the length of a couch standing there. Four years after we moved to that apartment, the neighbors got an addition—another boy. I recall the junior (who was two at the time) standing in his bed, wrapped in sheets and pretending to be an apparition, while his brother and I threw toys and other objects at him. Finally, we hit the boy with something hard, and the fun ended with him crying, and Marik and I being yelled at by the adults.

Like ours, the windows of our neighbors faced the street, while a single window in the common hallway overlooked an Italian courtyard with a fountain in the center, which had probably not functioned since the Bolshevik Revolution of 1917. Behind the fountain stood a latrine booth, and next to it was a water faucet. Our apartment had a single tap above the wall-mounted kitchen sink in the hallway, but that tap was dry most of the time, and we carried our water from the courtyard. Odessa received its water from the Dniester River via a conduit. The pipes in the ground were old, the water pressure was kept low to prevent them from bursting, so water barely reached the second floor.

The courtyard was the most interesting place where it all happened. Regrettably, my parents seldom allowed me to go there, trying to limit the street's bad influence. They had a point, as in the years following the war, the streets swarmed with juvenile delinquents growing up without fathers. There was a group of such youngsters on our block, too. Their leader was an urchin named Tolik[4], who lived in our building. But what bad influence could those youngsters have on a four-year-old? "Go tell

---

[4] Diminutive of Anatoly (Anatole).

Tolik he's got big balls[5]," engaged me one of Tolik's sidekicks. "What are balls?" I inquired suspiciously, being vaguely familiar with the implied meaning of the term but fully aware of Tolik's fearsome standing among the local youths. "It is this," replied the prankster, pointing to his flexed bicep, "Do not worry; he will be pleased." Not entirely convinced, I did as requested, to the great amusement of the gang and "boss" himself.

I remember Tolik well. He lived with his mother on the opposite side of the building. The entry to their apartment was on the second-floor gallery facing the courtyard. Tolik's mother shouted at him from the gallery, to which he paid no heed. Everybody in the building knew that Tolik was a thief. Occasionally, he got caught and was let go as a juvenile, although he never stole from the neighbors. He was no brute and exerted his authority via charisma and political skills, resorting to violence only in rare cases. When I was seven years old, my family moved to another apartment a few blocks away, but even in my teens, I kept returning to the previous address to visit Marik and his parents, or walked past it. By then, Tolik had graduated from the courtyard and hung out on the street corner in the company of petty criminals of the kind he had become. Of course, he did not remember me. He was a lean, handsome young man with long hair and a predatory smile. With his looks and demeanor, he resembled young Vittorio Gassman in the film classic *Bitter Rice*. One day, Tolik disappeared, and the neighbors told me that he had gone to jail, now as an adult. The next (and the last) time, I saw him years later. I was standing on a sidewalk when a trolley bus pulled up to the curb, and through the trolley's window, I noticed a scruffy, middle-aged man inside, staring into space. The man pressingly reminded me of someone, and then I realized who it was. It was Tolik. He looked much older than his age, stooped and unkempt, with a face that bore the signs of heavy drinking and emotional pain. By then, I must have seen the *Bitter Rice*, associating Tolik with the great actor's character, and was struck by the contrast between the person I knew and admired as a child and the wretch in the bus window. All of a sudden, I felt sorry for the wasted life, which, in other circumstances, might have been a success.

---

[5] The exact Russian term for that part of male anatomy was "eggs," although having them did not necessarily suggest bravery.

2. Sanatorium Lermontovsky

Yefim kept changing jobs, but his pay remained low. I counted pennies and finally decided to get a job myself. But who would take care of the child? He was too young for kindergarten—two and a half years old, while kindergartens admitted at three. I started looking, anyway. We had a woman neighbor in the building who worked as an accountant at the Resort Management Office[6], and she recommended me to the director of their central clinic for a secretary position. The clinic was situated on the territory of the sanatorium "Lermontovsky," one of the country's largest resorts, not far from where we lived. My neighbor also spoke to the principal of a kindergarten affiliated with the sanatorium and asked her to consider my son for admission. Micka was a bright and sociable child, advanced well beyond his age. After speaking with the boy, the principal agreed to take him, and I started at my new job.

The life of a working mother proved to be a challenging one. In the morning, I would drop Micka off at the kindergarten and go straight to the clinic, where I worked until six. After work, I picked my son up on the way home. At home, I cooked, cleaned the room, washed the laundry, and stood in bread lines. I toiled from the early morning till late at night. Yefim did not help me. He would come from work, eat supper, and lie down with a book or a newspaper. He became annoyed when I asked him to do something in the house, and argued about every detail. I did not recognize him. "Is this the man I loved and admired so much?" I asked myself, "No, it is a different person." No longer was I fond of him, and directed my love and attention to the child.

I was still good-looking, and men sought to meet me, but I was not attracted to them. Poor health and hard work at home and on the job were killing my desires. I only wanted to reach the bed at night and close my eyes. But with sleep came nightmares, and I woke up in a state of fright. One dream was especially terrifying: I was running away barefoot from German soldiers and Ukrainian policemen; they were shooting at me, and I was falling into the snow dead. That dream repeated again and again—I thought I might go insane. The home situation was not helping either. Yefim kept changing jobs, but things did not work out for him. He became frustrated, irritable, uninterested in my health and our material conditions. He would bring his meager salary, give it to me, and bow out. I had worn out my German clothes and had no decent coat or dress; everything was old, frayed, patched in places. I was ashamed to show up

---

[6] Government office in charge of sanatoriums and resorts.

at work like that. In the sanatorium, medical staff wore white coats. I was not entitled to such clothes, but asked my boss, the clinic's director, if I could have one set. As an exception to the rule, he ordered to give me two. I was happy since it solved my clothing problem. I wore one coat in the office while the other waited for its turn, washed, ironed, and neatly folded. I started my workday early and was already wearing a white coat when the first employees showed up.

Meanwhile, my health was getting worse. I lost a lot of weight and developed a chronic fever. Stomach pain and diarrhea wore me down. My hands were shaking, and horrific scenes tormented me in my dreams. I woke up in the middle of the night, gasping for air, trembling all over. Sometimes I got nauseous and vomited. The clinic's doctors examined me and concluded I had a nervous breakdown. Fortunately, my boss and coworkers treated me kindly and helped me through a difficult time. I mastered the new profession and was appreciated for my work ethic, diligence, and neatness. I gladly worked extra hours to get the job done. Overtime was not paid in the Soviet Union of those days, while my monthly salary was barely enough for two trips to the farmers' market, so I also had to stand in long lines to buy food in government stores.

My boss's name was Vladimir Artyomovich Cherednichenko[7]. He was an excellent administrator and a fine human being, but very ill. He suffered from emphysema (the result of heavy smoking) and died a few years later from a heart attack. I always remembered that demanding but caring man who did many good things for me. He understood my life was difficult and tried to help without ever showing it. "Do you know, Nadia, how much Vladimir Artyomovich loved you?" said to me his wife after he passed away, "He always spoke about you with great affection. You were like a third daughter to him…." Doctor Cherednichenko was buried in Odessa's interfaith cemetery, where my husband was interred, too, and when visiting Yefim's grave, I stopped every time at Vladimir Artyomovich's resting place to lay flowers on his headstone.

While working as a translator in Germany, I started a correspondence course at the Moscow Institute of Foreign Languages to improve my German. I finished the course already in Odessa. Besides my duties at home and at work, I also had to study. I graduated with top scores and received a certificate permitting me to teach German in a school. Such a job paid better than the clinic, but getting a teaching position without knowing someone was very difficult. Eventually, I gave up looking for a teacher's job and remained at the sanatorium… Meanwhile, my son was

---

[7] The first name + patronymic + last name.

nearing the age of seven and about to start the first grade in school. He was a bright and curious boy. All the kindergarten workers, including the stern principal, loved him, so when the time came to say goodbye, the parting was heartfelt. In almost five years there, Micka became attached to those people and remembered them for a long time.

I remember the kindergarten people and events even today. I recall a woman principal, bathroom sinks, open-air winter naps in sleeping bags, and a little girl in thick glasses who entertained other kids by inventing new words. One word was "over-toad," and everybody rolled on the floor laughing every time she said it. And, of course, I remember the clinic where my mother worked. The sanatorium occupied a large parcel of land with a park, dormitories, and medical facilities separated from the rest of the city by a high iron fence. The main entrance faced a one-block street, predictably named Lermontovsky Lane, while on the other side, the complex was naturally bounded by a steep drop-off descending to the rocky seashore. To get to the water, one had to use a long, narrow wooden staircase. The kindergarten was closer to the sea, while the clinic was near the main entrance.

Not far from the clinic stood the carcass of a building bombed out during the war. There were many such wreckages in Odessa in my early years, and gradually, they were razed or rebuilt, but one near the clinic was among the last to go. Growing up, I often visited the sanatorium and occasionally entered those ruins to spend some time alone. The building was burnt completely; only parts of the outside walls and short stumps from the inside supporting walls remained. There was no basement, and what used to be the ground floor was covered with grass, tall weeds, and wildflowers. I would settle on a stone stump and sit there, smelling the greenery and savoring the taste of solitude. I am not sure what attracted me to that place—perhaps the mystery of a bygone life, a lost connection, a purpose that strode steadily within these walls and now disappeared without a trace.

My mother worked in the sanatorium her entire Soviet career in various capacities and different buildings. In the clinic, she spent her first few years on the job when I was still in kindergarten. I remember the reception room, with undecorated white walls and high ceilings. There was little furniture. My mother, wearing a white coat, sat behind the desk at the back of the room near the door to the director's office. Behind that door, I could hear conversations and Dr. Cherednichenko's cough. Once in a while, he would come out to ask my mother a question or give her some instructions. Like that of Tolik from my first courtyard, Dr. Cherednichenko's physique was easy to describe—he resembled another famous actor, Sean Connery, albeit smaller in stature and gaunt due to illness. We did not know, at the time, who Sean Connery was and, while living in the Soviet Union, never saw his pictures. The Goskino[8] did an admirable job supplying Soviet audiences with bootlegged foreign films; however, James Bond was not among those reels. Only after coming to America did we get a chance to view that spy-adventure saga on TV, and the first time my mother saw the lead, she rose in her chair. "This man looks exactly like Vladimir Artyomovich!" she exclaimed. But I had already noticed the resemblance. I was a preschooler when I last saw Dr. Cherednichenko; yet, his image did not fade from my memory. I could not fathom then what kind of man he was or how much he did for my mother, but while in the reception room, I always wanted him to come out, and when he did, smiled, and spoke to me, it made my day.

I was still in kindergarten when Stalin died. That day left a lasting impression in my mind. We were on the kindergarten premises, readying for a daily stroll, when the news broke out. Of course, the great leader's image did not preoccupy our thoughts, but the significance of the event affected the children's mood, too. It was a late winter day—chilly, with the grey sky looking down through the leafless trees. The kindergarten population walked in pairs holding hands, somber music played over the loudspeakers, and I remember the anxious faces of the adults wiping tears in their eyes. I suddenly felt a tremendous uplift, almost an ecstasy, and switched to a marching gait, stomping buoyantly onto the asphalt. Where did that feeling come from? I always resented tyranny, yet didn't place the concept at the time, let alone associate it with Stalin's persona. Perhaps it was a natural reaction to a perceived threat, which causes people to mobilize their physical and mental resources, but I did not feel threatened at all.

My parents did not cry. My father was a thinking person who tried to understand the world around him, and I do not believe he was ever indoctrinated, despite his active part in establishing the Soviet State. And whichever ties he had retained with the official ideology, they already developed deep cracks. As for my mother, she was completely apolitical. She was concerned with the lack of money, poor living conditions, and other aspects of the daily struggle, and whether Stalin was alive or dead mattered little to her.

---

[8] State Committee for Cinematography, a governing body of the Soviet film industry.

3. Apartment Exchange

My aunt and uncle kept insisting that we exchange our apartments to live together. Tired of my stressful life, I finally agreed. They found a two-room suite in a communal apartment on the third floor of a four-story building. The apartment had two more families of neighbors, each family occupying one room. Our two-room suite consisted of a larger room with a terrace and a smaller room with an enormous single window above the building's entrance. The apartment began in a spacious foyer, where two doors on the left and a door on the right led to the residents' rooms. The foyer's right side also had wall-mounted electric meters and a passage to a long hallway leading to a shared (common) kitchen and bathroom. The first door on the foyer's left opened into a larger room of our two-room suite. Access to the smaller room was through the larger one. My aunt and uncle took the larger room, while Yefim and I chose the smaller one, which was more private.

Each family of the apartment neighbors had a table in the common kitchen to prepare their meals. The people who occupied our two-room suite before us were a single family, so they had only one kitchen table: near the window. My aunt took that table, and I timeshared it with her. Next to that table stood a Russian stove. The stove warmed the premises in cold weather, but in summer, I used it as my kitchen table. Yefim cut out two sheets of plywood and linoleum, glued them together, and placed the made-up board on the stove. I put a "primus" (kerosene burner) on that improvised countertop, where I cooked food, boiled laundry, and even baked pastries. Years later, when the city installed central gas and heating in the building, we demolished the Russian stove and replaced it with another kitchen table, which I could now use at all times.

The neighbors in the new apartment turned out to be very unpleasant individuals. One was an older woman who did not speak to anybody, and another was an unfriendly family of three. The head of that family was officially insane. He did not work, constantly screamed at his wife and child, and shouted at the neighbors. "Oh my god," I thought, "what place is this?" In the old apartment, there was less space and no bathroom, but we had only one family of neighbors with whom we were on good terms. Dora (the wife) did a poor job of cleaning the shared facilities, but she and her husband were good people, and our children grew up together.

Moving with the relatives was a colossal mistake, and that was when my worst problems began. My aunt announced that she wanted me to quit my job and stay home, cleaning, cooking, and doing laundry while she would go to work to earn a pension. "Why do you think I exchanged my apartment?" she told me, "I left a better neighborhood where I lived for a long time. I did it to go to work." "You can work," I replied, "There are only two of you. You will do your home chores after the job, like everybody else. I did not exchange my apartment to be your maid." After that conversation, my aunt started making trouble. She harassed Yefim and me—did not let us walk through her room in the evenings, affronted my coworkers coming for a visit, and occasionally locked the door to the foyer. Her husband tried to calm her down, but without success. She was pitting him against me, too... Several years after the apartment exchange, the crazy neighbor moved out and was succeeded in his room by an older couple, quiet and polite. The husband was a chief accountant at the city's largest department store, and the wife stayed home. I became friends with those neighbors; however, my aunt did not like that. She alternated between insulting them and slandering me. "Why are you pestering your niece and her family?" they once said to her, "She works so hard. What sort of an aunt are you? You are an evil woman."

When Micka was about to start the first grade in school, I went to our building's management office to get a proof-of-address note required for his admission. In the office, they looked at the records and informed me that neither my name nor the name of my husband was in the lease (register). "How is this possible?" I asked, "We exchanged two separate apartments. Our names should be in the register." It turned out that my relatives, to whom we entrusted the exchange's formalities, listed only their names in the lease, leaving Yefim's and mine out. We did not know it since my aunt paid the rent for both rooms while I was giving her my half. I told Yefim about the discovery, and he rushed to the building's office with the original exchange papers. They added our names to the register there, but later, we experienced occasional bureaucratic hurdles because those names were handwritten and not typed.

Another unfortunate fallout from the above exchange was our failure to qualify for a government apartment[9] when those apartments became available later on. To be eligible for such an apartment, a family had to report under six square meters of living space per member. My family

---

[9] For over fifty years after coming to power in 1917, the Bolshevik government built very few residential units. Post-revolutionary housing needs were primarily addressed through shared apartments, and the majority of urban dwellers resided in such communes. Human losses of WWII postponed the looming housing crisis; however, twenty years later, as the country's population was growing again, the government started residential construction on a fairly large scale. The new apartments were small, no-frills, and away from the center, but they had modern amenities and, most importantly, were private. Families that met eligibility requirements were placed on a waiting list, where they remained for years before securing the coveted accommodations.

satisfied that requirement in the old apartment and would have met the quota in the new room, too, but because of my relatives, the total area of both rooms had to be divided by five people, which put us over the limit. It did not matter that I had to walk through other tenants' spaces or get up at five in the morning to use a bathroom. An hour later, it had a line, and the neighbors banged on the door when someone stayed there a little longer. And like everywhere in the old city, we had problems with the running water. The water rarely reached our floor during the day and had to be hauled from the courtyard. Sometimes, in the middle of the night, the water would start running. I used those moments to do the laundry, filling all available containers beforehand to make sure I could finish the job if the faucets suddenly ran dry. We had a few professional laundries in the city; however, I did not use them because they turned out linens of a brown hue instead of white.

My existence in the new home became a living hell. The only place I could forget my aunt and neighbors was the job, but the very thought of going back home threw me into despair. It is hard to convey with words my frustration and feeling of hopelessness. Poor health, lack of money, disappointment in the man whom I had loved so much, and terrible living conditions added to my depression. There were moments when I thought of killing myself, but chased those thoughts away. I had to live and struggle for my child, my love and joy. I felt that the only solution was to leave my husband and relatives with their apartment, take the child, and start a new life elsewhere. Still, I could not find the courage to do it. I also felt sorry for Yefim, whose life went awry in part because of me. He sacrificed his career but was unable to adapt to a new environment and ended up with nothing. I tried to persuade him to leave Odessa and find a location where it would be easier to get a better job and a place to live, but he refused, maybe because he had lost hope. Eventually, I stopped talking about the move and pretended to be content. I lived for my son. I wanted him to become a decent, honest person, receive a good education, and never know scarcity.

Before the exchange was complete, my parents went to see the new apartment and took me along. The previous owners' furniture was still in place: mainly uninteresting stuff except for a baby grand piano of an odd oak color, standing in the middle of a larger room. The only piano I had access to before was in the apartment of Uncle Zinovy, my father's youngest brother, who lived with his wife and son in a different part of the city. They also occupied one room in a commune, but had even more neighbors. Electricity did not cost much in those days, yet it was not free, either, so each neighbor family in the commune had their own electrical meter, bulbs, and outlets, including those in the shared areas. When, for example, I had to go to the kitchen from my room, on the way, I would turn on *our* light in the foyer using *our* switch, turn on *our* light in the long hallway using another switch, and finally turn on the third switch to light up *our* bulb in the kitchen. And if a shared space was already lit by other neighbors' bulbs, the commune etiquette required turning ours on, anyway. The lights were turned off in reverse order on the way back. Our apartment had four sets of lighting fixtures in the common areas, while in Uncle Zinovy's commune, the number was six or seven ("Our switch is the second from the top," my uncle would remind a guest who wanted to go to the shared bathroom).

My parents and I visited Uncle Zinovy's apartment in the evenings and spent a few hours there, heading home when it was already dark outside. The tram's stop was at the end of the block. The tracks ran in the middle of a cobblestone street toward the earth's edge and were shared by several tram routes. Each route had its cars' marker lights in a distinct hue, so when the tram appeared far in the dark, like a huge, fantastic animal with marker lights for its eyes, I could tell the tram was ours by those lights' color. That late at night, the trolley was almost empty, and we traveled comfortably for half an hour to our stop... I enjoyed those trips. I liked my uncle, a thick rug on his floor, multitudes of bulbs and switches in shared areas, but the biggest draw was an upright piano in the corner of my uncle's room. The adults and my cousin (who was four years older than I) would gather behind the dinner table while I would settle at the piano and spend the evening playing with the keys.

Thus, I was excited to see the piano in the new apartment, hoping it was a part of the exchange deal. My mother told me later that the owners were willing to sell the piano cheaply, but my parents did not have the money, and my mother's relatives, in whose room the instrument would have remained, did not care for the extra furniture. "I will buy him an accordion," my mother's uncle said about me, but never did. Perhaps he and his wife did not want to be disturbed by a piano or other musical instruments, yet had they known I would be playing Wagner records in their room one day, they might have chosen the piano. I held no grudge.

4. Uncle Zachary and Aunt Rose

The name of my mother's aunt was Rose, and uncle's name was Zachary. They spoke Russian with a pronounced Yiddish accent and never fully mastered Russian writing. I became acquainted with Uncle Zachary's literary style in my twenties when he showed me a letter he had written to the building's management complaining about a leak in the wall. I laughed all week… Uncle Zachary and Aunt Rose were observant Jews, especially Uncle, although it wasn't easy to follow the custom in Odessa under Soviet rule. The city, with a Jewish population of over a hundred thousand, had only one synagogue located in a remote, industrial section where few Jews lived. But it was where Uncle Zachary worked, selling tap beer to the workers. The beer arrived in a large wooden cask, and the plug was replaced with a faucet from which Uncle Zachary poured the drinks into glass mugs. The inexactness of such a distribution method was mainly responsible for Uncle Zachary's above-average income, as well as the necessity to keep most of that income secret.

Although not a person of high culture, Uncle Zachary was a very musical man. He did not play musical instruments or sing "Volga River;" his specialty was cantorial art. In those pre-television times in the Soviet Union, people employed short-wave radios to receive their daily dose of information and entertainment. My family had such a device, a vacuum-tube Telefunken my father brought from Germany after the war, and Uncle Zachary had one of his own. He tuned in to Western radio stations broadcasting Jewish religious services and individual cantors and sang along at a half-voice. Sometimes, he sang prayers by himself, also mezza voce. What beautiful singing it was! All the passion and longing, every inflection, every little detail, Uncle Zachary reproduced with absolute precision and commitment. Every word was deeply felt. I often preferred his versions to the originals. I do not know if Uncle Zachary had the true cantorial voice (he never sang at full volume, perhaps afraid to be heard by the neighbors), but he could likely have sung professionally in his younger years and sung very well.

In the new apartment's common kitchen, facing a long hallway to the foyer, stood a walk-in closet. Later on, in a rare moment of communal harmony, the neighbors chipped in and erected storage shelves along the closet's walls. Each of the other two neighbors got a side shelf, while my mother and her aunt received the one in the middle, which was a little wider and which they divided into two halves. But in the beginning, the closet was not in use and stayed empty or filled with debris. And as soon as Aunt Rose settled in her room, she went to the kitchen and hung a padlock on the closet's door. "Finders keepers," she told my astounded father, who tried to explain that the closet was a common facility and did not belong to her. The padlock did not stay long, however; the mentally disturbed neighbor took an ax and knocked the lock off. That incident did little to foster better relations with the crazy neighbor, who, to his credit, made a goodwill gesture by offering us some of his shared space when we moved in. And he was not really crazy—just faked it to collect disability benefits.

My parents were embarrassed by Aunt Rose's brazen action, but she was unconcerned. She thrived on discord and was frequently the one who sowed it. She was a difficult person, manipulative and controlling, with a distinct misanthropic trait, but I would not call her evil. When one thinks of the time she and her contemporaries lived in and what they went through, it is surprising that many kept some sanity at all. So, more likely, Aunt Rose was a little touched in the head. Her only child, a boy, died from a common illness before the war when he was ten. She never talked about him, but a few times when walking into her room, I saw Aunt Rose sobbing and muttering over her son's photograph, which she quickly put away. She liked to show me pictures from her younger years, though, before she got married, saying how pretty she was and singing favorite songs of her youth. And now, she was an old woman facing a hostile world, together with her husband, whom she sought to isolate and protect. "A poorly dressed man is looking for Zachary!" were her panicky words to my parents after she overheard a stranger on the street asking about her spouse. A few minutes later, the snooper rang our bell and turned out to be a handyman that Uncle Zachary had hired to do some work, but failed to tell his wife. Their affluence kept Aunt Rose in constant worry, as she expected the police to come and arrest Uncle Zachary for skimming illegal profit off the government's beer monopoly. My mother told me a story, from when we lived in our first apartment, about Aunt Rose bringing a wooden stool there and asking my parents to keep it for a while. The stool was heavier than normal and, when shaken, replied with a metallic ring inside. And almost twenty years later, Aunt Rose walked into my room, where I was alone, and handed me a bearer's passbook to put in a secure place. "I hold it for you," she explained its existence. The passbook remained inside my desk for a few months until she felt safe to take it back. Such alarms were regular occurrences in Aunt Rose's life, although what triggered them was a mystery to me. While her fears were exaggerated, they were not unfounded—according to my mother, Uncle Zachary was taken into custody once, but Aunt Rose paid someone off to get her husband out. She was good at those things, knowing what the powers-that-be wanted and how to approach them with a bribe.

But Uncle Zachary was a small fish in the boundless sea of the Soviet underground enterprise. The big fish lived in the apartment below and appeared as a short, older gentleman, soft-spoken and perfectly dressed, who walked slowly and looked with sad eyes. He was a major black-market operator, dealing in gold, jewelry, and foreign currencies. Such activities were among the most serious offenses against the Soviet State, punishable by long prison terms and even a death sentence (when on the books). Our downstairs neighbor must have been a very prudent man to reach an advanced age while practicing such an occupation, and still, everybody in the building knew who he was. At first, I did not believe those rumors, finding it difficult to reconcile the old man's dignified mien with a notion of crime, but one day, he vanished, never to return, and tenants whispered to each other that our downstairs neighbor had been arrested and hanged himself in jail, not to reveal whereabouts of his riches. He was the building's only household head who did not share an apartment with strangers, having it entirely for himself and his family. The family, which included his son, the son's wife, and their divorced daughter with a child, continued to live in the apartment below after their patriarch's death. And topping the bizarre sandwich of the Soviet commune was a retired military prosecutor in the apartment above, but he, too, shared it with other neighbors.

The former state security officer – my father, the former prosecutor upstairs, and the underworld baron downstairs maintained courteous relations, resolving matters of mutual importance in a calm, businesslike manner—it was inside the apartment where the trouble brewed, fueled by a widening rift between my mother and her father's sister, Aunt Rose. It seemed as though the Chudnov grandmother had come back to life to reaffirm her authority over the rebellious granddaughter (my mother often remarked on how much Aunt Rose resembled her own mother[10] in appearance and character). But the shy girl had grown up as a strong woman hardened by the hellfire of the war, like a piece of steel. "You are *ghettovskaya*[11]," Aunt Rose would say to her obstinate niece during arguments. Of course, my mother had words to describe her aunt, too. Uncle Zachary and my father tried to ease the tension, but to no avail,

---

[10] Aunt Rose's mother. For the less involved, Aunt Rose's mother was the *grandmother* introduced and frequently mentioned in the initial chapter of this title's first book.

[11] "From the ghetto," a term often used among the postwar Soviet Jews to characterize Holocaust survivors as stubborn and difficult to deal with.

and the intensifying aunt-niece strife was pulling the family apart. Soon, there were no more joint dinners, then acknowledging each other in the hallways, and finally, Uncle Zachary (who was a carpenter by profession before Aunt Rose directed him toward a more lucrative line of work) erected a plywood wall along the edges of his room, creating a passage around the slightly reduced living area (did a great job, by the way). The quest for a unified family was over.

I wondered why my mother and her relatives did that apartment exchange. My mother mentions her difficult life as a reason, but she had an ample preview of what might happen when she stayed with her aunt upon coming to Odessa from Germany. Perhaps the years passed and yearning for the lost family had eased my mother's worries, but the relatives' insistence on moving together also contributed to her decision. From a practical standpoint, Uncle Zachary and Aunt Rose did not need that exchange. They were not too old, were still active, and well off. Maybe they felt lonely, especially Uncle Zachary, whom Aunt Rose had pushed away from his own kin, and I do not remember them having friends, either. In those times, extended families comprising two, three, and sometimes four generations often lived together to cope with the housing shortages and other challenges of arduous existence. That was how my mother lived in Chudnov before the war, and Uncle Zachary must have lived even before the Bolshevik revolution. So, the appeal of such an arrangement to both of them could be understood; plus, Aunt Rose's inventive mind might harbor other reasons known only to her. But whatever those plans were, they had not worked out for anybody except one person who did not plan anything and barely knew what was going on. That person was I.

My parents decided not to involve me in the dispute with their relatives, who welcomed such a turn of events. The decision rendered both rooms to my unrestricted use, and even Uncle Zachary's Great Wall of Separation did not change that; moreover, it gave me a refuge from punishments imposed by my parents for my various misdeeds. My father was a strict disciplinarian who demanded good grades in school, proper behavior, and even a particular hairstyle (which was the opposite of what I preferred). Sometimes, he used corporal punishment, albeit infrequently. The examples could include a poor grade in school or a teacher's note of my bad behavior. The floggings were rather symbolic and did not leave a bad taste because they were conducted in an orderly, impassive manner. My father would announce the sentence in advance, setting a time (after supper) when I had to submit to the procedure. I would lie on the couch face down, and he would give me a few lashes with a belt, carefully landing it on my behind. It was not painful, let alone any marks, but I cried and screamed like I was being murdered. Perhaps I thought the beating was for real, but also exaggerated a bit to show that the punishment was working and to garner sympathy from my mother and her relatives.

An important aspect of the punishment was its certainty. I remember escaping judgment only once. The "execution" time had been set, and I was spending my last hour comforted by Uncle Zachary and Aunt Rose on the couch in their room when I spotted a small pillow on the bed on the room's opposite side. I stuffed that pillow into my pants, covering the lashes' receiving area, and went to the scaffold. My father, pretending not to see the bulge, administered the first blow. The pillow responded with a muffled sound and a cloud of dust. "What is this?" exclaimed my father, playing a surprise, and hit the pillow again. Then he laughed and let me go, fully pardoned, to return the pillow. The floggings stopped after my father realized that I had lost the fear of them, which happened before my third grade.

My mother disciplined me, too, but without getting physical, which I appreciated during my father's flogging sessions. However, my father's educational approach had one plus that outweighed all minuses: he left my soul alone. He could tell me what to wear or how to comb, but never what to think or how to feel. I did not owe him anything, did not have to take his side, favor people he liked, or keep away from those he didn't. He never demanded personal loyalty or affection—it was entirely up to me. I recall an episode when he had to go away for a month. I was twelve years old at the time and attended a boarding school. My parents went to the train station together, and I was supposed to come there from school to say goodbye to my father. One thing after another, plus a few miscalculations, and when I finally reached the station, the train had already left, and I was greeted by an angry mother. She told me how upset my father was, how he kept looking out the railcar's window to see if I might appear at the end of the platform. He probably worried that something bad had happened to me, and when the train moved, my father's eyes were almost in tears. Later on, my mother often reminded me of that incident as an example of my irresponsibility, but my father didn't say a word—not in his letters nor in person—as if it had never happened.

The relations of my father with my mother's relatives were distant in the beginning and nonexistent later on. Aunt Rose's self-serving attitude and penchant for causing trouble did not suit my father's personality. She picked on him, too. "Do you know why you are so unlucky?" she said to him once, while still on speaking terms, "Because she is unlucky" (she was my mother who told me that story), "She has passed her bad luck onto you." My father did not reply. Whatever his opinion of Aunt Rose and Uncle Zachary was, he never expressed it in my presence, and I believe my neutrality in the family conflict was largely due to his influence. I understood my parents' indignation after they discovered their names missing from the register. I am sure it was Aunt Rose's idea, but Uncle Zachary ought to take some blame for not standing up to his wife. And it was such a senseless thing to do. The deception would have come out eventually, resulting in my parents altering the lease, but it dealt a deadly blow to the idea of togetherness that the joint lease was to signify. Aunt Rose was not a stupid person, and she had hardly planned that action in advance, yet, when asked in the office for the leaseholders' names, could not resist her volatile, opportunistic nature. But whatever the reasons, the damage had been done. The seeds of the discord had been sown, and it was entirely Aunt Rose's deed.

By not erecting barriers between their son and unwelcome relatives, my parents showed wisdom and restraint that was commendable. They had no utilitarian motives. Since the third grade, I attended a boarding school, spending all day there, and did not require supervision at home during those hours. Uncle Zachary's money mattered little—both my parents were fiercely independent people, and their goodwill could not be bought. Neither did they want the relatives to spoil me with gifts, except for an accordion that Uncle Zachary had promised but never delivered (and thanks for that, or I might have become an accordionist). As for myself, I did not care whether Uncle Zachary and Aunt Rose gave me things. They were my family, too. Among the four grandparents, only my father's father was alive the year I was born. He lived with the family of Uncle Zinovy and died before I was two, so I did not remember him. Uncle Zachary and Aunt Rose became my de facto grandparents; I even addressed them as such. They were very liberal and did not impose any norms or doctrines on me. They just enjoyed my company, and I liked theirs. With my parents, there was a certain distance arising from their need to exercise parental duties. Such a reserve did not exist with Uncle Zachary and Aunt Rose—it was a relationship between peers: two big peers and a little one. Growing up, I spent more time in their room than my own. I listened to cantors on the radio with Uncle Zachary, ate Aunt Rose's chicken soup, played with the cat, read books on the couch, and, in warmer weather, sat for hours on the balcony…

From the balcony's northern vantage, adorned by the branches of surrounding trees, opened a view of our entire street stretching far into the hazy mosaic of the urban landscape. Throughout most of its length, the street ran along the city park. The park began two blocks away, its fence and main entrance lining up on our side of the street. The park's nearest section was hidden from view by the adjacent buildings, but I could see magnificent structures across the park's main entrance, farther away. Aunt Rose was not sincere, claiming she had lived in a better neighborhood prior to the exchange; the new neighborhood was better. Before the Bolshevik revolution, the buildings facing the park housed the aristocracy and the wealthy, befitting the structures' architectural chic. Our building, which bordered that one-time exclusive area, was also luxuriously built—with a sculpted facade, wide marble stairs, and high ornamented ceilings—but the buildings across the park had even higher ceilings and more vestiges of former splendor. Of course, it mattered little now, as the only difference between such quarters and less alluring ones was the former's ability to accommodate more residents. Still, for many, the beauty of the surroundings eased the pain of overcrowding and need. I do not believe my mother was among those many; however, she could walk to work. My father was getting to his job by tram, which stopped two blocks from our building. Aunt Rose did not work, going wherever and whenever she wanted, and Uncle Zachary did the same, having retired from his store unscathed.

Looking back at my relations with Uncle Zachary and Aunt Rose, I only wonder how simple they were. Even with Aunt Rose, who disliked nearly everybody, I do not recall a single uncomfortable moment. And I would have remembered it, as I remembered Uncle Zachary's emotional reaction after, in the heat of an argument, my mother called him a "wolf in sheep's clothing." "Your mother," Uncle Zachary said to me, almost in tears, "how could she say that? I am such a nice man," but then halted the phrase and changed the subject. And Aunt Rose did not complain in my presence once—just pursed her lips, bracing for future battles. Both tried to hold their side of the bargain, keeping me away from the quarrel, albeit it was my parents who made it possible. My father's commitment to that pact was unconditional, while my mother accounted for her son's younger age, expecting him to sort things out upon growing up. I guess she did not see a contradiction in that stance. Thus, after my father's death, my contact with the ersatz grandparents became more remote. By then, I had grown up and saw Aunt Rose and Uncle Zachary less often, yet retained the ease of interaction as when I was a child. That continued until my mother and I left the country. In those times of the Cold War, such a departure was deemed forever without return. My mother did not say goodbye to her closest relatives.

My farewell with Aunt Rose was cold, but it was warmer with Uncle Zachary, who better understood my predicament. For the past few years, Uncle Zachary had suffered from colon cancer and undergone several operations. He died soon after my mother and I left the USSR. After his death, Aunt Rose exchanged both rooms for a smaller place in a different part of the city. We learned those details from a woman émigré who had met Aunt Rose and spoken with her shortly before leaving the Soviet Union, but that woman did not know Aunt Rose's address, either. Aunt Rose mentioned in the conversation that she lived alone and had no relatives except a nephew in America. That nephew was I, then hearing from Aunt Rose for the last time. As of this writing, she would have been well over one hundred years old. People in the former Soviet Union did not live that long unless, according to legend, they were villagers high in the Caucasus Mountains. Aunt Rose was not such a villager.

5. Boarding School

Shortly after we exchanged the apartment, Micka started the first grade in school. The school was across the street from our new residence. At one in the afternoon, he was already home and remained alone until his father or I came from work. Despite his high aptitude, Micka did not like doing the homework, so I often checked his school journal to see if he had completed the assignments. However, Yefim and I never helped him; he did everything himself, albeit without great enthusiasm. He enjoyed solving brain teasers and did it well.

The school across the street was elementary, and after the second grade, we transferred Micka to another school, a boarding one. Many students in that school were the children of prominent citizens, including military commanders, industrial managers, and Party and government officials. The school had an advanced English language program. Micka passed the entrance exam (interview) and was admitted to the third grade. The school was far from our home, about an hour's ride by two trams, yet it was convenient for us, as Micka remained there all day. The children ate lunch, did their homework, and were supervised at all times. The school charged tuition, which was a small percentage of the family income, so we paid very little. I was glad my son got into that school—it had strict discipline and good teachers, but most importantly, he was not out on the street with juvenile delinquents. Early in the morning, before work, his father or I would drop Micka off at school and pick him up on the way home at night. A few months later, Micka began to travel on his own, so we no longer had to accompany him.

Micka studied in the boarding school for six years. He was good at mathematics and attended advanced math classes administered by the city's Pedagogical College. He participated in mathematical contests and often ended up among the winners. He was interested in history and read a lot, but paid less attention to other subjects (although he received good grades, anyway). Besides academic disciplines, the school emphasized physical education, offering a range of sports programs. Micka chose gymnastics and later became a team member with one of the city's major sports clubs. The coach of that team once worked at the boarding school as a part-time gymnastics teacher; he had known Micka since the fourth grade and invited him to the club. Micka did well there, too, traveling to tournaments in different parts of the country.

The sport was good for Micka's health. In his early years, he was a sickly child who often caught a cold and had stomach problems. While in kindergarten, he developed chronic sinusitis, which caused him much discomfort, especially during the illness' acute phases. Several times, the doctors rinsed his sinuses with antibiotics, and once, he stayed in the hospital. I was worried—that illness sometimes took an aggressive form, requiring complex surgery. The practitioner who treated Micka was Dr. Tartakovsky, one of the best otolaryngologists in the city. He was a top-notch physician and a brilliant surgeon who performed the most difficult operations. I asked him for a prognosis, and he replied that Micka would likely grow out of his condition. "He must be physically active, do sport, be in the sun, swim in the sea, and the problem will go away," the doctor said. And his prediction turned out to be accurate—by the time Micka reached the eighth grade, the ailment disappeared.

Dr. Tartakovsky, I shall never forget. He was a scrawny, middle-aged man, bespectacled and wearing a surgeon's hat with a head mirror in front. The reason he admitted me to the hospital (where he was the chief of the otolaryngology department) was a small polyp on my palate that he wanted to remove. For him, it was a simple operation, which he did in minutes, but with one peculiar bend: he did it without anesthesia. Dr. Tartakovsky was a caring man, very good with his underage patients, so I would not suspect him of callousness. It probably had to be done that way, yet was a painful experience. When the nurse brought me to the operating room, there were several people inside, including a large man who sat next to the instrument table and looked like a wrestler rather than a medic. The man told me to turn around, tied my hands behind my back with a towel, seated me on his lap, and wrapped his powerful arms around my torso. Dr. Tartakovsky picked up a shiny tool from the table and told me to open my mouth. Still unsure of what was about to occur, I complied. The doctor pushed the instrument toward my palate and got to work... Perhaps my cries were heard over the entire hospital because when being transported back to bed, all shaken and in tears, I caught a conversation in the hallway between two patients from my ward. "Did you hear those screams?" asked one nervously. "What was that?" "Never mind," replied the other, "it was Lermontov giving a concert."

In her memoirs, my mother overstates the exclusivity of the boarding school, perhaps to parry a perception of such places as orphanages, and because she felt guilty that she had not provided me with tutoring beyond the regular school program. Many parents in Odessa, especially among Jewish families, tried to develop their offspring's talents early, hiring private tutors or sending children to places like music schools. Musical education was not a part of the general curriculum in the USSR; however, it could be pursued extracurricularly in special schools. Those schools charged nominal or no tuition, but they were few and had an admission test. Odessa was renowned for the many gifted musicians it produced, attesting to the popularity of music studies among the city's residents, so getting into those schools was not easy, as the competition was intense.

    Like Uncle Zachary, my father had a knack for the vocal arts, albeit his musical interests were broader. He enjoyed opera, symphonies, all sorts of instrumental music, and, of course, cantorials, having sung in a synagogue (where his grandfather was a cantor) choir as a boy. He may have passed on the diamonds in Germany, but brought back two multi-record albums of opera excerpts by Verdi, Puccini, Wagner, and other composers. Growing up, I played those records on Uncle Zachary's iron needle player in his room. The albums included a couple of single-sided Caruso 78s pressed by the Victor Talking Machine Company in the first decade of the twentieth century. Later, I learned that those disks were quite rare, partly because of their brittleness. Sadly, they did not survive my early interest in classical music.

    I was five years old when my father took me with him to a Caruso movie, which was playing in the city theaters at the time. It was one of those pseudo-biographical, melodramatic features serving as a showcase for whichever singer acted in the title role. I remember a sad figure in a white robe with a painted face, singing *"Ridi Pagliaccio"* and collapsing on stage. The tragic story, the music, and especially the singing blew me away, defining my musical preferences for years to come. At night, I tuned in to radio broadcasts of opera performances from Vienna, Rome, Milan, and listened to instrumental music. The shortwave reception was poor, with interference and static, but it did not diminish the magical effects of those sounds. One night, after listening to such a broadcast, I was already in bed when a melody appeared in my head, played by an orchestra, clear and detailed as if coming from another room. The music was in the style of Mozart but different from anything I knew. What was unusual, I could direct it in my mind, varying melodic flow, instrumental balances, dynamics, and phrasing to a desired effect. It was an effortless improvisation, which brought me a great sense of fulfillment and which I rode until the music faded into my dreams. I didn't tell anyone about that experience, but my parents decided to check my musical abilities anyway. My mother had a woman coworker whose brother was a low-number violin in the Odessa Philharmonic Orchestra, and that woman arranged for my audition. That meeting I remember well. The violinist checked my ear, let me hold his violin, and suggested that I be taught music privately or in a musical school. Private lessons, my parents could not afford, so they opted for the alternative. I do not recall who took me to the entrance exam—probably my father. The waiting room was full of wunderkinder flanked by their parents carrying all kinds of cases, big and small. They brought the instruments to demonstrate developed skills, and those who did not carry anything must have played the piano. I had nothing to show in that realm, so the examiners asked me to repeat a few keyboard passages and administered other tests. I passed them all, but was not accepted. Schools like that were few, with many applicants per seat; they had plenty to choose from and must have chosen some dwarf with a tuba.

I am sure my mother did not view the boarding school as the best choice for her son's education. She did not talk about it, but one episode revealed her remorse. I was already in high school, and we had an argument—some trivial teenage matter, where she scolded me for being ungrateful to my parents, who did so much for me. A little peeved, I blurted out that perhaps she was not such devoted a parent, having sent me to an "orphanage" (I used that word for a stronger impact) in the past. It was said out of spite, but my mother's reaction surprised me. I rarely saw her backing down or apologizing; however, at that moment, she shrank a bit and began explaining in a contrite voice her and my father's decision to send me to boarding school. I found such a response peculiar, as I seldom asked my parents for anything, preferring to be left alone. My father had no problem granting me that wish, but my mother could not fully comprehend it. She was more cliquish in general, and the tragic war experience conditioned her to overstate family relations, with higher hopes and greater disappointments. A cry for help, arising from the aching memory of her parents and little sisters, called for a response, and she was a mother, too. So when I tried to explain that my orphanage remark was not real, my mother did not believe me. In the following years, she occasionally touched on that topic, perhaps to see if I still held a "grudge," and every time, I went about saying how fortunate I was to have studied in that boarding school… but could not convince her.

And I was telling the truth. I loved that school during my attendance years and appreciated it even more as time went by. It was a very special place, which left me many fond memories and a sense of fullness of life that I seldom experienced later on. For a long time after leaving the boarding school, I had dreams where I walked the streets and suddenly found myself in front of the school's building. My heart leaped with joy, and I rushed through the gate toward the building's entrance, my eyes fixed on the windows of our classroom on the second floor. The entrance hall was empty, and I ran up the stairs. There were more stories inside than appeared outside, so it took me four or five flights to reach the second floor. The hallway had no people, either, and everything seemed strangely different; however, I was neither surprised nor confused, knowing exactly which door belonged to our classroom. The classroom looked like nothing we had studied in (it resembled a small college auditorium or a movie theater), but once again, I had no doubt it was the right place. A few figures were sitting in the rear, their faces obscured by the distance, their ages unclear. They were not moving and did not react to my intrusion. "What did you expect?" I said to myself, "Much time has passed. They don't know who you are." And the visit was over. I walked down the staircase past the library and back to the street… Such dreams repeated often, sometimes in the main building, sometimes in the dormitory, but they all carried a warm, nostalgic feeling I cherished for days. Why did those images appear to me so vividly and with such emotional thrust? I do not remember dreams about high school, for example, where I studied after the boarding one. Maybe because the boarding school was a microcosm of life, whereas the high school wasn't. My other lifelike dreams also featured microcosmic environments like college in Moscow and army service, but those dreams were far less frequent and did not leave such a bittersweet taste of happiness and sadness. Hence, I will take a detour to describe the boarding school in greater detail in the following chapter.

6. Summer Time

After the boarding school's eighth grade, Misha transferred to a high school with an advanced math and science program. He studied there for three years and received a recommendation to attend college. He chose the Moscow Institute of Physics and Technology (MIPT), one of the best colleges in the Soviet Union. Courses in that place were taught by the country's leading scientists. It was also one of the hardest colleges to get into, with the highest number of applicants per seat and the most difficult entrance exams. Yefim and I advised Misha to consider other colleges, with less competition and possibly better chances of getting accepted, but his mind was made up. The admission process at MIPT began a month earlier than at other colleges, and the next day after the commencement, Misha left for Moscow. We could not accompany him, but wished our son success. And our wishes came true: Misha received top grades on all tests, passed an important personal interview, and was accepted as a student. He got a bed in the dormitory and a stipend.

In high school, Misha befriended a classmate named Fima[12]. Fima was a wonderful boy—hardworking, talented, and honest. Fima's parents encouraged his friendship with my son, whom they treated like a family member. Fima's mother was a prominent physician, and his father was an engineer, a fine man who suffered from a debilitating illness. They had another son, a few years younger than Fima. Fima graduated from high school with a "Gold Medal" (straight-A diploma) and was admitted to Moscow State University's School of Mathematics. Once more, he and Misha would study in the same city and stay in touch.

I will never forget the day, one of the happiest in my life, when Yefim and I received Misha's telegram informing us of his acceptance to MIPT. He was coming home to prepare for his move to Moscow, as his college classes were to begin in a month. He returned to Odessa one day before his birthday. I cooked and baked for a little party Misha's friends threw for him in our apartment. It was a happy event, where everybody had a good time.

After Misha departed for Moscow, the home became empty. Little connected me with Yefim other than letters from our son, occasional conversations with him on the phone, his interests and successes. My other emotional outlet was my job; I developed cordial relations with coworkers and had many friends who helped me in difficult moments and who forever remain in my thoughts and heart.

---

[12] Diminutive of Yefim.

Fima's family lived around the corner in a one-story facade separated from the main building by a narrow courtyard. Their apartment was also a commune but had only one neighbor on the other side of the shared kitchen, so each family had private access to the street. Like ours, the entry to Fima's quarters was from the main tube, except that their door led directly into the residence. The apartment had three rooms, which, when we just got acquainted, were filled with people. Besides Fima, his parents, and his younger brother Vova[13], there were Fima's grandmother, the grandmother's sister, and maybe someone else. Fima's apartment had fewer occupants per room than mine, but it seemed more crowded because of the many visitors. They were the hosts' relatives, friends, and neighbors who had come for a social visit or to seek Fima's mother's medical advice.

The name of Fima's mother was Tsylia Ilyinichna[14], and she was a remarkable woman. One of the best physicians in the city, she combined broad cultural interests with high morals and practical sense. Seeking her help were people of all backgrounds, and Tsylia Ilyinichna did not refuse anybody. Several times, while in her home, I witnessed neighbors in the building coming in and asking her to see their sick family members, and she would interrupt a conversation or a meal, put on a coat, and walk outside. She did not charge fees or demand anything in return, but there was no lack of chocolates in her place, which I frequently enjoyed.

Both Fima and Vova were intelligent, erudite boys. Fima was very organized, hardworking, and striving to be the best, while Vova spent more time reading novels from his mother's library. Fima gravitated toward science, especially mathematics, while Vova favored liberal arts. Perhaps Fima's domineering attitude as an older brother discouraged Vova from paying more attention to that other knowledge. Occasionally, Tsylia Ilyinichna asked me to help Vova with his math, or he made his own request. "He yells at me," Vova said of his brother, explaining the preference for my advice. Despite his brilliance, Vova often received average grades in school, but Fima was a straight-A student and the first in our class overall. If he ever got a B, it had to be before I knew him. Such consistency was awe-inspiring, especially to someone like myself, who could never be sure of a test's outcome and needed hours to solve a problem in five minutes. I also found it hard to overcome my distaste for certain subjects and graduated with solid As and Bs only because of the negotiating skills of our class (and math) teacher, who had foiled an

---

[13] Diminutive of Vladimir.

[14] First Name + Patronymic.

attempt by her Ukrainian literature colleague to fix me with a C in the diploma by threatening to retaliate against that teacher's favorite pupil. And since a single C in a school diploma notably reduced a graduate's chance of getting into college, I largely owe my higher education to our class teacher[15].

Unlike my parents, I viewed my odds of getting into MIPT as better, and not worse, than getting into a lesser college. A few years earlier, the government changed college admission guidelines to favor high school graduates with the top GPAs (Gold and Silver Medal honors). Such applicants no longer had to take all entry exams (usually four) and, upon receiving As on the first two, were admitted automatically. MIPT was the only college exempted from that rule, and everybody competed on equal terms there. Thus, not being a GPA laureate, I viewed MIPT's admission policy as an advantage... Another important issue was the unofficial college admission quota the Soviet State administered toward its Jewish citizens. The quota was universally applied across the country, so its discriminatory effects were more pronounced in places with greater Jewish presence, such as my hometown of Odessa. "Jewish" in the Soviet Union implied a nationality[16] rather than a religion. The nationality of a child was determined by the nationalities of the parents, as a free choice between the two, meaning no choice at all if both nationalities were the same. During the war, the nationality succession chain sustained some damage. The destruction of Soviet archives left many citizens without records, and the authorities accepted any proof to reconstruct the lost identities. My mother, for example, entered the postwar Soviet world under the assumed name of Nadezhda Momot and carried it all her life, except for taking my father's surname after marriage. She could have kept the Ukrainian nationality, too, but changed it back to Jewish at my father's request. That predetermined my own nationality, making it a thing to consider in my college plans. And again, MIPT seemed to be the best place to skirt the admission quota, as in a school of that caliber, such matters had to play a secondary role.

If there is a higher power controlling every person's destiny, it must be some committee whose members fight and bicker with each other over their charge's every move, as it is hard to imagine that a single mind

---

[15] C. I. Gavril'chenko.

[16] Nationality in the USSR was akin to ethnicity in the West, owing its name to Lenin's insistence that every ethnic group in the Soviet Union had a "homeland." Officially, the Jewish homeland in the USSR was the Soviet Autonomous Republic of Birobijan in the Far East, but very few Jews resided there.

can be so conflicting... On my first test, in written math, I got a C. Such a result would have shattered all my hopes of becoming an MIPT student, but it was preliminary. The final grade was determined on a subsequent oral test, where the applicant could contest the written score. Yet by then, I had already adjusted to the new environment, and not only did I get an A on the oral math, but the examiner also changed my written score from a C to an A. Then, I received an A in written physics. On the oral physics, I floundered again, but not badly enough to halt the momentum of three As, and got away with a B, which assured a passing total. However, the ultimate verdict was rendered by a group of faculty members, known as a "commission," who interviewed every candidate fortunate enough to have survived four tests. Horror stories were told about the commission rejecting candidates with the highest scores, but its primary goal was to choose among those who scored below the passing average. Applicants with perfect or near-perfect (like mine) scores were almost certain to pass the interview and had to do something weird to get rejected. Therefore, considering myself a relatively normal person, I worried little when I walked into the interview room and stood, like an umlaut, before a long, U-shaped table with a dozen people behind it. The conversation started amicably—commission members asked about my hobbies, interests, and sports activities—and then, someone upstairs decided that I was having it too easy. The commission's chairman, who had been sitting quietly thus far, throwing at me suspicious glances, posed a question. It was something broad, intended to appraise my understanding of the special relativity principles, and I started the answer with the phrase, "Suppose we are moving faster than light." The chairman almost fell off his chair (I do not know if he was the chairman, or the commission had a chairman at all, but the inquirer sat in the middle and looked so important that I cannot refer to him by any lesser title). "How is it possible to move faster than light?" he cried in disbelief. I tried to explain that it was only a conjecture, but the emotional trauma caused by my unfortunate choice of words disabled the chairman's comprehension. He became agitated, kept repeating that the speed of light could not be exceeded, was turning helplessly to his colleagues, looking for their moral support, and did not listen to my arguments. It was so bizarre that I lost my speech. From both sides of the table, commission members yelled that I had said "suppose," and the chairman calmed down a little. Speaking about weird... In a couple of days, the college put up a list of new students, where I found my name.

7. Security Clearance

While studying in Moscow, Misha would come home for a recess, and so he did on a winter break after his third semester. On the second day of Misha's stay, Yefim suffered a stroke. He collapsed at work, was taken to a hospital, and died the next morning without regaining consciousness. Misha and I were at his bed when he departed this world.

Misha was very distraught by his father's death. After the funeral, he telegraphed the school he would be late for classes. He also asked his schoolmates, who were from Odessa and staying in the city for a recess (I recall one of them attended the funeral), to pass the message in person. However, when Misha's friends returned to Moscow, they discovered an official notice on the bulletin board outside the dean's office, stating that Misha had been expelled from college for nonattendance of the military classes. On the first day of the semester, Misha's schoolmates went to see the dean to inquire about the expulsion notice. By then, the school must have received Misha's telegram, and the notice was taken down. The students were told it was a mistake, and when Misha arrived a few days later, he did not suspect anything. Not willing to upset him more, his friends said nothing about the expulsion attempt. He found out about it months later.

The expulsion memo correctly stated that Misha had failed to attend the military classes; however, he did it not by choice. He was not allowed to attend. Military training for male students was a part of the curriculum in many Soviet colleges. Those who had completed the program received a lieutenant-of-reserve rank at graduation and could be called to military duty in the event of an emergency or war. In Misha's college, the military classes began in the third semester and required a security clearance. That clearance Misha did not get. No reason was given for the denial, but it likely had to do with my American relatives.

The piece of paper with her brother's USA address, my mother gave me during our Chudnov farewell, I carried throughout the entire war and, upon returning from Germany, wrote a letter to my uncle. In that letter, I described what had happened to his sister and her family in Ukraine. I received a reply, but the correspondence was interrupted by an outbreak of the Cold War and a new round of Stalin's repressions. Letters from foreign countries did not reach addressees in the Soviet Union, whereas outgoing mail disappeared without a trace. During Khrushchev's thaw, international mail resumed its flow, and I sent another letter to America, but it returned with the "Addressee Unknown" stamp. That ended my attempts to reestablish ties with American relatives. I rarely mentioned them at home, while Misha showed little interest in the family history written even before his mother's birth. So when filling out a college application form and answering if he had relatives abroad (it had such a question), Misha answered no. However, the authorities had a different idea of what it meant to have relatives abroad. One day during his first year in MIPT, Misha was called to the college's Special Section. "You stated in your application that you did not have foreign relatives," the Special Section official told Misha, "but we have information that you do." Apparently, my undelivered letter was intercepted by the KGB, leaving an imprint in their files. Misha replied that his family had no contacts outside of the USSR. "Check with your parents and get back to us," said the official. Misha wrote to me, and I gave him the particulars about my uncle, which he then conveyed to the Special Section. I was not worried, nor did Yefim believe it was a big deal. Still, Misha was denied his clearance, and I can think of no other reason other than my relatives abroad.

    I am describing these events as if I knew about them all along, but that was not the case. Misha did not tell his father or me about the security clearance problem. We did not know he was banned from the military classes, and after Yefim's death, I did not know about the expulsion memo. Misha completed his second year with excellent grades and spent the summer break in Zagorsk[17], doing construction work with a group of his fellow students[18]. He came home for a few days, left me his pay, and went back to Moscow. Six months later, shortly before his winter recess, Misha called me on the phone. He said he would not come to Odessa this time—he had failed one test and was threatened with expulsion. He would remain in the school during the break, trying to arrange a retest. I was very concerned but also perplexed: Misha had been studying in that college for almost three years, was considered a talented student, had never flunked a test before, and because of a single exam, he was being expelled? So, I decided to fly to Moscow to find out what was going on. Several months earlier, I had surgery and was still not feeling well, but that did not stop me. I asked for leave at work and called my brother-in-law, Aaron, who lived in Kiev and with whom Misha and I were close. After Yefim's death, Aaron often helped us financially, taking great interest in Misha's affairs. When I told him about

---

[17] Today's "Sergiyev Posad," a city 80 kilometers north of Moscow.

[18] A reference to the so-called *stroyotrjad* (construction brigade), a state-sponsored group of volunteer college students doing paid construction work on their summer recess. Most of those brigades worked in Siberia, but ours was sent to Zagorsk.

Misha's problem, Aaron said that he would go to Moscow, too, and we agreed to meet there.

Moscow greeted me with brutal cold and deep snow. I took a taxi to Savelovsky train station, boarded a train, and soon arrived at the MIPT campus twenty kilometers from the city. Misha was not in the dormitory, but his roommates were in the room. They told me the entire story—how Misha had been banned from the military courses, about prior expulsion attempts, and that the current trouble was likely the result of the same clearance issue. Starting in the fourth year, MIPT's academic program required attending the state's research facilities, many of which involved even higher security clearance than military classes. And if skipping the military course implied that Misha would have to serve in the army sometime after graduation, without access to research facilities, he could not continue in school at all. So, I decided to speak with the college's president. I waited in the reception room for several hours, but he did not receive me and redirected me through his secretary to Misha's dean. I got the impression that the president did not want to lie but could not tell the truth, either. And there was not much he could do—he had no power to override the security apparatus.

The dean received me right away. He was very polite and said that my son's only option was to transfer to another school that did not require a security clearance. He promised to help if Misha agreed to the transfer. After the dean, I spoke with the vice president of student affairs and the secretary of the college's Communist Party organization. They all echoed the dean's advice: transfer to another college. I tried to contact someone in the Special Section but was not let in. So, the following day, I decided to go to Lubyanka, the KGB headquarters in Moscow's center. I stayed with my distant relatives. When I told them about my Lubyanka plans, they became nervous and tried to dissuade me from going. "You will not be allowed into the building," my relatives said, but I went anyway.

The guard at the Lubyanka's entrance inquired about my business and directed me to the front desk in the lobby. A young lieutenant at the front desk gave me a form where I put my name, address, and reason for the visit. He then asked me to take a seat in the lobby's waiting area... In about half an hour, the lieutenant called my name. He handed me a pass with a room number on the second floor and told me to go there. I went upstairs. A KGB colonel was already waiting for me in the hallway next to his office. The office was a two-room suite consisting of a reception room and a large workroom in the back. The reception room was empty. The colonel took me to the workroom and offered me a chair. "How can I help you?" he said. I told him about my American relatives, how the

Special Section denied my son a security clearance, and that the boy was being forced out of the school. The colonel listened patiently. "How do you know it was a Special Section? What is Special Section, anyway?" he said. "You ask *me* what the Special Section is?" I replied, "You know it very well, as everybody else does. Why was my son denied access? He did nothing wrong." The colonel asked me to step outside for a few minutes and wait in the hallway. Behind the closed doors, I heard him shouting at someone on the phone—perhaps in the college's Special Section, for not handling me on their own. Then he opened all the doors and invited me back inside. "You may go home," he said, "Write us a letter explaining your son's situation. We will look into it and notify you officially. I think everything will be all right." I returned to my place of stay, wrote the letter, and brought it to Lubyanka the next morning. On the same day, my brother-in-law came from Kiev. He spoke with a few college officials, including the president, but to no avail. There was nothing else we could do, so I went back to Odessa, this time by train.

In a couple of weeks, Misha informed me that he had been called to the Special Section, where he signed a nondisclosure form. He was given clearance. A few days later, I received a letter from the KGB. "Your son has been granted access..." the letter proclaimed. However, it was all a smokescreen, and the authorities had no intention of letting Misha stay in MIPT. The school delayed his retaking the exam, and he remained under a constant threat of expulsion. His emotional state was terrible. He had nightmares, waking up at night many times. One of his roommates called me on the phone and described Misha's condition. Fima's mother urged me to convince Misha to leave MIPT; she worried about his mental and physical health. But Misha would not give up—he believed the security clearance issue had been resolved. Lastly, at the end of the semester, he received a failing grade on another test, and the school posted a notice citing Misha's transfer to another college as a reason for his termination. Of course, he never expressed any desire to transfer, and no arrangement had been made to do so. I begged Misha to stop fighting, and he finally agreed. After several attempts to get into a college in Moscow or nearby, he was accepted to the university in our hometown of Odessa.

If the above memoirs were mine, I would not have mentioned the security clearance story, as it paints me as a victim. Life has its ups and downs, and one cannot be sure [s]he did all to sway the outcome, or things might not have turned out worse if they had gone the other way. But my mother chose to tell her tale, and little can I do about that other than add my commentary. And the story was not just about me, as she played a sizable part in it.

My mother's trip to the KGB headquarters was viewed by many as a heroic act, but she had been to worse places before. And the KGB was not what it (or its predecessors) used to be. It was less deadly and more subtle, trying to project an appearance of fairness and civility. To me, the notion that a seventeen-year-old born and raised in the USSR could pose a security risk seemed absurd. The grip the Soviet government held over every aspect of a young person's life made such a risk implausible (I, for example, became familiar with liberal ideas mainly in college, the same MIPT with its high-security requirements, where those ideas were more widespread than in most other colleges in the country). But if the KGB cleared everybody, what would their use be? Therefore, they ought to disallow an occasional student to show vigilance to true believers and remind of the organization's presence to the rest. And why me? Nobody confirmed the reason was my mother's letter to her American relatives or my reply in the application form, but those circumstances had likely put me in the spotlight. Some suggested vengeance against my father by his former associates as my trouble's source, yet such a theory seems too conspiratorial to me.

It may be naïve thinking on my part, but if I had been an exemplary student, the KGB might not have succeeded in pushing me out of MIPT. The outcome of the last test I flunked was likely prearranged. The test was on a subject I considered boring and rarely attended the lectures. My foes must have known that and found an examiner who agreed to give me a failing grade, expecting it to be an easy task. However, before the test, I spent a few days and nights reading the textbooks and managed to absorb the contents of the course. So, during the exam, I answered all the questions and solved all the problems, only wondering whether I got an A or a B. The examiner gave me an F! That removed the last doubt about the authorities' plans for my MIPT future, but had I kept a consistently high academic standard, no examiner would have dared to pull such a stunt. I could complain, and there were independent, influential people in the school who would have spoken on my behalf. But I studied like in my pre-college days, ignoring unappealing subjects and cramming before exams, which, together with sporadic time-limit-induced mental paralysis, resulted in my grades being rather spotty (except for math, where they were always top).

I did not tell my parents about the military classes ban because I did not want to upset them, and also believed I could handle the issue alone. When the news of my exclusion from the military program appeared on the bulletin board (the school put up a list of military training groups, none of which mentioned my name), I went to see our department's vice dean. I wanted to know how serious the situation was and what my course of action ought to be. The vice dean told me that cases like mine had occurred before, and neither he nor his superiors had any say in those matters. He knew of a student who graduated from MIPT without ever attending military classes. "I suggest that you do not make waves," the vice dean said, "Keep studying, and everything should be alright…" Recalling that conversation, I now understand that the vice dean's was not good advice, if only because by not protesting the ban, I partially validated it. In all likelihood, the protests would have been useless and might have even ended my MIPT term earlier, yet it was the right thing to do. But I was still a kid, gullible and naïve. The ban did not affect my relations with instructors and fellow students, so I followed the vice dean's recommendation.

My other mistake was not accepting a transfer when it was offered to me soon after the clearance denial. I was summoned before an important school official, an Air Force general with a peculiar title: "Vice-President for Miscellaneous Affairs." The general was a legendary figure—one of the school's founders and its first president, a man of impeccable repute. At the time of our meeting, he was almost seventy years old and nearing retirement, yet still wielded considerable influence and wore a military uniform, in which he received me in his office. "I do not know why you were refused clearance," started the general, "that was not my call. There is nothing I can do about it. They decide those matters in other places and do not tell us the reasons. However, we must deal with it. MIPT is a very good school; however, it requires clearance. There are other good schools that do not have such a requirement. It is in our power[19] to transfer you to any of those colleges. Listen to my advice, pick one." If the general was sincere (and he likely was), I could transfer to Moscow University's School of Mathematics, the best math school in the Soviet Union and the one that educated Fima. I would have applied there after high school if not for that new GPA admission rule, which put me at a disadvantage, and now I only had to ask the general. But I did not ask him for anything. I felt agreeing to a transfer was like admitting my guilt. As if anybody cared whether I was guilty or not. At that point, it was a checkmark or a note in my KGB file, easy to put in but almost impossible to expunge, which determined the official attitude. In Stalin's time, such

---

[19] Having learned more about that general, I now realize he meant "in *my* power," as such a generous offer could not have come from the school itself.

a mark could have led to my arrest, but in the more benign post-Khrushchev era, it only cost me admission to a particular college. Still, I had no regrets. An institution of the highest standing, MIPT attracted the best and the brightest, multi-talented young people whose friendship and influence had broadened my horizons. It was also one of the most liberal periods in the Soviet Bloc's history, culminating in the Prague Spring, with the fresh air of freedom blowing through the school's halls. Communist ideological principles were questioned, incarcerations of dissidents loudly protested, and a surprisingly large portion of my non-Jewish schoolmates took Israel's side in the Six-Day conflict. But soon, the Soviet rulers began a new crackdown, and by the time of my MIPT exit (which coincided with the Soviet invasion of Czechoslovakia), the reaction was in full swing.

Having passed on the general's offer earlier, I had to find a transfer college on my own, which turned out to be a difficult task. Eventually, I ended up at my hometown's university. The school's officials dragged their feet and would have rejected me if not for Tsylia Ilyinichna, who used her connections to cement the deal. But before that, I spent a few months wandering around Moscow and nearby cities, looking for a place to continue my education. I slept in waiting halls of airports and train stations, listened to the confession of a petty crook, borrowed one rouble from a stranger, and even flew in the cockpit of a commercial airplane. That flight happened in Voronezh, where I came to discuss a transfer to their university. I finished early and went to the airport to catch a plane back to Moscow, but all the flights were booked. I then went to the train station, also to a sold-out event. It was my terminal call in a grueling sequence; I was tired, and the prospect of spending another night at the train station did not appeal to me. I sat down on a bench in the waiting hall, pondering the situation… and letting fate plot its little surprises. "Problems?" a male voice woke me from a deep thought. The voice belonged to a fellow traveler sitting next to me. I explained I was stuck in the city. "Did you try the airport?" the man asked. I answered that I had just returned from there. "There is one more flight to Moscow today," continued my neighbor, who must have traveled that route often, "You can still make it. Go to the airport and get near the aircraft[20]. You will see a guy loading baggage there. Give him twenty roubles, and he will put you on the plane." The notion of a stranger at the train station instructing

---

[20] In those days in the USSR, boarding an airplane was not much different from boarding a train or a bus, and passengers walked freely among planes, even at the main airport of a large city, such as the one mentioned here.

me how to bribe a flight crew at the airport seemed improbable, but I had nothing to lose. In the worst-case scenario, I would be sleeping at the airport instead of the train station, so I abided by the odd advice.

The baggage handler took the money without questions. "Wait here," he said. He returned a few minutes later, and we walked toward the plane. All seats in the cabin were occupied, so the captain escorted me to the cockpit. The second pilot was already at the controls, ready to go. He waved hello to me. "I will be back in a moment," the captain said and walked out of the cockpit. I thought he had gone to find me a seat among the passengers or in the luggage section, but he returned with a regular stool, put it behind the second pilot, and invited me to sit down. Then he proceeded with the takeoff… It was a clear summer afternoon. The four-engine propeller aircraft flew at a low altitude, allowing me to appreciate the cockpit view. "Help yourself," said the captain, and moved a tray with seltzer and candies toward me, the items only the crew could enjoy, as no refreshments were served to the passengers. I felt like on a private plane, and it didn't cost me more than a regular ticket. After months of a draining odyssey, that flight was a welcome relief and brought me such pleasure that it made the entire MIPT ordeal almost worthwhile.

8. Postgraduate Distribution

At university, Misha studied well, receiving an increased scholarship for academic achievements. He did not discuss his reasons for leaving MIPT and, when asked, replied that he had transferred to be closer to home. Misha's MIPT malady affected not just him but also me. Troubles with relatives, bad neighbors, and worries about my son had worsened my health and state of mind. I was often ill, had fevers, and stayed a few times in the hospital, but worked and smiled, hiding my true mood. At my job, I was treated well by the management and employees, among whom I had many friends. Their moral support had helped me a lot, for which I remain in my coworkers' debt.

His graduate thesis, Misha wrote in Kiev. He stayed with Aaron, his uncle, and later Fanya, Aaron's sister, who also lived in Kiev. Upon the work's completion, Misha brought his thesis notes back to Odessa, and I typed them myself to save money. After graduation, he was assigned a schoolteacher's job in some village in the countryside. Most university graduates received similar assignments[21]. They had to work there for two or three years before being allowed to pursue their own careers.

There was a duty to the Soviet State more urgent than postgraduate distribution. That duty was military service. College male students who had served in the army before enrolling in the studies were exempt from postgraduate obligations, while those drafted after college received the same deal upon the service's completion. Having skipped military classes at MIPT (the university did not offer a military program), Misha was to be drafted before his twenty-eighth birthday[22], so he wanted it to happen sooner rather than later. Enlisting early, he would avoid the postgraduate distribution while incurring the army routine at a younger age. But going to *Voenkomat* and asking to be drafted was not an option, as they did not accept volunteers—one needed contacts to make it happen. Luckily, we found such a contact, and a couple of days after his graduation, Misha was drafted into the Navy. He served near Sevastopol in Crimea in harsh conditions of physical strain, scant food rations, and lack of sleep. Every other day, he performed 24-hour guard duty on the top of the mountain

---

[21] All Soviet college graduates were required to do stints at state-designated workplaces commensurate with schools and specializations. MIPT graduates, for example, were often sent to research facilities around Moscow (where they usually stayed after the mandatory period), graduates of medical schools were assigned to provincial hospitals and clinics, and those with a university diploma taught in rural schools. Here, I shall refer to such mandate as "postgraduate distribution," which is a literal translation of its Russian term.

[22] The draft's cutoff age.

above the sea. In winter, his boots had worn through. The weather was chilly; Misha caught a cold, developed a fever and cough, but kept going to guard assignments. He may have even gotten pneumonia, as his later X-rays showed tiny lung scars.

During Misha's service, I visited him three times. His troop was in a restricted area, where I could not go, so he would take a few hours' leave and come to Sevastopol to meet me. Despite a challenging environment, Misha served with distinction. Upon the service's completion, he was honorably discharged, received a commendation, and came home. To the place of graduate distribution, he did not go but found a job in Odessa, acting on my tip. That summer, I spent my vacation in Yessentuki[23] to treat my stomach problems. My roommate in the dorm was a woman from Odessa who worked as an accountant at an engineering firm in the city. She mentioned that her organization sought people for the newly created automation group. Upon returning to Odessa, I told Misha about the opportunity, he told his friend, and they both got hired. In those days, Soviet industries were beginning to automate, so the demand for workers in that field was very high. At the new job, Misha became involved with computers and, in a few years, transferred to his firm's parent company, where he worked until we left the Soviet Union.

A bottle of cognac was all it took to get me enlisted. A few weeks after the main draft, the Navy requested several more conscripts, and the enlistment office included me in that group. I was handed an envelope with my papers and a transit pass, boarded a ship, and showed up the next morning at a military training camp in Sevastopol. There, I met other members of the special draft—a dozen college graduates mainly from Odessa, including my former university classmate (who also used to be my sports colleague). In the camp, we spent a few weeks learning basics, then were dispersed among the navy divisions to serve the rest of the term. I ended up in one of the Soviet military's toughest units and owed it to my mother's concern.

In every society, connections play an important role in advancing individual interests; however, in the USSR, with the country's lack of economic opportunities, connections were a way of life. Everybody had to know somebody to get something. Influential people had powerful connections, which translated into cushy jobs, private apartments, cars, and other big-ticket items, while members of the general public used

---

[23] A resort town in the northern foothills of the Caucasian Mountains. The town is famous for its mineral springs considered beneficial for gastrointestinal health.

their able acquaintances to obtain things like meat, clothes, and instant coffee. My family belonged to the second category, had no friends among the military, and had never been to Sevastopol, so it was remarkable that my mother found a contact there, and not just any, but among the top brass of the army command. It so happened that relatives of our Odessa friends were related by marriage to the late Sevastopol commandant, whose family was on friendly terms with his successor (and other high-ranking officers). Thus, without informing me, my mother put a word through that channel, asking to place her son in a "good" unit, and the commandant (or someone else) obliged. I think he did, because the unit I got into was certainly a good one, from the standpoint of someone like him. The troop belonged to an elite, "combat-ready" division notable for its iron discipline and heavy demands on the soldiers. Every other day, we carried out twenty-four-hour guard duty, and the rest of the time did not lack exertion, either. Forty-five seconds after the reveille, sailors had to stand in line, belts fastened and beds partly made (seems impossible, but if a soldier was a moment late or missed a belt or had his bed open, he was punished, so everybody managed somehow). After the roll call, the troop ran outside for a thirty-minute workout, in any weather and without tops; only striped undershirts were allowed on the coldest days in winter. Scanty breakfast was followed by a morning inspection and assignment of tasks, at which point the daily grind began. The individual task could be a minor guard duty or a military patrol, but most of the time, it involved some physical work in the compound, and if the effort required only half a day, there was another round of assignments after lunch. Sometimes, the regiment conducted a drill, where the sailors were raised in the middle of the night and ran a mile up the hill toward the installation at the top of the mountain. After the drill, it was business as usual, with no respite to make up for the lost sleep. Consequently, we averaged about five hours of sleep and were kept awake by unceasing physical activity and an acute sense of hunger.

Nobody among my special-draft comrades ended up in a troop as strenuous as mine. My university schoolmate, who had no military connections, was sent to a submarine base to man their store (which, unlike ours, stocked canned food) and gained twenty pounds by the time he was discharged. Others got lighter duties, too. I also believe I did not land in my unit by mere chance because I was the first college graduate there, and in the beginning, the command did not know what to do with me. At first, they exempted me from the most onerous duty—a twenty-four-hour shift guarding the installation. Perhaps they thought I was too old to perform such a task (I was twenty-three), or too educated, or my presumed benefactor expected them to go easy on me. Unfortunately, such an arrangement soured my relations with fellow sailors, which was unnecessary, as I did not seek preferential treatment in the first place. So, I went to the regiment commander and asked him to lift my dispensation from the 24-hour duty, as well as other exemptions he might think of. "Are you sure?" inquired the commander. I replied that I was. "You've got it," the commander said. I sensed he was relieved, as my special status placed him in an awkward position, too. The immediate effect of my request was an increased physical strain, but emotionally, I fared much better. The sailors' hostility disappeared overnight, and during my first 24-hour mission's lunch, my most vocal critic, who happened to be in the same detail, emphatically served me a tray with food. And the commander owed me a favor, which he later repaid by discharging me with the first batch.

Perhaps the psychological difference between the ages of seventeen[24] and twenty-three is greater than it seemed to me then, as I did not adjust to army life as quickly as my younger comrades. I grew accustomed to scarce food rations, lack of sleep, physical exertion, and nightly drills, but could not fully accept the submissive constraints of the martial order. That stance was summed up in a dream I saw repeatedly after my army service. In that dream, I hiked in the beautiful, bottle-green Crimean Mountains and wandered into my navy compound. A pleasant surprise turned into horror, as the next moment, I was in a uniform, standing in a row with other sailors. I tried to explain that it was a mistake, that I had already served my term and was just enjoying the scenery, but nobody listened. The sergeant shouted a command, and the platoon marched toward the barracks, taking me with them.

But the army is an army, and I did not go there to protest its rules. I viewed the service as a contract, where I gave the state my time and effort in exchange for being left alone later, and the army's rules were the contract's terms. I might have even gone too far with that contract notion when I took a 24-hour guard assignment while stricken by the flu. Our unit operated a rocket battery as part of the Navy's defense. The silos and the bunker sat on a mountaintop above the sea and were under construction at the time, so the sailors' primary duty was to maintain and guard the site. Every morning, a new guard detail took occupancy of a small hut near the bunker's entrance. The hut had two rooms: one at the front, with a table, chairs, and a wood-burning stove; and another at the back, with sleeping cots. Sailors guarded the posts outside, sat in the

---

[24] The draft's age.

front room, and slept in the back—two hours each phase. That sequence repeated four times, making up a 24-hour shift. In winter, the guards sometimes received a sheepskin coat to wear at their posts. Regulations called for such a coat when the outside temperature was below minus four degrees Celsius with wind; however, most of the winter, the temperature was just above that mark, so we wore regular coats, freezing in the strong wind from the sea. I remember donning the sheepskin coat once, where I understood the command's reluctance to give the coat out —it was too easy to fall asleep in that thing.

What I cannot recall were sailors with the flu, stomach aches, and similar issues. Perhaps nobody got sick, or, like me, the afflicted ignored the symptoms. The harsh army routine was the best medicine for minor ailments. Twice, I took a 24-hour assignment while experiencing acute signs of the flu, and by the shift's end the following morning, they were totally gone. Thus, my mother's suspicion that I had pneumonia was baseless since that disease did not have enough time to set in. As for the scars on my lungs, they were likely the result of a faulty X-ray film.

My inflated sense of contractual obligation resulted in the holey boots my mother mentions in her text. She did not check my soles, so I must have told her the story... A single pair of boots was the only footwear a sailor had. The boots were very sturdy and supposed to last for a year; however, our combat-ready routine accelerated their demise by about six months. Mine arrived at the end of their life in winter. I mentioned to the regiment's storekeeper that I needed a new pair, but he ignored my wish. I did not press the issue and wore the old boots, as discomfort from the holes was a trifle compared to the lack of sleep and chilling winds from the sea. One day, I was standing at my 24-hour post when the regiment commander came with an inspection. He approached me and suddenly asked to see the soles of my boots. I raised one foot. The commander looked at the holes, turned around, and walked away. The next morning, when I returned from the assignment, the apologetic storekeeper was waiting for me with new boots (in fact, they were reconditioned, as a brand new pair was not due for another six months).

I was surprised that the regiment's commanding officer expressed an interest in my boots. Neither did I know what prompted him to make that inquiry. Perhaps a good officer ought to know such things, and our commander was undoubtedly a good one. All our commissioned officers were top-notch military men—intelligent, educated, and well-trained. All graduated from a naval or military academy, and many had a second degree in engineering. I was on good terms with most of them, especially the political chief (a position that originated from the early Bolshevik era's "commissar"). The commissar was our second-in-command, with an army rank of a major; however, as a liaison for the ruling political party, he embodied a shadow authority chain. He was low-key, well-mannered, yet competitive and strict. Despite his title, he was not overly ideological. We occasionally chatted about various subjects, and during one of those conversations, he asked me if I wanted to become a Communist Party member, in which case, he would provide me with a testimonial. In those days of mature communism in the USSR, party membership was mainly a career booster, not readily available to citizens of my background, so the major's offer was well-intentioned. "Thank you very much," I replied, "but I do not feel I have earned that honor yet." The major laughed and changed the subject.

A few times, I had the opportunity to ease my burden by enrolling in the officer-of-reserve program (an eight-month course for conscripted college graduates, counting toward the term of service) or becoming a sergeant, but those moves would have reinforced my ties with the army, something I tried to avoid. So, I turned down an officer-of-reserve offer and sabotaged the sergeant-hood by giving orders in an inaudible voice when asked by an officer to direct a group of sailors. The commander did promote me to a lead seaman, which I could do nothing about, but it was just a stripe with no bearing on my rank-and-file status. It only meant that if the enemy killed all the officers, sergeants, and other lead seamen, I would be in command. But it is unlikely anybody would listen to me in those circumstances.

During my service, my mother visited me twice or thrice. On her first trip, she met a woman on the ship who traveled to Sevastopol to see her husband, also serving in the Navy. The husband turned out to be my friend and a fellow special draftee who had landed at a submarine base as its storekeeper. The submarine base was located in Sevastopol proper, while my troop was half an hour's drive from the city. The soldiers in my unit were allowed six leaves per year. Each leave lasted five hours and occurred on a Sunday afternoon. A military truck would pick the sailors up at our compound's gate and drop them off near the commandant's building (Kommandatura) in Sevastopol. The reverse took place on the way back. When my mother was arriving for a visit, I would take a leave (which did not count toward the allowed six) and come to Sevastopol to meet her. We walked around the city, sat on a bench, ate the food she had brought from home. One time, we met in the apartment of the late Sevastopol commandant and had dinner with his widow (the one I suspected of conspiring with my mother to "help" me into my unit) and their children. My mother stayed at the commandant's home overnight and went back to Odessa the next morning.

Occasionally, I went to Sevastopol on regular leave to see a movie, walk the city's streets with my fellow sailors, or visit my submarine-base friend, who would open for me a small container with jam or a can of sardines. But despite our unit's isolation, coming to Sevastopol was not a big thrill. The main base of the Soviet Southern (Black Sea) Fleet, the city swarmed with officers and military patrols. One could not walk a block without saluting somebody, moving the right arm repeatedly up and down like a mechanical toy. And if a soldier neglected a military greeting or had his jacket unbuttoned or hat askew, he could be detained by a patrol and spend the rest of the afternoon goose-stepping around the Kommandatura's courtyard, practicing a salute.

Wearing civilian clothes was strictly prohibited for enlisted men, and patrols were constantly on the lookout for violators; yet, some recruits did it anyway, eager to escape the pressure of a uniform. One violator was my submarine friend. Ten years older than an average conscript[25] and uncharacteristically heavy from his military duties, he was less likely to be stopped by a patrol and frequently slipped into the town in civilian garb. That activity resulted in a surprising encounter to which I was an indirect party. One morning on my mountain, the sailors were washing up after a workout when the major (who was a duty officer[26] that day) walked into the washroom. He came to a sink next to mine and opened the faucet. "Good morning," the major said. "Good morning," I replied. "Regards from your buddy," continued the major and uttered the name of my submarine friend. For a few seconds, he savored the expression of astonishment on my face, then explained that he had been to Sevastopol and apprehended my friend wearing civilian clothes on the street. "I escorted him to the *Kommandatura*," the major added, "On the way, we had a conversation and discovered a common acquaintance who was you. He asked me to say hello to you." "I asked him to let me go," complained my friend later, "He was so affable, but in the end, delivered me to the commandant and filed a report."

Looking back at those navy days of mine, if I could choose between my combat-ready unit and something less taxing, such as a submarine

---

[25] My friend was a late starter and was drafted shortly before his 28th birthday.

[26] Officers did not stay in the compound at all times. Most of them lived in the military town at the foothill of the mountain. They would come in the morning and leave in the evening, except for a duty officer, who remained on the base's territory throughout his 24-hour shift. During our nightly drills, the officers were awakened in their homes and brought to the installation by a truck.

base, I would have chosen the former without hesitation. A memorable experience in itself, it provided me with a glimpse into human behavior under harsh conditions. I also acquired some useful habits and derived indisputable health benefits. Clean air, intense physical activity, and a low-calorie diet, so valued by today's medical science, were ample in my navy routine. Since boarding school, I had always done sports and, coming to my unit, believed I was in excellent physical shape; however, when my first drill commenced in the middle of the night, and we ran up the hill, loaded with military gear, I thought I would die halfway to the target. I did make it to the mountaintop, but had blurred vision and was gasping for air like in an asthma attack. By the end of the service, I did those drills without breaking a sweat. Never in my life was I that fit, and the first clothes after the uniform felt like the finest silk. Hence, my mother's unsanctioned attempt (to which she never admitted) to do me good worked out, after all, although not in the way she envisioned.

9. Moscow Vacations

When my husband died, we had no savings. There was no money even for the funeral. My brother-in-law, Aaron, who had come from Kiev, paid the burial expenses. A few months later, I installed a metal fence around the grave through my job. Putting up a stone was too costly; we did it when Misha started working.

I received a job promotion and was in charge of personnel affairs in an organization with over a thousand employees, but my salary remained low. With those wages, I had to buy food, pay rent, and cover other living expenses. To buy clothes, there was no money left. My son kept telling me I would be able to afford those things when he started working. And so it happened—he would bring his pay home and give it to me. He was glad when I bought something for myself.

There were no quality clothes or shoes in the Soviet stores. Only in major cities—Moscow, Leningrad, and Kiev—could one buy something decent (usually imported) after standing in line for hours. In Odessa, commercial sailors brought clothes and other goods from abroad. They sold the merchandise to resellers, who sold it at the flea market. Odessa had a large flea market in the outlying borough of Peresyp, but clothing was expensive there and hard to find in the right size and style. Thus, many chose to buy fabric and look for a tailor who would custom-make the garments and do a good job, as fine fabric was costly, too. The work itself was not cheap, either, so people ordered "heavy-duty" items, such as coats and suits, that would last a long time. Could an average Soviet woman come to work in a different dress every day, like in America? Of course not. I wore the same dress and blouse-skirt combination until they became dirty, then washed or dry-cleaned them and put them back on.

My social life was nonexistent. I dwelled in one room in a communal apartment. How could I receive guests in a place where relatives behind a plywood divider watched my every step and neighbors stared at the visitors in the common hallway? I preferred to spend more time at work, leaving early in the morning and returning late at night. On weekends, I cooked, cleaned the apartment, and did the laundry. After work, I would sometimes go to the movies or a theater with friends, but most of my leisure time, I slept, being too tired to do anything else. On vacations, I often traveled to Moscow, where I stayed in the apartment of my distant relatives with whom we were close. Those trips were my respite, but time passed quickly, and I had to go home...

Chapter 2

THE BOARDING SCHOOL

1. Primer

Within the boarding school's student body, we did have the offspring of government officials, Party leaders, and military commanders; however, the school was not conceived for them. It was created soon after the war[1] to house and educate the sons of fallen soldiers. The school was not an orphanage, but it had many orphans, especially in the years immediately following the war. From its inception, the school was a closed, all-male institution where students lived on full government sustenance. For many, it was the only home they knew. The predilection for delinquency, common among boys without fathers, was countered with an army-like routine, high academic standards, and disciplinary methods that often went beyond verbal persuasion. And those few who could not be straightened out were sent to real orphanages—dismal places in the city outskirts, where crime spills into the neighborhood could be ignored[2]. The boarding school's emphasis on English was also new and hip at the time. Foreign languages played an important role in Soviet educational programs, but the prevailing choice before the war was German, with English replacing it after the Allies' victory. Academic proficiency and early maturity led many boarding school graduates, especially in the earlier years, to successful careers in the military, management, and foreign service, thereby enhancing the school's reputation. The advanced curriculum, good teachers, and strict discipline attracted the powers-

---

[1] The Great Patriotic War of 1941–1945.

[2] The number of such rejects had to be minimal because, in the early days, the boarding school drew on those very orphanages to fill its student ranks through careful selection.

that-be, who occasionally enrolled their scions in the school's program. The school's location also helped, being in a newer, desirable part of the city where some of those powers lived.

By the time of my enrollment, the school had already lost some luster, although it was still a good place to learn. A decade after the war, there were no more first-graders whose fathers died on the battlefield, and the number of truncated families had diminished as well. The eligibility pool was drying up, and so was the quality of new recruits. Thus, in the year of my entry, the school decided to open its doors to the general public and also become coed. Children from single-parent, lower-income homes received admission preference, but they still had to meet certain criteria to get accepted. The bulk of the new enrollees went to the lower grades, while vacancies in the higher grades were filled mostly by girls… The majority of students with both parents did not live in the dormitory or receive any keep from the school, but neither could they go home after classes—the extended day was mandatory for everyone. We ate lunch in the cafeteria, played in the schoolyard a little, and spent the rest of the afternoon doing homework under the watch of our class supervisor. The homework was followed by recreational activities and manual tasks, after which the extended-day crowd would go home while the full board headed to the cafeteria for supper, accompanied by the class supervisors. Class supervisors did not teach subjects, but monitored students after that. They would come in the afternoon and leave late at night, passing their duties to night watchmen.

2. First Impressions

My first schoolyard trip gave me a glimpse of the indigenous population, and it was not an encouraging sight. I could not believe how big and scary those youths were. At least one grade my senior, many sported a year or two over their grade's normal age (a big difference for a nine-year-old), and their rough demeanor made them look even scarier. One of the aborigines approached me. "Do you live at home?" he asked. I replied that I did. "Your mother cooks some tasty stuff for you, doesn't she?" continued the student, "Bring some of it to me, and I will make sure nobody bothers you." I was not thrilled by the proposal—not by its sharing part, but by the prospect of becoming somebody's vassal—yet did not dare to say "No" on my first day on the extortionist's turf. I nodded silently and walked away. Not wishing to upset my parents, I told them nothing and the next day went to school empty-handed, ready to bear the consequences. Surprisingly, when we met in the schoolyard, my new "friend" did not request his due and pretended that he hardly knew me. I knew that some of my extended-day classmates received similar proposals, but there were no follow-ups on those either. Someone must have told their parents, who informed the school's administration, which foiled the fledgling protection scheme.

The exhilarating smell of new textbooks had not faded yet when I became a witness to a scene that shook me to the core: between the main building and the dormitory, next to the schoolyard, two male teachers chased a student, cornering him like a calf that had broken out of a pen. One teacher grabbed the fugitive's arm, but the student freed himself and ran across the lawn toward a low fence edging the schoolyard. He jumped the fence over, pursued by the second teacher, who tackled the student to the ground and held him until the first chaser arrived. The teachers lifted the captive off the grass and, clutching his arms on both sides, led him inside the building... To me, like most pupils of my age and upbringing, even arguing with teachers was a serious offense, but fighting them was unimaginable. Yet, it was not so rare an occurrence in the boarding school, whose older students (or "autochthons," as I will refer to them further down) were tougher and more mature than their typical coevals. Among themselves, autochthons maintained a power structure based on seniority—older students exerted authority over their junior mates, affirming it on every proper occasion. The introduction of the extended-day program, as well as the opposite sex, set limits to the oppressive regime's reach; however, it had little effect in the dormitory, where the majority of interactions between classes took place.

Challenges to the seniority rule happened infrequently and were crushed without delay, sometimes with frightening brutality. The drastic measures were taken when the rebellion turned physical. I recall one such case involving an autochthon, a grade my senior. His nickname was Agrippa, and he was among the toughest, most fearless students in the school. Agrippa was overage, tall and strong, and with a face that bore the marks of many fights. He wasn't especially bright but was composed and not a troublemaker; still, he often got into trouble because of his reluctance to accept authority. One day, I saw him in the schoolyard, all black and blue. It was evident he had undergone a severe beating. My full-board classmates informed me that Agrippa had gotten into an argument with an older student, and when the latter tried to enforce the "law," a fight broke out, which Agrippa won. The following night, a group of the humiliated party's classmates entered the dormitory room where Agrippa slept, pulled him out of bed, and pummeled him with their feet until there was no resistance. That incident happened in my boarding school's middle period. Occasionally, I fought with other kids, too, but felt no anger toward them, and under no circumstances, at the time, could I hit another person in the face. But those youngsters did that with their feet, which was very disturbing.

The school made little effort to soften its students' character or break the clasp of the tyrannical code. The country's greatest ills were alcohol consumption and physical violence (committed under the influence). Maybe the school prioritized addressing those issues, which it did rather successfully. I never heard of anybody drinking on the school's premises, and a smaller share of the autochthons ended up on a criminal path than of my own class, where several went to jail later on. Perhaps the seniors laying down the law was viewed by the administration as a form of self-governance, which helped maintain discipline and, in appearance (if not in purpose), was not much different from what some teachers and class supervisors did. The school staff's male faction had several war veterans who were willing and able to enforce the rules. Several of them were quite unorthodox educators, and their antics were legendary. One such eccentric was the school's head teacher[3], a former Air Force gunner, who awed students by doing a "flag" pose on a pole in the middle of the schoolyard. The head teacher was in his late thirties or early forties, short, bald, muscular, and wearing a wartime bomber jacket, which he sometimes traded for a custom-made suit. He was a harsh disciplinarian, and even the most chronic violators tried not to end up in his office.

---

[3] School's deputy director (principal) in charge of the studies.

Occasionally, he stayed overnight, sleeping in the dormitory, and in the morning, rushed to teach a class, often lacking time to shave. When that happened, he would bring shaving utensils to the classroom, lay them on the table, send the monitor to the cafeteria for hot water, take off his shoes, and shave methodically while conducting a session. After the school opened its admission, the head teacher halted his public shavings, so I did not witness them in person but heard a story from an old-timer reminiscing how he was called in front of such a class, stood shifting legs, stepped on the head teacher's foot in a stocking, and got smacked with a soapy hand. I did not know that head teacher well—he left the school soon after my enrollment, and was followed by Geography in English as a curriculum item.

3. Keeping Promises

The boarding school's tougher image entailed one benefit, which was particularly useful—it kept street gangs away. There were many such packs in the city. A typical street gang comprised several teenagers who hung out in front of some building in the middle of a block (corners were occupied by older thugs), harassing younger passersby and jumping them when fewer people were on the street. The hooligans also enjoyed attending school parties and making trouble there. Even teachers were afraid of those youths since the trespassers carried brass knuckles and knives. Widespread alcoholism, with its destructive effects on a family, assured a steady supply of such youngsters. As their leaders grew up and moved to street corners (and then usually to prisons), the old gangs dissolved, and new ones sprang up. Police paid little attention to teenage ruffians, getting involved when they hurt someone badly or committed other serious offenses. The state-controlled media did not report crime incidents or publish crime statistics, so it was hard to determine how many gang attacks resulted in severe injuries and even deaths; however, based on my experience, such outcomes were not so rare.

One gang-related episode occurred inside the boarding school. I was in the eighth grade then, and we had a school party (which I missed but later got a full account of). The event took place in the evening in the main building's auditorium. The party was winding down, and most attendees had already left the hall when a group of local toughs showed up. We knew them—they were a nasty lot, but did not bother us, afraid to start a war they could not win. However, that night, the visitors must have had a few drinks and were overly aggressive. They started hassling our girls, and when one of the students intervened, he was punched in the face. Another student ran to the dormitory for help. Agrippa was the first on the scene. Without a preamble, he knocked the gang leader to the floor, but another intruder came from behind and stuck a knife into Agrippa's back. In the ensuing commotion, the perpetrators escaped into the darkness, and when the reinforcements arrived moments later, they could not find anyone. Luckily, Agrippa's wound turned out not life-threatening, and the stabber was later apprehended by the police, but it is easy to see how that attack could have been fatal. Of course, none of the party crashers set foot on the school's grounds again.

I did not tell my parents about Agrippa's stabbing, afraid that they might get alarmed and place additional constraints on me; however, my parents found out on their own or knew the overall situation, realizing I had entered a perilous age. I was almost fifteen, and my sports activities were paying off, which, together with a good adrenaline pump, made me a formidable adversary (within my age group, at least). Not that I was looking for a fight, quite the opposite, but my confidence had grown considerably. So my father, who understood such matters well, requested that I not engage in a confrontation when accosted by teenage ruffians on the street. He asked for my word, and I gave it to him. It didn't take long before I had a chance to keep my promise.

In my first grade in school, we had a student named Vasya (Vassily), who studied in a parallel class. The word "studied" did not accurately describe that pupil's activities, as it was the second time he tried to finish the first grade. The previous attempt was thwarted by the program's knottiness (how one could flunk the first grade is beyond me), so he was given another chance. Scholastic ineptitude of that degree is frequently accompanied by bad behavior, and Vasya was no exception to the rule. Now a year older, he bullied the first-graders, scaring them out of their wits. Even at such a young age, his mien revealed a sociopathic persona, especially his eyes—puffed, light blue, almost white—which did not blink, staring like those of a predatory animal. Perhaps to some adults, Vasya appeared like a cute, rambunctious kid, but I always perceived him for what he would become: a repulsive thug. Our paths did not cross in first grade, and by the second, I no longer saw him at school. Maybe he failed to clear the first grade again and was transferred to a special facility.

Although no longer sharing with him educational space, I sometimes saw Vasya on the street since we lived a block apart. As he was growing up, the vitality of youth had masked, to some extent, his developmental problems, permitting him to reach a certain level of self-assurance and athleticism. He wore fancy shirts with sleeves rolled up to show off his biceps. By then, he must have had a juvenile record and was a leader of a gang of six or seven youths, with whom he hung out in front of the building where he lived. Unlike Tolik from my first courtyard, whose clout rested on intelligence and charisma, Vasya was a primitive goon who needed a show of brutality to impress his acolytes. I had a stomach-churning feeling when I saw him, and tried to avoid close encounters, not to let that sensation spark trouble. My regular itinerary rarely took me past Vasya's lair, but sometimes I had to go that route and, one day, ran into the entire gang. Vasya sat on an iron post[4] at the building's

---

[4] Many older buildings in Odessa had a short iron post (the size of a fire hydrant) on each side of the main gate. I am not sure what the purpose of those posts was—maybe to anchor an iron chain across the entrance, controlling vehicle access to the courtyard—but in my time, people used them as rather uncomfortable stools.

entrance, flanked by five or six sidekicks. One of them—a big, fat youth with a deliberate expression of ferocity on his face—was Vasya's second in command, who frequently accompanied his master. The fat lieutenant was sitting on the opposite post, and the rest of the pack stood between their leaders.

As I passed that group, Vasya hailed me. "Come here; I want to tell you something," he said. I approached him. Without a word, he punched me in the stomach. It was a light punch, intended not to cause damage or pain but to challenge me to a fight. I automatically responded with a similar ersatz blow. "You are brave," uttered Vasya, rising from the iron post, "you are brave." I stepped back while the gang repositioned itself, too—Vasya got in front of me, the fat lieutenant took a spot behind me, and the others moved to seal the sides. "So, it is seven against one?" I said. Vasya signaled his crew to stop the advance, but the fat lieutenant remained behind me, blocking the retreat... Vasya then stepped forward and punched me in the face. This time, he did it with full force, trying to knock me down in front of the admiring audience. I staggered back but remained on my feet. Despite his athletic appearance, Vasya was not very fast or agile, as generations of watering his family tree with alcohol had slowed my foe's reflexes. Although he had the advantage of a bigger size, I would have taken him apart in a fair fight, but there was no chance of such at the moment. I knew the rest of the gang would join the skirmish, and in the heat of a battle, someone might stab me with a knife, as it happened to Agrippa. I imagined the grief of my parents and stood paralyzed by that sight.

From behind, the fat lieutenant pushed me toward Vasya, who threw another punch but once more failed to dislodge me (in a way, those attempts mimicked his efforts to complete the first grade in school years earlier). Suddenly, in a blow-induced daze, a vision appeared in my mind, clear and detailed, like a motion picture. In that vision, Vasya went for the third blow, but this time, I did not wait. I leaned against the fat lieutenant, forcing him to step back so that his foot came under me, and drove my heel into his toes. The fat lieutenant shrieked from pain while I, using his body and the unfortunate foot as a springboard, threw myself onto Vasya. I punched Vasya hard, then again and again, until he fell onto the ground. It all happened in seconds. The fat lieutenant moaned behind me, incapacitated by the suffering, while the rest of the pack stood motionless as if they had seen Medusa's face. With their leaders out of commission, the rank and file did not know what to do, and had I offered them to join my gang, they might have accepted the offer... But I did not have a gang, and, back in the real world, Vasya hesitated. He stood with an air of frustration, unsure about the next move. Maybe he saw the backside of my vision, but more likely, realized that he had used all his "free" shots. Now, if he failed again to drop me, his reputation among the followers would suffer greatly, while a likely counterattack might topple it altogether. He squinted as if something got into his eye, indicating he would not take a chance. "Go," he said to me, and waved the fat lieutenant to clear the way. "Go," Vasya repeated. I turned around and continued on my route.

Perhaps the outcome of the Vasya episode was a happy one, but I did not feel satisfied. It wasn't unfulfilled vengeance that bothered me. Life took care of my attacker in its own way. He soon disappeared for years, probably went to jail, and then I saw him only a few more times, every time alone and closer to the ruin—face swollen from drunkenness, barely visible eyes, slow body movements, and scarred hands permanently red from hard labor in cold weather in prison. Even if I wanted to view Vasya's downfall as a reprisal for my beating, the punishment was far greater than the crime… What troubled me was the sense of a missed opportunity, which my motion vision had almost commanded me to seize. It was not a cop-out on my part since the suggested reaction was contingent on Vasya's keeping up with the attack; still, I felt like I had foolishly declined an invitation to an important social event. "What happened to your lip?" asked my father when I came home. I replied that I had been assaulted on the street. My father said nothing.

4. Teacher's Chair

The boarding school was not large—three hundred students or so. Other schools were bigger, with several parallel classes, but ours had only one class per grade. Perhaps the lower count was the result of many pupils living in the dormitory, whose size and number of beds limited the total capacity. It was also a Ukrainian-English school—all subjects were taught in Ukrainian, except for the Russian language and literature (taught in Russian) and a few others, such as English and geography, which were taught in English in higher grades. But by the time of my enrollment, the only course taught in English was English, so it was a Ukrainian school[5] with an extended English program. Because of the school's smaller size, individual instructors covered a broader range of subjects and grades. Such versatility required proficiency in multiple disciplines, and most of our teachers met that requirement, especially holdovers from the pre-coed era. They were likely better compensated, being good enough to find an easier job within the school system or even in college, as some later did. Overall, the school must have cost the government a bundle, but who counted?

The teachers recruited after the school's "liberalization" were more specialized, carried a smaller load, and did not stay long. Coming from traditional schools, many lacked experience dealing with disruptive students (who were several among us)—the teachers became frustrated, overreacted, and made things worse. I remember one such teacher, a woman who taught Russian literature. She was nice, relatively young, a little overweight, and unable to project authority. Whenever a challenge to her command arose in the classroom, she became upset and flew off the handle, unable to measure her response. We quickly recognized the teacher's weakness and paid little attention to her demands... One day, before the Russian literature class, someone "borrowed" the teacher's chair in our classroom, and the monitor went to look for a replacement. The monitor's duty was to prepare the classroom for the class, ensuring there was a chair for the teacher to sit on. The chairs were in short supply (because of their poor quality) and frequently disappeared, so monitors looked for them in auditoriums and empty classrooms.

After spending the entire break looking, the monitor came back with a stool, which seemed a little shaky, but following a brief inspection, was deemed okay. Had the teacher received a warning of potential hazard,

---

[5] Most schools in Odessa were Russian. Ukrainian schools were few, and they typically offered some specialized studies, such as an advanced English program.

she might have been more careful sitting down, but as it was, the chair collapsed under the woman's weight, sending her to the floor amidst a pile of wooden chunks. The class erupted in a burst of uncontrollable laughter… I still see the teacher's face as she got off the floor—red, with an expression of surprise, embarrassment, and dismay over the class' heartless reaction. Even today, I feel sorry for her and a bit ashamed that I laughed too; yet, this is how kids are: mostly good individually, but collectively, a bunch of monkeys devoid of compassion.

The monitor put the chair back together and invited the teacher to give it another try, this time with greater caution, but the poor thing was so upset by the unfortunate accident that she spent the rest of the class on her feet, letting everybody do what they wanted… The next class was mathematics. It was taught by Mikhail Isayevich Maximchuk, one of the most feared and respected teachers in the school (and its one-time principal). Tall, heavyset, with short grey hair and a dour face, he cut an imposing figure that no wobbly stool, like the one waiting for him in our classroom, could support. Of course, the monitor should have replaced that chair with a more structurally sound device, but he, like the rest of the class, was too intoxicated by the recent triumph to worry about the future. The sparks of laughter popped up in the classroom as details of the spectacular fall were being recalled, and the stool stood in its place, looking totally harmless, when the bell rang, and the massive frame of Mr. Maximchuk appeared in the door. The class rose. Mikhail Isayevich paused suspiciously, sensing the room's elevated mood, then nodded to everybody to sit down and started toward the stool. It was like a dark, stormy cloud moving toward the bright sun, swallowing a bigger and bigger portion of the blue sky, and casting a shadow of fear upon the people on the ground who were us… The class froze, waiting for the monitor to act. "Mikhail Isayevich," cried out the monitor as the teacher reached the chair, "do not sit on this stool. It may collapse." "What?" growled the teacher, "Everybody's up!" The class rose again. "You go find me another chair," Mikhail Isayevich ordered the monitor, "and while you are looking, nobody will sit." "If I have to stand, you will be standing, too," he said to the class and sat on top of a student's desk, starting the lesson, while we continued to stand until the monitor came back with a new chair fifteen minutes later.

According to rumors, Mikhail Isayevich was badly wounded during the war. He had all his limbs in order but saw a doctor regularly, as once revealed under rather peculiar circumstances. He was a good teacher and a skilled mathematician. After leaving the boarding school (which happened in the year of my departure), he went to teach mathematics at the city's polytechnic college. I do not know if he had an advanced degree, but his admittance to a college faculty bespoke his qualifications. In school, Mikhail Isayevich took his job seriously, trying to teach his pupils in earnest. Not typically in a good mood to begin with, he would become particularly irate when a student could not answer a simple question or solve a trivial problem, and in those moments, the teacher's path was not to be crossed. I recall a scene where one of my classmates stood in front of the class, struggling with an assignment, while Mikhail Isayevich sprawled in his chair, half-turned toward the blackboard, waiting for an answer. As the minutes passed, the teacher's face turned sullen, and he began fidgeting in his seat. At the same time, another student in the middle of the first row peeked into the class journal, which lay open on the teacher's table. Small and quick, with a pointed nose, that classmate reminded me of a sparrow. He stretched his neck as far as possible but could not read upside-down and rose above his desk, leaning over the teacher's table. Mikhail Isayevich noticed the move with his peripheral vision. "Sit down, or I will punch you in the head," he uttered through his teeth, barely turning around. The student retracted but, in a minute, hovered over the journal again, finally getting the teacher's full attention. Mikhail Isayevich rose to his feet and stepped toward the nuisance. "Yes," he yelled at the birdlike pupil, who slumped in his seat in horror, "I am undergoing treatment!" (and that was when I learned of our math teacher seeing a doctor, maybe even a psychiatrist, as the Russian expression "to be treated," used in such context, often implies the mental side). "And you ought to be treated, too," Mikhail Isayevich bellowed, "Because I can punch you, and no veterinarian will piece you back together."

Mikhail Isayevich seldom realized his threats of physical violence, but once or twice, he slapped a student in front of the class, perhaps to show those threats were not empty. The student was my friend and sports teammate, not a star in the studies department, but not a laggard either. I never understood why Mikhail Isayevich disliked him so much; in some way, my friend ticked the teacher off... Like most men of his generation, Mikhail Isayevich saw nothing wrong in slapping boys who misbehaved, considering such punishment a useful educational tool. As an overseer of many fatherless children, he filled the void of parental authority with its presumed right to administer smacks. Thankfully, he did not abuse that privilege and never laid a hand on those who had fathers, preferring to communicate the infractions along the chain of command.

Despite being feared, Mikhail Isayevich was widely admired for his authority, fairness, and sense of humor. He had no favorites among his students and, when in a relatively peaceful state of mind, cracked jokes in Ukrainian that were repeated in the class and dormitory for months. Other times, he could be quite nasty. I recall when he once walked into the classroom and, instead of teaching math, conducted a thorough search of the students' belongings. The class stood in a row in front of the auditorium while Mikhail Isayevich went through the bags and desk compartments, sarcastically commenting about their contents. I do not know what he was looking for—perhaps he had received a tip about illegal items such as cigarettes—but found nothing.

Luckily, I had few problems with our esteemed math teacher, being the first in his class. His subject came easily to me. I didn't have to sacrifice my time-wasting activities to keep up with the program, and when the homework remained unattended and Mikhail Isayevich called me in front of the class, I solved the problems on the blackboard. He did not smile or dole out praises but spoke to my father, with whom he was on good terms. "Mathematics?" said my father to my mother after the conversation with Mikhail Isayevich. "Who did he (I) inherit it from?" Of course, my father did not study enough to know his own aptitude, but he could look at his younger brothers, who did go to college to become accomplished engineers... Mikhail Isayevich was the one who told my parents about a new school with advanced math and science programs, and he also wrote me a recommendation to that place, but then, in my eighth grade, I was just thankful to him for not yelling at me in class.

5. Parking Space

Not every school staffer was a role model, however idiosyncratic, like Mikhail Isayevich. There were some unpleasant individuals among the teachers, and, oddly enough, they were mostly women. I remember two such teachers: one was scornful, with a boa constrictor's gaze that sent shivers down the students' spines, and the other projected a steady aura of barely controlled rage. Both were antisemitic. They did not express it openly, but their occasional remarks toward Jewish students revealed unmistakable prejudice. I believe the snake-eyed teacher was an average antisemite, her snide ways responsible for letting it out, but the other woman sported a more toxic attitude, and if anybody doubted that, they might look at her son. He was a full-board pupil in our school, a grade or two my senior, and while other autochthons chose protégés among the lower graders, the teacher's son had chosen a victim. The victim was my classmate and later friend, Dodik[6]. He was also a full-board student from an impoverished Jewish family without a father. His widowed mother worked several jobs to make ends meet, living with a couple of younger children in a rathole of an apartment, so Dodik's attendance at boarding school was essential to their keep. Dodik was thin, neat, very organized, and stubborn as a donkey. He always had to have the last word, which often got him into trouble with teachers and autochthons alike; however, they handled those episodes casually, except for the antisemitic teacher's son, who persecuted Dodik on a regular basis. "You are a filthy Jew," he scoffed at my classmate in the hallway, slapping Dodik's face. "And you are even worse," Dodik replied, raising his hands to fend off more blows.

Why didn't Dodik complain about such treatment? Antisemitism was commonplace in the post-World War II Soviet Union, affecting younger generations who no longer strongly identified with their Jewish roots. Having abandoned the protective confines of an old tradition for a new society's ideological mainstream, Soviet Jews were caught by surprise when that society turned against them. They were left anxious, confused, torn by a foisted sense of shame and guilt—a sentiment Dodik's defiant reply to his tormentor curiously revealed. Still, the latter's conduct was unacceptable, and had someone reported it to the school administrators, they would have ended that travesty. Unfortunately, such a turn would have made it worse for Dodik, rendering him a snitch. Thus, he had little choice but to keep growing up, harassed perhaps at a lesser rate as time went by… One day, when we were already in the eighth grade, Dodik

---

[6] Informal of "David."

came to me with an absent look on his face. "I beat him up," he said almost indifferently as if not fully realizing what had happened. He was referring to his persecutor, the teacher's son. The bully must have had a bad day and decided to take it out on his old punching bag, only to discover that the latter had grown a few barbs. David vanquished his Goliath.

In a surreal conclusion to the Dodik story, he and his longtime foe became pals. Like his mother, the teacher's son had a few strings broken in his mental harp. He was shunned by his peers and did not have close friends. After Dodik defeated him in a fight, nobody among the loser's classmates tried to retaliate—they may have even gloated over the black sheep's ignominy. Ironically, the reviled Jew was the nearest soul the teacher's son had, and the possibility of severing that lone social tie frightened the latter more than the humiliation of a defeat. Thus, the teacher's son reached out to his former victim and was not rejected. As tough and unyielding as Dodik had been in his struggle, he was kind and generous in his victory.

I do not imply that antisemitism was a big issue at the school. Like everywhere, it simmered in the background, surfacing from time to time via casual remarks, but was a small factor in personal relations. Dodik's case was rather an exception, viewed by many as a personalities' conflict. Most school staffers were fair people who did not condone overt bigotry, and some were Jewish themselves. Not that it mattered much, as the only school employee who tried to hit me was Jewish, and had he not missed, we both would have been in a lot of trouble—I from the blow, he from dealing with my father afterward. My attacker was not a teacher; he was in charge of the school supplies, including food for the cafeteria. Students worked under his command, unloading provisions for the kitchen, or observed him walking on the school's territory—the reddish face crisscrossed chaotically by deep furrows like the channels on the planet Mars—as if it all belonged to him. The supplies manager lacked the civility I came to expect from the school's personnel, as well as most Jews I knew. He seemed to have stepped out of Isaak Babel's Odessa gangster stories[7] and, as I was later told, had two sons who were real thugs. And he had a car. The car was a "Moskvich[8]," a two-door clunker assembled at a former Opel factory that was transferred from Germany after World War II, giving rise to the Soviet consumer auto industry. The car was old and had completely shed its sheen, but even in such a state,

---

[7] *Odessa Stories* by Issac Babel.

[8] Translates as "Muscovite," a popular model in those days.

an auto was a luxury available to a select few. The supplies manager drove the car to work and parked it at his convenience on a single-hoop asphalt playground, which our students used as a basketball court. The car interfered with our game, but we avoided the vehicle until one day, found it right under the hoop. It was impossible to play, so I suggested moving the obstacle. We were in our fifth or sixth grade, not very strong individually, but succeeded together in pushing the car out of the way[9]. When the automobile reached its destination on the other side of the court, I noticed that the headlights we had been pressing against were a bit recessed, which I did not recall seeing at the beginning. But maybe I wasn't paying attention, and the recessed headlights were part of the car's original design. Either way, they did not look so bad.

The game started. A few minutes into the play, we heard a loud voice screaming obscenities, and the enraged supplies manager appeared on the court. He approached our group as we stopped playing and stood skittishly next to each other. "Who moved the car?" yelled the supplies manager with an insane expression on his face. Nobody answered. Of course, it didn't matter who moved the car—all he wanted was a trigger sound to unleash his fury. "Who moved the car?" the manager shouted again, and I realized he was addressing me. "We all did," I replied. The supplies manager emitted the sound of an opening dungeon door that had been shut for fifty years and took at me a huge swing. I ducked, the manager's fist zoomed above my head, and while he was trying to regain his balance, the players scattered in all directions... I wondered why, among a half-dozen suspects, the manager chose me to inquire about the vehicle. Yes, it was my idea to have the car moved, and it was I who pressed against the headlight, but he did not know that, and none of my playmates had yet had an opportunity to betray me. It must have been the intuition of an owner. Anyhow, after that incident, the supplies manager stopped parking in our court and may have switched to public transport altogether.

---

[9] The car was not equipped with a parking brake, or the latter did not work.

6. Full Board

What was special about the boarding school that caused me to enjoy and miss it so much was the school's free-spirited atmosphere and variety of characters. Perhaps members of other collectives I happened to be a part of were smarter, better educated, more focused or diverse, but they all carried a stamp of homogeneity molded by the group's rationale. If it were a school for the gifted, one would be ranked by scholastic aptitude; if it were an elite college, one had to conform to its reputation; and if it were the army, homogeneity was the rationale itself. Yet, nothing of the kind existed in the boarding school, whose purpose was to turn out more or less normal humans. I, for example, did not feel superior because I was good at math, as others did not feel inferior because they weren't. We sang no anthems, carried no standards, and nobody tried to coerce us into any particular creed. At one time, we wore a uniform, but the school was giving out clothes and would not ask for wardrobe preferences. In the third grade, like all my classmates, I became a young pioneer[10] and was given a red silk tie, but after a few days of narcissistic delight, I took the tie off and (except for a few official occasions) did not wear it again. *"Nekhtuvav nosinn'am pioners'kogo galstuku"*[11] wrote our class teacher in my annual review, and that was the extent of it. But the benefit I valued the most was the lack of parental control. Of course, we were supervised, but it is one thing when a single adult watches thirty kids and another when a couple watches one.

Other than in my dreams, I never visited the boarding school after we left it. There was nothing to go back to. My classmates were no longer there, relations with the teachers had been distant, associations with the autochthons too brief to produce lasting ties, and the circumstances of our exit precluded expectations of the school's future rise. Thus, I started (and ended the first version of) this chapter, believing that the boarding school was long gone and forgotten and my memoir could be the sole recorded tribute to that unique institution, only to discover later that the school was still in place and had been restored (save for the full board) to its former glory, with the ancient roots revered and acclaimed. Perhaps the resurrection happened still in the USSR through the efforts of earlier graduates who had accumulated enough clout to alter their alma mater's fate; plus, recent school administrators once studied there, too. Despite the drastic changes that befell Soviet republics in the 1990s, the school's

---

[10] Soviet political youth organization for middle schoolers.

[11] Ukrainian, "refused to wear a pioneer tie."

history was viewed as an unbroken whole, with the early years (which adjoined my time there) exemplifying unimpaired virtue; however, this is not how I remember it. There were instances of cruelty and oppression that deeply troubled me, but the drawbacks were offset by minimal intrusion into the pupils' inner worlds. Instinctively or by intent, we were trusted with being ourselves—perhaps the highest praise to a forming character. In a way, it was similar to how my father treated me. And maybe at some point in its creation, the school received a blessing from above that no human decree could override.

The spiritual autonomy of our students reflected the ideas of Anton Makarenko, a renowned pedagogue whose method was a gospel among Soviet educators, especially as it applied to post-apocalyptic milieus. What distinguished the boarding school from other implementations of Makerenko's blueprints was the moderation of the collectivist message the system also conveyed. So it was natural that individuality flourished in such a setting, which could be compared to an uncultivated field, not as practical as wheat or as pretty as a tulip one, but with different flowers and plants, sometimes unremarkable, sometimes bringing a surprise. Perhaps because of that miscellany, more of my classmates displayed entrepreneurial flair than what could be expected of the time and place we were in. One classmate became a busy tailor who, before my leaving for the West, had sawn me a pair of pants (we lived a few blocks apart, traveled home together after an extended day, and remained friends long after the boarding school) and another, a birdlike fellow whom Mikhail Isayevich once threatened with destruction, came to renown as a black marketeer buying foreign goods from commercial seamen and selling them to the public. The latter was not a close friend of mine in school; still, we readily acknowledged each other afterward and often stopped to chat. He would offer me his wares, such as nylon socks, at a discount or as a gift, and I would gratefully decline the offer. Neither the tailor nor the trader (nor my many other classmates) could be mistaken for role models from the boarding school's idealized past, but it did not diminish our appreciation of the time together, which made later encounters such happy events.

In my seventh grade, the school announced the termination of the extended-day program. Those enrolled in it were given a choice—to join the full board or transfer to another school. That was quite a turnabout since, before the announcement, the extended-day students could not get into the full board even if they wanted to, but now, the only alternative was to leave the school altogether. Most opted for the full board. My parents asked me what I wanted to do, and I replied that I would stay. It was my full-board term that caused my mother's later penitence, so had I decided otherwise, she would have been relieved despite the strain on the family's finances and overcrowding in the apartment; however, for me, the prospect of living six days a week away from home was a major draw. I did not reveal it to my mother, not to hurt her feelings, but other reasons could be cited instead, with family relief at the top of the list. There was one problem, though—the autochthons. While on an extended day, I did not interact with them much, but now, it would be difficult to avoid contact and likely conflicts. How would I react in a confrontation, back away and let humiliation mar my brand new freedom, or stand up and become a target of sustained harassment? My full-board classmates had already adjusted to dormitory life, and some developed closer ties with the autochthons, but these were associations of patronage rather than true friendship, something I wouldn't be happy with, either.

The majority of class interactions occurred between adjacent grades, and our next-door neighbor up the street was soon to be the ninth, the rowdiest class in the school, and the one that listed Agrippa. Even before his stubbing, which happened during my full-board term, Agrippa was a celebrity admired by younger schoolmates for his toughness, bravery, and sports achievements. The school's physical education emphasized classic sports, such as gymnastics and fencing, over coarser ones, like wrestling and boxing. Among games, basketball was very popular in those days, partly because soccer and hockey required training facilities that most schools lacked. But whichever sport it was, our students were among the best. The fencing team dominated the city's tournaments year after year, my gymnast-friend (the one disliked by Mikhail Isayevich) later became the province's champion and a national team member, and the basketball teams (middle and senior) were legendary, with Agrippa among the middle team's top scorers[12]. Their game was a pleasure to watch, proceeding like a well-oiled mechanism whose parts interacted efficiently and precisely. The player I admired the most was not Agrippa, but his classmate, nicknamed Scola, who played as a midfielder. Scola was the team's brain, and his surprising moves and total vision of the game were truly exciting. In physical appearance, he was Agrippa's opposite, short and powerfully built, with muscles bulging on the back of his neck. Scola was also a more sociable type, always surrounded by sidekicks. He matched Agrippa in notoriety, though, having compiled an impressive record of rule-breaking and teacher-fighting. Both teens were

---

[12] I made that team in my eighth grade, although the team was already in decline, as my recruitment indicated; however, to the coach's credit, he kept me on the bench.

overage and, in their eighth or ninth grade, did not submit to any other student in the school. By then, they no longer wrestled with teachers or committed other serious offenses but remained a daunting presence to their immediate juniors.

7. General's Daughter

Like many observers before me, I often noticed that life situations feared the most occurred with frustrating regularity as if attracted by those very fears. The encouraging part was that such occurrences did not have to end badly, and in many cases, they ended quite well. And so it happened in my full-board term—the confrontation I was afraid of did take place, and with no other than Scola, but in a surprising turn of events, it solved my autochthons' problem once and for all.

In the eighth grade, we got a new classmate: a girl whose father was an army general. The general endowed our school with not one daughter but two, the other enrolling in the next (ninth) grade. The older sibling was strikingly beautiful—slender, with milky skin, long black hair, and sparkling black eyes. She was already a young woman whose mysterious half-smile revealed awareness of her powers, but the younger sister was still a child, pure and sweet, with a touch of melancholy in her dark eyes. Maybe the general sent both of his daughters to the full board because something happened to their mother, or he got temporarily assigned to another location or tried to make up for the absence of sons—I do not know, as I never saw the girls' parents in the school; however, I never saw my parents there, either, since parental visits were discouraged by the administration. Anyhow, I didn't ask the new classmate about her family situation. We soon became friends. I had a minor crush on another girl, a youthful fixation that kept a certain part of my brain occupied, so the relations with the new classmate were less affected by romantic awkwardness, and we had a good time together. She was such a lovely girl, a type often found among the families of military commanders (one wonders what can be achieved with discipline). Our rapport did not go unnoticed, and the class supervisor paired us for classroom cleaning duty. The classrooms were cleaned every night by two students, a boy and a girl. The girl did lighter tasks, such as wiping dust and washing the blackboard, while the boy moved furniture and scrubbed the floors. The entire procedure lasted an hour. The cleaning team worked for a week, and then another pair took a turn according to a rotating schedule.

The first two evenings of the new assignment were uneventful—we would finish our job, my partner would go to the dorm to freshen up, I join my friends in the schoolyard, and then we all would meet for supper in the cafeteria—but on the third night, the classroom's door opened, and Scola walked in, accompanied by three of his classmates. The reason for their visit was the pretty char. Had her sister been a lesser star in their class, the visitors might not have known of my partner's existence, but as it was, the glow from the popular classmate reflected off the younger sibling, attracting a notable interest. Paying no attention to my presence, the uninvited guests began the courtship, and I realized that chivalry was not among their strongest points. They did not cross the line but came close, acting aggressively and making suggestive remarks that got their aim upset. I saw how troubled she was by the bawdy pursuit... and suddenly felt a wave of outrage pounding the wall of fear inside me. Thankfully, that wall was thick enough to hold the tide till the intruders left.

The following night, Scola came again, but this time alone. Without a company, he seemed less cocky and a little coy. So when my partner told him she had work to do, Scola did not persist and headed for an exit, mentioning that he would wait for her outside. He did not mean it as a threat—perhaps wanted to talk in a more private setting—but after the previous night, a greater reassurance was needed to secure the girl's trust. She took Scola's words as bad news, and so did I. "Would you accompany me to the dormitory?" she said to me when we finished the cleaning. The accursed radiance of the older sister had now touched my harbor with an eerie shine, pitting me against one of the most fearsome people in the school; however, I could not refuse my friend's plea. "You go ahead," I answered, "and I will follow you." My cowardly thoughts were that Scola might find something else to do, or call off the pursuit altogether, so the problem would go away without him ever knowing of my involvement. But if he saw me walking next to his romantic interest, I could become an object of his wrath. And if he intended to approach his target no matter what... I did not want to even think about it.

The streetlights were already lit when my workmate and I got out of the main building and headed for the dormitory, which was a few hundred yards away. My ward walked first, chin up and looking straight ahead, and I followed her at a distance, praying for a miracle. We cleared the main building without incident. The dorm's facade appeared at the end of the alley, and I inhaled some air for a sigh of relief when Scola jumped out of the bushes in front of my lead. For a moment, everything went dark before my eyes, and when awareness returned to me, I stood between the hunter and his prey, shielding the latter from the former. Perhaps there was something weird in my look, reflecting the blackout effect, but Scola withdrew as if he had seen a ghost, and the girl skipped past him toward the dormitory's entrance... Of course, Scola was not afraid of me, but he was startled by a sudden dash, and I also noticed an air of curiosity on his face—an odd reaction under the circumstances. We began to talk. To my surprise, Scola did not show any anger. Apparently, my hunch of him being a reluctant libertine was correct, plus he must have been embarrassed that the object of his attention had requested an escort. So when I asked him if that was how he planned to gain the girl's friendship, Scola answered that he was sorry about his behavior and would apologize to her. He would also make sure nobody disrespected her in the future. We shook hands and parted ways.

I felt triumphant. Not only did I escape being thrashed, but I stood up to Scola, gained his respect, and secured the girl's safety and comfort. I am not sure if she understood my sacrifice. She might have even been displeased that I did not walk next to her that night (we never discussed that incident afterward); still, I knew what had happened—she asked for my life, and I gave it for her. Luckily for me, it wasn't taken.

8. The Pitcher

The Scola episode marked the turning point in my relations with the autochthons. It probably coincided with growing out of childhood, but the barrier separating our groups disappeared. An amorphous mass of a hazardous substance that those autochthons seemed to be had splintered into individuals who were not much different from me. Most of my classmates went through a similar transition, and it was then that Dodik defeated and subsequently befriended the teacher's son. Scola and I became friends, too. He turned out to be an amiable fellow with a quick, inquisitive mind. It was that mental agility, where thoughts ran ahead of emotions, which might explain his air of curiosity during our standoff over the general's daughter. We had some common interests. Scola was a good chess player, notable for surprising combinations, which reminded me of his moves on the basketball court. We played chess on the school's team in city tournaments and against each other for fun. Our friendship was entirely natural. I did not seek any benefits from his formidable standing—it was an association between equals, and sometimes, I felt he looked up to me. What made me comfortable in Scola's company was his unprejudiced attitude. Unlike Agrippa, who could erupt in a bout of hostility for no apparent reason, Scola carried little anger inside him and sported an easygoing disposition. It was hard to believe such a person had fought teachers and caused trouble in the past, but when I asked him to explain that behavior, he laughed my question off.

The termination of the extended-day scheme was the first in a series of changes that befell the boarding school. The following announcement declared that the school would become a middle institution, with the eighth grade as the last. Grades nine through eleven[13] would complete the high school program, while the eighth (where I studied then) would graduate the same year. Hence, I wasn't going to remain in the boarding school for much longer. Not a big loss from an educational standpoint, as the school became a rather average learning body; however, it was the place where I lived and had all my friends. Luckily, changes at that age come easy… The announcement surfaced a few months before the end of the school year, but the administration must have known something in advance, as I noticed a laxity of oversight earlier on. The new leniency, combined with a diminished autochthon threat, had rendered my last boarding school year the most carefree period of my youth. No longer were we confined to the school territory and roamed the surroundings

---

[13] The full school term in the USSR was eleven years at the time.

unsupervised. In warmer weather, we would go to the seashore—a short walk from the school. I loved the water, but my parents would not let me swim without a lifeguard. Now, I didn't have to ask them. In those days, Odessa's shoreline, which later became a solid band of beaches, was mainly rocks with a few isolated sand strips. The water near the rocks was crystal clear, and the stones were colorful and varied. We looked into the sea's depths, basked in the salty breeze, but swam infrequently, as the water was too cold during the school months.

Occasionally, our forays into the neighborhood caused its residents damage. It was never the intent, but sometimes things got out of hand. I remember one such expedition, which luckily did not include me... In our class, we had a student blessed with a special talent. Most of my boarding school classmates had talents: some were good at sports, others at business; some built shortwave radios, others sewed pants. That particular student's genius was hurling objects, mainly stones, which he threw farther and with greater precision than anybody else I knew. Had he lived in America, he could have become a baseball pitcher, but in the absence of a similar sport in the USSR, all that his gift was bringing to society was sporadic destruction. One night, the "pitcher," with a few classmates, went into the town. On the way back, they took a shortcut across an apartment complex adjacent to our school. The pilgrims were halfway through the complex when the "pitcher" felt the urge to throw a stone. The stone went a bit too far and broke a window with a blue lampshade behind it. The gang ran, but when they realized that no one was chasing them, they went berserk and started hurling stones in other windows with blue lampshades. They broke some more glass before the complex's residents, who were many military officers, organized a posse and caught the perpetrators. The residents brought the captives to the school before our class supervisor. The supervisor was embarrassed and apologized to the visitors. The next half an hour after the neighbors left, he yelled at the culprits, who could not believe what they had just done. Consequently, the school replaced the broken glass, and the offenders were grounded for a month.

The slack in the school's discipline was partly due to a reduction in the auxiliary staff, including night watchmen. In the dormitory, our class' male faction occupied a large room on the third floor, with two rows of beds and nightstands lined up against the opposing walls. The class supervisor occasionally slept in that room, and when he was away, some other staffer watched the floor at night. However, a few months before the school year's end, we were relocated to an open hall on the second floor. Maybe the school did renovations or needed space and moved us early because we were leaving anyway, but our new quarters transpired in a remote floor section that the night watchmen rarely reached. Perhaps those in charge believed we were grown-ups enough to avoid trouble during our remaining short span in the school, yet that assumption was overly optimistic... In the beginning, we stayed up late, talking, playing games, and reading books, till someone noticed that a rug-covered aisle between the bed rows looked like a fencing strip. The missing part was swords, and we rectified that omission by lifting a few iron bars off the beds' headboards. No gear was employed to protect the swordsmen. For several years after those fencing bouts, I wore scars on my hands, but it could have been worse. Thankfully, before someone got seriously hurt, the ceiling collapsed on the startled low-graders who slept on the first floor below the fencing arena, and the administration dispersed our class all over the dormitory. But then, a handful of weeks remained before our departure, and the imposed solitude became a proper setting for the separation process—collecting memories, looking into the future, and bidding a final farewell to the best of times.

9. Pickle Factory

My last student days were not the final episode connecting me with the boarding school, as I spent the following summer alongside my former schoolmates working at a pickle factory. Summer work was the boarding school's old tradition. The school had an agreement with a couple of city enterprises that offered summer jobs to our senior students. Such an arrangement was not the norm in the USSR, and it possibly violated the country's labor laws (child labor, I believe, as Soviet propaganda often mentioned exploitation of children as one of capitalism's cardinal sins); however, the authorities exempted certain groups from those rules to let teens from poor, single-parent families earn some income (and satisfy the industry's needs for seasonal unskilled labor)… The requisition from the pickle factory came to the ninth grade, whose students worked there the prior year; however, maybe because of a better crop, the ninth-graders could not muster enough volunteers among themselves and offered the vacant spots to a few male pupils from my class, including me.

Before the pickle factory, I had a chance to earn money only once. I was ten years old then and hanging out with a couple of friends in my mother's sanatorium park. We were watching a dominoes game played by the sanatorium's guests. The players were strong, unsmiling men, perhaps farmers and industrial workers whose efforts at collective farms, mines, and factories had been rewarded by the government with month-long sanatorium vacations, all expenses paid. Oblivious of their younger audience, the men played with great concentration, crashing the tiles down on the wooden tabletop and smoking like chimneys. As the game progressed, one of the players ran out of cigarettes. I think he was a coal miner (because of his grayish skin and soon-to-be-revealed uncommon generosity—coal miners were among the highest-paid workers in the Soviet Union). Unwilling to interrupt the game, the miner looked around and saw me. "Hey, kid," he uttered in a raspy voice, "go buy me a pack of cigarettes," and he handed me a five-rouble bill. Honored, I ran to the nearest kiosk, coming back with the order and the change. The miner counted the change, took out one rouble, and gave it to me. It was a very generous tip, more than the price of cigarettes themselves and over one percent of my mother's monthly salary. I tried to refuse the money, but the miner insisted.

I recall the feeling of accomplishment and pride with which I walked into my mother's office and handed her the freshly earned rouble. She also remembered that moment and always mentioned it with a smile. Even then, I recognized my family's tight finances and tried to contribute as much as I could. So when the pickle factory knocked on the door, I welcomed the opportunity with open arms. Only this time, it was not a rouble or two but real money. In the centrally managed Soviet economy, wages were tied to job titles regardless of who did the work, which, together with manual labor's elevated standing, ensured that a fourteen-year-old working pickles at his summer recess was compensated at a rate comparable to that of an engineer or a nurse. It was no less than what my mother took home as a personnel director or what my father earned at whichever job he had at the moment. Such a payment oddity may also explain why an arrangement like that between the boarding school and the pickle factory was an exception rather than a rule.

The work at the pickle factory was hard, even for an adult male. The pickling cycle commenced at the time of the cucumber crop. Cucumbers were transported from nearby farms, placed in large wooden casks, and covered with brine. The casks were then sealed and put into storage. Our job was to cull the cucumbers, load the casks onto trucks, and unload those barrels into storage facilities in the basements of commercial and residential buildings around the city. The pickle factory was a primitive enterprise with no forklifts or other lifting machinery. To load a cask onto a truck, we would open the truck's tailgates, drop two wooden poles off the edge, and roll the cask up those improvised rails. Unloading used the same technique. The casks were heavy, requiring two or sometimes three people to handle. My gymnast friend worked next to me, and as unlikely as it seems today, a few times a week, after a day of lifting heavy casks in scorching heat, he and I would go to the gym for a training session.

That summer was hot and drinking water scarce, so we ate pickles and cucumbers to quench our thirst. For years after working at the pickle factory, I couldn't even look at fresh cucumbers, but pickles never lost their appeal to me—a great culinary invention. The long time the pickles soaked in that magical solution imbued them with a taste that never waned, attesting to the formula's indelible imprint, like one the boarding school had left in us, its pupils. I gave the earned money to my parents.

Chapter 3

THE OTHER SIDE

1. Provenance

My father was the oldest among four siblings, with two more brothers and a sister. The family hailed from a small town in Bessarabia, not far from Odessa. His father (my other grandfather) was a shoemaker. After the Bolshevik Revolution, the family moved to Odessa, and a few years later, my father left his home to start an independent life. He was fifteen.

After centuries of persecution and pogroms, the abolition of the monarchy gave Russian Jews full citizenship rights, and many eagerly embraced the new, short-lived democratic government, followed by the Bolsheviks, whose ominous nature was not very evident in those cruel, tumultuous times. One of those Jews was my father. In the years when my mother's grandfather escaped with his children to America, and her father was sent to the Solovki prison, my father built a socialist paradise, working at an industrial plant. Intelligent and well-read, he attended night school and was active in political life. He was promoted, became a member of the Communist Party, and received a recommendation to the state security forces. In the early Soviet Union, such a recommendation was among the highest honors bestowed on a young patriot. It meant a front-line position defending the fledgling workers' state against its many enemies. It also meant a position of power and elevated social status. Perhaps some vanity played a role in my father's decision, but I am sure his motives were mostly altruistic. And he may not have had a choice, as it was the Party's mandate.

Through the purges of the 1930s, my father was stationed in Central Asia, unlikely to participate in the mass arrests that were rampant in the western portions of the Soviet Union, and by the time of the postwar sweeps, he was already out of commission. During the war, he served in counter-intelligence, having fought on most major battlefronts, including Moscow and Stalingrad. In Stalingrad, his unit became encircled by the Germans but managed to break out. My father counted bullets to leave the last one for himself if captured by the enemy. The platoon walked for three days and three nights, and when they reached the Soviet side, my father fell asleep and slept so long and deep that he wet his pants like a small child. He was decorated with a medal for that march.

The Stalingrad account was my father's only response to my many inquiries of a boy hungry for war stories. He did not like to talk about the war, his military service, and past life in general—it was my mother who informed me of my father's time of yore... I always thought of him quitting the security forces as a defiant and dangerous act. My father was not a reckless person. He had to realize his action's consequences, among which the loss of a military pension was not the worst possible outcome. There must have been several factors that prompted him to resign. Of course, my mother being alone in Odessa and expecting a child was a major concern, but I also believe my father already had doubts about the organization and the cause he served, which contributed to his decision.

The army did not suit my father well, because of his independent nature. He was a good officer who followed his superiors' orders but did not seek their favors. There was innate dignity in him, which projected beyond a subordinate state, denying, in a way, the chain of command. Perhaps because of that, he did not progress very far in the ranks despite holding high-responsibility posts such as those in Germany. And there again, he passed up the opportunity to advance his career, refusing to concoct fictitious plots and phony spy cases. A relatively junior rank of a captain[1] may have saved his life, however, when a new round of Stalin's repressions hit after the war. The postwar purges were smaller in scale than those of the 1930s and more selective. One of the targeted groups was the military, who came out of the war feeling that their sacrifice and role in victory entitled them to a greater say about the country's future. Perhaps Stalin wanted to send a message that it wasn't the case—victory, *schmictory*. So, the secret police started the arrests with higher ranks and did not reach the captain level before it all ended.

After teaching the military a lesson, the ruthless dictator turned his attention to the Jews. The campaign against "cosmopolites," arrests and

---

[1] In fact, captain was not such a junior rank for a counterintelligence officer, given the influence that state security wielded in the USSR. In Germany, for example, my father reported to several senior officers, none of whom held a rank below colonel.

executions of Jewish cultural figures, and trials like the "doctors' plot," besides their direct impact, stirred antisemitic feelings among the country's population. The rumors had it that Stalin readied another mass relocation, this time of Jews to Birobijan in the Far East. My father was disheartened by such a development, but did not plan to go quietly. Upon discharge from the service, he surrendered his official weapons; however, he also owned a small Walther pistol, acquired as a trophy in Germany and never registered with the army. That pistol my father kept. He could have been arrested and jailed if the authorities had found out about the gun, yet my parents knew how to keep secrets. He hid the pistol outside, maybe buried under a tree in the park, so I never saw the piece, but when the new purges rolled in, my father dug his Walther out and brought it into the apartment. "I know they will come for me," he said to my mother, "but I won't be captured alive and may take a few of them along. It is unfortunate that I may shoot at my former comrades." My mother was terrified by my father's words and the sight of the weapon; she nagged him until he got rid of the gun. But then Stalin died, and the arrests stopped almost immediately.

In Central Asia, my father got married and had two sons. His wife was of a Christian lineage or, according to the Soviet ethnic taxonomy, of Russian nationality. Their sons (my half-brothers) were born a few years apart, a decade earlier than me. I saw their pictures in the home of Uncle Zinovy (my father's youngest brother, the one with the piano), whose wife stayed in touch with the boys' mother. The faces in the photos looked pretty much like my father's at that age and like mine. My father never mentioned his other family in my presence—it was Aunt Rose who brought me up to date (hoping perhaps to annoy my mother that way). I did not ask my parents questions or reveal any knowledge of the family's "secret," but my mother told me about it a few years later when she decided I was old enough to understand such things. Of course, I already knew of my father's prior marriage; however, my mother provided more details.

The breakup between my father and his first wife was a bitter one. She wrote to his superiors, accusing him of moral misconduct and other sins. Those letters contributed to my father's problems, especially getting permission to marry my mother. The accusations were baseless and even bizarre, as by then, my father and his first wife had not lived together for several years and were either divorced or in the final stage of the divorce procedure. Besides, she already had a suitor, a higher-ranking military officer who married her soon after my parents tied the knot. The children remained with their mother but kept in touch with my father via mail.

My father loved them and waited impatiently for their letters. They still carried his surname, whose "Jewish" character was becoming an issue amid the rising wave of antisemitism. Still, surname or not, their mother wanted my father out of the picture and requested his consent to the boys' adoption by the new husband. My father refused. He probably felt he was abandoning his offspring, but had little choice, if only because of his financial situation. The way things were, he could barely provide for one family, and paying child support to another would have ruined him. With no role in his children's lives, he would have agreed to the adoption eventually, but his former wife did not wait. She dictated to her sons a letter, which she then sent to my father. In that letter, the boys called him a "traitor," an "enemy of the people," writing that they were ashamed of such a father and did not want to bear his name. My father was very upset and (as per my mother) even cried. Then he signed the consent, severing the ties with his flesh and blood forever.

2. Family Photograph

I know little about the man who replaced my father in the latter's sons' lives, but he was probably a decent person who raised his adopted children and provided them with a good education. The older son chose a military career, while the younger earned a doctorate and worked as a scientist or engineer. The older son was never curious about his origins, but the younger one had a greater interest in his biological father and an obscure other sibling that was I... Soon after my father's death, while still in Moscow, I had a phone conversation with my mother. She told me that my father's younger son from a previous marriage wanted to meet me. He had contacted Uncle Aaron (who was his uncle, too), and Uncle Aaron wrote to my mother. I was excited by the opportunity to meet my unbeknownst brother. My mother seemed to want that meeting, too. Coming from a larger family, she must have regretted that I grew up as the only child. But then Uncle Aaron changed his mind. I do not know what transpired behind the scenes and what his motives were. Of course, he remembered the hostilities and the pain my father had gone through during the breakup, but it happened long ago, did not matter anymore, and had no bearing on my brother, who was a child at the time. All my uncle had to do was give his other nephew my coordinates and bow out. However, my uncle must have lived the old strife, treating the proposed event as a parley, and started setting preconditions. He might have even insisted on being present at the meeting, or perhaps he did not want that get-together from the start and passed the message, hoping it would be ignored. "I think it is too early for them to get acquainted," said Uncle Aaron to my mother, and she communicated that decision to me. "Your uncle..." she added disappointedly, "he thinks he knows better than the rest of us."

How would my father react to the above encounter if he were able to observe earthly events following his departure? He probably would be happy for his sons from different marriages and also relieved to see the broken pieces of his life coming together. Alas, that meeting never happened. I soon left Moscow and didn't hear from my brother again. I did hear from his mother, though, years later. She was in Odessa, staying in Uncle Zinovy's home. There, in a conversation, she mentioned that she wanted to see me, having heard I looked very much like her former husband, my father, when he was young. And maybe she did see me, as, not knowing what she looked like, I would not have recognized her in the crowd.

The reason I suspect that Uncle Aaron over-negotiated the powwow between my brother and me was my uncle's temper and preoccupation with detail. He was a sensible man, but sometimes, his spleen obscured a bigger picture before him. Compared to my father and Uncle Zinovy, he was far more prickly and confrontational—he was not someone to be taken advantage of. I recall stopping at his place in Kiev on my way to Odessa from Moscow. I stayed with him for a day, and then he took me to the train station. We got on the train and entered my compartment, which had two passengers inside. Uncle Aaron raised my berth to put my luggage into the storage bin below, but the space was occupied by another passenger's bag, probably by mistake. My uncle flared up. "Whose bag is this?" he shouted at the suspected trespassers, "Remove immediately!" The stunned violator hastily withdrew his belongings, and Uncle Aaron installed my suitcase in its rightful place.

I was nine years old when my parents took me to Kiev for the first time. We stayed with Uncle Aaron. He had two rooms in a communal apartment, sharing them with his sister and her daughter. I remember the building's courtyard and the street, but strangely, not my uncle's quarters or him and other relatives. I do recall Uncle Aaron's neighbor, though, a charming, middle-aged man who occupied one room in the same commune. That room I picture vividly in my mind. It had a huge bookcase filled with volumes of adventure stories that were very popular among the youngsters of my generation and also extremely hard to get. The neighbor's books were originally intended for his children, who by then had grown up and moved away. Those books were impossible to find in stores, and the libraries' waiting lists stretched to infinity. My uncle's neighbor must have had some special access because he stocked them all. There, across the room, stood a high wall of red, green, and blue hardbacks, heralding in gold letters any title one could dream of. Luckily, I struck a good rapport with the book's owner, and he not only granted me full use of his room and library but also offered me a cot to sleep on at night. Everybody was happy with such an arrangement, and I spent most of my time devouring those novels, one volume per day (which may explain why I remember little else from that trip).

Both rooms in the Kiev apartment belonged to Uncle Aaron, but he took his sister (my aunt, Fanya) and her daughter in when they needed a place. That happened long before my first Kiev trip, and Uncle Aaron looked after both women, especially his niece, until she got married. In fact, the occasion of our visit might have been the girl's wedding. After Aunt Fanya's daughter moved out, a rift developed between my uncle and his sister. I do not know the nature of the argument and who was right or wrong, but my aunt went to court, which affirmed her claim to half of the apartment. Uncle Aaron was furious, and my father, with Uncle Zinovy, called a family meeting to reconcile the feuding sides. The meeting took place in Odessa, my father presiding. Aunt Fanya stayed with Uncle Zinovy at the time, and Uncle Aaron came from Kiev to join the summit. Uncle Zinovy and my father sympathized with their sister as the only female sibling, but they sincerely wanted to settle the matter to everyone's satisfaction. So when Uncle Aaron arrived at the meeting, my father greeted him with an amicable reproach, saying jokingly, "Here is our rascal." But my uncle was not in a humorous mood (if he ever was). "I am a rascal?!" he cried angrily, "Very well," and stormed out of the room. He went back to the train station, returned to Kiev, and started cropping family photographs... When my father and his siblings were in their twenties and thirties, they took a photo of themselves together. The photographer made two shots (smiling and serious)—one where Uncle Aaron stood on the left of the group and another where he was on the right. Thus, upon returning from Odessa, my uncle took scissors and excised his siblings from the first photo, then from the second, and put the carved-out images of himself side by side on display. That was his family now. He exchanged his apartment for two rooms in separate communes—one for Aunt Fanya, another for himself—and did not speak to his brothers for years. Only when my father died did Uncle Aaron come to Odessa; he arranged the funeral and reconciled with Uncle Zinovy, but his sister he never acknowledged again.

Uncle Aaron could be annoying at times, but when he did not lecture or split hairs, my uncle was good company and an upstanding man, generous and fair. The row with my father did not affect Uncle Aaron's relations with my mother and me. He wouldn't visit our apartment in the summer, like before, but my mother and I were always welcome in his home, staying there when in Kiev. On his part, my father made sure we did not feel uncomfortable with his estranged brother... My college degree thesis I wrote in Kiev and, for the first few months, stayed with Uncle Aaron. The apartment he received from the unfortunate exchange was not bad—one room, but in a good neighborhood and a fine building. The room was spacious, clean, nicely furnished, and had only one neighbor in the commune. The apartment exchange happened long ago; my father had been gone for several years already, and Uncle Aaron was back on speaking terms with Uncle Zinovy, but mangled fragments of the family photograph stood prominently on the buffet, touching along the violent zigzags of the scissors' cuts. Perhaps the composition now symbolized Uncle Aaron's attitude toward his sister, my Aunt Fanya, who remained persona non grata. She also lived in Kiev, and I sometimes visited her while staying with Uncle Aaron. One day, she told me that her neighbor in the commune had gone away for an extended time and left his room in her care. Aunt Fanya said that I could live there. It was great news. I would have my own place, coming and going as I pleased. I would not inconvenience anybody and could even choose when to hear my uncle's next sermon. The only issue was breaking it to him. We had no photographs of us together, but I still did not want Uncle Aaron to view my acceptance of his sister's offer as having anything to do with their quarrel. Yet, that was how he initially reacted, assuming I took Aunt Fanya's side. I saw that he was hurt and disappointed. "What for?" he exclaimed fervently upon hearing my plans, but quickly realized the nonpartisanship of the new arrangement and cooled off before I had a chance to answer his rhetorical question. After moving to Aunt Fanya's commune, I regularly visited Uncle Aaron at his home and met with him for lunch, but did not sense in him any grudge or change in attitude, then or ever.

Among the three brothers, Uncle Aaron was the only one who did not spend time in the trenches during the war. Uncle Zinovy joined the combat as a young lieutenant, while Uncle Aaron, who already had a few years of work experience, was sent to the Ural Mountains to build a manufacturing base for the war. He was a good engineer and later held a prestigious post at an industrial research institute in Kiev, although it was Uncle Zinovy who advanced the most, professionally, becoming the chief technologist at a large construction-engineering firm. In physical appearance, Uncle Aaron resembled my father—the same size and complexion, but a little slimmer and with sharper facial features. He was a ladies' man in his younger years and had numerous affairs, which prompted much gossip among the relatives. What Uncle Aaron lacked was a major commitment, and logic may suggest that he never married, but he did, at the ripe age of seventy. It happened a few years after my mother and I emigrated to the United States. Uncle Aaron's new wife was his one-time girlfriend, who had become available for an official relationship. She was younger than he, although not young enough to have children. But having children was not the point. As my uncle grew older, the empty space around him was getting bigger. He had patched things up with Uncle Zinovy, but the relations remained distant, never reaching the pre-fallout warmth. His friends drifted away. My mother and I now inhabited another universe, accessible through rare phone calls and unreliable mail service, and then, his other nephew, Uncle Zinovy's son, died of a heart attack. He was thirty-nine. That tragedy had likely pushed Uncle Aaron away from his prolonged bachelorhood. After the marriage, he and his wife lived together for nearly twenty years until my uncle's death.

My mother respected Uncle Aaron for his candor, punctuality, and sense of duty—the qualities he shared with my father. She was less enthralled with Uncle Zinovy, who had a softer character and, according to her, did not always deliver on his promises. In addition, my mother did not get along with Uncle Zinovy's wife, Aunt Manya, so interactions between our families were not as frequent as my father and his brother probably wanted. Nonetheless, when my father was alive, we exchanged visits regularly, and after his death, I often stopped at Uncle Zinovy's home, passing regards from my mother (whether she asked me or not). "Give our best to your mother," Uncle Zinovy and Aunt Manya would say on my way out... Uncle Zinovy was a gracious, mild-mannered man who treated me kindly, and his wife was ecstatic when I happened to drop by. I was also on good terms with their son, my cousin Tolik, who departed this world too early. We were not very close, as my cousin was older than me and lived in a different part of the city, but the relations were never less than cordial. Almost never—he did threaten to kill me once, but I was two years old then, and he was six. That summer, our parents spent vacations together, renting rooms in the country, and while roaming in the nearby bushes, I found a wooden stick. It was a beautiful piece of wood, very straight—I still recall the thrill of holding it in my hands. When Tolik saw the stick, he became so enamored by it that he attempted to annex the item, wringing it out of my grasp. I ran into the house, screaming for help. Uncle Zinovy promptly intervened: he returned the stick to its rightful owner and disciplined his son. Tolik was furious and blamed everything on me. "I will kill him anyway," he whimpered through tears, "He is not going to live much longer." That attitude changed dramatically as we grew up, and when my college trouble resulted in the loss of a stipend, Tolik (who was already working) and his father had covered the shortfall. For his part, Uncle Aaron helped my mother financially after my father's death until I graduated. All that assistance was provided with no conditions or expectation of payback. Conversely, my uncles would have been offended if they were turned down on their offer and would have refused repayment unless they needed money badly. Both lived well, receiving good pay at their jobs and decent pensions after retirement. They also had savings in the bank's passbook accounts (the only official investment vehicle in the Soviet Union), and then, everything changed...

My mother and I had lived in the United States for over ten years when the Soviet Union fell apart, and so did the country's economy. Retirees were hit hard. Rampant inflation wiped out their savings, while pension increases did not keep up with the prices. The first post-Soviet years were particularly tough when, according to eyewitness accounts, the neatly dressed elderly rummaged through garbage in search of food. My uncles, who had by then retired, did not reach such a desperate state; however, their fiscal advantage practically disappeared. Now, in their declining years, they were facing uncertainty and need. Uncle Zinovy fared somewhat better, receiving small government aid as a war veteran, but Uncle Aaron had only his pension to live on. So, my mother and I arranged a courier delivery of a few hundred dollars to Uncle Zinovy in Odessa, who split the money with Uncle Aaron. That was enough to support both families for several months, and later, I sent them more. My uncles did not ask for my help, as I (or my parents before that) never asked for theirs, but that they accepted the money bespoke the direness of the situation. Hence, those parcels made a difference, allowing me to partially repay my uncles' kindness.

3. Old Watch

I sometimes think of my assistance to my uncles in their later years as the extension of support my father rendered them when they were young. Both struggled financially, and my father helped his brothers as much as he could. He was generous to a fault, sending, for example, a motorcycle from Germany to Uncle Zinovy when the latter settled in Odessa with his wife and small child after the war. But my father had means and clout then. He also had no reason to believe that fortune might abandon him and did little to secure his family's future. Thus, when confronted by the harsh reality of postwar Soviet existence, my father mustered few resources to soften its blow. He was probably surprised by how quickly disappeared the items of some value my parents brought from Germany for personal use. By the time I became fully aware of the material world around me, most of those things were gone, sold to buy us food, shelter, and other necessities. A few articles I remember, such as a Singer sewing machine and a porcelain jar, were kept as reminders of happier days, but eventually, they were sold, too. Only a wristwatch remained. It was a stainless-steel Swiss chronograph my father had worn since the war. The watch was not new when it came into his possession, but he liked it and may have replaced the case to save the timepiece from liquidation. The alteration was discovered by a watch repairman a few years after my father's passing. I stayed in Kiev with Uncle Aaron at the time, writing my thesis, and wore that watch regularly. We were having breakfast, and the watch lay on the table when Uncle Aaron accidentally swept it onto the floor. The crystal came off, the minute hand bent, and the movement stopped. The next day, I visited a few repair shops nearby, but nobody knew how to fix it. Finally, I found a newspaper ad for a shop claiming they could repair any timepiece and decided to give that place a try.

The repair shop was an hour by tram from my uncle's address. The receptionist directed me to an older man in thick glasses, sitting behind a desk in the room's far corner, amidst a great variety of timepieces and parts. I handed him the watch. "It fell on the floor," I started to expound, but the repairman interrupted me. "Thank you for helping me out," he uttered sarcastically with a pronounced Yiddish accent and continued to inspect the item. "Whose watch is this?" he asked, raising his head and staring at me with squid-like eyes behind the powerful lenses. "It is Swiss," I replied (in Russian, "whose" may refer to an item's owner as well as its maker). "No!" the man exclaimed impatiently, "Is this *your* watch?" I explained that the watch used to belong to my father. "I can fix it," said the repairman, "but this will take a while and cost you a fair amount of money. Makes no sense for an old piece like this. Buy yourself a new watch." The master's advice seemed sound—the watch no longer kept good time, but I did not know if it was because of wear and tear or some fixable flaw. "It was a very good watch but has served its purpose," added the master, "It used to have a gold case." Surprised, I replied that I did not recall any other case except the stainless-steel one. "Look," said the repairman, pointing at the watch's open back, "the clearance between the rim and the mechanism is too big; it is not the original case." Perhaps the repairman was right, and my father had sold the gold case to avoid parting with the entire timepiece, or maybe it was how he obtained the chronograph—my mother did not know, either. I was disappointed by the master's verdict, as I grew attached to that clock like my father once was, but what else could I do? There was only one person in the entire Ukrainian capital who could fix it, and he recommended buying a new one. So, I followed that recommendation.

Selling personal possessions was not my father's primary source of income—like all the able-bodied Soviet men, he had to work at some government-owned enterprise. However, without a profession or proper connections, finding a good job was difficult, and his earnings were not enough. While his younger brothers advanced in their stable engineering positions, my father kept changing jobs, trying to escape scarcity and grind. He had many talents, knowing how to make things. He was an early automobile enthusiast in his younger years, who combined the prowess of an accomplished driver with a mechanic's know-how. When the city installed new electric meters in our building, my father replaced the apartment's old, threadbare wiring[2] himself. He bought the materials and did an excellent job, even by professional standards. But my father attempted such a big electrical job only once, further using his skills to fix broken light switches and frayed appliance cords. The other time, he got someplace a length of striped fabric and made me a suit. He took my measurements, drafted the pattern, cut the material, and sewed a jacket and pants. I remember him sitting behind the Singer sewing machine, driving it with his foot, and humming a tune. The suit came out perfect and remained my favorite garb until I outgrew it. Naturally, I expected more clothes from my father, but he never tailored anything else and soon sold his Singer.

Another story, from a time that I have little recollection of, told me my mother. In the immediate years after the war, when the country was in shambles, the government decided to prop up the economy, allowing

---

[2] Older buildings in Odessa (and other Soviet cities) had open wiring.

some private enterprise. The new initiative transpired on a smaller scale than its predecessor, NEP, and involved manufacturing a limited range of consumer goods. My father's expertise in operating a sewing machine landed him a position in one of those enterprises, making hats. After a few months, he improved on the process and was crafting hats so well and fast that other shops sent their representatives to learn how he did it. But shortly, the job lost its appeal to my father, and he quit. In that case, quitting was a fortunate decision, as the government soon closed those franchises, sending some of their partners to jail. "Your father could do anything," my mother finished her story, "but he did not want to."

Why didn't my father use his considerable faculties to earn a higher income? After all, the official stance favored blue-collar occupations over other forms of productive activity. A factory worker could be making more money than a physician or an engineer. Manning a mechanism at an industrial plant or a tractor at a collective farm opened an easier path to political and management careers, while the proletarian perspective was force-fed to the intelligentsia, whose members had to spend a few weeks a year doing physical work such as picking tomatoes in the fields or clearing construction sites of debris[3]. Still, a typical attitude viewed manual laborers as a lower class, a stance reinforced by a general lack of upward mobility. Of course, the potential benefit of a blue-collar job as a career stepping stone was not in the cards for my father, and what remained were diminished social status and physical exertion, for which he was too old already. So, he opted for a job in the service sector—retail sales. At the same time, he kept writing petitions, asking to complete twenty-five years of military service to receive a pension.

Wages in the retail sector were low, but workers helped themselves by redirecting a part of the revenue to their pockets. That was not an option for my father, who would not steal a penny. In addition, he was pursued by bad luck. Although no longer a member of the Soviet ruling clique, he retained his Party affiliation, which gave him an advantage in obtaining supervisory positions, and one of his first civilian jobs was managing a small store. We still lived in that little apartment with a huge Russian stove and no bathroom. The store was across the street. It was a tiny place with tall, empty shelves and a high counter, behind which stood my father. There was another employee, a woman, who worked different hours and whom I never met. For the time being, my father was content with the job—as a manager, his pay was somewhat higher, and the store

---

[3] Most of those "duties" also addressed the temporary labor needs of the full-employment Soviet economy.

was close to home—but one day, came auditors and found a shortfall. The inspections of small shops, like my father's, were rare, and there was not supposed to be any impropriety, so my mother suspected a setup. She believed that the woman employee, whom my father trusted (as he trusted most people), took the money and anonymously alerted the authorities. That was a credible scenario. The way the system worked, nobody would have bothered to investigate such a minor case, and at that point, it was my father's responsibility to cover the deficit or face a prison term. But if he had discovered the shortfall on his own, the woman employee would have been in big trouble, so tipping off the inspectors allowed her to keep the loot. The deficit was small, maybe six months of my father's salary, yet for my parents, it was an impossible sum. Uncle Aaron came to the rescue, putting up the money, but my father was so distressed by the incident that he never sought another management position in retail again.

Nor well were going my father's efforts to secure a military pension. His requests to complete the twenty-five years of army service were repeatedly denied. Sometimes, the authorities asked for more data, and my father's spirit sprang up, as he thought his case was being reviewed, and this time, the response might be positive, only to get disappointed again. The closest my father came to securing the coveted pension was when he contacted his old war comrade, who by then had reached the rank of general and held an important post in the army command. They even met in Odessa, or my father traveled to Moscow. I remember him in a good mood, telling my mother how well he was received by his former commander, who promised to help. However, that attempt ended like all others. I believe the general sincerely wanted to aid his former associate, and the matter was not an unusual one—the government did allow army officers who interrupted the service with a year or two remaining to complete their terms and receive a military pension, but not rebels like my father. Somewhere in the darkened vaults of his one-time employer's archives, I picture my father's file with a "no favors" stamp on the cover, making further consideration unnecessary.

Perhaps, deeper inside, my father realized that he had no chance of attaining the desired pension verdict, but continued the pursuit to delay an admission of his failure as a breadwinner. Meanwhile, he was getting the puny pay of a sales clerk. Most in his place would blame prejudice or rail against purported crooks who enjoyed the best in life while honest folk struggled to survive, but my father made no such pronouncements. He did not complain about his misfortunes or express hostility toward more fortunate ones. Through his work and family, he interacted with several such "prosperous" individuals, whose entrepreneurial zest was matched by their willingness to circumvent the rules, and showed no envy or resentment toward them. Having served as an instrument of intolerance and oppression in his younger years, my father now revealed a surprising understanding of life's complex pathways. At the same time, he remained true to himself. He recognized that, without a profession or economic freedom, his principles hindered his ability to earn a decent living and never preached them to me; yet, I somehow shared his values. Even as a child, I recall the confidence and pride that manifestations of my father's character filled me with. He was no failure in my eyes, and I couldn't care about the material possessions missing from my life (albeit I wasn't the one who charted the family's budget).

4. Lucky Break

The years of frustrations and setbacks took their toll on my father's personality—balanced and optimistic by nature, he became irritable and withdrawn. Unlike my mother, who got things off her chest quickly, he kept his grievances inside and was usually on the receiving end of their arguments. They argued often. Both were fluent in Yiddish, which they spoke when quarreling in my presence; however, not understanding the words made me feel no better. The changes in my father's character affected our relations, too. Somewhat distant during my childhood, they became increasingly antagonistic as I entered my rebellious teens. The reason for my father's earlier reserve was, I believe, a traumatic history with his sons from the previous marriage; as for our later clashes (which we both regretted in their aftermath), they stemmed from his growing sense of frustration and despair. He was pushing sixty and worked as a sales clerk in some store, facing the prospect of humiliating poverty to his days' end. His dream of me going to college did not look realistic either, as my school grades were not good enough to make up for an unlucky nationality and lack of connections. It seemed the last glimmer of hope was fading for my father when his life's grim countenance cracked an uneasy smile. All of a sudden, he landed a decent job, and a few months later, I was admitted to MIPT. My father's new job was managing a warehouse at an industrial plant. The pay was not excessive, but it was better than anything he had earned in his civilian career, and the slot itself was a solid, respectable position that carried no stigma of corruption. I do not remember the details, but he got that job almost by chance. Someone mentioned the opening in a conversation; my father went there with little hope of getting the job and was hired on the spot. It was a time of political thaw when employers no longer needed every approval to fill lower management roles, and maybe the interviewers at that plant were impressed by the applicant's desire to trade a job in the retail sector for one in their own.

To better illustrate the sector juxtaposition mentioned above, I shall describe my gymnastics coach's reaction to my father's job change. I was in my last high school year and already curtailed my sports activities, but had the coach's open invitation to participate in training sessions. I took advantage of that offer and, even when studying in Moscow, would come to the gym during recess Odessa stays to break a sweat and meet my former teammates. Our coach was a remarkable man: professional, hardworking, and devoted to his pupils. He practically substituted for a father to my boarding school friend, who was his most talented student and one of the neediest, with a single mother and two redhead-sisters living in a small room in a commune. The coach had his own family to feed, but he supported my friend financially, placed him in college, and later helped his protégé launch the latter's own coaching career. The coach offered the same college deal to me. It was similar to a sports scholarship in the United States but semi-official in the Soviet Union. Thus, my parents' worries about their son not getting higher education were misplaced—I did have a solid college option, but was interested in neither that college nor tying studies to sports, and never mentioned the coach's offer to my parents, afraid that they might force me to accept it.

My first gym visit as a warehouse manager's son occurred after a pause, so the coach asked me how I had been and how my parents were. I told him about my father's new job. "Why?" exclaimed the coach with surprise, "What didn't he like in the old place?" The question zapped me like an electric current. "What is he implying," I thought, "that my father is a crook?" The coach had known me since the fourth grade of boarding school (where he briefly worked as a part-time gymnastics teacher), and of course, he knew my parents, but had never been to my home and was unfamiliar with our financial situation. He must have thought we were doing well, not in the least because of my father's prior job. For the past few years, my father worked in a so-called commission store, which sold goods (clothing, jewelry, electronics) procured from the public. The items were second-hand but in good condition and usually unique. They could be heirlooms, electronic calculators that merchant sailors brought from overseas, and even wartime articles from Germany, such as my father's Singer. Perhaps my parents liquidated some of their assets through a commission store (although not the Singer, which was bought by my father's tailor, I believe). There were maybe one or two commission stores in the city, and like most businesses in the USSR, they belonged to the government. Odessa had a flea market where people could trade with each other directly, bypassing the government middleman, but that market was far away and open only on Sundays, so many preferred to sell through a commission store for less money (or buy there for more) rather than subject themselves to the inconvenience of the lost weekend and tiring travel.

Dealing with the public on both ends of the retail cycle made it easier to circumvent financial controls, and commission store employees were presumed to take advantage of those opportunities, or why would they be working there? The presumption of fraud was so blanket that people in my situation might not have even known what to be embarrassed about—that their family member was looked upon as a crook or that

[s]he wasn't one. Hence, the coach's surprise was natural, yet I wished he had not expressed it. My enthusiasm for a workout disappeared; I packed my bag and left. I was not angry at the coach, whom I always respected, yet I could not help feeling smeared. The coach must have sensed that something had gone wrong—he kept passing me (through my boarding school friend, with whom I stayed in touch) regards and invitations to come. When my father died, the coach sent condolences, asking whether I needed help or wanted to meet him. I conveyed my thanks and the message that I did not need anything, but had to go back to Moscow, and the meeting never happened.

My father took attitudes like the coach's philosophically; still, they must have bothered him, if only as a reminder that he held a position meant not for him but for someone more adept at utilizing its dubious benefits. The warehouse job relieved my father of that nuisance, helping him thaw. The protective shell built up over years of setbacks and a lack of understanding had softened, revealing his tender side. Our relations also improved, becoming more even and heartfelt. "I may have spanked you a few times when you were a boy," my father said to me during one of the sincere conversations we started having more often, "but it was how my parents disciplined me. I only meant well…" Yet, I held no grudge. I was more upset, as a child, by my father's aloofness than by those beltings and, in my teens, was saddened by bouts of hostility that erupted between us. Now, I welcomed the opportunity to annul past grievances and was surprised at how fast they were gone. My father enjoyed our new friendship, too, and there were more things he could look forward to. After losing all hope, life was worth living again.

He even kicked his smoking habit. My father was a two-pack-a-day smoker since the age of fifteen. He did not smoke inside the apartment, going to the staircase or leaning out of the window instead, but I recall a pleasant smell of tobacco and my father's morning cough. Despite such a heavy intake, he did not develop lung problems; however, his vascular system was badly affected. In those days, the link between smoking and a heart attack or a stroke was not well realized, and few attempted to contain or reverse the effects of the addiction. And although my father eventually quit, the damage had been done, resulting in his death from a stroke two years later. He had a meeting at work when he complained of a headache, collapsed on the floor, was taken to a hospital, and died there the next morning. My mother, Uncle Zinovy with Aunt Manya, and I were at his deathbed. The doctors told us my father did not suffer and never knew what had happened to him.

My father did not fear death, but he was terrified by the possibility of spending the last months or even years of his life bedridden, helpless, unable to care for himself. He would become withdrawn and depressed when witnessing such a condition. My mother told me once how they had visited the home of a person incapacitated by a deadly illness. On the way back, my father was silent and then spoke. "I only ask God to send me quick and easy death so I would not suffer myself and be a burden to others," he said. And his wish was granted. The curtain fell on the happy scene.

Chapter 4

RETURN TO CHUDNOV

1. Personal Salary

Starting my first job improved our finances considerably. Not that I felt deprived before, but my mother, with her high sense of responsibility, appreciated the changes the most. She continued to live in the same hated apartment; however, her material condition was better than it had ever been—I supplemented my salary with tutoring receipts while my mother clocked in extra hours at her job. She continued to work in the sanatorium, now as its personnel director. It was a junior nomenklatura position, usually reserved for retired military and KGB officers. The job did not pay much, but its typical holders had other sources of income, such as a military pension. It was a position my father could have aimed for if he had completed military service and not listed his nationality as Jewish. My mother was Jewish, had never served in the military, and was not even a Communist Party member, so how did she end up with such a title?

After the passing of her boss at the clinic, Dr. Cherednichenko, my mother transferred to the sanatorium to a medical statistician's position. Her new responsibilities included keeping business records and writing reports. From an early age, my mother showed remarkable diligence and commitment in anything she did. Those qualities were enhanced in the service of Herr Hunke, who could not have made a better choice at the Berlin "job fair" in the summer of 1943… Everything in our home was clean and organized: pots emitted a bright shine; dishes were spotless; clothes were ironed and arranged in stacks; and so were the linens. The rationale behind ironing bedsheets had always escaped me, as the moment they were first used, all wrinkle-smoothing efforts became a waste; however, for my mother, such an activity was an integral part of her lifelong crusade against chaos. And she brought that cause to the workplace, doing a far better job than what was perfectly acceptable. The management noted the unusual zeal and started assigning my mother more tasks, eventually asking her to handle the records of a few hundred sanatorium employees. The employee count was too small to warrant a dedicated personnel position, so my mother did that work within her statistician's duties. Meanwhile, the sanatorium grew, absorbing the old clinic, then other facilities, until it reached a size requiring a personnel department ("cadre department"), and as the sole member of a new administrative unit, my mother automatically became its head. But still, it took a few more years before she received the official title. The cause of the delay was her unsuitable background, including a "Jewish" surname, which sounded to the apparatchiks' ears like nails on a chalkboard. The sanatorium's chief physician confided to my mother about the hard time the Party bosses and central-office bureaucrats were giving him because of an improper individual in charge of personnel affairs. However, in the Soviet Union, the land of full employment and one employer, firing a worker was unheard of. I recall a story from my own place of work about a disturbed woman employee getting so upset with her boss' demands that she hit him over the head with a chair, knocking the poor man off his crutches, and she still kept the job—just was transferred to another department. Thus, it would be difficult to force my mother out right away, and later, the chief physicians did not want to do so.

As a personnel director, my mother reported to a chief physician. In the years she worked in the sanatorium, the chief physicians changed two or three times. I remember those events, as my mother complained at home about confrontations with the new bosses. Perhaps the early briefings at the Party offices fueled the chief physicians' antagonism, although my mother's direct, uncompromising manner also contributed to those clashes. She had little use for diplomacy and told her opinions about people to their faces. Every time a new chief took control at the sanatorium, relations with the personnel director began on a rocky footing, only to improve significantly over time. Chief physicians were doctors who chose administrative careers over practicing medicine, and those in the sanatorium were competent managers with a good measure of common sense. Whatever their initial attitude toward my mother was, they were won over by her commitment, character, and work ethic. But even chief physicians could do little to address my mother's primary concern—her salary. The same rules that obligated a pickle factory to pay full loader's remuneration to a fourteen-year-old boy at his temporary summer job precluded the chief physician from paying more to the boy's mother at her prestigious, permanent position. The only proper way to get around the wage-scale constraints was the so-called personal salary, which the sanatorium's management attempted a few times to arrange for their personnel director. A personal salary rewarded workers for outstanding performance and was conferred by ministry-level officials, who based their decision on the executive's recommendation as well as other aspects of the candidate's background. Those "other aspects" accounted for my mother's failure to get personal pay. "They did not give it to you because you were Jewish," whispered to my mother her central office counterpart, who, despite his former military career, proper nationality, and Party membership, was outraged by the unfair verdict. But the Soviet State's partiality toward its Jewish citizens was no secret and had been factored into people's expectations, so my mother took the rejection calmly. The setback did not affect her status as a key member of the sanatorium's administration, and the chief physician used overtime to bring my mother's pay to a more acceptable level (although she had to work more).

2. Kidney Stone

All those years, my mother did not visit Chudnov but kept in touch with her fellow townsmen Jews, also teenagers at the time of the war, who had survived the catastrophe. Their families perished at the hands of the Nazis, but the youngsters slipped through the cracks, finding refuge in the homes of a few heroic locals. I knew of two such survivors: one was a girl, two years my mother's junior, and the other was a boy, my mother's classmate. The girl was taken in by a Ukrainian woman, who adopted the orphan and christened her in church. Not that it mattered to the persecutors, but had they asked who the girl was, the woman could have honestly replied, "My daughter," and had the question been if there were any Jews in the house, the answer would have been a confident "No." The woman lived in a village near Chudnov and stayed under the radar throughout the German occupation. After the war, the girl (now a young woman) remained in Chudnov. She and my mother knew each other before the war and reestablished contact while trying to pick up the pieces of the shattered past. They exchanged letters and may have met in Odessa, but I was too young to remember such a meeting. I do remember my mother's classmate, though, the only other Jewish student in her class who survived the occupation. He was hidden by a local farmer's family, living with them until the Soviets returned. Later, he graduated from college and worked as an engineer at a factory. A few times, he visited Odessa and once stayed in my mother's sanatorium as a guest. My mother helped him with a pass. He was one of my favorite people, and I rejoiced when I saw him in our apartment or at the sanatorium during his stay there. I was a preschooler then, but still remember his face—high forehead, soft, straight hair flowing on both sides, and a kind smile. His eyes were sad when he smiled. Perhaps, like many children of the Holocaust, he heard the cries of angry Moloch calling on the escaped prey. I sometimes got a similar impression from my mother's looks and her reactions. But she had a strong will to live, countering the ghosts from the past with a flurry of daily activities. Her classmate, who was a sensitive and gentle person, could not muster such resistance. One day, he put on a clean shirt, a tie, and a suit, went outside, and threw himself under an oncoming train. He left no note, will, or other explanation. I recall my mother crying after receiving the dreadful news, and my father comforting her.

Through the renewed Chudnov contacts, my mother learned about the town's events after her departure and the fate of its many residents. She learned that when Stepan came home, leaving her in Zhitomir to wait for his return, he planned to go back the following day but was taken into custody by the police (probably at his parents' request) and kept there for several days. The rumors of him helping Jews spread around. He was detained by the police once more but got out aided by his boyhood friends who worked there. Realizing it was only a matter of time before he got arrested again, Stepan went to the woods and joined the resistance. His thorough knowledge of the forest was helpful to the fighters. When the advancing Soviet troops freed the area, Stepan joined the Red Army and continued westward. He was killed in battle in what is now the Czech Republic, a couple of months before the war's end. His family survived his death. I do not know what happened to the forest ranger, Stepan's father, but he died soon after the war. Stepan's older sister got married and moved to Zhitomir, while his mother, with the younger daughter (whose birth certificate my mother carried during the war), continued to live in the same isolated ranger's house a few miles from the Yagodinka village.

My mother was less successful in finding those who had helped her during her wandering years in the Ukrainian countryside and especially in Kiev, where she spent many months. It would have taken a miracle for Aunt Yelena and Masha to survive the arrest, but there was no trace of Maria Ilyinichna and Olen'ka either. The latter had more to fear from the returning Soviets than from the Nazis. Olen'ka's father-in-law's ties with the Germans placed him in the collaborators' category, casting a shadow of treason accusation on the entire family. I hope both women left Kiev with the retreating German troops and safely reached the free West, or their likely destination would have been some labor camp in the eastern parts of the Soviet Union. The two mother-daughter pairs were similar in their disposition and role in my mother's survival, yet, by mere chance, they found themselves on different sides of the great divide, vulnerable to the merciless winds of hostilities blowing in opposite directions. Mass displacements caused by the war had made it difficult to trace anybody beyond one's close circle of relatives and friends inside the USSR, while the slamming of the Iron Curtain after the fighting's end rendered all inquiries abroad futile. Thus, my mother's wanderings over occupied Ukraine and her life with Zum Dortmunder's owners in Berlin became a discarnate past; still, her Chudnov experience might be revisited.

Perhaps the reason my mother did not visit Chudnov for over thirty years was her difficult life, which suppressed any desire to rekindle the traumatic past, but as things got a little better, she began contemplating the trip. She wanted me to accompany her, to show me the places of her youth while having someone to support her emotionally. I was intrigued by the idea, yet didn't see it as a priority, and neither was my mother certain that she wanted to go. She kept mentioning the trip as a distant possibility until a confluence of events made it a reality.

That summer, I spent a few weeks on a job assignment in Moscow, working long hours and traveling long distances, often lacking time to eat or even drink. I stayed with my friends in their apartment in the city center. One night, I woke up from a sharp pain in the abdomen, as if someone was going through my intestines with a knife. I lay quiet for a while, hoping the pain would go away, but it was getting worse. Finally, I had to awaken the hosts. They saw me shivering from excruciating pain and called an ambulance. The ambulance arrived in half an hour. By then, the pain started to ease and, by the time we got to the hospital, was almost gone. The ER doctor told me that I had passed a kidney stone. He said it was one of the strongest aches humans could experience. It had to be true because after the pain went away, I felt such an uplift that I took a long stroll through predawn Moscow, reaching the apartment when it was already daylight. My hosts joyfully greeted me at the door.

I returned to Odessa in a poor physical state—had lost weight, felt tired, and the passed stone kept reminding me of its exploits inside my body. The condition persisted, so my mother arranged for one of their specialists to see me. "You are exhausted," the doctor said, "You ought to go to the country, breathe fresh air, drink raw milk, and everything will get back to normal." The doctor's advice reawakened the Chudnov dilemma, tipping it in favor of the trip. Before then, I visited the country with my parents twice—the first time as a two-year-old and the second when I was ten. The outings took place in the Ukrainian northwest, the area where Chudnov lay. Relative proximity to Chudnov did not make the town more accessible, though, as the lack of good roads rendered the detour a days-long adventure. Either way, my mother was not ready to go to Chudnov, but she enjoyed the climate, scenery, and lifestyle that were similar to those in her birthplace. I liked those sites, too, memories of which I saved with freshness and immediacy of a child's perception. Not much was remembered from the first trip[1] besides a few puppies and a wooden stick, but the second outing yielded more reminisces and even some photographs. We lived on a small farm, from where opened a

---

[1] My mother liked to tell a story about losing me there at a local farmers' market. She was talking to a seller, looked down, and did not see me next to her. My mother became scared as she heard (false) rumors about Gypsies stealing children with blond hair and blue eyes. She started running between stands, calling my name, but there was no answer. Finally, she found me on the other side of the market, sitting on the top of a fruit stand and enjoying the cherries the woman owner treated me with.

breathtaking view of rolling hills stretching all the way to the horizon line. The forest started on the left, and a tree line appeared on the right, planted there to slow the wind. I often went to my observation point at the farm's edge and sat there for hours, watching a colorful patchwork of fields, changing cloud patterns, and remote thunderstorms occasionally followed by a spectacular rainbow. The thunderstorms were the most exciting part of the show that nature staged before my eyes, with huge cracks of lightning illuminating the lead skies. The thunder was not always heard because of the distance, but sometimes the tempest turned toward the farm, and I could see an approaching wall of rain painting the ground dark. Despite growing up near the sea, I did not particularly like the beach but was beguiled by memories of the countryside and needed little persuasion to choose Chudnov as a recuperation point, while my mother now had an excuse to brush aside her doubts. So, we packed our bags, got onto the train to Zhitomir, took a connecting train there, and soon arrived at the Chudnov-Volynski station, a few miles away from Chudnov.

My mother made no advance arrangements, and nobody met us at the station. Such planning may appear too adventurous to a modern traveler, especially in the West, but it was commonplace in the Soviet Union of the time. Even on my business trips to Moscow, I rarely secured accommodations ahead of time and started looking for a place to live when already in the city. Despite the late start, I always managed to find something—a room in a hotel, a bed in a friend's home, and, when it all failed, stayed in the apartment of Uncle Zachary's distant relatives. Upon arrival in the capital, I would put my suitcase in a locker at the train station, take a small bag with essentials, and roam the town in search of shelter. Individual reservations were unavailable in Soviet hotels—one had to show up at the registration desk to discuss the stay. The reason for such a personal approach was the country's lack of a retail payment system other than by cash, plus room-seekers had to show an internal passport to prove they were out of town, as hotels were not allowed to lodge local residents. Moscow had more hotels per square kilometer than any other city in the country, but not enough to satisfy the demand. In the central part of the city, hotels rarely accepted random guests. Some places catered to foreign nationals; others housed individuals and groups in higher standing (for whom arrangements were made in advance at the behest of government officials and organizations), and, in certain cases, hotel managers extended favors to the properly introduced. The rest of the public (regular citizens with no suitable connections) scoured the capital's outskirts, searching for rooms. For complete outsiders, the best bet was a few massive buildings far from the city's center that offered "two-star" accommodations—four or five beds per room, a bathroom at the end of the hall, and no meals. The lodgers were a diverse contingent, with different habits and regard for other people's comfort. Most rooms had only a ceiling light, which stayed on as long as some roommates talked or read. In addition, many guests were heavy smokers who filled ashtrays with cigarette butts and the entire premises with smoke so dense that, according to an illustrative Russian expression, "one could hang an ax in the air." And despite all those headaches, getting such digs was considered a stroke of luck.

Having traveled to the Soviet capital many times, I was no newbie in the room-seeking business and, more often than not, found alternatives to the big "bunkhouses" described above. Once, I got a private room in a hostel, acting on a tip from my boss, who had stayed there before. The hostel occupied one floor in an office building and belonged to some ministry (probably the one that governed our firm), which used the place to house not-so-special attendees of special events. I mentioned my boss' name to the woman manager, gave her a box of chocolates, and she took me in. The room was plain (a bed, a nightstand, a closet, a table, and a chair) but clean, quiet, and, most importantly, for my sole use. Before then, I always shared living quarters with others. The room where my family lived, the common facilities in the apartment, a dormitory, and sleeping compartments on a train... all involved people who did not need my permission to come aboard. That hostel room was the first proper residence where all four walls and everything in between were at my complete disposal. I had a separate room in Aunt Fanya's commune when I wrote my graduate thesis in Kiev, but that room felt like it was shared with an absentee owner, plus my aunt overwhelmed me with her care. And if there were other instances of sequestered living, they ought to be too brief to note.

Like sleep, being alone is a physiological need, albeit its level varies markedly from person to person. Perhaps my own such requirement was relatively high—I had always handled isolation well, yet did not fully realize its deficit until that hostel stay. I lived there for ten days, and every morning, I woke up with greater energy, confidence, and a sense of fulfillment. Pity it ended so soon.

3. Bed and Breakfast

Despite their system's emphasis on the predictable (or maybe because of it), in private matters, Soviet people left a lot to chance. They had few tools to help them schedule affairs, yet often disregarded what they had, opting for more romantic paths. Case in point, only a tiny fraction of Soviet subjects had a phone at home, so social visits rarely involved prior notice (as it was everywhere before the rise of telecommunications), but even when phone service was available, most showed up unannounced. After all, a phone call was akin to asking for permission to come, which implied such permission could be denied—an inconceivable scenario among relatives and friends. I, for example, was never annoyed when at home by the sudden appearances of my associates, and if I happened to be occupied, I would invite the guests in, offer them a drink, a magazine, or a book to read, and continue with my business. And it was less formal in places like Chudnov, with its simpler lifestyle and greater hospitality of residents, where a similar welcome extended to strangers. My mother made no reservations seeking shelter during the war, and now her story was known in the area, where some still remembered her family, so we did not worry about finding a place to stay.

It was late afternoon as we got off the train at the Chudnov station. The last time my mother trod on that platform was over thirty years ago when she returned from Zhitomir on the second day of the war. She went into the town on foot then, but now, there was a bus service. The bus stop was in front of the station. Across the street stood a large house with a sign "Hotel" above the entrance. My mother had the coordinates of her former Chudnov neighbors' kin, with whom she corresponded after the war and who many times invited her to come. That was where we were heading; however, so late in the day, if the hosts happened to be away, not much time remained to find another place to sleep. Thus, I suggested checking the guest house across the street to find out if we could stay there overnight. My experience with Moscow hotels did not entail high expectations—perhaps the place across the street had no vacancies, or it had no water, or the door was padlocked—so we were pleasantly surprised when greeted by a baba[2]-concierge, who offered us a full choice of accommodations. The hotel had only three or four rooms, yet it was tidy, quiet, and even had a shower (it must have had one, as I recall a pleasant sensation of clean sheets touching my unsoiled skin). My mother and I were the only guests that night, but we were too tired

---

[2] A country woman of middle or old age, no longer concerned with her appearance.

after the long trip to fully appreciate the luxury of having the entire hotel to ourselves. We quickly fell asleep, waking up the next morning, rested and ready to face the formidable past.

I wouldn't have minded staying in that hotel a little longer (at least until we finalized our itinerary). I felt uncomfortable lodging in other people's homes, plus the hotel was close to the town and cost us very little, but my mother was eager to dive into the Chudnov-remembered, and the hotel's management would likely have balked at the extended stay. Anyhow, even one night was a nice touch, a reflection of small-town hospitality unheard of in larger cities. Thus, I did not voice my wishes; we took our belongings, crossed the street, and boarded a bus, which, in about twenty minutes, arrived at Chudnov proper. As the bus entered the town, my mother clung to the window, trying to discern familiar objects, but could not find any—the old structures had been destroyed during the war or razed later, giving way to new development. "I was told I would not recognize Chudnov," my mother kept repeating… until we reached our destination.

I do not remember if the woman who opened the door had met my mother before, but she instantly acknowledged the visitors and warmly invited us inside. The news of our arrival spread quickly, and by the afternoon, people began to assemble in the living room. The hosts set up a dinner table. The majority of guests were of my mother's generation: Chudnov Jews who evacuated as children at the beginning of the war and returned after the liberation. They had selective memories of the prewar Chudnov and did not experience German occupation; however, they knew the stories of death and survival, and they knew the people who could tell more. There were no accounts of my grandmother and her younger daughters' capture by the police, but it was known that their remains lay in mass graves in the park, among fifteen hundred other Jews, victims of the Chudnov massacre. We visited that site the following day. Finding my grandfather's burial place was a more difficult task. My mother did not remember where in the forest she and Stepan had laid to rest her father's body that awful night. There were no markers, and the small mound raised by Stepan had leveled off long ago. Stepan's mother and sister lived nearby, but it was unlikely Stepan had told them the grave's coordinates. Someone at the table mentioned Stepan's friend Ivan, who lived in Yagodinka. He grew up with Stepan—they went to school, fought in the resistance, and later joined the Red Army together. Ivan probably knew more about the events of those days and even the location of the grave. My mother was glad to hear about Stepan's friend, but she hoped to get some answers from that evening's audience and possibly meet someone who used to know her family.

Requiring perhaps a larger space than our hosts' living room, the Jewish population of Chudnov was rather small, especially compared to its prewar size. The low total and human losses in the war had made Chudnov Jews of my grandfather's age (who could be the most helpful guides into the past) a rare find; however, there was one such individual in the town, whom our hosts had sent for soon after we knocked on their door. He showed up late, bursting into the room as if being chased by wolves. He was a strange man, about seventy years old, skin-and-bones, short and stooped, with a large, bald head and a long, hooked nose. The lone seniority rendered him a de facto community historian, in which capacity he attended the gathering. He escaped the Nazi occupation but endured his share of woes and likely lost many family members. At the table, he sat immovable, staring at one point and waking up in feverish response when drawn into a conversation. Mixing Russian and Yiddish words, he started saying he remembered my mother's parents. I saw an expression of distrust on my mother's face—she suspected the old man was trying to put on airs. "Did you know my father?" she asked. "Of course, I knew your father!" upped the old-timer. "What was his trade? What did he do for a living?" my mother continued the test. "He, he," stumbled the old man, "he was *abisl speculant*[3]; he sold bluing!" "No," replied my mother satisfactorily, "my father sold horses."

The next day, our hosts took us around the town. A small regional center, Chudnov offered few tourist attractions; however, our sites of interest were what my mother knew, such as her old house. The house was no longer there, like most other places she remembered, but our guides were able to pinpoint the locations of the former shapes. They brought us to where my mother's home used to be. "This is where we lived," my mother said to me. The area had been cleared, paved with asphalt, and now contained a granary with a parking lot in front. My mother's eyes became teary. For a moment, she saw another picture: a dusty road, ramshackle houses, her relatives and neighbors—a vibrant community wiped out by the beast's fiery breath. We visited the park where mass executions of Jews had taken place, the site where my mother's school once stood, and other spots, such as the old market. The market was still active but closed for the day. We also met a few people who couldn't make it to the reception the day before… and returned home in the evening, tired and full of impressions.

---

[3] Russian-Yiddish, "a hustler."

4. Ranger's Farm

My mother did not forget the other reason for coming to Chudnov—my health. We had several offers to stay, including one from our Chudnov hosts, but despite its quaint atmosphere, the town was not what the doctor had ordered. Hence, the village of Yagodinka became the next logical step in filling the prescription. It was the place my mother knew well, where her family spent summers before the war, where her father was still remembered, and where he was buried under the forest trees... The village lay ten miles north of Chudnov, not far, if away from main roads. Our Chudnov hosts arranged the transportation, a light pickup truck from someone's place of work, and the following morning, we set out for Yagodinka. The woman my mother and I had been staying with accompanied us on the trip.

The weather was perfect as we rolled out of Chudnov: clear and mild, with white puffs of clouds adorning the blue skies. Soon started farm fields intermixed with forest patches. A grain elevator appeared straight ahead. As we passed it, the truck turned onto an unpaved local road and continued toward a tree mass in the distance. The village was behind the trees—a cluster of neat houses and little orchards. We asked at the first house where Ivan (Stepan's friend, mentioned at the initial Chudnov gathering) lived, and the owners directed us to his address... Nobody answered the door. "They are not home," said a woman who came out of the neighboring house, "They went to Kiev to see their children and will be back in a week. Anything I can help you with?" We explained who we were and the purpose of our visit. The woman invited us to her home and brought refreshments. My mother was disappointed she had missed Ivan. We still had time to meet him, as we planned to stay for more than a week, but my mother was eager to locate her father's resting place as well as get other information Ivan might provide.

We all sat down at the table. A lifelong resident of Yagodinka, a small village where everybody knew each other, Ivan's neighbor had heard about my grandfather, and of course, she knew Stepan's mother and sister. My mother asked how the two women were. The host replied that they were alright. Stepan's sister had a history of mental illness but was now in remission and lived with her mother, helping tend the farm. "You are welcome to stay in my house," Ivan's neighbor said to my mother and me, "or I can assist you in finding a place." Her house was small (like most houses in the countryside) and likely crowded when filled with all its occupants, so my mother replied she preferred the second option. Finding a room in Yagodinka ought to be even easier than in

Chudnov. The smaller the locality, the friendlier its people were, plus we intended to pay for the lodging. The only issue was convincing the future hosts to accept the money, as most would have offered a free stay due to my mother's story and her connection with the place... It was still early in the day to look for accommodations, as most residents were at work, and suddenly, my mother expressed a desire to visit the ranger's house. "It is so close," she said, "and we have a car. I will talk to Stepan's mother and go back." Everybody at the table got up and walked toward the truck. The driver got behind the wheel, my mother and our Chudnov host sat next to him in the cabin, Ivan's neighbor and I climbed into the back, and the truck started toward the ranger's farm.

Had Ivan not been absent at the time of our call, we would have lodged in his home, and my mother would not have rushed to meet with Stepan's mother that day. They would have met later or not at all. The tragic circumstances of my mother's last stay at the ranger's house did not invite repeat visits, while recollections of the ranger's wife's frenzied attempts to stop Stepan from leaving made their place an even less appealing destination. But the passage of time had dimmed my mother's memories and dulled her aches. Her return ought to be a triumphant event impervious to the living tokens of old torments, and she also pined to connect with the past, which hushed the rumbling echo of the ancient farewell.

The truck skirted the forest, entered a gap in the trees, and, in a little while, came to a halt at a wide glade. It was the ranger's farm. In the center of the glade was a corral with a few fruit trees nearby. Inside the corral was a cow. A small house was perched at the farm's edge, about a hundred feet from where the truck stopped. Chickens and ducks flocked around the feeder on the house's side. Two female figures in long dresses and headscarves stood in front of the house. The closest one was an old woman; she stared at the vehicle, trying to discern the people inside. The other female, who seemed my mother's age, kept behind, half-turned toward the house as if ready to retreat at any sign of danger. The women were Baba Olya and Nadja, Stepan's mother and sister. They had heard the sound of an engine and came out to meet the visitors.

Baba Olya recognized my mother right away. She knew the latter had survived the war and likely knew of my existence, but was unaware we were in the area. Nonetheless, there was not the slightest hesitation in the old woman's response, as if she had been waiting for that moment all those years. She threw her hands up, stepped toward my mother, and embraced her. At that point, Nadja figured out who the visitors were and approached to greet us. My mother introduced me to Stepan's family, then presented our Chudnov companions. Ivan's neighbor needed no introduction. Baba Olya invited everybody in the house. She told Nadja to look after the guests and retreated with my mother to the woods. They returned half an hour later with their eyes still wet. "Baba Olya wants us to lodge here," my mother said to me, "She promised to take good care of you." Later on, when recounting that conversation with the host, my mother told me how Baba Olya apologized for her actions during the war, for holding Stepan back many years ago. "Now that you have a son of your own," she said to my mother, "you must understand how I felt then. But God has punished me. Had I let Stepan go with you, he might have been alive today." I noted how cleverly Baba Olya framed her case. Despite lacking basic education and spending most of her life on a farm, she was intelligent and lucid, capable of reading people's minds while skillfully masking her own. I liked the old woman. She had an aura of lightness that often comes with advanced age, when passions and fears recede, revealing the crux of the years passed and an arched passage ahead, which is just another juncture in life—inevitable, natural, almost desirable—with every step toward it marking the return of innocence. In physical appearance, Baba Olya was not a typical Ukrainian peasant, either. Unlike her children, who must have taken after their father, she evinced features commonly attributed to the Nordic type: slender, with a narrow face, nicely sculpted aquiline nose, and a net of fine wrinkles around her eyes, arranged in an agreeable pattern. When I picture her today, standing in a long dress, she reminds me of a female incarnation of Boris Godunov, as portrayed by Boris Christoff in the famous opera during the tormented character's more peaceful moments.

    I gladly agreed to stay. Even before Baba Olya's invitation, I thought of the ranger's farm as a perfect setting to heal my wounds. It was as close to nature as one could imagine within civilization's confines. Any more of the countryside would have been wilderness. The place did not even have electricity. Lenin's electrification plans[4] did not presume, I trust, pulling a power line for two miles from the nearest village to light a single house. Another advantage of the farm's location was its privacy and abundance of space. Had we rented in Yagodinka, more time would have been spent inside the premises, while the house's lot would have felt like an animal enclosure in a zoo. But the ranger's farm had no neighbors and no fences, with the entire forest as a backyard. The only things that worried me were my mother's bad memories and her rough history with the host. I knew then of Baba Olya's histrionics during my

---

[4] A much-lauded Lenin's program of electrification of the country.

mother's and Stepan's departure from the ranger's house years back, but not of the woman's antisemitic diatribes and her threats to report the unwanted lodgers to the police. I learned about those remarks from my mother's notes when already in the United States. Perhaps my mother had those memories suppressed until they came to the surface, pulled up by the chain of events that made her story, but then, at the ranger's farm, she seemed happy and looking forward to spending time with the former opponent. Therefore, I hoped that the bitter part would remain dormant throughout our visit.

My mother's and my belongings were still in the truck. We took them out, said goodbye to our travel companions, and started settling at the ranger's place. The absence of electricity compelled the farm's dwellers to live by the sun—wake up at sunrise and go to bed upon the onset of darkness. There were candles and kerosene lamps in the house, but they did not make enough light to sustain daytime activities such as reading. The house was small—two or three rooms. There used to be a barn on the property (where my grandfather was hiding from the police), but it burned down during the war. The other structures included a storage shed and a pen where the farm's animals were kept in winter. Baba Olya set up a cot for me in her room, which she divided by a curtain, while my mother and Nadja shared the other room.

It was getting dark. My mother and I were tired and drowsy, and we parted to our beds. I was almost asleep when Baba Olya came from the yard. She walked to her side of the room, and I heard her lie on the bed. For a few moments, it was quiet. "Misha," she spoke suddenly behind the curtain[5], "have you ever seen a camel?" A bit surprised, I replied that I indeed had observed such an animal. Baba Olya then explained that she had visited her older daughter and grandchildren in Zhitomir, and they had gone to the zoo. There, for the first time in her life, she saw a camel. "What an amazing creature," she added. I was amused by the old woman's reaction, which I would normally expect from a child. My only question was why a camel, and not an elephant or a giraffe, impressed Baba Olya so much. There were other animals in the zoo, I am sure, some more exotic and rare. Perhaps she had been told that a camel was a domesticated animal, like a horse, and fantasized about having such a

---

[5] People in that part of the country spoke mainly Ukrainian. Some town residents spoke Russian, too; however, it was all Ukrainian in the village. Baba Olya and Nadja did not speak Russian but understood it well, while my spoken Ukrainian was rusty (I had not used it since boarding school). So, the farm's owners talked to me in Ukrainian, and I talked to them in Russian. My mother communicated the same way.

horse. But I was too tired to probe Baba Olya's infatuation with camels—I wished her goodnight and sank into my dreams.

The next several days were almost idyllic. We enjoyed the beautiful weather, rejuvenating air, peacefulness of the serene environment. My mother looked happy. She and Nadja spent hours in the forest, picking mushrooms and berries. A few times, I joined them, and once went with Nadja by myself—she taught me how to tell edible mushrooms from poisonous ones. I did not notice in her any signs of mental illness; she seemed normal, only very quiet and shy. She never argued with her mother, obeying the old woman's every command. During that forest expedition, we found a huge, meaty mushroom, and Baba Olya made from it such a tasty soup that I remember even today. She did take good care of her guests. Most of the day, she stayed busy, tending the garden, feeding animals, and cooking meals. Sometimes, she rested in the house during the day—my mother and I were outside then. We all got together for dinner. Perhaps that was Baba Olya's daily routine, but it gave my mother enough space for comfort. After the first emotional exchange, the two women spoke little about the past.

The food we ate was mainly from the farm and the forest. The hens laid eggs, the kitchen garden supplied vegetables, and the trees near the corral provided the fruits of the season, while the forest added berries and mushrooms. Early in the morning, Baba Olya or Nadja milked the cow. The cow did not like me personally, but its milk contributed to a delicious breakfast. The milk surplus was used to make butter, farmer cheese, and sour cream. Like most villagers, Baba Olya and Nadja ate little meat in summer, but on the occasion of our visit, they slaughtered a duck. All that food could be labeled organic today and, thanks to the abundance of fresh air and Baba Olya's culinary skills, engendered some of the most enjoyable meals I've ever had. Items such as salt and bread were bought in the village, which was Nadja's job. During our stay, she went there once or twice. My mother accompanied her.

Despite its many resources, the farm was not self-sufficient. Two women, one in her seventies and another mentally ill, could hardly run it that way. They received help from relatives who lived in the area and brought coal in winter, made house repairs, and checked on the farm's residents from time to time. But even with such assistance, it ought to be tough and lonely in that place, especially in winter. I did not understand why Baba Olya had not sold the farm or exchanged it for a house in the village years ago. She likely collected a pension, while Nadja received disability benefits, which should have been enough for them to live on. They sold some farm produce on the market, but I doubt the proceeds could justify such a harsh, primitive existence. Perhaps, having lived that way their entire lives, Baba Olya and Nadja saw things differently; still, it was difficult for me to explain their choice as mere habit.

5. Tall Grass

While at the ranger's farm, I did not go to the village or anyplace beyond the farm's close surroundings. As a convalescent, I wanted to absorb nature's medicine to the fullest. And there was not much to do in the village, anyway. On the trip, I took with me a few books and often read them in the tall grass at the farm's edge. The air was so quiet, so full of aroma, it made me sleepy. One afternoon, about a week into our stay, I was having such a repose and succumbed to the sleeping spell. I woke up from the sound of my mother's voice calling my name—she yelled at the top of her lungs. I got on my feet, rising above the grass. My mother approached me. Her hands were shaking; her eyes shifted from side to side. "I have been calling you," she exclaimed, "Why didn't you answer? I thought something bad happened to you…" My mother's behavior astonished me. I would retire with a book every day, sometimes dozing off in the grass, but it did not bother her before. Why didn't she assume I was asleep or had gone to the woods for a minute? And what could have happened to me in such a place? My mother's outburst was irrational, and I realized that she had used up her tranquility quota. The peaceful surroundings suddenly revealed their other side, that of treachery and mortal danger. "I was asleep and did not hear you," I replied. My mother calmed down a little, but something bothered her. "Did you see the bed Baba Olya sleeps in?" my mother said, "It is my parents' bed. It was among the things Stepan took with us when he smuggled my father and me out of Chudnov. She appropriated them. I must tell her," and my mother began recounting other items Stepan had put into the horse cart thirty-five years ago. "What do you need this bed for?" I said, "We are not going to haul it to Odessa. The other items are long gone, and there was nothing valuable among them, anyway." "Of course, I do not need that bed," my mother replied, "but she should have offered to return it." I agreed, adding that my mother could not say anything now, since she had effectively settled the matter by accepting Baba Olya's invitation to stay. The old woman refused the rent money, hoping perhaps to pay her debt that way. "Alright," said my mother, "I will not mention the bed. We are leaving soon, anyhow." Our stay at the ranger's farm was almost over, so I hoped proper etiquette would be observed until the end, although it seemed a little creepy that Baba Olya slept in the bed once owned by a person who slept forever in the ground a couple of hundred yards away, murdered in her home.

Our hosts did not know where my grandfather was buried, or that was what they wanted others to believe. I am sure Stepan did not tell his parents the grave's location, but the ranger, who knew every tree in the forest, could not have missed a fresh mound of earth nearby or not realized what it was. I doubt, though, that he told his wife about the find. She must have discovered the mound on her own but said nothing to her husband, and they never discussed what had happened the night the mound appeared or mentioned who lay under it. They did not want to know. The initial relief of the unwanted boarder's riddance was followed by remorse for the rest of their time. They probably told themselves they had no choice, as the presence of that man around the house threatened their lives. They could have even blamed him for their trouble; however, he had not come uninvited, and even if he had, it was still a betrayal of human life. Thus, more than thirty years later, Baba Olya wished the episode that my grandfather's resting place was a reminder of had never happened. And as long as nobody pointed out the grave's location to her, she had a choice of knowing or not knowing where it was. She chose not to know. So, my mother planned to go to the village to see Ivan, but he preempted her...

We were having breakfast with Baba Olya and Nadja when we heard footsteps outside, and a tall, lean man walked through the door, almost touching the casing with his head. He greeted the hosts unemotionally, then introduced himself to my mother and me. The man was Ivan. He returned from Kiev yesterday, was told by his neighbor that my mother was looking for him, and decided to walk to the ranger's farm to meet her. Yes, Stepan showed him where her father was buried—he would take us there. Baba Olya invited Ivan to the table, but he replied that he had already eaten and would wait outside. My mother and I finished our meal and got out of the house. Ivan was sitting on the porch, plucking grass. He rose as we approached him. "Follow me," he said and started toward the forest. I remember the helpless expression on Baba Olya's face as my mother and I walked away. By all accounts, she should have joined us to partake in honoring my grandfather's memory (and to make sure Ivan did not say anything unflattering about her), but couldn't overcome the thirty years of denial, and there was another reason, not known to me at the moment, that kept her behind.

I do not recall Ivan's occupation, but he was not a farmer—maybe he was a mechanic or a manager. He was collected and tactful, with probing eyes that revealed intelligence and insight. Ivan had not been near the ranger's farm for a while and wandered in the forest before stopping at the gravesite. He seemed uncertain, as if considering the nearby spots, which looked exactly like the one we were standing on. "It is here," he said. "Are you sure?" my mother asked. Ivan answered that he was.

Nothing distinguished that forsaken patch of land. There was no mound or sign—just grass strewn with pine cones and tree bark. We stood quietly for a minute; then, each of us stuck a small tree branch into the ground. "I wanted to invite you to my home," said Ivan, "Pity we were away when you came, but you still have a day or two. Pack your things, and go with me to Yagodinka. You will stay at my house, and then I will arrange a lift for you to Chudnov."

Ivan's invitation could not have come at a better time. We had to go to Yagodinka, anyway, and his company would have made for an easier trip. Besides, after the panic attack the day before, my mother showed increasing signs of restlessness, which could further strain relations with the hosts. As for my condition, I felt much better already and was eager to resume regular activities. Another reason for my mother's enthusiastic embrace of Ivan's offer was the chance to interview him at length, to ask questions only he could answer. And finally, Ivan's presence might smooth the farewell between my mother and Baba Olya, preventing it from taking a wrong turn... It all went well. Baba Olya asked us to come again, and my mother replied that she would, but both women knew they saw each other for the last time. As we reached the forest, I looked back. Baba Olya stood in the middle of the field, staring in our direction. She waved goodbye to me, and I waved to her back.

6. Disclosure

Ivan's house was small but well-maintained. The stucco exterior was painted white, with decorative blue shutters adorning little windows. The house's lot was not big, either. It had a kitchen garden and several fruit trees, but no animals other than a dog. The house's interior was spotless. Ivan introduced us to his wife, a pleasant, kindly woman. She and her husband lived in the house alone and gave us a separate room. The rest of the day, Ivan spent with my mother in the garden, answering her many questions. He told the details of her father's death, how the ranger prodded him out with a pitchfork, how the policemen shot my grandfather in the back. "But why did the police come in the first place?" inquired my mother, "Who alerted them?" Ivan paused. "Stepan's parents did," he said, "The ranger and his wife." My mother gasped in astonishment. Despite Stepan's accusatory words to his parents after her father's killing, she did not believe the ranger couple was involved. She thought their threats to go to the police meant only to force Stepan to relocate the inconvenient lodgers; plus, Baba Olya had sworn to my mother during their initial chat in the forest that she had nothing to do with the raid thirty-five years ago. "His wife?" my mother repeated after Ivan, "Do you mean the ranger did it?" "No," said Ivan, "they both went to the police." "Is there any proof?" my mother continued in disbelief. "There is no proof," Ivan replied, "but everybody in Yagodinka knew it, and Stepan told me himself that his parents were responsible."

My mother could not believe what she had heard, and I had doubts, too. The story did not square with the behavior of the policemen who had ransacked the farm. There was no doubt the ranger had exposed my grandfather to the executioners during their search, but if the original tip came from the farm's owners, how could the policemen not know my mother was also hiding there? After killing their victim, they entered the house, not looking for her in particular, but asked pro forma about "more Jews" and left when told there were none. And neither did it make sense for Stepan's mother to bring the police and then lie to them (although one can only guess what she might have said had Stepan not been in the room). There were others who could suspect my grandfather was at the ranger's place and who had motives to report him. One such individual was Ivan Chernenko, who took my grandmother's jewelry, promising to conceal her and the twins, but did not keep his promise and likely gave them away. At the time the police raided the ranger's farm, Chernenko was a policeman himself. He knew of Stepan's attempts to help my mother's family and could have sent the hounds on the trail to ensure nobody was left to claim the ill-gotten jewels.

Other signs pointed to Stepan's parents' involvement. The authorities did not retaliate against the couple, even though hiding Jews was a capital offense. Of course, the ranger was known in the area, with friends and associates who now held important posts in the local government and might have swept the matter under the rug; however, Stepan's admission of his parents' complicity was the strongest evidence of their guilt, and there were other clues, such as Baba Olya's conduct during our sojourn at the farm. Her inability to visit my grandfather's grave, her willing isolation and pronounced fatalism signaled a remorse pleading for a sentence. She enjoyed my company, and we often talked about subjects beyond camels (albeit not about the events of the war). During one of those conversations, Baba Olya told me how she was struck by an illness a year earlier. "I could not stand on my feet," she said, "had a high fever and was coughing my liver out. I was sick for several weeks and prepared to die, but suddenly felt better and soon recovered. God gave me more time in this life." What astonished me in Baba Olya's story was not her belief that one could cough the liver out but that she had not sought medical help and must have refused one, as I cannot imagine that nobody offered to take her to a doctor or a hospital. She did not want any interference. It was between her and the Creator now, and nothing was to tamper with his judgment, which she would accept unquestionably and with great relief. I sensed she wanted me to know that.

Thus, if Ivan's story was correct and Stepan's parents did inform on my grandfather, the only explanation for my mother's "luck" was that they did not mention her to the police. My grandfather's presence on the farm posed a far greater danger to the owners than the presence of his daughter. Everybody in Yagodinka knew my grandfather, who had worked there for years. He was also well-known in the greater Chudnov area because of his past horse-trading activities. The ranger's farm was isolated but had many visitors, and even if my grandfather's face had not been such a familiar entity, his looks, demeanor, and speech revealed him as a Jew. I am sure he spoke Ukrainian and Russian with a heavy Yiddish accent, and in case any doubt remained, there was the ultimate test to diagnose a Jewish man. On the other hand, my mother spoke Ukrainian and Russian perfectly, was little known in the village, and, when appropriately dressed, looked like any other country girl. Besides, Stepan's parents knew that if she got arrested and their son discovered their involvement, they would lose him forever. But if my grandfather was exposed alone, it could be viewed as protecting not just their family but the Jewish girl on the Russian stove, too, a sacrifice any father would have made to save his daughter. That might be how the ranger and his wife justified their action; as for the victim, he was doomed, anyway, since nobody would have offered him asylum. My poor grandfather—he had no place to hide.

We stayed in Ivan's home for another day. The gracious hosts made our time very comfortable, but there wasn't much left for us to do in Yagodinka; plus, we had to go back to work. In the morning, a light truck arrived at Ivan's house, and the driver took my mother and me to the train station. There was no time to see our Chudnov acquaintances—my mother wrote them after returning to Odessa. She was happy with the trip, telling her friends about its many details. As for my kidney stone problem, it was completely gone.

7. Nadja's Letter

A year had passed since our trip to Chudnov when my mother received a note in the mail from an investigative government agency (I do not recall which one) requesting her to come. She was received by an official who offered her a chair and opened a folder on his desk. "Do you know Nadja Momot from Yagodinka village in the Zhitomir oblast?" he asked. My mother replied that she knew such a person. "She wrote us a letter where she mentioned you, and I am not sure what to make out of it," continued the official. He took a few handwritten pages out of the folder and handed them to my mother. It was a letter from Nadja. She wrote about my mother, who had a birth certificate in Nadja Momot's name but was not the real Nadja Momot. The real Nadja Momot was she, Nadja from Yagodinka—and the letter went into an incoherent, semiliterate account of the events that had led to the mixup. "I don't understand what she is saying," said the official. My mother told him the story. "So, why is she writing about it now?" the official asked, "What does she expect us to do? She sent this letter to Kishinev, a different republic[6], and they forwarded it to us. Is she normal?" My mother explained that the letter's author had been treated for mental illness in the past. "It surely looks that way," said the official, "I am going to close this case. Thank you for your help," and he saw my mother to the door. "I have an extra copy of this letter," he added, "would you like it as a souvenir?" My mother took the copy to show it to me. I read it with a mixed sense of amusement and pity. The letter was not so much about my mother as an attempt of a wandering mind to reclaim itself. As if the author felt that, together with the birth certificate, she had been deprived of her entire life: work, family, friends, and whatever else the poor woman never had. The remission was over, and I realized what had triggered the relapse: Nadja was alone now; Baba Olya was no more.

---

[6] Kishinev was the capital of the Soviet Republic of Moldova, while Odessa was in the Soviet Republic of Ukraine. Although geographically close, the two cities belonged to different national formations and are in different countries today.

Chapter 5

THE RUPTURE

1. Tectonic Shift

The nineteen-seventies in the Soviet Union marked the rise of a new phenomenon: emigration to the West. For the first time in the country's history, people were allowed to leave. The trend started soon after my army service, reaching a peak in the last year of the decade. The majority of emigrants were Jews, so the emigration was viewed as a Jewish one, but other nationalities, primarily Armenians and ethnic Germans, also joined the flight. As the patriotic zeal of the early Bolshevik and Great Patriotic War years fizzled out, Soviet citizens demanded better living conditions, presenting the government with a quandary. Having built a society on a materialistic promise, the communist rulers could no longer ignore those demands, while the centralized, planned economy was hardly capable of satisfying them. In addition, the State's customary waste and massive military outlay had rendered catering to individual needs an even more difficult task. Thus, the Soviets reached out to their adversaries—the capitalist West—for food, technology, and a favorable trading status. In return, the West, and especially the United States, requested from their reluctant partner liberalization steps, the most notable of which was allowing certain nationalities to emigrate. The Soviets agreed. They presented the new policy as a humanitarian gesture of family' reunification, and the flow began. No announcement had been made, but the word spread among the affected groups, whose members started to apply for exit permissions. Armenians were going to France, Germans to West Germany, and Jews were leaving for Israel, but after crossing the border, many of the latter changed their destinations to Canada, Australia, and the United States.

Looking back at those early emigration trickles, I now realize they were the first pieces falling off the crumbling edifice of communism—a process that took twenty more years to unravel—but then, inside that very structure, one hardly could foresee its downfall. If Soviet authorities were humbled by yielding to Western demands, they did not show it to their subjects, and especially to the beneficiaries of the new agreement. Those applying for exit visas were ostracized—denounced publicly at their workplaces and let go. The denunciations occurred at departmental meetings, where the prospective emigres' coworkers decried their former comrades' treasonous act. Naturally, the gravity of the offense warranted a dismissal. After all, every job in the country was a courtesy of the State, so an emigration visa application could be viewed as a resignation letter from the job.

Losing a job did not imply permission to leave, however, as the visas were occasionally denied. The denials could occur because of bad timing (when the emigration quota had been filled or relations with the West hit a snag), or they might happen randomly without any apparent reason. No explanations were given, but the unlucky aspirants could try again. Processing a visa application took three to six months, so the rejected applicants who had lost their jobs faced a lengthy period of uncertainty and hardship. All those issues rendered an attempt to leave the USSR a risky and stressful proposition, which was deliberate on the authorities' part. Their obstructionism was motivated not so much by malice (albeit there was a distinct whiff of it) as by a desire to make an example. The question raised before potential emigrants was whether the arguable benefits of living abroad in the future justified the real trouble now. And the answer was a loud yes, which further weakened the despotic rule.

2. Prince of Order

If there were a poll of which Soviet leader contributed the most to the eventual demise of the communist state, my vote would go to Nikita Khrushchev. His exposure and condemnation of Stalin's brutalities changed the country profoundly and without return. The disclosures did not question the regime's principles, though. Khrushchev was an idealist whose grandiose plans professed the communist system's superiority. He viewed Stalin's terror as an anomaly, a consequence of one man's flaws, whose repudiation would strengthen Soviet rule and bolster its moral authority. Besides, he likely remembered the unsettling sensation that the proximity to his late boss frequently produced. Others in the Party's higher echelons understood the danger that Khrushchev's reform posed to their power, so when he was removed from his post, they toned down Stalin's criticism and made a few attempts to rehabilitate the dead dictator's legacy. However, a return to mass repression was no longer possible. No more could the authorities crush dissent before it actually happened, which opened the door to a crucial agent of political change: passive resistance.

A remarkable case of passive resistance I encountered in the army. Our unit occasionally served as a punitive destination for privileged conscripts who had fallen out of grace or for higher-profile delinquents whom their prior command had failed to reform. Strict discipline and a grinding routine, distinguishing our troop, provided an effective tool for straightening out the violators, and it was aided by the threat of court-martial, which the regiment's combat-ready status made a more likely event. I was unaware of anyone being court-martialed, but witnessed a procedure that might have led to the charges. Such a procedure was invoked when a soldier disobeyed a direct order. It involved gathering four or five servicemen, in whose presence the commander repeated the directive. If the offender still refused to comply, he was arrested and brought before a tribunal.

The recipient of the court-martial warning I happened to observe was a rowdy sailor who argued with his superiors and violated the rules. The rule-breaker was already in his last "semester[1]" when I came aboard, so it seemed odd that he had managed to preserve bad habits in a strict environment like ours. My comrades-in-arms told me that the unit's old commanding officer, a navy commander, favored the rogue. Perhaps the soldier's look—he appeared younger than his age, almost a kid, with a

---

[1] The draft/discharge cycle occurred every six months.

round face and an innocent gaze—evoked the commander's sympathy, or the young man reminded the officer of his son (if he had one), I do not know, but the troublemaker enjoyed some slack.

The old commander retired soon after my debut in the unit, and his second-in-command took the helm. The new chief was an interesting man—intelligent and sophisticated, but coldly efficient and ruthless. He did not share the emotional attachments of his predecessor and held a particular dislike for the former favorite. All the baby-faced delinquent reminded the new commander of was a spoiled, angry brat, a nuisance to handle decisively and quickly… For a month, the commander pushed the rebellious seaman's buttons, scolding him at morning inspections and punishing every breach, and then ensued our regular drill, where the unit rose in the middle of the night and raced up the hill toward the installation. The regiment commander, who was a duty officer that night, instructed sergeants to load his disciplinary target with a few extra pieces of gear. Halfway toward the mountaintop, before we even reached the most challenging part of the climb, the overloaded sailor halted and slumped on the ground. The commander, who trotted along in a light jacket with a handgun on a strap, leaped toward the slacker. "Why did you stop?" he yelled. "I cannot run anymore," the sailor replied. He was puffing and wheezing, and sweat rolled down his face. With an extra load, he must have felt as I did during my first such exercise. "Run!" the officer commanded. The soldier's face flashed with anger. "I will not!" he cried out. The commander then stopped a group of marchers, lined them up, and turned toward the rebel. "I am ordering you to run!" he shouted. And the soldier ran.

The commander's crackdown did not end with the drill. The next morning, he sent the mutineer to the "*Hauptwacht*[2]," a military detention center in the Kommandatura building in Sevastopol. The *Hauptwacht* confinement was a disciplinary measure with a maximum term of fifteen days, and the officer in charge of the facility (the warden) could add up to fifteen days more. That was what happened to the disobedient sailor, probably at our commander's request. The additional fifteen days the violator spent in solitary confinement. He returned a changed man. Gone were the bravado and temper tantrums. He was quiet and had sadness in his eyes, which he lowered when crossing them with other sailors as if ashamed of something. That something was the realization he was not the man he strived to be, not strong enough to remain defiant, to deserve the respect and admiration of his fellow sailors that he enjoyed in the

---

[2] A guardhouse. In the Soviet army, a German derivative was used to name the facility.

past. The punishment had broken him. I never liked the fellow, but was sorry to observe the agony of a crushed ego. Still, one couldn't fault the commander, who took the necessary steps to affirm his authority. And he was successful, as nobody dared to challenge him after that... until the events I am about to describe.

Several months before my scheduled discharge, our unit received an addition: two soldiers transferred from other divisions as a punishment for their sins. Both were from the Caucasus region and, like me, about to complete the service that coming summer. The first newcomer was an Ossetian, a handsome fellow with an eagle-like profile and fierce eyes. Before the army, he played professional soccer in the league's second division in his native Georgia and, upon enlistment, was given a spot on the Southern Fleet's soccer team. Soccer was the most popular sport in the Soviet Union, and the players were idolized, so the new forward's life was not much different from that of a civilian. He did not have to dig dirt, get up at night, or freeze in the winter wind, clutching a submachine gun. All he had to do to fulfill his military obligations was to mark his presence daily, but could not abide even by that simple requirement and went AWOL for almost a week. Any other conscript would have been court-martialed as a deserter for such an offense; however, the soccer player got a break and was exiled to our mountain to learn what real military service looked like and better appreciate his former privileges. And the only soccer he would play was an occasional Sunday game on the base's rocky field with other sailors in army boots... The demotion did not dispirit our luminary, though; he quickly adjusted to the new environment and even seemed to welcome the experience. Although sybaritic and a little spoiled, he did not try to evade hardship and was a good company and a generous soul. He often told me of the pleasures awaiting him after the military service and would unlikely risk those prospects by causing trouble during his last months in uniform.

The second transplant was also a celebrity, but of a different kind. His claim to fame was having spent one-third of his army service in a detention unit, half of that in solitary confinement. He had been bounced from regiment to regiment, but nobody could alter his behavior. In a way, his transfer to our unit was a promotion (as a delinquent) for him and a compliment to us. The reputation preceded the man, so when we first met, I expected a muscular figure with a square jaw, steely gaze, and several tattoos, but in front of me stood a short fellow with a head of black hair, well-mannered and soft-spoken. He was not athletic and seemed well-groomed despite the army life and months of incarceration. His name was Arik. He was an Armenian from Baku who spoke perfect

Russian (as did the soccer player), which indicated a better upbringing in those parts of the USSR. Arik was assigned a bunk in my wing of the barracks. The following morning, forty-five seconds after the reveille, the roll call revealed his absence in the line. He probably was late the first time around. The sergeant went to hurry him up while the rest of the troop ran outside for a workout. When we returned to the barracks and started finishing our beds, I noticed a commotion on the other side of the aisle. The sergeant and a few seamen gathered between bunks, talking loudly and struggling with something (or someone). I came closer and, to my amazement, saw that they were trying to get Arik out of bed. He had never risen after a wake-up siren and now was holding onto his blanket, which a sergeant tried to pull away. Finally, Arik got up. At the morning inspection, the violation was reported to the duty officer, who punished Arik with a few hours of peeling potatoes in the kitchen.

A couple of days later, Arik did not get up in the morning again. This time, the sergeant was prepared and issued a direct order in front of an improvised sailors' line. It was unlikely one could be court-martialed for not getting out of bed on a regular day; however, Arik complied. He was given the assignment to clean the base's territory, but did nothing and, when asked about the litter on the ground, replied that it had been deposited after his efforts. Evidently, Arik was no combat material, so the commander made trash-picking the sailor's permanent duty, appointing a staff sergeant to supervise the endeavor. Arik's new boss was the most hated sergeant in the troop. He was a re-engaged serviceman about forty years of age, stocky, short, and with a voice that could drill a tunnel under our mountain. That voice was the primary reason Arik's sergeant was so disliked by the rank and file but valued by the officers. Even when spoken low, it was one of the most disturbing sounds I ever heard, and at a higher volume, the voice drove everybody insane. I still cringe when recalling it... Condolences started coming Arik's way, but, to everyone's surprise, he withstood the sonic assault without blinking an eye. I remember a scene where Arik walked down the compound's alley on a trash-picking mission, followed by the sergeant, who shouted in the sailor's ear. Arik would approach a few pieces of litter, pick up one piece, and continue walking. The sergeant would yell about the remaining trash, and Arik would pick it up, too. That routine repeated, again and again, assuring that the overseer made no less effort than the overseen. Arik was wearing the sergeant down.

A few more weeks passed, and at every morning inspection, Arik's name was brought up in conjunction with some breach (usually minor) of discipline. And every time, the duty officer reacted to the report with greater anger and menace. Meanwhile, Arik befriended several sailors, including me. "The command is pretty mad at you," I said to him once, "Aren't you worried they might cause you serious trouble?" "What can they do to me?" Arik replied, "I am not going to do anything stupid to get court-martialed; otherwise, the worst punishment is fifteen days in a military prison. I have been there many times and already miss it. Will relax in the solitary. The warden is my friend." I was skeptical, at first, about Arik's claim of friendship with the feared jailer, but changed my mind after seeing the former in a remote part of the base in his usual company of the stentorian sergeant. Both men bathed in the sunlight, chatted, smiled at each other, and the sergeant patted Arik on the back like a bosom buddy. In the evening, I asked Arik what was happening between him and the sergeant. "We are buddies now," Arik replied, "We drink wine[3] together."

Like his fellow exile, the soccer player, Arik developed a good rapport with many sailors and sergeants; still, his relations with the regiment's commanding officer remained tense. The commander kept receiving reports of Arik's violations, which did not please him. He was not a vindictive man, yet mindful of the troop's reputation and his own career. A military officer had to serve twenty-five years before he could retire with a pension. Most officers became eligible for retirement in their late forties, and for those who by then had not reached the rank of army colonel or navy captain, retirement was mandatory. That was how our old commander retired (although he was already a wreck, health-wise, and mostly absent during my short stint under his leadership). When the new commander took control, he held the rank of a major but was immediately promoted to lieutenant colonel[4]. He was in his mid-thirties, physically fit, and very bright, and had a good chance of receiving a colonel's star someday and continuing along the military path. Serving in an elite corps like ours could help an officer's career but hurt it, too, and which way it might go sometimes depended on the rank and file. A serious mishap caused by a conscript could tarnish his superiors' record. Perhaps it was why our officers fiercely proscribed alcohol (smuggled into the compound, sometimes) and were eager to crush other violations. The regiment commander came down on the earlier dissenter hard not to avenge the soldier's effrontery but because he viewed the latter as a potential embarrassment source. That sailor was a troubled young man with alcoholic tendencies. He was full of anger, whose self-destructive

---

[3] Strictly prohibited to conscripts.

[4] The rank associated with the position.

effects the commander used to break the unruly subordinate. Arik, on the other hand, was sensible and well-adjusted. He did not argue with his superiors, did not see them as enemies, did not hate them. It would be difficult to throw him off balance. The higher command sent Arik to our unit to punish him, but they cared little about what would happen afterward. They did not saddle our commander with reforming Arik and did not require any progress reports—they would rather not hear about that disciplinary nuisance ever again.

Arik's misdeeds had few consequences beyond our mountain, but inside the compound, the issue of insubordination remained. There was no chance that others might copy Arik, as he was an impossible act to follow; however, continuous violation reports and ineffectiveness of the response made a mockery of the military order. So, one day, the regiment commander came up with an ingenious solution to his Arik problem. He was a duty officer and received a report at the morning inspection of another Arik's breach. The commander erupted in a fit of pretended rage. "Such and such!" he shouted Arik's surname, "I've had enough! I do not want to hear this name again!" It sounded like something terrible was going to happen to the object of the commander's wrath—perhaps a strike by lightning or a fall into a suddenly opened precipice—but while waiting for such an event to occur, the sergeants stopped reporting Arik's misconduct. They left him alone. No longer was he bothered in the morning by wake-up attempts, sleeping as long as he wanted. After breakfast, he would disappear, supposedly to do some work under the supervision of the loud sergeant (who must have come to appreciate his assignment), but nobody knew what they were doing, and nobody cared. Soon began the discharge cycle, a two-month window, where conscripts with a better service record were released before those with a poorer one. Arik was let go with the first batch.

3. Political Education

Arik's case was unique, enabled by his exceptional persona—a mix of geniality, rational mind, and unshakable self-assurance. He could have become a successful businessman; I somehow picture him as a shipping magnate. His motives concerned me little. He did not volunteer to serve in the army and belonged to an ethnic minority subordinate to imperial dictate, so one might not expect him to be a patriot. Neither his behavior could be seen as passive resistance; it was more like civil disobedience. Arik did disobey, after all, albeit civilly. To me, passive resistance meant exercising freedoms already written into the law—not a trivial task in the old USSR. One such "freedom" involved a so-called political education program, a government propaganda initiative bombarding every citizen from cradle to at least retirement with a message of the Soviet system's supremacy. In kindergarten, that message was delivered via verses and songs; in schools and colleges, it was taught as a part of the curriculum; in the army, was communicated during nightly political studies (which our sailors slept through with open eyes); and could be heard at after-hours meetings convened explicitly for that purpose in workplaces. The meetings at work were considered optional, but everybody understood they had to participate.

Not every organization enforced the political education mandate. My mother, for instance, did not go to those political gatherings. When my father worked in retail, nobody cared if they had such meetings, and, as a warehouse manager, he conducted them himself, turning foreign policy topics into geography lessons. Before my last job in the Soviet Union, I do not remember attending political meetings at work. I am sure I was asked to, but I ignored the request. Those were smaller, more liberal workplaces with laxer Party oversight, where management preferred not to bother employees beyond the job requirements. However, my latest place of work belonged to a different category—a showcase government enterprise with all attributes, including a full-blown cadre department. The latter even had a Special Section. And they took political education seriously...

For a while, I managed to avoid the undesired after-hours pastime. My boss, a talented engineer, would have been perfectly fine with it, but as a department head, he was pressured by the Party's overseers. So, one day, following another missed political symposium, he asked me why I hadn't been there. Our department occupied a medium-sized hall where employee desks faced the desk of the department head in a typical classroom layout. My desk was in the back, so the department head shouted his question across the hall. I yelled back some excuse, hoping he would leave me alone, but my boss pressed on. A bit annoyed, I asked him whether he knew that attending those meetings was voluntary. "It is voluntary," replied my boss, "but everybody must come." And when I voiced my surprise over such an interpretation of the term "voluntary," he went for the jugular. "Will you be going to those meetings or not?" he hurled an ultimatum over my coworkers' heads... Of course, I had no desire to ruffle feathers and would not have minded wasting a few hours at those meetings if all I had to do was sit there. However, just sitting there was not an option, as every participant had to make a presentation denouncing the corrupt capitalist system and American imperialism. I am certain the Soviet rulers no longer believed such agitprop, and they knew that most of their subjects did not believe it either; however, what one believed did not matter. What mattered was that people went places they did not want to go and said things they did not want to say, thus bowing to the authority. And now, I faced public humiliation by replying "Yes" to my boss' demand. I opened my mouth, not yet knowing what would come out of it, and the answer "No" echoed in the hall.

The following few weeks were uneventful—nobody mentioned the political classes incident, relations with my boss remained normal—and then, I received a call from the personnel department. They asked me to come. I went downstairs to their offices on the first floor. The receptionist took me to a room where an unfamiliar, thirty-something man in a suit and a tie rose from the chair to greet me. He smiled, shook my hand, and introduced himself as a KGB officer (I do not recall his rank, possibly captain). The surprise visitor paused, watching my reaction, but I had dealt with a KGB officer before. It happened soon after I transferred to Odessa University. That officer approached me similarly through the university's cadre department. He was a young man who must have just started on the job and seemed not thrilled with the assignment—perhaps wished for something more exciting. I am unsure what the purpose of his visit was; he never stated it. Maybe the local KGB received my file from Moscow and sent him for a routine follow-up. The only relevant question he asked was what I thought had happened to me at MIPT; otherwise, we spent an hour walking the streets and talking about immaterial stuff. In the end, he said that he might call again, but never did, and the KGB had not contacted me... until now.

The receptionist left the room, closing the door behind her. "You may be wondering about the purpose of our conference," said the KGB man after we sat down, "I heard many good things about you and, while visiting your company for unrelated matters, decided to meet you in person." He did not mention my refusal to attend the political classes, but I am sure it was what caused our encounter. My boss must have reported the incident to the company's *partorg*[5], who went to the Special Section, which then passed the word to headquarters. And it was all my boss' fault—had he talked to me in private, we could have reached some compromise, or at least my refusal would not have looked so seditious. On the other hand, he had to make it public to have witnesses to his effort… The political classes' episode was not on the KGB guest's mind, though. It gave him an excuse to approach me, but as I soon learned, the man had broader interests. Our conversation was brief and unspecific; he kept switching topics (as his predecessor used to do). His manners were measured and polite, but one could sense behind them hours of training. Finally, the visitor got up. "It was nice meeting you," he said, "I may have a few more questions; you won't mind me calling, will you?" We shook hands, and I went back upstairs, a bit relieved.

A few more weeks had passed. My new acquaintance did not call, and I began to think that he had left me alone. After all, what was there to discuss? He wanted to meet me in person, and he did. Of course, the political classes remained unattended, as going there would have been like putting money into a meter after getting a parking ticket. I was almost sure I had gotten off scot-free when the KGB representative gave me a ring. He said he wanted to meet again, suggesting the city park as a venue. We met there in the afternoon. It was late fall; the trees had shed their leaves, and the park was deserted. We walked through the empty alleys and, to a casual eye, might look like two friends. He addressed me respectfully by my formal name (the first name plus patronymic), and I responded in kind, which is how I will mention him in this narrative. I do not remember his name and will use "Pyotr Ilyich" as the shortest example of such a form of address I could come up with. There was something Dostoevskian[6] in our exchange, so addressing each other that way seemed fitting.

This time, Pyotr Ilyich was more concrete. He began to mention names, revealing surprising knowledge of my friends, former associates, and various details of my life. "Do you know such a person?" he said and uttered the name of my high school mate who had studied in a parallel class. I answered that I knew the individual, albeit remotely. "He lives in Moscow now," informed me Pyotr Ilyich. "I didn't know that," I said. "You travel to Moscow on business," continued the KGB envoy,

---

[5] "Communist Party Organizer," a workplace "commissar."

[6] "Crime and Punishment" was very popular in those days.

"Would you like to contact him there? I can give you his coordinates." I was astonished by the absurdity of that proposal—to pop up like a lost relative before someone I had spoken with maybe two times in my life. "Why would I do that?" I replied, "And what am I going to tell him? That you have sent me?" Pyotr Ilyich laughed. "Of course not," he said, "We believe he is involved in the dissident movement." "Nice try," I thought humorously, "He wants me to become an informant so that I would have no choice but to start going to those political meetings." It was getting dark. I said that I had no immediate plans to go to Moscow, to which Pyotr Ilyich showed no reaction, and we parted ways.

Apparently, the KGB had a plan involving me, but whatever that plan was, I hoped to stall them gently until they gave it up. I did not want to antagonize an organization that could make my life difficult. They were not the people to take rejection lightly. Hence, when Pyotr Ilyich called again in several weeks, we convened in the park once more. This time, the conversation focused on my friend who had emigrated to the US a few years earlier and with whom I maintained correspondence. Before leaving the USSR, my friend had a run-in with the authorities, and the KGB got involved, so they knew him well. "How is your buddy doing?" started Pyotr Ilyich, calling my friend by his first name. I replied that my buddy was doing fine, working on his doctorate at one of the American universities. "And is this all he does?" said Pyotr Ilyich with a twinkle of mystery in his eyes. "What do you mean?" I asked. "We have information he engages in anti-Soviet activities there," said Pyotr Ilyich. I replied I doubted the KGB information was correct because my friend's studies would not allow him to do much else and because, unlike in the Soviet Union, where anti-Soviet activity was a hobby, it was a profession in the United States. "Don't you believe me?" said Pyotr Ilyich, "Then ask him in your next letter." Again, I was stunned by how crazy that proposal sounded, on par with one from the previous meeting. "Is he out of his mind?" I thought of my companion, and then it struck me what was going on. The KGB inquisitor was not interested in my friend's pastime in America or my one-time schoolmate. The story about the former's anti-Soviet activities he had made up and the latter's dissident links, too. What he wanted was my cooperation—that I agreed to do something for him, even as a symbolic gesture. And as soon as I did it, out of fear or to end the suspense, I would be working for his employer, like so many others, including the anonyms who had provided the KGB with all that information about me and my friends. It wasn't my American pal or former schoolmate the KGB was after; they were after me. "By the way," said Pyotr Ilyich amicably, "are you planning to emigrate, too?" I replied that I had not decided yet, and we called the day.

The realization of the KGB's strategy was bad news, as it implied that they would not let me off the hook voluntarily. I ought to break with them myself, and soon enough before our relations became too habitual. Even if I did not do Pyotr Ilyich any favors, our walks in the park were beginning to resemble regular meetings between an informant and his runner. I needed to talk to someone and called on my friend, a fellow special draftee who had served on a submarine base in Sevastopol. Pyotr Ilyich warned me not to tell anybody about our conversations, but I trusted my friend completely. "I also received a visit from a KGB guy a few days ago," exclaimed my friend when I told him the story, "He was asking questions and said he might call again." It didn't take us long to figure out we dealt with the same person. The KGB was looking for some conspiracy, and our mutual acquaintance was their field man... The new information reinforced my decision to sever ties with the notorious representative. If he had spoken with my submarine friend, he likely talked to other people, some of whom might know me, see us together, and conclude I was a snitch. "So, what are you going to do?" asked my friend. I replied that I would try to end my relationship with our KGB liaison the next time I saw him, but was unsure how to proceed. "Let me know the result, " said my submarine friend, "and I may get rid of him, too, if he contacts me."

Now, I was certain Pyotr Ilyich would call again, expecting the timing of the call to emphasize the periodicity of our meetings. He called as expected. I went to the park, determined to rebuff him at his first attempt to give me another "assignment." As we exchanged greetings, I noticed my date was a bit distressed. It had nothing to do with me—maybe he had a fight with his wife or was reprimanded by his superiors for tearing a discarded document into four pieces instead of the required eight—but he asked me no questions, preferring to talk himself. I listened, making occasional comments, to a fascinating exposé of the new KGB mindset. Pyotr Ilyich lamented the lack of strong leadership in the country, referring to Brezhnev and the Politburo as old, senile relics holding to power. Of course, he could be saying it to gain my trust, yet I sensed it was sincere. Such criticism by a member of the Soviet apparatus's most powerful institution surprised me; still, it already foretold the decline of the Communist Party and the rise of the KGB as a political force. "Stalin was a strong leader," I said, "and look at the sufferings he wrought on this nation." Pyotr Ilyich admitted the cruelty of Stalin's reign but attributed it to the dictator's ethnicity. "Stalin was Georgian," he said,

"He did not feel for Russians and Ukrainians; they were not his people." I found such an explanation simplistic and rather "unfair" toward a man who, in a major departure from the Bolsheviks' principles, resurrected Russian nationalism, yet I said nothing. "Anyway, those were things of the past," continued Pyotr Ilyich, "They will not be repeated. We will not allow it to happen."

The enlightened speech lifted my companion's spirit, and he recalled what he had come for. "Have you received any new letters from your American friend?" he asked after we sat on the bench. I did not answer. "We live in a different time now," continued Pyotr Ilyich, sensing my tension, "It is up to you to cooperate with us. If you do not want to have these meetings, say so." He was still skating down the liberal slope, but my biggest surprise was a sudden realization that, in the course of our acquaintance, he had completely misread me. Where I was polite and cautious, he interpreted it as signs of weakness and fear. Of course, I was nervous, but at no time did I consider his "proposals," and as I was building the resolve to end our relations, he thought that I was fast approaching a capitulation point. And he construed my silence as an internal farewell to moral chastity, whereat decided to ease my pain by making the surrender a free choice. So sure was he of the outcome, he engaged in a cat-and-mouse game where opened too wide an escape path, to which I rushed almost instinctively. "All right, let's not do it," I said. "Let's not do what?" asked Pyotr Ilyich bewilderingly. "Let's not have these meetings anymore," I elaborated. The face of my companion turned red. For a few moments, he tried to grasp what had happened. Had I cut him off in the beginning or refused to meet during our phone conversation, the KGB could have summoned me to their headquarters, made threats, brought up the political classes' episode, or pressured in some other way. But none of that was possible now after the company's official representative had granted me an absolution. The game was over, and the only option my opponent had was to beg, which was not going to happen. "Very well," uttered Pyotr Ilyich angrily, as speech returned to him, "do as you wish, but remember not to talk about our encounters, because if you do…" he paused for a second, "we may not put you in jail, but you will feel our presence." His words and unfriendly tone annoyed me. "Do not threaten me," I shot back involuntarily. But Pyotr Ilyich had already regained his calm. Perhaps, downright hostility was not within his mandate, plus he had to stick to the progressive tone assumed at the beginning of the meeting. "I am not threatening you," he said. We sat in silence for a while. "Let's walk," said Pyotr Ilyich, and we started toward the park's exit. "I want you to know," said my escort as we reached the gate, "I hold you in high regard and have no hard feelings." He seemingly regretted his outburst. I diplomatically replied that I had enjoyed his company and was sorry I could not be of greater assistance. We shook hands. "One more thing," said Pyotr Ilyich as if remembering something, "if you do decide to emigrate and encounter visa or other problems, give us a ring; we might help you."

4. Physical Exam

The last words of the KGB emissary were properly ambiguous. They could mean a threat to cause me problems if I tried to leave the country or an assurance that no such problems would come my way. My reading leaned toward the second. I did not believe the KGB wanted to help me (not without asking for anything in return), but they were not going to create obstacles, either. Had Piotr Ilyich wished to threaten me, he might have used something more substantive. In fact, his utterance sounded almost like a suggestion—that it would be better for all of us if I left or that, at least, I would not be missed… But Piotr Ilyich did not decide on emigration matters, and although my mother's and my visa approval went without a hitch, it would be presumptuous to attribute that ease to the KGB's interference on my behalf. After my mother and I received exit permission, I went to the emigration office to pick up our papers and, while in the waiting room, recognized a few individuals with whom I was applying for visas three months earlier. And both times, we were called in the same order. Such a correlation pointed to the absence of special treatment by the KGB or any other authority, which was rather fortunate; who knows how things might have turned out if I had been singled out during the approval process?

I did not tell my mother about the KGB affair, but the immigration topic began to come up between us more often. She looked at the matter favorably, if that of a distant future. In the sanatorium, she had become a key administration member, respected by her superiors and fellow staff members. She was on good terms with the chief physician, as well as his deputy, a prominent medical practitioner and a gifted organizer. Their support made my mother's life easier, as the authorities never fully accepted a Jewish cadre director in the Odessa resort system (or possibly in the entire city). The higher-ups did not deal with my mother directly, but they seldom failed to show their displeasure when they had the chance. One such display involved the earlier-mentioned personal salary. The central bureaucrats refused to give it to my mother, and later, they slighted her again, from a different angle… As the sanatorium grew, my mother got an assistant. The assistant was a young woman, diligent and hardworking. My mother liked the girl and often praised her to the chief physician, who must have communicated that praise to his superiors. And after less than a year at her new job, the assistant was awarded a personal salary, an honor my mother had been repeatedly denied. The story reminds me of the "Secretary" episode from the Seinfeld sitcom series, but my mother was not amused. She did not blame the assistant, who happened to be an unsuspecting apparatchiks' tool, yet was upset by the snub. The years of commitment and hard work had no bearing on the regime's disdainful attitude.

Besides the KGB, there were other factors to ponder in my emigration plans, the most consequential being military service (or the restrictions of its aftermath). In the classic Soviet Union, these restrictions involved a nondisclosure pledge, but after emigration burst onto the scene, they added a waiting period before a former serviceperson could leave the country. There was no official acknowledgment of a waiting period's existence, nor was there a published schedule of any kind, so people relied on rumors that were often true. The rumors had it that my troop's waiting time was seven years. Other rumors stated that the government tried to extend the waiting terms for Jewish reservists by calling them up for military exercises and changing their army classification.

All able-bodied civilian men in the USSR comprised the army reserve, having undergone some form of military training. The training could be a mandatory military service I went through or the college's officer-of-reserve program, which I skipped. Active reservists could be summoned for training exercises, typically a few-week event. Officers of the reserve were called once a year, sergeants every few years, and the rank and file almost never. In addition, the rank and file's active-reserve status expired at a younger age. Those disparities accounted for my refusal to advance beyond the rank of a lead sailor. I preferred to endure the full hardship of the army routine and be done with it. Most of my fellow servicemen who faced a similar dilemma did the same.

"Almost never" still implied that the rank and file could be called up for training exercises, and such cases did occur. Nobody knew why any individual might receive such a rare distinction, so when a call-up note requesting my appearance in the *Voenkomat* (enlistment office) turned up in my mailbox, I ignored it. The note did not necessarily mean they were going to send me to the training grounds, but I was not taking any chances. A few weeks later, I got another note, screaming in red letters of severe punishment for failure to come. I disregarded that one, too. After all, how could they prove I had received it? Someone in the post office could be stealing all my call-up notes. They had to notify me by a courier. The enlistment office ran its own courier service, where they retained reservists to deliver notices or asked done-with random callers to make a delivery on the way home. Knowing that, I stopped answering the door. I was approaching, age-wise, the end of my active reserve term and planned to hold on until then, but an unlucky happenstance frustrated those plans... I was at home, waiting for a friend with whom we had scheduled a meeting. Precisely at the time slated, the doorbell rang, and I rushed toward the apartment's entrance to let the guest in, but instead of the expected visitor, there stood a young man with a stack of papers in his hand. He was a military courier. He handed me a call-up note and ran downstairs, almost colliding with my friend, who was coming up.

I walked toward the enlistment office, telling myself it could be a routine matter—perhaps they needed another courier—but realized the chances of that were slim. It was unthinkable for the adverse forces of fate to set up such an elaborate trap to get me to *Voenkomat* so that I could deliver a few notices. My fears were justified—the clerk collected my draft card[7] and directed me to undergo a physical exam (or "medical commission," as it was known) conducted at another location, in some school, I recall. The enlistment office assembled such commissions a few times a year, usually in the course of the draft cycle. The military would requisition a space and local physicians to perform the evaluations. The examinees would go from doctor to doctor with a checklist stating the proposed fitness level, and each specialist would mark "Fit" or "Not Fit" against the organs [s]he was responsible for. If all the checklist items had been marked "Fit," the suggested fitness was confirmed.

The clerk handed me a checklist; I looked at it, and my heart sank. The checklist proposed the highest fitness level in the Navy—that of a submariner. While on active duty, I qualified a notch below, permitting me to serve on surface ships. Perhaps the Navy did not award me the top fitness then because I was a few years older than a regular draftee, but more likely because the enlistment officer in Odessa, who had arranged my recruitment for a bottle of cognac, doctored my file. He said nothing, but I recall him shuffling papers, his self-congratulatory smirk, and a conspiratorial wink, with which he handed me an envelope containing my file. That envelope I surrendered at the training camp in Sevastopol, and saw it the next day on the desk of an army physician, looking at my chart. "How is your arm? Any problems?" the doctor asked. "What arm?" I replied with surprise. "It says here you had your arm broken in the past," said the physician, and I realized that the enlistment officer back in Odessa had taken a few pages from someone else's file, probably the results of a physical exam I missed (I was among the last special draftees, and the commission had been already disbanded then). But regardless of the reasons for my prior qualification, raising its level now

---

[7] Every adult male in the Soviet Union had such a card (military ID), which indicated his military (draft) status and ought to be shown alongside an internal passport in many situations. So, the enlistment office's taking away a draft card effectively put its owner under military control until the document was returned.

made no military sense. Even if undergoing a full physical exam was routine (and it was not for a regular sailor like me), it should have been to determine whether I still performed on the same level, since people usually move down the fitness scale with age and not up. Hence, the only purpose I could think of for bumping up my fitness grade was to send me to a training camp, change my army classification, and extend the waiting period, precisely as the rumors stated.

I started the examination, ready to fake every ailment known to men. Most of the examiners were women. Several times, I asked the doctor who tested my hearing to repeat what she said and deliberately called the wrong letters on the eye chart, but the hearing specialist pretended not to hear me, and the eye examiner did not listen to my answers. The latter poked her pointer into the chart while looking in the opposite direction and talking to her colleagues. She did not know herself, which symbol she was pointing to, so what did it matter what I answered? Both marked me fit. The next specialist dealt with the breathing apparatus. I had a history of chronic sinusitis, with years in Dr. Tartakovsky's care, and could describe the old symptoms I claimed to still experience from time to time. The woman doctor inquired what I felt, and I embarked on an unpleasant memories' path. "Do you suffer headaches?" the doctor asked sympathetically. "I do," I replied with glee, believing my luck was about to change. "Well, who doesn't?" said the woman and checked the "Fit" box... The fitness carnage continued until I reached the internist. There, I complained about chest discomfort and a racing heart (which, at the moment, was not hard to demonstrate). Apparently, it was acceptable to serve on a submarine while having poor eyesight, bad hearing, and clogged sinuses—those were not life-threatening ills—but a weak heart would be more difficult to ignore. So, the internist played it safe and sent me to my local clinic to undergo additional testing and to bring back the family physician's report.

The internist's decision had calmed and encouraged me. It wasn't over yet; however, I bought some time and postponed my ascent to the Chomolungma of physical fitness. Now, I had to see a family physician. Our city was divided into several administrative districts, where every district had a clinic serving the residents' outpatient needs. The clinics belonged to the government, and all their employees were government workers. The districts were further broken down into areas, each area covered by a family physician from the clinic's staff, so that a family's address determined which physician they had. Our family physician was a woman who had served in that capacity for many years and who knew us very well. She was friendly with my mother, but as far as my fitness problem was concerned, our physician had a flaw—she was Jewish and could (or thought she could) face greater scrutiny if she tried to help my case. I did not ask her for anything, but it was obvious what I wanted. To my chagrin, she sent me to a cardiologist, who found nothing wrong with my heart despite several cups of strong coffee that Tsylia Ilyinichna had brewed for me in her apartment... I returned to the clinic with the cardiologist's report the next day, but instead of our family physician, there was another woman sitting behind the familiar desk. The woman was the clinic's chief family physician, covering for her subordinate who had suddenly called in sick. I met that family physician before, also in the role of a substitute. She had a reputation as a good doctor and fine human being; however, I tried not to set my hopes high, remembering the sinusitis complaint fiasco. And it seemed to be a hopeless situation, anyway. "Are they drafting you in the army?" asked the chief family physician, reading the cardiologist's report. I explained I had already served, but the military was trying, inexplicably, to raise my fitness level. A quick air of inference ran across the woman's face. "Let me listen to your heart," she said, putting on a stethoscope. She then returned to her desk and started writing...

I walked out of the family physician's office in a grave mood, certain that the note in my hand reflected the cardiologist's opinion, but did not believe my eyes when I read it. Nowhere in the note was the specialist's conclusion even mentioned. The family physician wrote instead that she had heard suspicious noises in my heart, and more tests were needed to determine their cause. Someone upstairs had finally woken up just in time to arrest the submarine juggernaut. The military could still order those tests, but the commission's term was ending, and they were not going to extend it because of me... The next day, I went there in the afternoon to give my foes less time to maneuver. The commission was winding down, and the doctors in white coats were moving furniture, prompted by a stern man in an army major's uniform. I found the doctor who had requested the family physician's note. He was in a hurry. I handed him the report. He hesitated for a moment, perhaps looking to fulfill his "Fit" mandate, and then checked the "Not Fit" box. With such an imperfect checklist, I rushed to the enlistment office, where they returned my draft card, and the next time I set foot in that place was before leaving the country, to surrender the above card permanently.

5. Exchange Rate

The spike in exit permissions in the mid-1970s was followed by a lull, when the authorities accepted very few requests to emigrate. The pause continued for a couple of years, resulting in long lines of mainly Jewish citizens who contemplated the big move. In Odessa (as in other places), the line was self-organized. Several volunteers maintained a waiting list, which, at its peak, had over ten thousand entries. The list was updated every weekend—new members signed up, and the old ones registered their presence. Those who did not register (in person or by proxy) twice in a row were removed from the list. All that activity took place in a small park near the government offices that handled visa applications. On weekends, the park became busy. People were coming and going. Some registered their presence and left in a hurry, trying not to be noticed; others joined various discussion groups to hear the latest news and socialize with fellow aspirants. For many, it became a favorite pastime. They basked in the promise of a better future, new places, and coveted freedom, shrugging off the risk, pain, and turmoil that such uprooting would bring to their lives. The unpleasant part could be safely ignored, for now, as visa applications were not accepted anyway. The authorities tolerated those gatherings, maybe because it was easier to keep an eye on the emigration movement that way. I am certain the KGB periodically reviewed the list and had informants among its members... But a public assemblage of so many people eager to escape "the greatest society in the world" embarrassed the country's rulers, and eventually, they had to let the steam out. Hence, one day, the doors of the visa office opened widely, taking the line by surprise. As it turned out, the majority was not ready to proceed with an application, and, in a matter of weeks, I advanced from a number in the thousands to the head of the list. It happened so fast that I had no time to develop cold feet. I spoke with my mother, we gathered the necessary papers, and, a few days later, applied for emigration visas.

The visa application required a note (proof of employment) from the applicant's workplace. Asking for such a note marked the moment when an organization became aware of its employee's attempt to emigrate. For those of my mother's and older generations, who had worked at the same place for years, it was an especially challenging step. The stigma of official disapproval made breaking the news to the management and coworkers a highly emotional affair, while the denunciation meeting was deeply feared despite the event's obvious buffoonery. Even if the visa seekers continued on the job, the sense of being an outcast created a displacement trauma, unmitigated by new impressions and the necessity to act. "How am I going to tell it to my boss and those I have worked with for so long?" said my mother. I suggested that she blame everything on me. But blaming was not necessary. The chief physician shook my mother's hand and signed the note she had prepared herself. Of course, the infamous forum was out of the question... I met that chief physician once in my mother's office—he walked in to discuss some sanatorium business. My mother introduced me to her boss. "It is quite a muscular neck you've got," complimented me the chief physician. He was in his mid-forties, tall and thin, with low, combed-back hair. His behavior was erratic, even manic, yet indicative of high energy and a quick mind. I can envision him as my boarding school's alumnus. As his "neck" comment suggested, he had little trouble starting up a conversation and counted many influential friends, including city government officials and Party bosses. Those connections permitted him ample leeway in directing his administrative duties, occasionally sparking protests from my mother, who insisted that things be done properly. "He is such a desperado, not afraid of anything," she once said to me after another argument with her boss. His audacity worked out well for her, however. The chief physician allowed my mother to stay on the job as if nothing had happened until she and I left the country.

By the end of the nineteen-seventies, most emigration visa applicants were no longer dismissed from their jobs. I was not fired, either, yet underwent a denunciation procedure. Our company's *partorg*[8] was an ambitious man, determined to advance his management career through political activism, and he ordained the ritual. The first attempt to arrange it was unsuccessful: the *partorg* communicated to my boss the meeting's date and time, so I knew when not to come. A week later, when leaving the office at the end of the day, I got caught in an unusual counterflow—people were returning to the room as if driven by an external force. That force was the *partorg*, standing outside the door and turning everybody around to partake in a surprise meeting dedicated to me. It was the only way he could make my coworkers participate in that spectacle. I imagine many of them were praying they would not be called to speak out. Among the meeting's attendees, I must have felt the most comfortable.

The *partorg* made a speech, calling me a "traitor" and accusing me of going to the other side of the "barricade." He seemed vexed, maybe because of the trouble I had given him with setting up the meeting and because he saw me trying to suppress a smile. But I was not laughing at

---

[8] A Party Organizer, a workplace "commissar."

him. As he spoke, an amusing thought popped into my mind—what if I phoned the KGB and complained that the *partorg* was giving me a hard time? After all, Pyotr Ilyich told me to call if I had emigration problems. I doubt the KGB would have appreciated the humor, though. And there was little to complain about. The *partorg*'s influence did not extend far beyond the denunciation meeting, and nobody bothered me after that. My work pattern did not change, and neither did my relations with coworkers, including my boss. He even sent me on a business trip to Tallinn[9], which I enjoyed. Another eagerly anticipated trip, to Yerevan, was already in the works when my mother and I received a letter from the visa office stating that our emigration request had been granted. The entire wait took three months.

From the day of receiving exit permission, emigrants had one month to pack their bags and leave. The quantity and contents of those bags were strictly regulated. Two suitcases with personal possessions were allowed per adult, and one small container per family could be shipped via freight. No Soviet money was permitted across the border except for a few coins, but the government exchanged one hundred rubles per emigrant for US dollars at almost parity. The Soviet rouble was not a freely convertible currency, so such an exchange rate was arbitrary (it even fluctuated slightly to look authentic), reflecting the national pride rather than an economic condition ("our rouble is no less than your dollar"), but in reality, the rouble was much less, as I found out after crossing the border. On the way out, I accidentally smuggled a twenty-five-ruble note—forgot it in the wallet compartment, and customs did not check. I discovered the unintended contraband in Vienna, where I attempted to exchange the note for US dollars or Austrian shillings, but nobody wanted the unfamiliar banknote. Eventually, I found one small bank that took the bill. They gave me four US dollars for it.

Obviously, the Soviet government was losing big on those hundred-rouble exchanges but recouped the losses via confiscatory emigration rules, which often left the exchanged sum as the largest portion of the departing family's estate. Thus, emigrants packed things they could sell abroad, such as linens, record albums, and cameras... within allowable limits. One camera, one bottle of champagne, and one small jar of caviar (for example) were allowed per adult. Of course, domestic products sellable abroad were hard to find in Soviet stores, requiring a concerted effort to procure. Over the vast Soviet territory, Moscow (and, to a lesser degree, Kiev and Leningrad) was the only place where, with some luck

---

[9] The capital of Estonia, then a Soviet republic.

and after standing in line for hours, those items could be purchased off the shelves. I had to travel to Moscow to obtain Israeli visas at the Dutch embassy[10], so I did some shopping, too.

---

[10] The Netherlands embassy represented the State of Israel, with whom the USSR did not have diplomatic relations at the time, and since Soviet Jews were officially leaving for Israel, they had to have Israeli visas.

6. The Parting

The day of our departure had arrived. Friends and relatives came to the train station to bid us farewell—Uncle Zinovy with Aunt Manya and Tolik, Tsylia Ilyinichna with Fima, and many others. Fima and I had already said goodbye to each other during my last trip to Moscow, where I stayed in the summer house of his in-laws. Fima also lived there at the time with his wife and two-year-old daughter. He was coming to Odessa that summer, but I did not know my exact schedule and was unsure if I would still be in the country. He came two days before my mother's and my departure. We tried to persuade him not to go to the train station because of the uncertain political climate in the country. The autocratic pendulum had already swung in another direction. As I was going through the visa formalities, a wave of refusals hit applicants who had not yet reached the safety of exit permission. The reaction was setting in, and it was rumored that KGB agents at the train station logged those who saw off departing emigrants. Such rumors seemed far-fetched, but so did the army waiting-period-extension ones, which, as far as I could tell, turned out to be true. Common sense was a poor guide in predicting Soviet authorities' behavior, and since Fima's job required clearance, coming to the station might pose a risk to his career. He showed up anyway. It was the last time I saw him, as well as most others at the station. After the collapse of the Iron Curtain, I felt no desire to go back for a visit, while letters and phone conversations were infrequent, even with the closest left behind. And it wasn't because my attitude toward them changed—I appreciated our relations more—but because those people were a part of life that took much pain to disengage. My fellow countrymen who emigrated after the USSR's collapse did not have to endure the aches of forsaking their birthplace. They knew they could come back at any moment and resume their prior existence. Few did, but that knowledge made emigration an easier choice. It was different in my time when the regime tried to assure the departing that they would never see their homeland again. We were stripped of Soviet citizenship (for which, ironically, we had to pay a substantial fee), and the entire process was devised to leave the most uninviting aftertaste. Little did I realize, then, that the authorities did us a favor by shortening the period of bereavement. Before leaving the old country, I thought that I would miss it until my days' end, only to discover, upon crossing the border, that I had done all the missing on the other side. The perceived finality of the emigration action accelerated the breaking with the past, making it more painful but also more complete. Sadly, the rupture affected ties I wanted to preserve, which could have kept me closer to friends and relatives, especially my uncles. Now that they are gone, I regret not speaking with them more often. Only after Uncle Zinovy's wife died (Uncle Aaron died a few years earlier) did I begin to call Uncle Zinovy regularly on the phone, but never came to Odessa, unable to cross the barrier created by the circumstances of our exit. Who knew that in just ten more years, the regime that wielded such a sway over its subjects' lives would disappear in a puff of smoke?

Uncle Aaron was at the station, too, but he was not on the platform. He was inside the train, accompanying us to the border town of Chop, a major railway crossing to the West and the last stop in the Soviet Union. In Chop, my mother and I would go through customs and board the Vienna train. Crossing the customs line placed the now stateless emigres in a no-man's-land, so most brought with them relatives and friends who would collect rejected items at the baggage search or help in other iffy situations. That was why Uncle Aaron got on the train with us, and we were joined by another uncle, Uncle Simeon, who volunteered to go to Chop, too. Uncle Simeon was the husband of my father's cousin, Aunt Shura. They also lived in Odessa, and our families stayed in touch. Uncle Simeon belonged to the extended family's entrepreneurial side. He had worked many jobs, endured government persecution for unlicensed economic activities, and settled down as a deputy director of a large food store. The store's largeness was relative; it was no larger than an average American drugstore (and stocked far less merchandise), but was among the largest in Odessa. Like in many such businesses, the store director (manager) was a figurehead—a retired military or apparatchik who did not involve himself in day-to-day operations—and Uncle Simeon ran the place. Such a position, combined with chronic food shortages, let Uncle Simeon accumulate a lofty balance in the favor bank, a repository of bona fide Soviet currency. Of course, the nominal currency was the rouble, and the government set prices an average family could afford... if the products were available in stores. Not that the stores never got good stuff, yet the shipments were rare and in quantities too small to satisfy the demand. As a larger outlet, Uncle Simeon's store sometimes received fresh meat, instant coffee, cognac, and other sought-after items. When that happened, the store's employees were permitted to buy a little for themselves; the director set aside a measure for his clientele and gave some to Uncle Simeon for his. The rest of the shipment would go to the store's shelves and sell out in minutes to a lucky few who happened to be in the right place at the right time.

After my father's passing, Uncle Simeon included my mother in his client list. He would call her once in a while to offer a kilo of meat, a few cans of sardines, or whatever else was available, and I would go to the store to pick it up. Even if the items were of little interest to us, we took them anyway to give to our friends. For example, my mother and I rarely drank coffee, preferring tea, but Tsylia Ilyinichna, who had hypotension, needed coffee to stay alert, so we bought some for her. On the other hand, when Uncle Simeon sought an expert medical opinion, my mother asked Tsylia Ilyinichna to see him. Several times, my mother helped out Uncle Simeon and Aunt Shura with monthly passes to the sanatorium[11], which was quite generous since those passes were in high demand. Of course, Tsylia Ilyinichna did favors for my mother as a friend, and Uncle Simeon did them as a relative, but my mother would not have accepted those favors if she could not respond in kind.

Uncle Simeon was the one who arranged my army enlistment, and he did it without leaving his store or making a phone call—the officers in charge of military recruiting came to him. The military recruitment office (*Voenkomat*) was a few blocks from Uncle Simeon's store, and the chief recruiter, with his assistant, was a frequent guest in the store's basement, where the deputy director had a small office. Perhaps the recruiters stumbled upon Uncle Simeon while looking to quench their thirst, or they approached him through the store's director, who asked his deputy to take care of the new acquaintances. And now they were regulars in Uncle Simeon's little room, occasionally stopping there after work for a free drink. So when my mother mentioned that I wanted to get drafted, Uncle Simeon replied that he knew the right people and would speak to them. Speeding up enlistment was not as big a favor as deferring it and posed no risk to the involved, yet merited a bottle of cognac. Uncle Simeon delivered the bottle to the chief recruiter, and I paid its listed price, as I did with every item procured in that store.

Several times in Uncle Simeon's office, I observed peculiar characters coming from the street (the store had no security guards) and attempting to bluff or bully the deputy director into selling them some valuable artifact, usually a bottle of liquor. The enterprising visitors mentioned bogus references, and one even claimed to be sent by a doctor. Uncle Simeon handled them with admirable aplomb. Baldheaded, sleepy-eyed, and with a broken nose, he sat motionless behind his desk, like a sphinx or a Buddha, projecting a mysterious authority that quickly shattered the intruders' confidence, causing them to abandon the pursuit.

---

[11] A month-long course of healing and rehabilitation procedures with no room or board.

Uncle Simeon's temperate rationality complemented Uncle Aaron's hotheaded energy, so having both uncles on the train could be a big plus in case of a problem. Luckily, no such problem occurred. The customs rejected a few items from our load, although they did it to everybody, perhaps following some percentage guidelines. My mother and I were "under-stuffed," having three bags out of the allowed four, but it didn't matter to the checker; he took a few kitchen towels and other minor things I planned to sell in Italy and put them aside. We did not argue or ask questions—just passed the items over the fence to the uncles. After the baggage search, my mother and I proceeded to the international waiting hall to board the Vienna train in a couple of hours. The hall was isolated from the rest of the station, with armed soldiers guarding the doors. The uncles had already left. Uncle Simeon rushed to catch the Odessa train, while Uncle Aaron, whose train to Kiev was leaving in the morning, went to look for a place to sleep. My mother and I were now alone, suspended between worlds, but I did not feel any sadness or abandonment—the rising tide of the new beginning had picked us up.

Chapter 6

EN ROUTE

1. Across the Barricade

The waiting hall had no benches—we put our bags on the ground and sat on top of them. The premises were filling up with emigrants arriving from various parts of the Soviet Union, and in a few more hours, the place was packed. Families with suitcases and sacks scattered all over the floor. A stocky, powerfully built man with a purple face and crew cut rushed past my mother and me, aiming at a free spot on the other side of the hall. He hauled two enormous suitcases, pushing everybody out of the way and shouting at his wife and two kids (a girl of about fifteen and a boy of twelve, also with bags), who tried to keep up with the family's head. "Look!" my mother said in amazement, "This man is like a tank."

It was late at night when the station radio announced the boarding. My mother and I got on the train, reached the first empty seats, and sank into them, totally exhausted. Several more minutes passed, and the train moved, taking us across the border to the West—the first time in my life, the second in my mother's. We fell asleep almost immediately. I did not want to miss the Prague stop, as the city held a special significance for me. On my tenth birthday, Uncle Aaron gave me a book of Prague's photographs (which I still have). I enjoyed those beautiful black-and-white photos, looking at them for hours and imagining myself at those sites. There was no chance of getting off the train now, but I hoped to discern familiar shapes in the railcar's window. I did open my eyes as we paused in Prague, perhaps awakened by Czech soldiers walking through the car, but it was still dark, and all I could see were trees and a water tower. I went back to sleep and did not hear the locomotive resume its movement...

When we woke up, it was already light outside, and the train was approaching Vienna. There were a few emigration-aid workers in the car, who must have boarded the train after it crossed the Austrian border. The aid workers were telling everybody to prepare for an arrival, and soon, we entered the Vienna station.

The arriving emigres settled under the auspices of the Joint (JDC) and HIAS[1], Jewish humanitarian organizations with a long history of helping the displaced and distressed. The Joint provided relief to Jews (and non-Jews, victims of various disasters) worldwide, while HIAS took care of immigration matters. Perhaps the same organizations aided my great-grandfather and his children on their way to America sixty years earlier. Besides HIAS and Joint, assisting the transients were smaller agencies, such as the Tolstoy Fund and Rav Tov. The Tolstoy Fund handled a small faction of mainly Christian refugees from the Soviet Union, including exiled dissidents, while Rav Tov, an Orthodox Jewish charity, represented the religious part of the world's Jewry. All those groups worked together, using Joint as a common gateway. They were Joint guides who got on the train earlier and now directed the passengers to a gathering point where the initial briefing would take place.

Most of the Joint guides were young men who emigrated from the USSR a few years before me. Some were Israeli citizens living in Vienna; others remained in the city since their arrival from the East. All spoke German, English, and, of course, Russian. After a welcoming speech by the Joint's representative, the guides started calling out new arrivals, who were then escorted to buses parked nearby. The buses took emigres to their places of stay. Our bus headed north. The morning sun rose over the horizon and blinked cheerfully between buildings. The passengers clung to the windows, breathing the air of a new life and, perhaps for the first time since their decision to emigrate, realizing the extraordinariness of what was happening to them… In about twenty minutes, the bus stopped near a two-story building in a modest, well-kept neighborhood. The guide called out several names, including those of my mother and mine. It was our terminus. Another guide waited in front of the building, which turned out to be a small hotel. I do not recall any signs above the building's entrance—there were probably none, as the hotel was booked by Joint entirely.

The bus pulled away from the curb, continuing on its route. The new guide took the debarked passengers inside the hotel, where, in a dimly lit lobby, he delivered an orientation speech. He warned about terrorist

---

[1] American Jewish Joint Distribution Committee and the Hebrew Immigrant Aid Society.

threats (radical groups, such as the Red Brigades and Baader-Meinhof, were active in Europe at the time), asking everybody to be cautious and stay away from the windows. I doubt that terrorists were interested in poor emigres like us, though, plus the danger claims were unsupported by the negligible police presence (during the ten days in Vienna, I saw a policeman in the streets maybe twice). More likely, the guide wanted to scare the emigres off a little so they would keep a low profile and not disrupt the customary atmosphere.

After the orientation, the transients were shown to their rooms. Each family received accommodations according to its headcount. My mother and I got a small room with two beds and an electric range, while the panzer-like fellow, who had impressed my mother in Chop's waiting hall and now was our neighbor, received one of the largest rooms for his family of four. The guest rooms had no baths. There was one shared bathroom at the end of the hall. That bathroom had a shower. We had not eaten since the previous afternoon, but felt no hunger after the frenzy of the past few days. My mother was tired and sleepy. She lay down for a nap, and I rushed outside.

2. Vienna Connection

Shortly before emigrating from the USSR, I became acquainted in Tsylia Ilyinichna's apartment with a woman who had started there as a home aide. Her duties included some cleaning and cooking, but, for the most part, caring for Tsylia Ilyinichna's ailing husband. I wondered how Tsylia Ilyinichna had come across that woman, as the new helper did not fit the occupational profile. She was over sixty, rather old for such work (albeit younger people were gainfully employed by the government), and too cultured for it. She clearly needed money, and I got the impression that Tsylia Ilyinichna had hired the woman out of sympathy for the latter's circumstances. Most times I visited Tsylia Ilyinichna's home, the aide was gone for the day or on the way out, but one night, Tsylia Ilyinichna was late from work, and the helper, who had answered the door, offered me to wait for the host inside. We began to talk. The woman knew I was leaving the country, which made me a trusted ear to her unusual story.

She was a native of Latvia, born before the Bolshevik revolution into a Russian family of certain means. Latvia, like the other Baltic states[2], had often been a target of Russian expansion and, in the past few hundred years, came, a couple of times, under the control of its eastern neighbor. After the overthrow of the last Russian tsar, the Baltic states declared independence, which was recognized by Lenin's government. Thus, my host grew up in the free West and traveled all over Europe. In Paris, she met her future husband, a Ukrainian expatriate. He had an older brother in the Soviet Union, with whom corresponded by mail. Soon, broke out the Second World War—the newlyweds continued living in German-occupied France. After the war's end, they received a letter from the Soviet brother, who wrote he was alone and in poor health, had nobody to leave the house to, and was asking his sibling to come live with him. Europe lay in ruins; life was difficult everywhere. Latvia had become a part of the Soviet Union, while the Russian-led victory in the epic battle against Nazi Germany stirred ethnic pride in Slavic people around the world, inducing sympathy toward the communist state even among its staunchest detractors. Thus, moving to Soviet Ukraine did not seem like such a losing proposition, yet the woman was apprehensive. "I did not want to go," she said to me. But the husband insisted.

The reunion between the brothers, who had not seen each other for many years, was a joyful one. Perhaps the happy moment softened the cultural shock the newcomers undoubtedly experienced (I recall my

---

[2] Latvia, Lithuania, and Estonia.

mother's own account of her dreadful impression when she came to Odessa from Germany, and she grew up in the Soviet Union), but they soon realized they had bought a one-way ticket. And the worst was still to come. The couple's arrival coincided with a new round of repressions, which disproportionally affected people like them, former residents of foreign countries. They were arrested on trumped-up espionage charges and sent to Siberia. The husband did not survive the cruel conditions of the labor camps, while the wife was released after the gulag's shutdown, having spent almost a decade there. During her incarceration, the brother-in-law died, and the house was seized by the authorities, who gave it to someone else. "They did it to me, and I had never lived under the Bolsheviks before," the woman concluded. She was still unbelieving after all those years.

As her helper and I were talking, Tsylia Ilyinichna came home. She was in the mood for company and went straight to the kitchen, returning minutes later with teacups and a box of chocolates. We all sat down at the table and continued the earlier theme. Growing up in Soviet history's relatively benign period, I was often amused by the caution with which people of older generations discussed delicate matters of politics and living abroad. Tsylia Ilyinichna, for example, could not help lowering her voice, even among the closest of friends, when telling an opinion that might have been heretical in Stalin's time, and the home aide had experienced the regime's fury firsthand. But in the intimate atmosphere of that evening and in the presence of a person with one foot over the border, everybody was comfortable. Flooded with memories, my new friend reminisced about her younger years and life in Europe's great cities. "Do you know which city I enjoyed the most?" she said to me, "Vienna—a beautiful, charming place. I won't see it again, but you are going there. Give the city my love. When I think of you walking its streets, I will feel like being there myself."

I recalled the conversation with Tsylia Ilyinichna's helper as I got out of my Vienna hotel and immediately felt that special atmosphere she had spoken about. The hotel was situated on Taborstrasse, not far from the Prater amusement park. It was still early morning, and few people were on the streets. I walked, savoring the harmonious surroundings and the air of contentment, dispelling the uncertainty that had pursued us since the Soviet Union. But the most unusual sensation was my having been to these places before, and of yet unknown purpose for being there now. As if the buildings whispered in my ear to go that way, and maybe straight ahead, around the corner, which looked so familiar, I would discover the mystery that tied me to this place. It felt so exciting and so surreal, like those dreams about my boarding school. That strange awareness stayed with me the entire time in Vienna and was particularly strong in the offbeat areas where common folk lived. Of course, it was my first time outside the USSR, but later, I traveled to other cities and liked them, too, yet never experienced such a strong sense of belonging. Were I a believer in the paranormal, I might have assumed a telepathic connection with the woman in Odessa, where my perceptions were relayed to her and, by some malfunction, her emotions transmitted back to me. However, being rather scientifically inclined, I explained that peculiar consciousness by my pre-birth or genetic memory.

Genetic memory did not inform me where to buy food, though, so I walked around the hotel, noting the locations of grocery stores. When I came back to our room, my mother was awake. She was calm and in a good mood. Usually apprehensive of unfamiliar places, she did not seem worried at all. The relaxing Viennese atmosphere had soothed her, too. We went out to a grocery store. After thirty years of nonuse, my mother's German was rusty, but she could still express herself and understood everything. "It looks like Berlin," she summed up her impressions from the first Vienna stroll… After breakfast, I went down to the lobby, where the hotel guests assembled to socialize and share information. Our guide was there, too. His duties included answering the transients' questions and communicating to them Joint's directives, such as when to come for an interview. My mother's and my appointment was the next morning. It was a routine meeting where a Joint representative would review the emigres' papers, give them a few schillings, and ask which country they wished to go to. Those who chose Israel were put on the next plane to Tel Aviv, while the rest remained in Vienna for a week before going to Rome, where further differentiation would take place. My mother and I did not know anyone in Israel, but we had friends in the United States or going there, so we remained in Vienna.

3. Champagne and Caviar

As the first order of business, I had to unload champagne and caviar, the only items from our stock to be sold in Vienna, where for them existed a niche market. Selling goods on the streets was prohibited in the city, and if there was a flea market, it had to be beyond the transients' reach, as I never heard anybody mention one. Perhaps the pleasure of staying in Vienna was too brief to mix it with business, plus proper natives would have balked at buying from unsanctioned sources. Alternatively, steep fines deterred those who had a lesser regard for the local laws. It was different with champagne and caviar, which went straight into the cellars of cafes and restaurants. I doubt that traditional Viennese establishments used those channels, but there were many places run by foreigners who did not mind a competitive advantage. The continuous flow of Soviet emigrants created a steady supply of such delicacies, as well as a small industry to procure them. We did not look for buyers—buyers were looking for us. Our Joint guide in the hotel was also a part of that trade, strategically positioned to advise emigres on the matter. Occasionally, he bought champagne himself, acting as a middleman, as some other guides did. Joint paid little attention to its workers' extracurricular activities as long as nobody complained. I do not believe those activities were even illegal; after all, they were exchanges conducted on private property of personal possessions lawfully brought into the country. One could find the same items imported from the Soviet Union in select stores at much higher prices. Perhaps there were improprieties in the ensuing stages of the merchandise's trajectory below the radar of governmental statistics, but it did not concern us.

Selling through our guide was the easiest way to offload the bottles, but also the least profitable. Fortunately, the champagne trade was big enough to accommodate smaller operators who offered better deals, and such an opportunity presented itself on our second day in the city. I was standing outside the hotel with several other emigres when a dark-haired, thirty-something man approached our group. His appearance could be described as Persian, suggesting origins from one of the Soviet Union's Central-Asian republics, such as Turkmenistan or Uzbekistan. He spoke Russian without an accent. The man told us he would buy champagne and caviar at prices noticeably higher than our guide's. He could not conduct business on the street (which was illegal) or inside the hotel (a territory controlled by the competition), so he left his home address and stated that he would be there after six in the evening.

A trip to the unknown with valuable merchandise appeared riskier than trading inside the hotel, plus the terrorism scare had a numbing effect on the transients' taste for adventure, so the majority chose to sell locally. Only Leon (which was the name of the resolute "shover" from Chop's waiting hall) and I decided to take the Persian man up on his offer. Leon was an energetic and audacious person, while my confidence stemmed from that odd sense of a special affinity with the city. Besides, my mother's and my tight finances made every schilling count.

The Persian man lived within walking distance of the hotel. Leon and I decided I would go first, and he would follow after my return. My mother expressed a desire to go with me. She needed time to get ready, so I put the bottles in the bag and said that I would wait for her outside. The heavy load stretched the bag, revealing its contents to a trained eye, like that of our guide, whom I passed in the lobby on the way out. The guide promptly trailed me onto the street. "What do you have in your bag?" he inquired aggressively. I replied that it was no business of his. "You are going to get caught," the guide said with anger, "will pay a huge fine and then know whose business it is." He was clearly irked by a slipping income. "Why would anyone want to catch me?" I said. At that moment, my mother emerged from the hotel's entrance, and the guide rushed past her back inside. "What were you talking about?" my mother asked me curiously. "Nothing important," I responded, and we walked toward the Persian man's address.

The Persian man answered the door himself. He was in the apartment alone. The first-floor residence was spacious, clean, and well-furnished. The windows faced the courtyard, softening the sunlight. I pulled the bottles out of the bag; the Persian man took them to another room and returned with the money. The transaction was complete. As my mother and I prepared to leave, the Persian man's wife came home. We made an introduction. The young woman also looked Central-Asian, with raven-black hair and sparkling black eyes. Her demeanor conveyed warmth, buoyancy, and curiosity about fellow human beings. She probably felt that the guests had not been extended the hospitality customary in her native land, and offered us tea. I was eager to go back to the hotel, where Leon was waiting for me, but the woman's charm was hard to resist, plus my mother wanted to spend time with compatriots experienced in living in the West. We all got behind the table and began to chat.

As I had already guessed, our hosts belonged to the famed group of Bukharian Jews who had left the Soviet Union in the mid-1970s and soon became the Soviet propaganda's poster child for disillusionment with Western values. The city of Bukhara (located in today's Uzbekistan) had been Central Asia's important cultural and economic center for centuries. Sitting on the Silk Road, it used to be a major trading hub. The city, as well as other parts of the former Bukharian Emirate, had a sizable Jewish population that dwelt there for over a millennium. It was a close-knit community, distinct enough to be called "Bukharian Jews" rather than simply "Jews." They were viewed by the Soviet laymen as wealthy. I am sure there were many poor Jews in Bukhara, yet considering the city's history as a center of commerce and Jewish prominence in that orbit, some Bukharian Jews might have acquired substantial wealth, part of which they preserved even under confiscatory regimes such as the Bolsheviks. Also, Jews in Bukhara had largely escaped the influence of communist ideology and faced less antisemitism, being a part of the local culture, itself sidelined by the communist state. Thus, on the whole, Bukharian Jews in the USSR lived rather well.

After the fall of the Soviet Union, Bukharian Jews abandoned their ancient homeland, settling in Israel and the United States, but fifteen years earlier, only a tiny faction, including our hosts, had ventured to explore the newly opened trails. They went to Israel; however, the new country did not agree with them. Perhaps they grew nostalgic or could not adjust to a different lifestyle—our hosts did not specify—but the Bukharians left Israel, came to Vienna, and applied in the Soviet embassy for permission to return to Bukhara. However, the Soviets were in no rush to restore the applicants' citizenship. A positive response would undermine a key deterrent to potential emigrants—the irreversibility of their action. Among a small number of emigres who requested to return, the Soviets admitted a select few, but the latter had to become a tool in an anti-Western propaganda campaign. They were put on TV, decrying the horrors of capitalism, asking for forgiveness, and thanking the Soviet government for letting them back.

Incredibly, as it was so rare an event, my mother and I knew one such returnee family and, at one point, listed them among friends. They were husband and wife, maybe in their forties. The wife used to work with my mother. She was a polite, phlegmatic woman with a college degree. By the time my mother and I applied for exit visas, she no longer worked at the sanatorium but stayed in touch with my mother. It so happened that the woman's family had also applied for permission to emigrate, and our waits overlapped, so we spent some time together, discussing emigration issues and hunting for trading supplies. It was when I met her husband, a tall, emaciated man with big, red hair and the quick reflexes of an ostrich. His name was Alex. He grew up in a small town (or even village) in the Odessa province and did not finish high school, starting a job after the eighth grade. My mother often mentioned the educational disparity between Alex and his wife, but what the former lacked in scholarship, he made up for in entrepreneurship. When free from his occupation as a factory worker, he traveled to surrounding villages, trading goods, or moonlighted in the city, doing various odd jobs. I do not know if it was because of those activities, but Alex owned an automobile, an item few could afford in the old Soviet Union. It seemed Alex had to be thrilled going places that rewarded qualities like his, but he had some surprising concerns. "I do not know what to do with the English language," he told me, "I study hard, yet nothing registers in my mind. It is so difficult." I tried to assure him that English would not be a problem, that he was still young and would eventually learn it, but Alex remained unconvinced. "I am worried," he kept saying, "very worried."

Alex's family left the Soviet Union a few months after my mother and me, so we did not cross paths in Vienna and Rome. From Italy, they came to Los Angeles, where their relatives lived. My mother was delighted to receive a phone call from her former colleague. They spoke often, and I was kept informed of Alex's progress. Within a year, he changed several jobs, working as a janitor, a cook, and other similar professions. English remained a problem. Finally, he found a position as a restaurant chef and, according to his wife, was happy with the work and the money. My mother and I were happy for them, too, so it came as a surprise when Alex called us on the phone to announce their decision to return to the USSR. He was going to the Soviet embassy in Washington, DC, and wanted to spend a few days in New York if he could stay at our place.

He came on the weekend, and I went to the airport to meet him. My mother and I did not ask our guest about their motives, nor was he eager to explain—just mentioned the difficulties of assimilation and issues with the English language. The next day, Alex and I took the subway to the Port Authority bus terminal, where he bought a ticket to Washington. On the way back, we walked along Forty-Second Street, which, at the time, was a dilapidated, crime-ridden quarter swarming with derelicts, drug dealers, and sex shops. The dismal surroundings did not affect my companion's spirit, though, as he engaged in a lively discussion with a hooker standing outside of a sex shop. "Service, service," I heard Alex repeating. He did not exaggerate his English language problems, but they were not going to stop him now. I pulled him away. We headed toward a subway station, past a row of vagabonds, mostly blacks. "I do not understand these people," said Alex with absolute seriousness about the vagrants, "They can get such good jobs. They speak English so well."

The Forty-Second Street episode, however grotesquely, showed that Alex had not probed the new country deeply enough, and their decision to return to the Soviet Union was premature if not a sad mistake. He must have sensed it, too, even more so after a fresh dose of impressions that our trip to the bus station and the subsequent few days in New York City brought him. He seemed withdrawn and confused when leaving for Washington. I offered to accompany him to the bus terminal, but Alex said he would have no problems getting there. It was our last contact. They got the return permission unusually fast and were gone in a couple of weeks. Several months later, my mother received a letter from her former coworker in Odessa, who wrote that she had seen Alex and his wife (with a few more returnees) on local TV, keeping their side of the bargain. "How can anybody go back to a country like that?" my mother (who had adjustment issues of her own) reacted to the news, "I would rather die than be subjected to such humiliation."

Unlike Alex, our Bukharian hosts had been waiting for their return permission for several years already. Occasionally, the Soviet embassy would hand them a refusal, but they would promptly reapply. Perhaps the Soviets did not view the Bukharians as proper TV propaganda stars because the characters were too different from the intended audience to easily relate to. They served a more useful purpose as far-off sinners doomed to damnation for betraying the motherland. The authorities played on anti-Asian xenophobia to insulate the public from sympathy for the alleged sufferers while maintaining a reliable source of doubts for potential emigrants. I remembered frequent mentions in the Soviet press about desperate Bukharians huddling on the embassy steps in Vienna, begging to be allowed back, and now, I drank tea with those very people.

They did not strike me as desperate; on the contrary, our Bukharian hosts appeared quite content. Of course, the husband did not have a steady job, doing things like our champagne deal, but the wife worked at some reputable firm and seemed happy and well-adjusted. They had two children in full-day kindergarten, so everything looked good. "Do you really want to return to the Soviet Union?" my mother asked. The hostess paused. "We would like to stay here," she said, "but it is hard to get a permanent status in Austria." That was true; Austria did not accept immigrants, allowing foreign-born permanent residents mainly through sponsorship, and even then, with little chance of becoming citizens in the foreseeable future. The country did allow temporary stays, though, for transients like my mother and me… and like our hosts. Only we were going in opposite directions, and they got stuck in Vienna. But that delay was what gave them a legal right to live there. As long as they waited for permission to return to the Soviet Union, the Bukharians could remain in Austria and work to support themselves. Perhaps the earlier returnees, like our hosts, arrived in Vienna with a genuine intention to go back to the Soviet Union, but I am not so sure about those who came later, when it became apparent that one could simply apply for return permission to remain in the country. "But what if the Soviets let you back?" my mother asked. "We hope to find a sponsor here, maybe through my job," the woman replied, "otherwise, we will go to the United States or back to Israel. We will not return to the USSR." "And what about the locals?" my mother continued, "How do they treat you?" The husband answered first. He started to complain about uppity Austrians, inhospitable to foreigners, especially from Asia. I saw an expression of protest on the wife's face. "It is a two-way street," she interrupted her spouse, "People are apprehensive of the unfamiliar, but if you respect their laws and learn their ways, they will accept you for what you are."

It was time to go. My mother and I thanked our hosts and headed back to the hotel. Leon was waiting for us, pacing impatiently in front of the hotel's building. He probably thought that I had been arrested. He carried two heavy bags (I am sure the Joint guide did not confront *him* regarding their contents). My mother went upstairs while I paused at the entrance to brief Leon on the trip's details. He then took off with the bottles, and I went inside. As I entered the lobby, the earlier guide at the concierge desk waved to me to come over. I approached him. "I am sorry for my outburst," said the guide in a conciliatory tone, "but you are new to this country, and I am sort of responsible. I only wanted to warn you for your good." That explanation might have been more convincing had he not participated in the champagne trade himself, but I was not going to make a fuss about it. I thanked him for his concern and went upstairs to my room.

4. Briefness of Stay

The transients who proceeded to Rome stayed in Vienna for one week, but our squad remained there for ten days. I spent most of that time exploring the city and relishing every moment of it. Occasionally, my mother accompanied me. She enjoyed those jaunts, which reminded her of Berlin. Sometimes, we teamed up with Leon and his family, with whom my mother and I became friendly. Perhaps my companions did not feel as drawn to Vienna as I did, but they valued the public comfort typically associated with a private home. The city was clean and well-maintained. There were no homeless and drunks, no breadlines, no scrambling for limited resources. One could always find a seat in the tram or an empty bench in the park, in a seeming contradiction with population-density statistics. Locals were distant but civil and helpful. Nobody had to worry about being cheated because of a poor knowledge of the language and local currency—whether in a store or a street kiosk, the merchant would take the right amount from the customer's hand and count the exact change. Maybe such a prodigious display of honesty and efficiency had a less appealing side, the one of conformity; however, it was barely detectable from our quasi-tourist perspective. For most of us, the Vienna stopover was like a vacation in a fairyland, but it passed quickly, and we had to continue our journey.

5. Road to Rome

The weather in Vienna also contributed to a pleasant experience, with comfortable temperatures, invigorating clouds, and light breeze. Things began to change as the train moved deeper into the Apennine Peninsula. We left Vienna in the evening and woke up in Italy to the clear sky and luscious landscape, bracing for the midday heat. Our railcar was fully occupied by emigres, and so were the cars adjacent to ours. Between the cars, shuttled an agitated, older man with an expression of disdain on his face. He was the train's "commandant," a Joint worker in charge of the convoy. Strangely, he spoke neither English nor Russian. I do not know if that was a special train or a regular one with a transients section, but the train made few stops, and they were short. The next stop was Florence, which we reached early in the morning. As the locomotive approached the station, several passengers opened their bags and pulled out camera tripods conveniently packed at the top. Despite the early hour, the platform was full of people who looked like they had come to greet some dignitary. As soon as the train stopped, the platform crowd rushed toward the cars, waving American dollars. Inside the cars, the emigres lifted the windows, and the trading began.

Soviet-made optics and photographic equipment sold in Italy very well. Those products were of good quality, and their prices made them real bargains. The entire selection was available in Rome, where Soviet emigrants based their Italian stay, but certain items could be traded on the way. In Florence, they were tripods. The locals would have gladly procured cameras and other gear; however, those were complex devices requiring thorough checking, for which the train's brief pause left no time. Tripods, on the other hand, were simple instruments (one, maybe two models) with prices known in advance, so the deals took seconds to complete. At the time of our passage, the demand was still strong, so not all the tripod seekers could secure the coveted accessory, but there was another train. Those who did not get a tripod often settled on consolation prizes, presenting an opportunity for tripod-less emigres like my mother and me. Of course, I knew back in the Soviet Union about tripods' popularity in Italy, but did not want to haul the bulk. They were easy to sell but difficult to carry, so I considered something more compact (albeit less profitable), such as binoculars. We brought with us two theater binoculars (opera glasses), retro style with brass rims and a faux-ivory body. I still have one of them, and the other was sold at the train stop in Florence. After all the tripods were gone, I moved to the window, timidly holding the binoculars in my hand, and a man on the platform snapped them for three US dollars.

"*Nicht bazaar! Nicht bazaar!*" sounded a hysterical cry, and the train commandant burst into the car. He started running between the car's sections, screaming and swearing in German, trying to stop the tripod trade. His anger puzzled me. Of course, a "bazaar" like that would have been improper in Austria, but we were in a different country now. The Italian public welcomed such a mobile flea market, and if the authorities wished to end the trading, all they had to do was to put a policeman on the platform. Perhaps the old man was not happy with the assignment, which involved long hours in the summer heat, poor sleep in a rambling car, and undisciplined plebeians from the East who paid no attention to his demands. They ignored him now, politely pausing when approached by the stickler and resuming the commerce as he moved away. Finally, the commandant recognized the futility of his efforts, threw his hands in the air, and ran out of the car. A minute later, the train moved, speeding toward its destination: the great city of Rome.

Rome was lying in ruins—at least, I saw some as the train entered the city. The ruins were surrounded by more functional buildings of a yellow-brown color, like that of a riverbed dried up by the burning sun. The buildings' windows seemed disproportionately small. Cypress and palm trees contributed to the disquieting exotics of the place. I surely had not been here before, not in this life nor a previous one… The train slowed down, entered a tall glass enclosure, and came to a stop. It was Roma Termini, the city's main railway station. Local Joint representatives waited for us on the platform. I saw our train commandant talking to them, and then he tumbled into the past.

The arrivals got off the train and assembled in front of the Termini station. From the outside, the station looked more reassuring—a modern structure of white stone, albeit counterbalanced at the square's opposite end by a large classic building resembling a gigantic chest. The weather was very hot. Like in Vienna, the emigres were split into several groups and taken by buses to temporary staying places in Rome and its suburbs. The bus carrying my mother and me was moving away from the city. The freeway ran up the hill, past sunlit orchards and grapevine fields. In half an hour, we entered a town that looked like a scaled-down version of Rome, with narrower streets and shorter buildings but of a similar style and tawny color. The town's name was Frascati. The bus crossed the town, continuing the ascent. The incline became steeper, and in ten more minutes, we reached another settlement on the mountaintop. It was the town of Monte Compatri, our destination. The bus turned, flashing a spectacular view of the Alban Hills below—a tapestry of gardens, roads, and house clusters—circled a small piazza with a sculpture-decorated fountain in the middle, and stopped near a contemporary, two-story building: our hotel. In front of the building's entrance stood a plainly dressed, middle-aged woman with a cabbage-patch face wrapped in a light headscarf. She was surrounded by a dozen kids, mostly girls. The woman was the hotel's owner, and the children were friends of her eight-year-old daughter, who was also among the spectators. They waited for us—guests from a distant, mysterious land.

6. Anna's Inn

In the early years of Soviet emigration via Italy, the transients stayed in Rome and Ostia, but as their numbers increased, they started settling in the town of Ladispoli, and in the year of my exit (the most prolific of them all), the first busload of Soviet emigres landed in Monte Compatri. My mother and I were a part of that group.... The Joint's choice of the town was accidental because the hotel we were about to check into was idle at the time. It was not even a hotel—more like a boarding house, where Roman retirees (the same people from year to year) rented rooms in summer to escape the city heat. Earlier in spring, the hotel underwent renovations, which were completed a few weeks before the start of the season, and the gap was filled by the Joint, trying to cope with a record influx of emigrants from the USSR.

We got off the bus and entered the building. The hotel had a dozen guest rooms on the second floor, while the first floor housed a kitchen, a dining hall, and other service facilities. The owner's name was Anna, and the place was predictably called "Anna's Inn" (or something like that). Anna handled all the hotel's business herself. She did not speak English or Russian, but our Joint guide spoke some Italian. Anna and the guide showed the emigres to their rooms. The cortege was tailed by the local children, who soaked every detail of the guests' appearance and behavior. After dropping luggage in their rooms, the arrivals assembled in the dining hall for a meal and orientation. The meal was simple and tasty, but we were hungry enough to enjoy any food. The dining hall had an elevated stage (probably used to provide live entertainment to Anna's regular clientele), from where our Joint guide delivered his address.

After the guide's speech, my mother and I returned to our room to unpack the necessities. The Joint provided accommodations for one week, during which time the transients had to find private rentals for the remainder of their Italian stay (three months for those going to the US), so we were not about to get cozy. As soon as we opened the bags, there was a knock on the door. It was Anna. She was accompanied by our Joint guide. "Do you have a camera for sale?" asked the guide. "She's looking to buy one," and he nodded toward the hotel's owner, "She will pay the going price." My mother and I had two cameras: a rangefinder and an SLR, two models most emigrants brought to Italy for sale. The cameras were Soviet-made but of German ancestry, with Zeiss-designed lenses. The rangefinder went for thirty-five thousand Italian lire, and the SLR for eighty-five thousand (thirty and eighty-five US dollars, respectively). I asked which camera Anna wanted. The guide replied that she needed a rangefinder. I took the camera out of the bag, handed it to Anna, and she gave me thirty-five thousand lire. Then she and the guide left.

The unexpected sale pleased and encouraged me. I always recognized the reciprocity of free commercial exchange, yet, having grown up in a country where those exchanges were improper and often illegal, I could not help aggrandize the buying side. Such a feeling, besides placing me at a haggling disadvantage, added a chronic worry that locals might not be kind enough to buy my stuff. The sale of binoculars in Florence and Vienna's champagne trade did not suffice to dispel that annoying sense of mercantile inferiority, but Anna's purchase was a big step toward remedying it. I am not sure why Anna chose my mother and me to buy a camera from, perhaps by chance; still, buying from a hotel guest was a smart move on her part. That way, she would not have to travel to Rome and would have enough time to thoroughly check the device. She was a good businessperson, competent and tough. I do not know if she was married then, but she had a few children, all grown-ups except for the eight-year-old we met upon arrival at the hotel. The girl was a late child and her mother's miniature copy. Anna worshiped her.

By any measure of human achievement, Anna was an accomplished person—she ran a gainful business and raised a family—yet her social status was not particularly high. One day, she showed up wearing huge sunglasses that covered half of her face. News travels fast, so when my mother inquired about the masquerade, she was told by other emigres that Anna got into an argument with her older daughter's fiancée, and the future son-in-law had given Anna a black eye. The following day, as the swelling came down, she took the glasses off and wore the bruises openly, framed in the expression of solemn acquiescence… Italy of that time was torn by a political debate, with communists making strides in the elections, but I doubt it affected the public's attitude toward small-business folk like Anna. The town my mother and I eventually settled in had a mayor who owned a bar, and the grocery store's owner was an elected official, too. They were well respected, and I can hardly picture them with a black eye. Perhaps being a woman of humble origins in a title-revering society contributed to Anna's lack of recognition, but she seemed unaware that anything was wrong or could be different. And few examples better illustrate that deficit of self-esteem than the bizarre "engineers" episode I will describe next.

7. Engineers

The decade of emigration from the USSR preceding our exit created a body of knowledge that guided travelers on their journey. Which items to sell, what prices to ask, where to buy food—all those questions were answered, and many more. The information was constantly updated and passed along by word of mouth. One important topic dealt with renting rooms in Italy. The landlords usually asked prospective tenants about past occupations, and there, for an answer, the unwritten rule suggested something respectable, such as an engineer. An engineer's degree did not mean much in the Soviet Union, where egalitarian government policies devalued the title (similarly to how a college degree has been devalued in the United States). Of course, there were brilliant engineers in the USSR, but also less skilled ones, and they were all called engineers. It was different in Italy (as well as many other European countries), where an engineer was a professional title comparable to a doctor, a lawyer, or a university professor. Thus, although most Soviet emigres who claimed to be engineers had a diploma, they, in a way, misrepresented themselves. At the time of my Italian passage, the "engineer" card had lost its magic, as most emigres no longer dealt with landlords directly, taking up rooms vacated by their peers; plus, the locals in transients' enclaves had learned what a Soviet engineer was. I remember visiting a friend in Ladispoli, a temporary home to many Soviet emigrants. My friend and I went to the beach, where we struck up a conversation with a sand neighbor, a local lady. She spoke good English, had traveled a lot, and was very friendly. The woman asked which places in the Soviet Union my friend and I were from and about life in the old country. "And what did you do for a living there?" came the inevitable question. My friend replied that he was an engineer. The woman laughed. "You are all engineers," she said.

Our Monte Compatri emigre colony had engineers, too, yet despite the town's unfamiliarity with the Soviet version of the esteemed title, the presence of its holders among Anna's guests should not have caused a stir, as most did not plan to rent in the town. Nonetheless, the "engineer" topic did come into play and in a rather comical fashion... Our group had two related families—two brothers (or cousins) with their wives and children. They kept together and apart from the rest. I do not know what the brothers did in the Soviet Union or which school went to, but at the first opportunity, they let the innkeeper know they were engineers. I am sure nobody asked them about their former occupation (nobody asked me about mine or other members of our Monte Compatri party about theirs). Perhaps one brother stepped in front of the hotel's owner, stuck a finger in his chest, and said, "Ingegnere," then pointed at his sibling and said "Ingegnere" again. Anna was mightily impressed. Never did she imagine that a casual Joint business deal would grace her establishment with such high-class individuals. When making the arrangements, Anna overbooked the hotel by a couple of families, intending to place the surplus in homes of her relatives, but when she learned of the brothers' alleged occupation, she gave them her own apartment and moved in with the relatives herself. For the next few days, she was brimming with pride, telling everybody that she housed very important people whom she referred to only as "engineers." If Anna had inquired about other guests' professions, she might have found a few more engineers, but couldn't fathom more members of that shining elite in her little hotel. It would have been too good to be true.

I understood my fellow emigres when, pressed by the circumstances of a difficult transition, they stretched the truth or cut a corner; however, few of them would have delighted in exploiting others' innocence. That did not include the "engineers," though, who enjoyed the landlady's adulation and apartment as much as their own "savvy." The strangest thing, they morphed into the role that Anna had unwittingly assigned to them. She was a practical woman and a good judge of character, so her falling for a meaningless title surprised me. It also surprised our Joint guide, from whom I learned the intimate details of that affair. The guide was a Soviet emigrant going to Australia, to where the wait was almost a year—he had prepared for an extended stay and learned Italian. He was a big, amiable man, intelligent and educated. The guide was Anna's Joint contact; he knew what went on around the inn. He sounded frustrated and annoyed when telling me the "engineers" story, but trying to explain the truth to Anna would have embarrassed her. She had to learn it on her own. The situation reminds me of the "Touch of Class" episode from the *Fawlty Towers* sitcom, save Anna's case was more benign. Eventually, she realized her mistake. She said nothing to the "engineers" but stopped mentioning them on every occasion, and when they asked to stay in her apartment for a few extra days, Anna said no.

8. Rental Blues

The day after settling in Anna's hotel, my mother and I traveled to Rome to meet with Joint officials. We also wanted to use that visit to locate a couple of Soviet emigrant friends who were in Italy at the time. The Joint kept track of emigres in its care, sharing that data with new arrivals. My mother had a letter from a woman coworker to that woman's daughter, who had left the Soviet Union shortly before us and was still in Rome, so we confirmed the addressee's coordinates. But the most urgent task was finding a place to live, as Joint did not keep transients in hotels for more than a week and provided no help with permanent abodes (I cannot fathom why—they knew who was to leave Italy and when, and so could compile a list of potential rental vacancies). Going from door to door with a limited Italian vocabulary entailed a lesser chance of timely rental, so most transients learned about vacancies through personal contacts and in places of assembly, such as a small park near Joint's offices. After a Joint interview, my mother and I spent time in that park with fellow emigres, looking for referrals and other rental information. The reports from the housing front were not promising—the transients' outflow from Rome had slowed to a trickle, for some reason, while inflow continued at a normal pace, resulting in a severe rentals' shortage.

Disheartened by the bad news, my mother and I headed back to Monte Compatri. We walked toward Porta San Giovanni, from where our bus departed. Uncharacteristically, I felt no desire to explore the city, maybe because of the housing worries, but also because I found the Roman scene discomforting. Besides awkwardly proportioned buildings, there was an alarming proliferation of sculptures. Eroded marble figures of scantily clad humans clustered in unbearable heat, making the place look like a sauna and—when combined with noisy, dirty streets and suffocating vehicle exhaust—like hell. My mother did not fare much better, so we were relieved when our bus stopped in front of Anna's hotel. It was almost evening. We got off the bus and immediately felt a cool breeze from the nearby woods. Local children played in front of the hotel's entrance. They greeted us in Russian.

At the time of our Italian passage, the majority of Soviet emigrants settled in Rome, Ostia, and Ladispoli. Each location had its merits and drawbacks. Rome and Ostia provided easier access to the Joint and HIAS offices, historical monuments, and the flea market. The disadvantages included higher rents in better neighborhoods and more crime (mostly pickpocketing and purse-snatching) in cheaper ones, while summer heat had rendered the proximity to cultural sites less of a benefit. Ladispoli, on the other hand, was a pleasant town and relatively inexpensive. The inconvenience of a greater distance to Rome (about an hour's ride) was partially offset by excellent public transportation, including regularly scheduled buses and trains. In the late 1970s, the town became popular among Soviet emigres, especially during the beach season, but regardless of their pluses and minuses, that summer, all three locations were full, resulting in the transients' spillovers into neighboring towns. Among those spillovers was my mother's coworker's daughter (to whom we carried a letter), and the place her family settled in was the coastal town of Passoscuro, ten miles from Ladispoli.

The same day we arrived in Monte Compatri, I thought about renting there, and that idea became more appealing after a few days of grueling room searches amidst the trodden emigre enclaves. Renting in Monte Compatri made every sense. The ancient town exuded a special charm, sitting picturesquely atop a hill. The climate there was perhaps the most bearable around Rome at that time of the year, with cooler nights and fresher air of the highlands. Even the flora was different from the lower grounds—more northern, with taller trees and denser forests. Finding a room in Monte Compatri should have been easier, too. There was no competition from Soviet emigrants, as none rented in the town. Local landlords might be cautious about leasing to unfamiliar types, but I hoped Anna would vouch for my mother and me and even help us find a room. The "engineers'" experience had likely left the innkeeper with a sour aftertaste; however, it should not have affected her attitude toward the people she bought the camera from. One issue was the "engineers" themselves, who also entertained the idea of renting in Monte Compatri, but the town was big enough for all of us. Hence, had my mother agreed to remain there, I would have talked to Anna and gotten a room or small apartment in no time. But my mother did not agree.

The reason my mother refused to rent in Monte Compatri was the very absence of Soviet emigres, which would have made finding a room in the town an easier task. Perceived seclusion among strangers with a different language and customs alarmed her. Adding to those fears were the Joint's warnings about terrorists and other hazards. The dangers stated by the Joint were exaggerated; however, the risk of having my mother removed from her compatriots was real and rather serious. She did not handle isolation well. Outside of familiar companionship, her worries would amplify, negating the advantages of living in a Castelli Romani town. Thus, I did not pressure her, which, in hindsight, was a mistake. Out of our entire Italian stay, the week spent in Monte Compatri left the fondest memories for both of us. Later in America, my mother often reminisced about the town, the hotel where we lived, its owner, and the local youngsters who mingled with the guests or played outside, screaming at the top of their lungs all day long. The town we eventually rented in was modern, cosmopolitan, and bland. It had no allure of Anna's home place—a slice of great civilization fermented over the centuries like an aged cheese—and living there might offer other benefits not yet known to me at the time of our hotel stay…

Living in Monte Compatri would have spared my mother the annoying neighbors that our first rental gave her. It could have also provided us with extra income. On my first visit to Rome's Joint, I ran into an Odessa friend who worked there. He was about to leave for the United States and recommended me as his replacement. The pay was small, but it would have made a big difference to my mother and me. My friend's supervisor introduced me to the Joint's Italian chief—a neat, older lady. She and I spoke in English, and the woman said that I could start the job as soon as I rented the room. Joint was giving free transit passes to its temporary employees so those living in Ostia and especially Ladispoli would not have to spend much of their salary on commuting to work. The passes were accepted on commuter trains but not buses, and the town of our choice (or absence thereof) connected with Rome only by bus. I tried to make a deal with Joint—perhaps an allowance in the amount of a transit pass' cost—but was unsuccessful. There were only a few such positions and hundreds of emigres willing to take them, so Joint went with the next candidate… Monte Compatri did not have a train either, but it was closer to Rome, and there was a train station in Frascati, a few miles down the hill. Hence, had we remained in Monte Compatri, I would have kept the Joint job, my mother and I could have afforded a few luxuries such as eating out once a month or going to Rome more often, and the most of all, we would have had a unique experience of cultural immersion warming our hearts for the rest of times. And had my mother wished for more compatriots—working at the Joint, I might have advised selected emigres to rent in the town. But the events took a different course.

9. Balcony Apartment

The town my mother and I rented a room in was Passoscuro, where the addressee of the above letter lived with her husband and child. The letter was not a high priority, and I initially planned to deliver it after finding a rental, but the search was not going well. Our Joint-sanctioned stay in the hotel was ending, yet my mother and I had nowhere to go. "Signore Lehrman!" exclaimed Anna in an urgently reproaching tone on the last evening of the official term when she saw me in the hotel's lobby, coming from the city after another fruitless day of rental-hunting. I gesticulated that I would pay for the extra nights and rushed upstairs. In those days, Italy was cheap, and a room in Anna's Inn cost ten US dollars per night; however, paying it out of pocket would have set us back financially a painful distance. Just three more nights would have wiped out the proceeds from the camera sale. But money was not the only issue; Anna needed the rooms to prepare for her regular guests. So, the following day, I went to Passoscuro.

Although close to the major hub of Ladispoli, the town of Passoscuro was inconveniently removed from the main roads and rail tracks. My Roman bus exited the freeway onto a local lane and continued through little groves and farm fields for ten more minutes to Passoscuro, which was the last stop. I quickly found the address, on the second floor of a two-story apartment building on the town's opposite side. A young woman opened the door. I introduced myself and handed her the letter. The woman invited me inside, where I met the rest of the family. The room they lived in was spacious and had a large balcony. My hosts told me about Passoscuro and its small (a dozen families) Soviet emigrant population. The hosts knew of a room down the street that was coming up for rent in a few days. My mother and I could sleep on their balcony until then. The husband offered to accompany me to see that room, and we took off right away.

The upcoming vacancy was in a newly built, two-story private house. The house owners occupied the ground floor, while the second floor was shared by two emigre families. Apartment sharing was commonplace among the Soviet emigrants. The Joint allowance was too small to pay full rent, so the transients shared apartments in Soviet-style communes. That did not present an inconvenience to former Soviet citizens, most of whom had lived in similar conditions all their lives. In Italy, an emigre commune usually had one family that dealt with the landlord, collecting rent and utilities from other neighbors and sometimes deciding on new tenants. With such a family (or with its head, whom I will call a "primary tenant"), I was about to meet.

An Italian male opened the door. I said the word "Appartamento," and he invited my escort and me inside. As we got in, I heard the hum of many voices coming from the house's depths. The Italian fellow yelled someone's name, and a tall man about sixty years of age appeared in the foyer. He was the primary tenant. The man confirmed that his neighbors were moving out, and the room was up for rent. I could have it if we agreed on the terms. My companion interrupted the discussion, saying he ought to go home and would wait for me there. He then left while the primary tenant and I went inside the house... The house's interior was airy, sparsely furnished, and surprisingly cool. All rooms had ceramic floors, and the outside walls were made of a porous stone that felt almost cold to the touch. The windows were relatively small, like in many other Roman buildings, but I already understood the purpose behind this disproportionality—it helped keep the summer heat out, contributing to indoor comfort. As in most Italian homes, there was no air conditioning, and none was needed.

The primary tenant took me upstairs to show the room. The room's occupants were away (in fact, I never got to meet them), so my guide opened their door to look inside. After that, we came down to the dining hall, where, behind a big round table, sat ten or so people having dinner. Theirs were the voices I heard in the foyer when I entered the house. The primary tenant introduced me to the party. The Italian man who had opened the front door was at the table, too. He was the house's owner. He owned the house with his younger brother, who was also present. The brothers were in their late thirties or mid-forties and looked much alike—of average height, with dark receding hair and dark eyes. Both were a little overweight but seemed healthy, and their deeply tanned skin emitted a matte glow, which added to the overall impression of well-being. The owners were flanked by their wives and possibly a child or two. The rest of the diners were the primary tenant, his wife, and their two adult sons.

I do not remember (or never knew) the occasion of that dinner and which side, Italian or Russian, initiated it. Perhaps the primary tenant celebrated a birthday or an anniversary and invited the owners, as I witnessed no more joint meals during our stay there, yet found that gathering to be a heartwarming example of Italian congeniality. Not all the locals were friendly all the time (albeit more often than I anticipated), but even when conflicts did arise, the transients were treated like equals, for better or worse. During our Passoscuro stay, the town's Soviet emigre population almost doubled, putting a strain on the city commute. If, in the beginning, the rush-hour bus accommodated the seating needs of all passengers, now a few people had to stand, and those standing were frequently Italians. Perhaps some of them blamed the newcomers for the discomfort, yet I never observed any overt hostility, and when the locals decided to address the issue, they did it in a surprisingly civil manner… One morning, a group of Soviet emigrants at the Rome bus stop was approached by an Italian man holding a stack of papers. The man spoke English. He explained that the authorities had been slow to react to the town's population growth, so the local activists decided to petition for an extra rush-hour bus. The man was collecting signatures and asked the transients to sign the petition, which they did. A few weeks later, when I went to Rome in the morning, there were two buses at the stop, one behind another, ready to take passengers. That incident had an especially welcoming feel, as the petition organizers could have collected enough signatures from Italian residents alone, but chose to involve the emigres to make them feel like part of the community.

From his seat, the house owner waved to me to join the feast. I was eager to go back to Monte Compatri, but did not want to start the new cohabitation on an unsociable note, and decided to spend a few minutes in the diners' company. I was given a plate, served myself an appetizer, and ate slowly, studying the future neighbors… The primary tenant was an imposing man with a leonine face and a mane of grey hair. He used to be a prominent figure in the Soviet Union, possibly a company chief or a professional sports coach (I thought of the latter, as his sons mentioned playing professional hockey in the old country). His demeanor was stately and tempered. The sons, on the other hand, seemed hyped and craving a spotlight. Paradoxically, they fit the Italian stereotype, marked by overly emotional speech and excessive gesturing, far better than the house's owners. The latter behaved with an amicable reserve, speaking evenly in low voices, so it fell upon the primary tenant's sons to maintain the festive atmosphere. Their family was going to Canada, where the waiting period was half a year—they had been in Italy for three or four months already and had learned a few Italian words. But those words were not enough to drive the conversation; hence, the Soviet brothers grimaced, gesticulated wildly, and acted silly overall. In contrast, their mother was the quietest at the table. She must have been in her fifties, but looked older than that. During the dinner, she did not say a word and appeared absorbed as if tracking a fly trapped inside her skull. It was clear that the primary tenants had little in common with my mother and me. That would have mattered less had the house's layout allowed for a better separation between neighbors, like in our Odessa commune, but it was too much to ask of a place intended for one large family or, at most, for the related two. Yet, I had to take that room, as we could no longer stay at Anna's and had no other prospects.

It was time to go back to Monte Compatri. I thanked my hosts for the meal and headed for the exit to catch the bus to Rome. A few minutes remained to call on my new friends. I told them I had rented the room and would be moving to their balcony the next day, then rushed to the bus stop… I reached Anna's hotel late at night. My mother was already worried—she was glad to hear the good news. In the morning, we ate a quick breakfast and got ready to check out. I found Anna, told her we were leaving, and reached into my pocket to pay for the extra night, but she refused the money.

10. Sharing Arrangements

We slept two nights on our friends' balcony, then moved to the rented room. My mother did not like the new neighbors. She revealed nothing to them but shared with me her impressions, which mostly coincided with mine. We only disagreed about the primary tenant's wife. If our distaste for the male neighbors was muted—more of a disappointment that things had not turned out better (and I rather liked the primary tenant himself)—my mother's aversion toward the other female was unflagging. Such an attitude seemed irrational, as the two women had no history between them, yet it reflected my mother's tendency to form opinions about people in a flash. Perhaps the years of living on the edge, when decisions had to be made fast and mistakes could be deadly, had sharpened her perception of human behavior—tiny details, invisible to the average insight, that warned of danger. She sometimes erred, like when, already in the United States, she once claimed that she had heard my downstairs neighbors in the building curse Jews (the neighbors were an elderly Jewish couple), but in the case of the primary tenant's wife, my mother's hunches were justified.

A notable contrast between apartment sharing in Italy and the USSR was that in Italy, appliances were shared, too. The neighbors would establish a schedule of gas range and washing machine use, divide the space inside a refrigerator, and make other similar pacts. The primary tenant's wife violated those agreements. Just days after we moved in, when my mother went to the kitchen in her time slot to prepare a meal, she found the primary tenant's wife using the gas range. The woman explained that she had been delayed and needed a few more minutes to finish the chore. "I'll wait," said my mother, and went back to our room. She was annoyed. The time slots were sparse enough to avoid overlaps, so why did the neighbor woman pick that moment to do her cooking? Not that she was busy other times. My mother, who was punctual to a fault, religiously adhered to her promises and would have been ashamed to breach them. The primary tenant's wife had no such scruples.

A couple of days later, the primary tenant's wife committed another offense: she put her stewpot in our refrigerator section. My mother confronted the violator, and the woman removed the pot, but in a few more days, trespassed on our fridge space again… When renting that room, my mother and I believed our predecessors had vacated it because they were leaving Italy. However, as we later found out, those people were still in the country, just moved to another apartment in Ladispoli.

So, my mother concluded that the primary tenant's wife had driven them out. That may have been the case, as the woman had difficulty sharing things. She likely lived a comfortable life in the Soviet Union, protected by her husband's status and income, and never experienced the complex relations of the Soviet commune. Her husband was Jewish, while she was not, and possibly unhappy with his decision to emigrate, which she silently protested by making trouble. Even her demeanor conveyed not aggression but a confused mind, as if she barely understood what she was doing. However, my mother was not interested in the underlying psychology; she was furious and ready to let the sparks fly. Therefore, I approached the primary tenant and asked him to influence his wife. The primary tenant apologized (which she had never done) and promised to talk to her. He was a reasonable man, but seemed marginalized within his family, with his wife and sons siding against him. Still, in this case, the sons, who were present during the conversation, agreed with their father, and how could they not? The transients had fewer emotional outlets abroad than in the old country, where pressures at home could be relieved at work, in the company of friends, or just by walking familiar streets—remedies unreachable in a temporary state. Hence, in Italy or Vienna, everybody tried to avoid conflicts, which made even more sense considering the situation's evanescence. In such a context, the primary tenant's wife's little provocations were highly improper and would have embarrassed her family had they become notorious among the emigres. The house's owners might not have liked it, either.

The conversation with the primary tenant halted the intrusions into my mother's kitchen space but did little to assure her comfort. The antipathy she initially felt toward the primary tenant's wife was now reinforced by the woman's discourteous behavior, making neighborly relations between the two unattainable. They barely acknowledged each other in the house and tried to avoid being in the same place at the same time. My mother was particularly troubled by the situation because it echoed her old problems back in the Odessa commune, evoking dark thoughts that such a living was her destiny. On the plus side, the evasion routine was made easier by the house's owners being absent most of the time, which gave my mother and her nemesis more space to maneuver. The owners lived in Rome, coming to Passoscuro on weekends, and, when in town, occupied the first floor, while the tenants could use the living and dining rooms there at other times. However, my mother cared little about those amenities and tried to escape the house whenever possible. She spent a lot of time with her coworker's daughter (on whose balcony we slept the first two nights in Passoscuro). They talked, walked with the child, shopped for food, and often went to the beach. The young woman's husband and I sometimes joined them.

    I intend no harm to the area's tourism, but have to mention that I did not enjoy the beaches in Passoscuro and Ladispoli. The beaches lacked little in the department of sand and sun—the sand penetrated every item in its domain, and the sun scorched everything in its rays' path—but those were drawbacks I could cope with, if I derived a pleasure from dipping into the sea; however, that pleasure was noticeably missing. The culprit was the water itself, tepid and bland, like a salty mix that people rinse a sore throat with. Unlike the Black Sea in Odessa and the Atlantic Ocean in New York, that part of the Tyrrhenian Sea produced no ocean smell and provided little relief from the oppressive heat. Perhaps the shallow bottom extending far from the shore impeded fresh inflow, but whatever the cause, one hardly felt immersed in the miraculous solution earthly life had come from. Thus, I seldom attended the beach, despite having little else to do in a small coastal town. Luckily, Rome was an hour away, and we traveled there to buy food at the Round Market near Termini, where the prices were lower. And on the first few Sundays of our Italian stay, I went to the city to sell stuff at the flea market.

11. Flea Market

Not long before applying for an exit visa in Odessa, I had a chat with my submarine friend, where we talked about emigration and our mutual acquaintances who had made the big move. My friend's circumstances had rendered him an unlikely candidate to leave the Soviet Union, but I was nearing that decision and mentioned it in the conversation. "And you will be selling on the flea market, like other emigrants?" asked my friend disapprovingly, implying the disrepute of the said activity as a measure of my future lapse. Such was the effect of the Soviet propaganda thrown at us from a young age that even my friend, who could be quite unscrupulous when pursuing his interests, chose one of the oldest and most civilized ways to make a living as an example of a shameful trade. "I will do no such thing!" I replied indignantly to my friend's innuendo but thought that I might do it, after all, if there was no other option. And indeed, there was none.

Thus, I couldn't help the feeling of reluctance with which I traveled to Rome's flea market for the first time. I had a history of selling a camera in Monte Compatri and champagne in Vienna, but those were private deals with no public exposure, unlike what was about to unfold now... The flea market was set on a wide asphalt lot, a short bus ride from the Termini station. Every Sunday, early morning, long rows of merchant stands (portable tables) cropped up on the market's grounds. One by one, the sellers took available tables, laid out their wares, and waited for the customers. Market attendants then made rounds collecting fees. One table cost five US dollars per day. That busy summer, tables were in high demand, so I left for Rome with the first bus to secure a selling stand. My mother remained in Passoscuro.

I entered the marketplace with a distant fear of being recognized by someone I knew. That fear was utterly irrational, as the only people who could recognize me were other emigres doing the same business, but that feeling reflected a deeply rooted prejudice conveyed by my submarine friend during our conversation back in Odessa... Most tables were still available. I picked one in the middle, opened my suitcase, and started readying the shop.

The market was filling up with sellers; soon, all the tables near me were occupied. The first buyers also appeared (many locals attempted to come early to take advantage of a wider selection), and within an hour, trading was in full swing. My opening sale featured a record album. It was a concert performance of Aida conducted by Toscanini. I liked that recording and hoped it would attract no buyers, but the set was gone in minutes[3]. I got three thousand lire (three US dollars) for it. A few kitchen towels followed, and then came the turn of my collection's crown jewel: the SLR camera. An Italian man in his late twenties stopped at my table and asked how much the camera was. He looked a little testy, which raised a slight alarm in me, as most flea market shoppers were relaxed and in a good mood. "*Ottantacinque mille lire*[4]," I told the price. With nervous hands, the man opened the camera's battery compartment, took out the battery, and gazed into the viewfinder. "*Non funziona*," he said. The phrase did not need a translation. "*Funziona*," I replied, learning Italian on the fly. "Put the battery back in," I added in English, but the lad did not understand. "*Non funziona!*" he repeated angrily, trying to discern something in the viewfinder. "*Funziona*. Read the instructions," I said, pointing at the Russian-language booklet and getting angry myself. At that moment, another Italian—a slender, middle-aged man in a light jacket—appeared on the scene. I had noticed him before as he walked a few times past my stand. My fellow merchants told me he was a regular at the Sunday event, acting as a middleman and maybe buying for his business. According to them, he spoke some Russian and occasionally helped emigres negotiate sales. He certainly was not an ordinary buyer. Every time I visited the flea market, I saw him walking between rows, checking out merchandise, yet buying infrequently, if at all. He could be a reseller, as he knew the entire line of emigre-offered products very well, but also act as a steward hired by the Joint or flea market owners to watch the trading, resolve arguments, and safeguard sellers against local swindlers (one of whom might have been my camera buyer trying to lowball the price). The lively exchange at my table attracted the man-in-a-jacket's attention, and he approached to find out what was going on. The unhappy customer began to jabber in Italian, perhaps complaining that I tried to sell him defective merchandise. The man in a jacket took the camera, inserted the battery, and quickly tested the device. Then he nodded "all right" to the buyer, who promptly completed the purchase. The Italians walked away, talking to each other… and leaving me eighty-five thousand lire richer. At the market's close, one-third of my inventory was gone.

I returned to Passoscuro full of impressions, calm and confident, like I had not been in a long while. My mind kept replaying the events of the day, generating a stream of therapeutic emotions. The dreaded activity turned out to be my happiest Italian pastime. It was a pleasure to stand

---

[3] I have it now on video, whose existence I didn't suspect then.

[4] Eighty-five thousand lire.

in the open, watch a procession of colorful characters, interact with them, and, at the end of the day, have extra money in my pocket. But the most satisfying sensation was being a contributor, a participant in a societal spin, and not just a stranger in a strange land. There were other pleasant moments during our Italian stay—I enjoyed Rome's tourist attractions, for example—but only at the flea market did I feel totally assured and free. There, I provided services people wanted, transcending the barriers of language and culture. Later, in the United States, I became familiar with scholarly opinions accenting economic freedom as the foundation of a free and prosperous society, and recalled my flea market experience. The authors did not have to convince me.

An amusing case of commercial camaraderie described to me my former coworker, whom I ran across in Ladispoli. The town of Ladispoli had its own flea market, which served the selling needs of Soviet emigrants and was illegal. A black flea market, so to speak. That market had no stands or fees—the action took place in a street park, which curiously reminded me of that in Odessa, where aspiring emigrants once gathered to honor the "big list." The site in Ladispoli looked very similar, except that the emigrants were real and selling stuff. Most had only a few items unsold at the flea market in Rome and were no longer worthy of table fees and the cost of the commute. I had such items too (a couple of kitchen towels, a few drill bits, and a pair of opera glasses), which I brought with me to the United States, but other emigres, especially those living in Ladispoli, attempted to sell their leftovers on the "black" flea market. Not that they risked very much. The Italian authorities' liberal attitude toward minor infractions ensured that nobody was arrested or jailed; however, the police could seize the merchandise. The violators might get it back, I believe, by going to the precinct, paying a fine, and promising not to do it again. The casualties of the police raids were mostly sellers who peddled the full stock, being too lazy to haul it to the city or too stingy to pay the fees. Those sellers were an easier target, as a heavy load impeded their maneuverability. Alternatively, the light sellers could quickly hide their trinkets, which, even when impounded, were seldom worth begging for. One such fleet-footed seller was my former colleague. I used to work with him at the engineering bureau in Odessa, where he headed the precision measurements group. He was a scrawny, bespectacled, hollow-cheeked man whose jaws appeared clenched in a permanent spasm. He was abrasive and abrupt but well-respected by colleagues for his directness and professionalism. Thus, it was a pleasant surprise when I saw him in Ladispoli's park (which I visited because of the place's reputation as a Soviet emigrant community hub). My former coworker was selling an amber necklace. Like me, he must have valued the social side of the trading more than the financial one, being reluctant to close the deal. We walked in the park for an hour, my companion held the necklace in his hands, and buyers occasionally asked him about the price. *"Quaranta Cinque[5],"* he replied curtly and kept walking, seemingly disinterested in the response. He was the one who told me about the intricacies of the Ladispoli flea market and police raids. During one such raid, carabinieri interrupted a sale and impounded the wares, but the buyer (a local man) was so incensed by the frustrated deal that he got physical with the lawmen. He was arrested and taken away in a police van, together with the confiscated items.

My former colleague recounted the above police raid incident as a peculiar and humorous occurrence; however, I couldn't help noting the story's intrinsic message—about commercial interest's unifying power. And that message appeared even more pronounced amidst the political divide, which, at the time, was tearing Italian society apart…

---

[5] My friend was asking for forty-five thousand lire.

12. Political Divide

Passoscuro was a communist town—the town's key elected officials were members of the Italian Communist Party. The town's mayor, who owned a bar-restaurant, was a communist, and the supermarket's owner (a councilman, I believe) was a communist, too. Coming from a communist country, where all restaurants and stores belonged to the government, I found the mayor's and the grocer's political affiliation peculiar, as they advocated a system that would, if not delegitimize, at least sideline their trade. They likely had not studied the movement's history or the works of its masterminds and could espouse any version of communism that fit their tastes. For the restaurateur-mayor and his middle-class comrades, communism was a fancy facade of contemporary Western liberalism, and there ought to be some hedging, too. By then, the Italian communists no longer maintained close ties with Moscow and often criticized the Soviet government for the mistreatment of the dissidents, restrictive emigration policies, and lack of freedom. Most treated Soviet emigrants well. I cannot speak of the Passoscuro mayor since I never visited his bar-restaurant, but we frequently went to the supermarket (a small place by American standards, about the size of a drugstore, yet the largest grocery store in Passoscuro), and the owner was always friendly and helpful.

In Italy of those days, politics was a national pastime. The country was like a theatrical stage, with the citizenry acting in a play. The feeling of pretense stemmed from an impression that Italians lived a good life. A mild climate, scenic surroundings, authentic Mediterranean cuisine, and three-hour lunch breaks produced the happiest and healthiest-looking population I have ever encountered. The buses we traveled to Rome by had a crew of two people who alternated between the roles of a driver and a conductor. The crewmen were young males—smooth, laid-back, and always in a good mood. From an efficiency standpoint, I saw no reason one person could not handle both driving and ticketing, as it is done in other places, including the United States. The ride took only an hour, and the infrequent service left drivers enough time to rest. Perhaps the second driver was a concession won by their union, which, like most unions in the country, supported the Communists. Every commuter bus had such a tandem crew. I am certain other public employees enjoyed comparably generous benefits, so why not ensure the public paying for those benefits was served well? Unfortunately, the opposite was taking place. The flames of the class struggle burned hot, discharging flurries of strikes that impeded vital services and wreaked havoc on people's lives. The emigres were affected, too, especially those who lived outside Rome, such as my mother and I. The service we used the most was transport to and from the city, and it was constantly disrupted by the walkouts. Every time going to Rome, I did not know where I would spend the coming night—in my bed in Passoscuro or on a bench in the Termini's waiting hall. Sleeping at train stations was not new to me, but luckily, I never had to do it in Rome. If the Passoscuro service were on strike, I would take a Ladispoli bus, get off at the Passoscuro junction, and walk several miles to the town. If Ladispoli buses were not running, either, there was a Ladispoli train, followed by a hitchhike to the above junction, or, with any luck, straight to Passoscuro. Or one could wait for the strike's end, as most walkouts were meant to send a message and did not last more than a few hours.

The reasons for the bus strikes were usually unknown, as Rome did not have a bus terminal, and all the information had to come from the drivers; however, the train operators had Termini's electronic tableau and used it to tell the world about their grievances. For the most part, those complaints had nothing to do with the strikers' working conditions but represented general political statements… During one of my flea-market trips, I became acquainted with a fellow emigre selling next to me. After the market's closing, we left together and headed for the Termini. My countryman was taking a train to Ladispoli, where he lived, while the Passoscuro bus departed an hour later; hence, I followed the new acquaintance inside the train station to finish the chat. The Ladispoli trains were not running. There was a message on the tableau in Italian that we could not understand. My companion expected the tableau to display important travel information, such as when the service would be back on, so we started looking for someone to translate the text. Finally, we found an English-speaking[6] commuter who gave us the answer. The tableau stated that the railway union had called a walkout in solidarity with another union, striking in a different industry in another part of the country! The protests were getting absurd, burdening the public and the protesters themselves. After all, the strikers were the public, too. Outside their jobs, the drivers rode trains and buses as passengers, and garbage collectors wanted their streets to be clean, like everybody else. They had family members and friends who suffered from the disruptions, and whose patience, like the patience of the entire country, was wearing thin. I believe most rank-and-file union members felt uneasy about so many strikes, but they were bound by the organizational discipline.

---

[6] Few Italians spoke English in those days. Even in Rome, where many residents could speak foreign languages, the most common were Spanish, French, and German.

It must have been easier for us, Soviet emigrants, to cope with transit irregularities, as they entailed only a few adjustments among the many we had to go through. The chaos caused by the strikes added little to the upheaval that accompanied the emigration process, so rather than complaining, we sought solutions to individual travel hiccups. In Rome, the Passoscuro bus' last stop was near the Termini, whose surrounding streets collectively served as the city's bus terminal. I often could tell that something was wrong when too many buses were parked in the area or there were too few passengers inside, but regardless of these indicators, it became part of the boarding etiquette to ask the drivers if they were on strike... One morning, there were delays going to Rome, so I expected better luck on the way home; however, the strikers must have been in a playful mood and stretched the stoppages into the afternoon. I became aware of the problem when I saw numerous empty buses on the way to my street corner. The Passoscuro bus was there, but it had no passengers: only a crew. I walked up the front steps to the driver's cabin. "Strike?" I asked. The driver, a middle-aged, unfamiliar man, lowered his head and apologetically mumbled, "Si." I turned around to get off. "Wait," the driver halted me and started calling a dispatcher on the radio. He spoke for a while, then an expression of relief appeared on his face, and he waved to me to go inside. The strike was over.

I walked to the end of the bus and sat next to a window. Ten more minutes remained before the scheduled departure, a welcoming pause after an exhausting day. As I looked through the window, a woman on the other side of the street attracted my attention. The woman must have been ninety years old, short and thin, with a wrinkled crescent of a face crowned by a shock of white hair. Next to her stood a large shopping cart filled with bags and packages. She was waiting for her bus. In a few minutes, the bus pulled to the opposite corner, and the woman made an immense effort to cross the street, pushing the cart ahead of her. She reached the bus' front door and called the driver to help her with the luggage. The driver came out. He spoke in a low voice, but the woman's reaction revealed what she had heard: the bus was on strike and taking no passengers. The woman's posture changed to one of frustration and disbelief, and she began to yell. It was hard to imagine a so powerful sound coming from such a frail body. The old woman bellowed like a firetruck siren, filling the air of several blocks with her cries. My Italian was too limited to understand the entire tirade, but one word, repeated several times, I recognized with absolute certainty. It was "Mussolini."

13. *Arrivederci Roma*

Perhaps it was the summer heat, but the old woman's bus stop episode had marked the peak of the strike activity, which soon subsided together with the air temperature. Life was improving in other spheres, too. The transients' outflow jam, responsible for rental shortages, had cleared up, and my mother and I moved to another apartment. Our new quarters were in a two-story multi-unit building several blocks from the old address. The new apartment's layout was better suited to shared living: two family rooms, separated by a kitchen with a small dining hall (we used it as a lounge, as each family ate in their room), provided enough privacy for the occupants. Ironically, such privacy, which would have been so welcome at the previous address, was less important now, since the new neighbors turned out to be pleasant, considerate people. They were a family of three: husband, wife, and their four-year-old daughter. The parents were about my age, although individual relations formed not just by oldness and gender but also by a place in the family structure. Thus, my mother and the married couple connected as parents, while my counterpart was a four-year-old child. My mother became friendly with the wife—they chatted often, confiding in each other—while I socialized more with the husband and the little girl.

My association with the four-year-old did not get off to the right start. She was a bright, playful child who realized and took advantage of our peer status in the family hierarchy and my limits in controlling her. As a stranger, I presumed no right to discipline the girl, even raise my voice, but could not complain to her parents, either. It would have been farcical for a grown man to ask for protection against a small child; plus, as odd as it might seem, I felt bound by some children's *esprit de corps*. Hence, the little neighbor, who was going through a highly exploratory phase in her life, used our interactions to test the boundaries of her leeway, as well as those of my patience. She demanded my undivided attention and, when I sent her away, committed acts of poor manners that she knew would have been punished by her parents. Of course, had I been the girl's age, she would be the one complaining to her parents about me, but under the circumstances, my only recourse was to avoid the lounge (where we usually met) when the diminutive nuisance was on the loose.

One evening, I was reading in the hall when my tormentor appeared at the door. She had just finished dinner and held a piece of bread, which she occasionally chewed upon. She saw me and rushed to play, but I was tired after a day in the city and offered her a rain check. "We will play tomorrow; I promise you," I said. But the girl would not take no for an answer. She kept badgering me and, when she saw she was getting nowhere, showed her displeasure by spitting the chewed bread onto the floor. "Clean it up," I said. The little shrew burst into laughter. She did not realize she had already lost the match by leaving material proof of bad behavior. Now, if her father walked into the hall (which he usually did around that time of day) and saw the spittle, he would know right away where it came from, and if he asked me for confirmation, I would not be a part of any cover-up. So, all I had to do to get even was wait for the girl's father to show up, but decided to give my intermittent friend another chance. "If you do not clean this mess right now," I said firmly, "I will not play with you tomorrow or ever. I will not talk to you or want anything to do with you…" I saw that the ultimatum had an effect: my playmate stopped laughing and stood hesitantly, perhaps trying to imagine what her life would look like if my threats were realized. Then, she quietly left the hall. I continued to read. A minute later, there was a dragging sound, and the girl appeared at the door, towing a stand-up dustpan and a broom that were taller than she. Trying not to look in my direction and fighting tears of ignominy, she started working on the spittle. She cleaned up the floor, took the utensils back to the bathroom, and returned to the hall's entrance to see my reaction. "Good job," I said, "Will you behave then?" "I will behave," she replied. The girl's words were still in the air when her father entered the hall. He walked past his daughter and approached me. We exchanged greetings. "What did she do?" he asked curiously. Behind his back, the girl made me a desperate face, shaking her head side to side in a silent "do not tell" plea. "We had a slight misunderstanding," I answered her father, "but have sorted things out. Everything is alright now."

    The spittle incident was the turning point in my relations with the pesky neighbor, who overnight became an exemplary child. She was obedient and respectful, showing on every occasion that she valued our friendship. The moment of humiliation was forgotten, and the new order was happily embraced. Nothing after that clouded my coexistence with the neighbors. They were also going to America, to the West Coast, and we lost contact after the parting. My mother saved the phone number of their relatives in Los Angeles, but things got hectic after we arrived in the United States, and she didn't call. Similarly, we lost track of Leon's family, whom we also liked. Leon was a temperamental and boorish person, but dependable and sincere, while his wife made up for the charm her husband lacked, and the children were likable and well-behaved. The family was from Kiev, where Leon used to work as an auto mechanic, but not any auto mechanic—his specialty was luxury foreign cars, such as Mercedes and BMW brands. In the Soviet Union of that time, only top people in the government, the arts, and academia owned such vehicles. They were buying those cars abroad and, with no dealer networks at home, relied upon specialists like Leon (who were very few) to maintain the pricey possessions. "You would never believe who my customers were," Leon told me once. He had good connections and lived well in the old country. In addition, it was hard to recognize him as a Jew since, in appearance and behavior, he looked like a typical Russian or Ukrainian urban redneck, and only after closer observation did one sense in him a delicate awareness of limits that I associated with being Jewish in the USSR. Yet, his temper had to be an issue, or it was something else that caused his early exit... In Italy, Leon's family rented in Ostia. I visited them once, but the distance did not allow us to spend more time together. They were going to the United States, and there was a good chance we would end up in the same place, most likely New York City. An emigre's destination locale in America depended on a sponsor—an individual or organization that pledged support for a newcomer during the latter's first months in the country. Individual sponsors were usually relatives or friends, while organizations were local Jewish communities. But at the time of our coming, the local communities were overwhelmed by a massive influx of Soviet immigrants, and except for the individually sponsored, everybody went to New York (which was seen as the worst scenario because of the city's high crime rate and minimal assistance package). My mother and I did not have individual sponsors, so we were going to New York.

In Rome, Soviet emigrants not only sold things; they bought some, too, mostly sunglasses and shoes. Those items could be purchased very cheaply—sunglasses for as little as one dollar and a pair of shoes for ten. The majority of emigres had limited wardrobes. I, for example, left the Soviet Union with two pairs of shoes, which were pretty worn out, and my mother fared no better. It seemed cheaper to buy shoes in Italy and bring them to the United States than to buy in America. I still have a quarter-pound, metal-frame sunglasses that I purchased at the Round Market in Rome, and the shoes fell apart after a few months of wear in New York. My mother's Italian footwear did not last much longer. I purchased my pair at the San Giovanni flea market, the city's largest selection of cheap shoes, but there were other places that offered similar deals. One such place was a few storefronts across the Trevi Fountain, where my mother and I found ourselves another Sunday. I am sure they were shoes that brought us there and not the fountain itself. My mother was little interested in sculpture, while I had already observed a marble orgy of the famous composition; still, we approached the fountain. Suddenly, on the other side of the reservoir, I saw a familiar face. It was Leon. He saw me, too, and we walked toward each other. Leon must have sold his trading stock and was on a sightseeing jaunt with his wife and kids. We shook hands. Seconds later, Leon's family and my mother joined the gathering. Everybody was delighted by the encounter. I had not spoken to Leon since my last flea market trip more than a month ago, and my mother had not seen them since Vienna. We chatted buoyantly, then separated—the women and the children walked toward the stores while Leon and I continued talking near the fountain. "Perhaps next time we will see each other in New York," I said to Leon, knowing that he did not have an individual sponsor, either. "We are not going to New York," he replied, "We are going to Canada…." At that point in the process, if transients wanted to change their destination country, they had to find another organization to support them, as the current one would not permit the switch. "I begged them to send me to any place other than New York City," continued Leon, his face turning red with anger, "but they refused." However, the Joint was just one (albeit the largest) among several organizations that cooperated and sort of competed with each other, assisting emigres. Leon told Joint he would not go to New York, Joint dismissed him, and Rav Tov picked his family up (or Leon made the Rav Tov arrangement in advance, knowing he would be dropped by Joint). "I am not bringing my children to New York!" concluded Leon with his usual fervor.

The Trevi encounter happened in September, the last month of our Italian sojourn. The weather was still warm but tolerable and getting cooler. I sold most of our merchandise during the first month in the country, netting over two hundred dollars; plus, we had another two hundred, exchanged back in the Soviet Union. We were not going to spend that money in Italy, as we believed we might need it in America. So, having what looked to us like a decent sum made my mother and me feel more secure. And we already enjoyed the new apartment, which added to the sense that things were going well. Before then, my mother had avoided going to Rome, except to buy food at the Round Market near the Termini, partly because of transit strikes, but now that the strikes' danger had receded, she started traveling with me more often. We visited Saint Peter's Basilica, the Vatican, Castel Sant'Angelo, and the Colosseum, as well as other, less famous but no less impressive sites. On my first trip to the Joint, I bought an English version of Rome's travel guide, had studied it since, and was forearmed. Most places we visited had free admission, and many that did not, accepted museum passes the

Joint was giving to emigres. My mother enjoyed those trips, while I felt the city was growing on me; still, it remained a strange and somewhat unsettling place.

The happier part of our Italian stay was interrupted by a letter from HIAS informing us that we had been granted entry to the United States. The letter indicated the month's end as a departure date. The next day, I went to HIAS to pick up our papers. I finished my business early and decided to take a stroll through Rome, perhaps for the last time. The weather was perfect: not too warm, with clear views, a fresh breeze, and cloudy skies spilling showers onto the ground. I do not remember any other rainy day in Rome—there had to be some, but not when I was in the city. The showers were brief and did not cause discomfort; moreover, they washed the emotional lens through which I saw the surroundings. Everything looked different now—the streets, the buildings, and the monuments—revealing many details and the total meaning I had not realized before. My route took me through the old Jewish ghetto, with its shabby backyards and mesh of clotheslines, to the Tiber embankment. At a distance on my right, loomed the dome of St. Peter's Basilica and the cylinder of Castel Sant'Angelo with a silhouette of a cypress tree in between against a lighter backdrop of the clearing horizon. I had seen the two-structure composition before, from another angle, and maybe less the tree, but at that moment, with the wet pavement reflecting the pastel sky, the picture took on a surreal quality, and suddenly, it hit me where I was. The ancient ruins, the burning sun, the yellow-brown stone, the eroding marble… all came together to tell the story of human endeavor through glorious civilizations, their rise and fall, from generation to generation to the present day. History from books became almost material, as if I were a part of it. The eternal city revealed itself to me, as it would not have done to a mere tourist, but only to those who lived and struggled in its realm.

All good things come to an end, and so did my mother's and my Italian stay. Our neighbors departed for the United States a few days earlier, leaving us in the apartment alone[7]. Now, it was our turn. We were waiting for HIAS transportation to take us to the airport. I went outside with the bags to meet the vehicle. My mother remained in the apartment. I had already surrendered the keys and planned to use the intercom to signal her the vehicle's arrival. In a few minutes, a small van pulled up to the building, and the driver got out. He was in a hurry. I ran to the

---

[7] The beach season was over, plus the Soviet government put a hard stop on emigration, so few people were looking for apartments in Passoscuro.

building's glass door to buzz my mother down, but the buzzer did not work, and the lobby lights were out. A power outage had occurred while I was waiting for the van. We had no power outages before, so why did it have to happen now? As if someone tried to stop us from leaving. With no key, I could not get into the building, while my mother, on the second floor, with the apartment's windows facing the back, was unaware the conveyance had arrived and there was no power. I did not want to leave the bags unattended and shouted my mother's name, but she did not hear me. Meanwhile, the driver of the van was jumping up and down like a monkey, screaming in my face that he could not wait any longer. Still, he could not leave without us. I returned to the building's entrance, hoping that someone might be in the lobby to open the door. The lobby was empty, but the lights were back on. The power had been restored. In a minute, my mother came downstairs; we got in the vehicle and rolled toward the airport.

Chapter 7

THE NEW WORLD

1. Long Day

In Rome's airport, my mother and I boarded the TWA Boeing 747 plane to New York. The size of the incredible flying machine astonished me. The vast cabin was divided into several sections, with seating rows so wide that each section looked like a small movie theater. Apparently, the resemblance did not escape the jet's designers, who hung a movie screen in front of every section. From my aisle seat, I had a clear view of the screen and what transpired on it. A crazy-eyed man was talking to his hand, and two others were facing a firing squad. Years later, I learned the name of that movie—"In-laws," with Peter Falk and Alan Arkin—but on the plane, I did not bother to put the earphones on, as I would not have understood the dialogue. My mother was sitting next to me. For most of the flight, she was quiet, thinking perhaps about Odessa, Italy, and what awaited her in the New World. The hours were passing fast, and before long, we landed at Kennedy Airport in New York.

After picking up their luggage, the passengers proceeded to the customs area. My mother and I showed our white refugee cards to the customs officer. "Welcome to America," he said, and let us through the turnstile. In the waiting hall, the immigrants were greeted by NYANA[1] representatives, who divided the arrivals according to their place of stay and led them outside. As we reached the glass exit door, I saw the front of a yellow sedan pulling to the sidewalk. Three months in Italy, where roads swarmed with tiny Fiats, had formed in me an intuitive notion of how big an average automobile was, and how fast its front and rear

---

[1] New York Association for New Americans, a Jewish charity helping immigrants in NY.

bumpers might clear a given point. By those benchmarks, it took forever for the yellow car to show its tail, and there were many more similarly endless sedans… Right away, NYANA buses began to arrive; my mother and I boarded one of them, and we rode toward the city.

It was still daylight when the aircraft touched the ground, but with the added hours of deplaning, we left the airport at dusk, reaching our destination after dark. My body clock signaled bedtime already, yet there was much for us to do. Our staying place was a hotel, an old, twelve-story building of a pink color glowing under the nightly streetlights. We walked through the entrance door between two decorative pillars into the hotel's lobby. It must have been a fancy establishment, but had fallen on hard times—worn carpet, peeling paint, and scuffed, old furniture created an impression of insufficiency and decay… Behind the reception desk, which looked like a podium, stood a thin, balding, drably dressed man, probably in his fifties. He spoke good Russian, albeit with an accent I did not recognize. There was a security guard in the lobby, and, as far as I could tell, it was the entire hotel's staff for the night.

The arrivals gathered at the reception desk, where they received keys to their rooms. My mother's and my room was on the fifth floor; we took an elevator behind the concierge desk. The floor looked no better than the lobby, nor did it look much worse. We found our room, opened the door, and froze in disbelief: the room had only one bed. I saw the reaction of dismay on my mother's face—her worst fears, instilled by years of relentless propaganda, seemed to be coming true. The deafening sirens of emergency vehicles reverberated off the tall, dark buildings outside, evoking memories of war. The dour certainty of the old Soviet Union was gone forever, and left behind were cozy Vienna and sunny Italy. My mother sat down on the bed and cried.

I went back to the lobby to complain about the beds. The concierge looked at his records, which indicated that our room had two beds, and came with me upstairs to see what was going on. He entered the room and saw my mother sitting on a single bed, her eyes still wet. "It was a mistake; I am sorry. Please, go with me," said the concierge, and picked up our suitcase, which stood unpacked on the floor. My mother and I followed him. The concierge took us to the ninth floor, where he opened another room. "You will be staying here," he said and handed me the key. The new room had two beds, but it was also bigger, cleaner, and better furnished. The room's windows faced the street over the hotel's entrance. Across the street stood a modern, twenty-story apartment building. Some of its windows had blinds raised, revealing lit interiors: bookcases, pictures on the walls, and the residents going about their business. Life carried on, unhurried and undeterred. My mother calmed down a little. The concierge's friendliness and quick response helped improve her mood. It was already late. We had just enough strength to wash our hands (the room had a wall-mounted sink) and go to our beds. The long and tiring day, filled with places, events, and emotions, had finally come to an end.

2. Hotel Lucerne

We woke up early as we still ticked by the Roman time. I got out to the hallway, looking for a place to take a shower, and found one close to our room. It had an unusual access path: a door in the hallway opened into a narrow, long corridor leading to a small, closet-like chamber with two more doors, one of which belonged to the bathroom. The other door concealed a passage to a different part of the floor. As I was trying to figure out those portals, a lanky young man with long hair emerged from the bathroom and, keeping his head down, quickly disappeared into the second passage. I entered the bathroom. It was a small enclosure with a narrow window and a tiny, dirty bathtub, which had wet human hair all over it. The dirt on the bathtub's walls accumulated over a long time, but the hair was fresh and undoubtedly came from the young man I had just met on the way. I let the hot water run for a while, applied hand soap to disinfect the bathtub, and used the bathroom tissue to pull a ball of hair out of the drain. Then I took a shower, quivering with disgust. After I returned to our room, my mother went to inspect the newly discovered bathroom and failed it. She then came downstairs to get a brush and a scouring powder. Yesterday's concierge was still on duty—he gave my mother the utensils, and she proceeded to clean the tub, the sink, and the bowl to a condition probably not seen since the hotel's grand opening seventy-five years earlier. It was painful for me to even think of the hairy lad defiling my mother's effort, but there were no signs of him using the facility anymore. Perhaps the clean fixtures scared him off, or he checked out, or had not been a registered guest in the first place, sneaking in from the street to satisfy his bathing needs, but I never saw him again. In fact, it seemed that nobody else used that bathroom, maybe because of its labyrinthine access, so my mother and I had it to ourselves.

The name of the hotel was "Lucerne," and its locale was Manhattan's Upper West Side. Today, it is an upscale, trendy neighborhood, and the hotel has been restored, exacting lofty prices for its accommodations, but in those days, a room like ours cost twenty dollars, and the guests were people of modest means, from Soviet immigrants to local pensioners who lived there for years, preferring such arrangement to renting an apartment. The latest restoration preserved the building's pink color, as well as its peculiar architecture, which seemed inspired by a mix of styles dating back to the ancient Middle East. A heavy cornice trimmed the facade at the roof's edge, and every window had a cornice supported by a pair of decorated corbels. What made me think of an ancient influence was the main entrance, with a massive simulated pillar on each side, which, from afar, seemed wrapped in bands of sculpted human figures. The overall design appeared rather cheesy, but made the building stand out, contributing to its landmark status.

We waited for the NYANA representative to come; she showed up before noon. The representative was a woman in her forties, sociable and energetic, who emigrated from the Soviet Union a few years before my mother and me. She was a NYANA volunteer, I think, as she mentioned working in real estate. There were a dozen immigrant families in the hotel, and the NYANA woman went from room to room, talking to each family separately. Our meeting was brief: she explained some accounting basics, how to use the subway, and how to get to the HIAS office, where we had to appear the following day. She gave us a small cash advance toward that month's NYANA allowance—the rest we would collect in HIAS. I signed the receipt. After the official part, my mother asked the woman about life in America and our prospects in the new country. "Your son will find a job," the NYANA woman replied to my mother's concerns, "and you will stop pinching pennies."

It was still early in the day when the NYANA representative left, and my mother and I went out for a walk. I had already made a brief sally that morning, reaching a small grocery store around the corner. Now, we were going further. Our goal was to find "decent" bread similar to what we had in the old country. In most parts of the USSR, bread occupied a central place in people's diets. Grain production, which represented a major part of the country's economic output in czarist Russia, was still portrayed by the Soviet government as a vital indicator of the nation's well-being. Every day of the harvest season, newspapers, radio, and television reported how many tons of grain had been raked in so far, while lean crop years could result in food shortages. The main crop was wheat, although farmers grew some corn in the south of the Union, including fields near Odessa. The special attention the Soviet rulers paid to grain production often harmed the latter, sending tremors throughout the economy. The famine of 1932–1933, which my mother lived through, was the most lethal case of a socio-agrarian policy failure (in concert with bad weather), but it did not deter the authorities. In 1959, Khrushchev visited the United States and was so impressed by American cornfields that, upon returning to the Soviet Union, he ordered a wide adoption of that cereal, frequently at the expense of traditional wheat. However, corn did not grow well in the colder climates of Russia and Ukraine, which led to a decline in the harvest, made worse by a reduction in wheat acreage. Another Khrushchev brainchild was the Virgin Lands campaign, an attempt to cultivate the vast, arid lands of Kazakhstan. The misguided venture ended in a total fiasco but was hailed as a heroic achievement years later. All those experiments contributed to the situation where the possessors of the most fertile European lands, which had produced enough grain under the tsars to export to many countries, now imported it from Canada, the US, and other places.

The importance of bread in the Soviet Union manifested itself in how the product was sold to the public. Small towns and villages had bread sections in grocery stores; however, in larger cities, bread was offered in specialized outlets—bread shops. We had a shop like that in Odessa, on the street corner, one block from where we lived. Most of the time, the shop stood empty, bereft of customers and merchandise (except for a few stale, deformed loaves), but once or twice a week, the place was livened up by the expectation of a truck arriving from the bread factory. On those days, early in the morning, a long line formed outside the shop, although there was no guarantee the truck would come—sometimes it didn't, and the line dispersed to assemble on the next rumored delivery. Neither was it known which bread the truck would bring: dark (rye), white, or both. Dark bread was a preferred choice, but white was also acceptable. The truckload would sell out in an hour, with everybody getting something, as there was a per-customer limit. My mother often sent me, as a boy, to buy bread in that shop, and I remember a warm, elastic lump emitting a wonderful aroma on the way home. The dark bread was especially tasty, and I couldn't help but pinch off the delicious crust, despite knowing I would be reprimanded for it. That bread was likely healthier, too, since the Soviet industry's primitive food-processing capabilities assured higher whole-grain contents. One loaf weighed a kilo (two pounds) and lasted our family almost a week. We ate it with just about anything, as most others did. Such was the Soviet people's attachment to bread that, while standing guard on a mountaintop in Balaclava, cold and hungry, I dreamed not about chicken or borsch or my favorite Olivier (Russian) salad but a piece of fresh bread with a little butter on it.

One can imagine the frustration of Soviet emigrants, who, upon their arrival in the West, did not find the bread of the taste and consistency they had been accustomed to in the USSR. Most of the bread in Vienna was spongy and flavorless when fresh, turning into a half-dried putty the day after. The situation was no better in Italy, where supermarkets carried loaves of similar quality. Of course, sophisticated countries like Italy and Austria offered a wider selection of bread, but better types were sold in restaurants and upscale stores that emigres did not patronize. I doubt, though, that those more expensive offerings would have satisfied our bread connoisseurs. Even in New York, with the city's great variety of ethnic foods, nothing could erase the memories of that mass-produced Soviet bread. Shortly after coming to America, I moderated my bread craving, but my mother continued to search for the right brand, every time voicing unfavorable comparisons with the old favorites. Living in a Russian-speaking neighborhood in Brooklyn, she was exposed to one of the largest bread selections in the United States, with fancy names from imperial Russia evoking the old times' nostalgic wholesomeness, and tried them all. I tasted those brands, too, and may confirm that none could match the bread from our corner store in Odessa. Surely, bread recipes were not among the Soviet State's top secrets, and immigrant bakers knew and used them, but couldn't duplicate the originals.

In our earliest days in New York, neither of us yet realized the futility of trying to obtain the desired bread (a prospect even dimmer in the nineteen-seventies and eighties, when choices were fewer than today). During that first Upper West Side expedition, my mother and I visited a couple of stores on Amsterdam Avenue but found only supermarket-style baguettes, the kind that drew the sharpest criticism from Soviet emigres. We returned to the hotel's entrance and walked along Seventy-Ninth Street toward the block's other end. That end was an intersection of Broadway, a wide thoroughfare with a vegetation-covered median strip. A church on the opposite corner caught my attention—the church had two decorative towers above its entrance, symmetrically sited yet having different contours. Seventy-Ninth Street continued for one more block, then dived. Further ahead, an elevated plateau with isolated structures could be seen, making one curious about what lay between them. However, we postponed exploration of the lower grounds and concentrated on our primary task: the quest for bread.

As my mother and I surveyed the surroundings, we noticed a two-story Tudor building on the corner, one block up Broadway's opposite side. The building looked like a food store, with large display windows and a big "ZABAR'S" sign on the wall. We walked up a block, crossed the nature strip, and approached the building. It was a food store, and Zabar's was its name. An iconic New York City institution, it later took up the entire building, adding a café and a mezzanine, but then, the store was one-third of its present size, and the name told us nothing. The inside greeted us like an old friend, though, who had prepared a feast to celebrate our arrival, albeit we had to pay for it. Still, browsing was free and a pleasure in its own. Most merchandise was lumped chaotically all over the premises. Racks with cheese were scattered everywhere, while pots and pans, neatly shelved in the mezzanine today, hung off the ceiling, intermixed with salami sticks. And they had a wide selection of breads, so my mother fulfilled the purpose of our trip, and bought one loaf, but not before spending almost an hour in that store.

The following day, we visited the HIAS offices. Yesterday's NYANA rep had given us a printed subway map and a street-number calculator[2], which came in handy on the trip. HIAS was also located in Manhattan, but in a lower part of the island, around Union Square. We traveled there by train. The nearest subway entrance was on the northeast corner of Seventy-Ninth Street and Broadway, across the asymmetrical church. I noticed that entrance during our first reconnaissance trip, and now we were about to enter the world-under.

Designers of the underground transportation systems I happened to ride before tried to allay the part of the human psyche that relegated areas below the surface to the forces of evil, torture, and death. Vienna's U-Bahn, for example, was simple and clean, with neat, brightly lit cars and trains that were always on time. Kiev had only a few subway lines, but they were tidy and well-maintained, if slightly more luxurious than the Viennese. Neither could rival the Moscow Metro, whose builders went far beyond utility in architectural opulence and monetary expense. The New York Subway, though, seemed in full compliance with the old fables' imagery—austere interior, pockmarked floors, peeling paint, rat-infested tracks, winding passages strewn with derelicts, and graffiti-covered cars with brakes that sounded like screams of tortured sinners. As my mother and I descended to the train platform, we felt like taking an amusement park's horror ride, except that nobody was amused. The platform was full of straphangers, who looked completely unaffected by the grim surroundings, and we followed them onto the train.

Union Square looked different from the Upper West Side: more open, with shorter buildings and a greater variety of landscapes. It seemed like another town, except for the homeless sunbathing in a small park in the square's center. "However things may turn out, it won't be boring," I thought... HIAS was in a large office building on the square's north side. Their task of bringing us to America was complete, and the baton had been passed to NYANA, whose caseworker we were about to meet. NYANA had its own offices further down Manhattan Island but used HIAS' resources to handle new immigrants. In fact, we never went to the NYANA office, visiting HIAS instead. Those visits were infrequent and mainly involved receiving an allowance.

---

[2] A printed table, allowing to determine the nearest intersecting street of a given avenue address in Manhattan.

NAYANA supported the arrivals for three months, during which the newcomers had to find a job or other livelihood. The briefness of the assistance phase was among the drawbacks that rendered New York City an unwanted port of call. Guarantors in other places provided up to six months of financial support, with perks that included job counseling and referrals, while all that NYANA offered as an extra was a three-month English course. At the time of our entry, New York City was the only default destination, but legends were told about the VIP treatment that Soviet immigrants received in places like Cleveland, Baltimore, and St. Louis. Perhaps if given a choice, my mother and I would have picked one of those more welcoming locales, but already in New York, we had no regrets. I was even glad to have landed on barer ground, as lesser benefits implied lesser obligations, financial or otherwise. NYANA and other sponsors in the United States did not impose arrears on the assisted, nor did the Joint, but a feeling of indebtedness remained. It was easier with HIAS, which asked the emigres to repay what had been spent on them, mainly the cost of a flight across the ocean. The reimbursement requests were contingent on immigrants' ability to pay (which nobody means-tested), so many disregarded those HIAS letters, but I paid the loan off—took me a couple of years at thirty dollars per month.

Our NYANA caseworker was a woman in her thirties—slim, nicely dressed, and friendly. She did not speak Russian; there was a translator in the room. I do not remember that caseworker well, as I met with her maybe twice, where at the first meeting, she outlined the agenda for the next three months. The schedule required minimal involvement from NYANA—we had to sign up for an English class the following day, rent an apartment in one month, and find a job within three. The immigrants could call a NYANA caseworker for advice, but most did not use that lifeline, preferring to consult one another. Three months seem like a short time for the above tasks, not unlike the forty-five seconds between wake-up and roll call in the army, but as the soldiers did their part, emigres managed theirs. In his sci-fi short story "The Great Accelerator," H.G. Wells described a medicine that sped up human functions to a degree that it transported the recipients into a different time warp. The decision to emigrate from the USSR was like taking such a medicine, and what seemed a brief moment to an average person was a long stretch for us.

3. Cityscape

We stayed in the Lucerne for one month. I found an apartment rather quickly—went to visit my Odessa friends in Brooklyn, and they alerted me to a vacancy in their building. I did not like the neighborhood and would not have rented there on my own, but wanted to avoid the pressure of a deadline, considering my mother's fragile mental state. I took her to see the apartment the following day. The apartment was locked, and the super was nowhere to be found, so we asked the upstairs neighbor (an elderly lady) to see her place. The rooms were spacious and well laid out, the rent was low, and there were several Soviet immigrant families in the building, so we decided to take the flat. Unlike in Italy, where transients rented rooms month-to-month with few formalities and moved in right away, it was a minimum one-year lease in New York, starting on the first day of occupancy. Our lease began the next month, a couple of weeks after the signing, so we continued living in the hotel.

With the apartment secured, my mother and I plunged into the whirl of New York's life. Besides attending English classes, we were learning how to shop, travel, look for a job, and similar skills, taken for granted by the natives. The food we mostly bought at Zabar's, which, despite its gourmet status, was very inexpensive then. Our hotel room had a small electric range; however, it could not support my mother's kitchen, so our menu was simple. At the hotel, we socialized with other immigrants and sometimes talked to a concierge. He was actually the hotel's manager who doubled as a concierge, performing both duties from behind the reception desk. He worked with a partner. The partners leased the place from its owners and ran it on a shoestring. They managed another hotel, I believe, where our concierge's partner spent most of his time. Our concierge-manager liked to chat with the immigrants, maybe because they reminded him of his origins. He was from Romania, although never mentioned by which route he came to America, or where he learned to speak Russian so well. He lived in the United States for twenty years, which placed his arrival in the second half of the 1950s and may have something to do with the 1956 Hungarian uprising. The uprising was crushed by the Soviet tanks, sending a wave of refugees to the West. Romania neighbored Hungary, and the other neighbor was the USSR, with the once-Romanian territory of Bessarabia as the Moldavian Soviet Republic (where my father was from). Perhaps the concierge used to live there and crossed to Romania and then to Hungary, or maybe he escaped the Nazis to the Soviet Union before the war and returned to his native country after Germany's surrender—I only guess—but his knowledge of the Russian language was beneficial to the Soviet emigres who stayed in the Lucerne. He treated them kindly and never held back good advice.

Living in a closed society, Soviet citizens derived their knowledge of the Western world from movies and books. Access to that information was controlled by the government; still, there was only so much the censors could conceal. However ideologically compliant, say, a modern foreign film was, it depicted streets, apartments, transportation, stores, workplaces, human relations, and other details of everyday life, allowing Soviet viewers to make comparisons and draw conclusions. Based on those sources, the prevailing opinion stated that Europe was like the Soviet Union (its urbanized western parts), only nicer, and America was similar to Europe, only bigger. The journey from the Soviet Union to the United States, via Europe, presented an opportunity to put that theory to the test.

The notion of similarity between Europe and Western regions of the Soviet Union was reasonably accurate. Even outside the Baltic states and the Carpathian Mountains (which were essentially Europe), many larger cities in the Soviet Union displayed a strong European influence. It was not unexpected, considering the Russian elite's European roots and Peter the Great's Westernization push, which changed the country. The older cities, such as Moscow and Kiev, preserved a unique Russian character, while newer ones, such as St. Petersburg and Odessa, displayed a closer resemblance to their European counterparts. My hometown of Odessa, which was built after Peter's reign by French and Italian architects, was said to look like Marcellus. I have not been to Marcellus, but walked through some newer sections of Amsterdam that looked very similar to Odessa—the same architecture, colors, and even a tram in the middle of a cobbled street. Odessa's opera house was designed by the Austrian firm of Fellner & Helmer, while many residential buildings in the older parts of the city had an Italian layout, with the internal courtyard as the center of the building's social life. Where in America, one might refer to a person as living in a particular "building," in Odessa, the residential allusion often used the term "courtyard." Our Odessa street address comprised three adjoining, one after another, buildings with connected courtyards, and people would say a building resident was from the "first courtyard," the "second courtyard," or the third one.

The "building" and the "courtyard" reference distinction reflected lifestyle differences between America and many parts of the European continent, but there were other dissimilarities, which led to a surprising conclusion that the United States was farther, on a cultural plain, from the capitalist Europe than the Soviet Union was. Most apparent were

America's lesser regard for tradition and fewer constraints on individual expression. The departure from the conventional showed in New York's architecture, with the Lucerne Hotel and the asymmetrical church being my earliest examples. In Vienna and Rome, I noted their planners' attempts to preserve the character of neighborhoods. Perhaps not so much in Rome, where reverence toward the past took a few breathers over the ages—from city residents using the Colosseum as a source of building materials centuries ago to the construction of Roma Termini in modern times—but certainly in Vienna, where every newer addition to the city's landscape stood in perfect accord with the older surroundings. A similar approach was tried in the USSR's major cities, such as Moscow, Kiev, and Leningrad, and there was an analogous intent in Odessa, but a tighter budget did not allow the provincial town to keep up with the capitals. In New York, however, there seemed to be no desire to create a smooth architectural blend; on the contrary, everybody tried to put up something as distinct as money and zoning rules permitted. Especially impressive were the skyscrapers, one different from another, rising like upshots of a volcanic eruption. And what was remarkable, that such a denial of traditional harmony produced harmony of its own—the one of human enterprise.

It may be different in paradise, but here on Earth, people view events of their lives more favorably as they recede into the past. Bad memories fade, and good ones consolidate to form a more agreeable continuity. I was often bemused by my mother's lively accounts of her time in Herr Hunke's service and spirited childhood stories that mentioned her father during his rare appearances in Chudnov. My expectations were of the German memories to emphasize hard work in the above employ, as well as sad circumstances that had led to it, while of the childhood part being permeated with sorrow over her family's tragic fate. Those motifs did appear in my mother's narrative, yet they were infrequent and brief… Although not comparable to the wartime ordeals, our Lucerne sojourn also had its aggravations; however, I do not remember what they were. I do recall an occasional feeling of insecurity and frustration, but they left no emotional marks and, in retrospect, could have belonged to someone else. Today, I have only positive experiences to remember our first weeks in the United States by, and it was a wonderful time. Later, when already acclimated to America, I often envied newcomers because of their fresh perspective, which made my introduction to the manifold city a thrilling event. Our Hotel Lucerne stay happened in October, the best month in New York, weather and color–wise. The deep blue of the autumnal sky, the red gold of tree leaves, the patterned gray of boulders and bulwarks created a scintillating background against which the city paraded itself. I took advantage of the hotel's location, going to the Hudson embankment and Central Park, visiting the Museum of Natural History, or walking the streets. My mother sometimes joined me. That area remained among my favorite places in New York City, and I always enjoyed being there.

4. Furniture Store

My mother and I did not need a truck to move to our permanent address—we packed our bags, took the subway, and, in an hour, arrived at a six-story brick apartment building in Brooklyn, our new home. I found the super[3], who gave me the keys to the apartment. The apartment was bare; we needed furniture to help us with essential human functions such as sleeping and eating. The neighbors recommended a cheap furniture store not far from where we lived. The store was owned by Soviet immigrants, and many Russian-speaking locals shopped there. My mother and I went to the store together. We walked several blocks past Victorian houses, green lawns, and old plane trees onto a wide commercial thoroughfare. The furniture store was a few more blocks further down that avenue. A tall, middle-aged man with greying blond hair greeted us at the entrance. He was the store's owner. He made us out as Soviet immigrants right away, perhaps by hesitant gestures and wandering eyes, and spoke in Russian. A large showroom was filled with mattresses, tables, and chairs, and, at the moment, had my mother and me as the only customers. The owner showed us around. He reminded me of the Lucerne concierge: low-key, amiable, and deferential to the newcomers. He asked what part of the Soviet Union my mother and I had come from and told us about himself. He was from Kiev, where he worked as a lawyer (a profession not very portable across countries) before emigrating to the United States with his family. In the US, he changed several jobs, saved some money, and opened (with a partner) a furniture store. The neighborhood was not what one might call desirable, but the rents were low, and the business was good. That street had numerous stores selling electronics, clothes, and other goods at a deep discount, so my mother and I often visited the area, especially in the beginning. Sometimes, we stopped at the furniture store to say hello to our new friend and chat with him when he was not busy. Occasionally, his partner minded the place. The partner wasn't very chatty, but we got to know him, too.

Years later, when we no longer lived in that area, I read a newspaper on the train and saw a tiny article about a Brooklyn store robbery where the owner was killed. The article gave the store's address but not its type or the name of the victim. The address looked familiar, so upon coming home, I checked my Rolodex, which still had a card from the furniture store, and it turned out to be the one mentioned in the newspaper. A few days after reading the report, I traveled to the old neighborhood, where I

---

[3] Building's superintendent.

had not been in a long while. I got off the train, walked past our former residence, and continued toward the furniture store. The store was open, and through the window, I saw our friend-owner talking to a customer. The owner looked older and still shaken by the tragic incident, but very much alive. He must have drawn the long stick in life's lottery, and it was his partner who happened to be in the store that fateful night. The merchant did not resist and gave the robbers all the money, but they shot him anyway.

People often refer as heroes to those of uncommon valor in military action and police work, or to good Samaritans who put their lives on the line to help total strangers... but rarely speak in the same terms about merchants, like the furniture store owner and his partner, who go to dangerous places to start a business there. Of course, those merchants do it for themselves and their families; yet, like a traditional hero type, they risk their lives while improving the lives of others. The latter notion of heroism occurred to me still in middle school. We studied *Taras Bulba*, a novel by the great Russian writer and avowed antisemite Nikolai Gogol. The textbook version of the novel had all antisemitic references edited out (as they were omitted in the Hollywood film by the same name with Yul Brynner in the title role, although the movie's producers had leveled the field a bit by casting a Jew as Taras' son); however, the full text was available in the library, and one day, I laid my hands on it. An important character in the novel was a Jewish tavern keeper. In Gogol's and his hero's time, Jews dominated the liquor trade in Ukraine and Poland. They did not distill the alcohol (which was done by the landowners from their grain) but sold it in taverns all over the country. It had to be a good business, not unlike a gas station on a busy road in America today. The negatives included a hostile drinking public (carping about dilutions) as well as accusations by teetotalers of causing widespread alcoholism, a charge the book's author did not fail to repeat. But Gogol was unbiased when driving a narrative outside of his opinion. He could remark that Jews had devastated the entire area, yet would not invent a circumstance to demonstrate it. The genius could not betray the truth.

I do not recall how much of the textbook I had consumed beforehand, but I started the library version, expecting to fully share the author's attitude toward his characters, only to discover that my sympathies and dislikes formed differently. Despite numerous insults thrown at him by Gogol and Taras, the tavern keeper was growing in my eyes as he took a substantial risk to assist Taras in the latter's attempt to see his son in a Polish prison. At the same time, the protagonist, although a courageous and sincere man, repelled me with his rudeness, lack of self-control, and utter disregard for himself and those trying to help him. Of course, the tavern keeper needed a cutthroat of Taras' repute for protection, but was helping the Cossack primarily out of the goodness of his heart, realizing that someone like Taras was unlikely to return from Poland alive. As for protection, it was needed badly. There was a mention in the novel of a small pogrom sparked by a rumor so ridiculous that the author himself seemed uncomfortable describing the episode. I imagined the tavern owner's predicament after the Poles had disposed of his occasional defender and thought that an obsequious Jew selling vodka to Cossacks in his tavern showed bravery comparable to that of the heroic Taras fighting enemies on the battlefield.

On our first visit to the furniture store, we bought two mattress sets and a kitchen table with two chairs. The entire purchase cost us less than two hundred dollars, shipping included. The items were delivered the same day, and my mother and I had something to sleep on and eat at. The table doubled as a desk where I worked on my resume. A few weeks later, I found a job as a computer programmer. The economy was weak and unemployment high, but businesses aggressively pursued computer automation, and workers in that field were in high demand. Employers hired applicants with poor English and little experience as long as the recruits could learn on the job. There was not much to learn (on the technical side) in my case, as I had worked with similar platforms in the Soviet Union, and the first job interview brought me an offer. There was a second offer from another company, but I went with the first one, maybe because I liked their building more. The pay was about the same in both places, not much, but enough to live on, as the city was very inexpensive back then. In addition, the new employer provided various perks, such as an advanced English class, which my boss offered me a few months into the job. "Would you like to take an English course to improve your conversation," he said, "or rather have us learn Russian? The company will pay for it." I gladly agreed. My English was better than that of most newcomers—I had attended English school in Odessa and studied the language in college and on my own, so I could read and write pretty well—but conversing was a real pain. I often asked people to repeat their words and took time to construct sentences. That English course was designed to address such issues. It was taught by a language-teaching company in the old World Trade Center. The course's length was three months; I attended evening classes, walking there after work. My group had a dozen students, immigrants from several countries (a girl from Germany, a man from India), and an instructor who spoke only English. The instructor was a young woman, amicable and enthusiastic.

In the class, she staged short playlets, suggesting a plot, assigning roles, and letting students improvise their parts. Those little acts were the most enjoyable moments of the learning process and also the most helpful.

Besides myself, our class had two more Soviet immigrants: a woman and a man. The woman was pleasant, but the man annoyed everybody by constantly mentioning his wife. Maybe he felt guilty that he couldn't share all the fun with her; however, the rest of the group was uneasy about the odd imposition. Especially irritating were those mentions during our acts, with the proverbial wife crashing almost every scene her husband was a part of. I wondered what he told her after the classes. "Today, we did a sketch where we ate at a fancy restaurant, but worry not, my dear, you were there, too." The instructor wasn't happy either, as the excessive spousal references disrupted the communion atmosphere she was trying to create, yet she was too polite to say anything. It was an impasse until the setting's very theatricality came to the rescue. We were doing a scene where the German girl and I acted as a couple receiving a guest. The guest was played by the devout husband. He rang a fictitious bell, I opened an imaginary door, and, of course, the wife was there, too. After the "this is my wife" introduction, I turned to my co-star and whispered in her ear so everybody could hear: "Our friend is not well. He seems to believe he has come with a wife, but is clearly alone. Maybe his wife ran away, and he lost his mind. Let's call an ambulance." The audience (including the "guest") burst into laughter, and no make-believe relatives appeared in the class after that.

The playacting technique employed in my nightly English class was very effective in liberating students' verbal expressions and helped me a great deal. It would take years for my English to reach relative comfort, but I no longer feared to converse… My mother learned the language via more conventional methods in the NYANA classes and a job-training school afterward. She had the disadvantage of an older age and the lack of prior exposure to English; however, she had been multilingual since early childhood, was proficient in Yiddish, Russian, and Ukrainian, used to be fluent in German, and was a motivated and diligent student, which allowed her to learn English reasonably well. But in the beginning, I had to help her with translations.

As I began to receive paychecks and my mother started a job-training program, we tackled the last part of the apartment's interior that needed improvement—the floor. When we just moved in, the apartment's floor was covered with a carpet that must have been there since the building's construction forty or fifty years earlier. In those days, it was common for New Yorkers to rent an apartment in a new building and live there without changing anything until they died or moved to Florida. I do not remember which of the two caused our apartment's vacancy, but the carpet had rotted there for many years and ought to go. I threw it out with the help of my neighbors. Under the carpet, lay a hardwood floor. It was damaged in a few places by carpet rot, but not severely. Those six-story, brick apartment buildings had one flaw my mother and I found highly annoying—they lacked soundproofing. Acoustic waves traveled freely through hollow walls and squeaky floors, so the carpeting and furniture helped absorb the sound. Laying a new carpet was too costly; hence, we decided to lacquer the floor and put a rug in the living room. Most Soviet immigrants did a similar upgrade, even when the old carpet was in good condition, as they were not used to carpeted floors and did not like them. Apartments in the USSR had better sound insulation, especially in older buildings, like where my family lived, plus popular images of the Hermitage's interior[4] and the insides of other former homes of nobility, with shining floors and Persian rugs, inspired Soviet citizens to mimic those looks in their quarters; and lastly, such lacquered floors were more hygienic and easier to clean.

A neighbor gave me the phone number of a local floor man whom I then hired to do the work. He came with a helper, his son, an unbound fellow about eighteen years of age. "Leave me the keys," said the floor man to my mother and me, "and go for a stroll." I was ready to comply, despite the uncomfortable feeling that the keys' suggestion should have come from us, but my mother did not like the idea of having a stranger in the apartment alone and replied that she would stay in the kitchen. She was suspicious by nature, and the new environment heightened her wariness. The floor-man's and his son's odd behavior was not helping either... I saw that the floor man took offense, but continued with the job. He sanded the floor and said he would come tomorrow to varnish it. The following day, only his son showed up. Telling how he would go to college to study "Business Administration," the son applied the varnish, some of which ended up on the walls. After he finished, I paid him in the hallway, and my mother and I did go for a stroll to let the lacquer dry. Now, it was the rug's turn. My mother's schoolmates recommended a warehouse in Borough Park[5], where the prices were lower. It was not far on the map from where we lived, but still an hour's walk. We took a bus. The warehouse building had no windows and no signs—we circled it,

---

[4] The Hermitage Museum in St. Petersburg, Russia, located in the former Winter Palace of the Russian tsars.

[5] A Hasidic neighborhood in Brooklyn.

found the door, and got inside. A spacious hall was filled with rugs hanging from the ceiling and stacked on the floor. Next to one stack stood a Hasidic man. He was a salesman. I told him we were looking for a nine-by-twelve rug, and he showed us what was available. The prices were good; we selected a pattern, and I reached into my pocket to pay, when my mother pushed me aside and stepped in front of the salesman. She was going to haggle with the Hasid. I thought they would converse in Yiddish, which both spoke fluently, but my mother wanted to test her English skills... and show me how to negotiate a deal. "How much?" she asked incredulously, strongly accenting "much." The salesman repeated the price. "Too cheap," said my mother. Of course, she meant to say "too expensive," but confused the antonyms. "Cheap? Buy," responded the Hasidic man. I gave him the money, picked up the rug, and my mother and I headed home. It was an inexpensive polyester rug with a bright floral pattern on a dark green background, but it looked good on a freshly lacquered floor.

5. Classified Ad

The year was 1921 when my Chudnov grandfather put his in-laws in a horse cart and smuggled them into Poland on their way to America. The passengers were the family patriarch Jacob Moskowitz and three of his children—Sam, Morris, and Rose—all in their teens. Jacob's oldest daughter (my grandmother) remained in Chudnov, while my mother had not yet been born... Jacob was not the first in the family to embark on the American route; his two eldest sons emigrated years earlier when Russia was still under the tsars. The misfortune of leaving behind his daughter weighed heavily on Jacob's decision, but had he postponed the departure, none of the travelers would have reached the American shore; they would have joined my Chudnov grandparents in the misery of early Soviet existence. Poor mastery of the Russian language, combined with late adolescent age, would have limited the children's mobility and chances of advancement. Perhaps in a couple of years, the oldest, Sam, would have teamed up with my grandfather in the latter's horse-trading enterprise, gotten arrested with his senior partner, but received a lesser sentence as a juvenile. In a few more years, the siblings would have started their own families, adding to Chudnov's Jewish population. Most would have survived the famine, but barely so, requiring more American help than my grandmother got while having fewer family members to provide it. The repressions of the nineteen-thirties, which miraculously spared my grandfather, might have plucked Sam and/or Morris out of compensatory life or sent them into hiding like my grandfather and his brother-in-law. After the German invasion, there would have been a fiery debate on whether to leave Chudnov until the closing of a small window of opportunity, when such escape was possible, ended the discussions. A few unspeakable months of fear and confusion would have followed, and then, they all would have lain in a mass grave next to their older sister.

The fate that would have likely befallen her aunt and uncles had they remained in Chudnov accounted in part for the pause my mother took before attempting to find them. She doubted they were alive. All three would have been in their seventies, and although my mother realized that reaching such an age in the United States was far more likely than in the Soviet Union, her years of hardship and personal losses negated that logic. Nor encouraging was her failure to locate the American relatives while in the old country. The last attempt to learn their whereabouts she made a few years before our departure. At the time, relations between the Soviet Union and the West experienced a thaw, resulting in a higher number of people leaving the communist state as well as an increased (but still tiny) flow of tourists traveling in the opposite direction. One of those tourists was an American cousin of my mother's coworker, a woman physician. The American guest stayed in Odessa in a hotel and visited his cousin in the sanatorium, where the latter introduced him to my mother. He was a singer by profession—a performer of Yiddish songs. The singer did not speak Russian, while his cousin spoke little Yiddish or English, so he felt more at ease with my mother, who spoke Yiddish fluently. My mother told him about her American relatives and prior attempts to locate them. The singer offered his help. He said he would make a few inquiries upon returning to the United States and write to my mother a letter. He gave her his stage bill, with the artist's bio and discography, and took the last known address of her uncle; however, no letter from the singer ever appeared in our mailbox, and his cousin did not hear from him either.

During our first months in the United States, my mother did not bring up her American relatives, but as her life became more orderly, she made a cautious attempt to locate them. "My aunt and uncles are likely no longer with us," she said to me, "but their children must be around and not far away. Let us place a newspaper ad and see what happens." I put together a few lines of text, which I sent to the Classifieds section of the Sunday Times. The advertisement space was costly, so the ad came out small, albeit listing all the information, albeit in an abbreviated form. A few weeks passed with no response... Even before placing that ad, I doubted it was the right way to do the search. Why would my mother's cousins read that paper section at all? They were born and grew up in the US, lived a life of unbroken continuity, and did not expect to be sought in the Classifieds by anybody, least of all some mythical relatives from a faraway land. The audience my mother's ad should have aimed at was people like her aunt and uncles, who had left the old country at a conscious age and still remembered living there. As they grew older and spent more time with their thoughts, childhood memories would visit them more often, each time with greater clarity and impact. They would recall the places of their youth, whose mention they would look for in Yiddish periodicals. Hence, I suggested publishing the ad in such a paper. My mother liked the idea, except this time, she wanted to search not for her relatives but for the Yiddish singer she had met in Odessa several years earlier. She always wondered why she never received the promised letter—the singer seemed eager to help and even volunteered to make the inquiries. Maybe he got ill, or the letter was not delivered, or there was something else my mother ought to know before contacting her American kin. She wanted to talk to the singer first. Also, as a better-known personality, he should have been easier to find.

The newspaper, where we placed the second ad, was the Yiddish Forward, the largest Yiddish daily in the United States. I visited their offices in Manhattan to make the arrangements. The advertising space cost much less than in the Times, so there was no need to abbreviate… The day after the ad went into print, we received a phone call. The caller was a woman who clearly belonged to the targeted demographics. She and my mother spoke in Yiddish. The woman lived in the Midwood section of Brooklyn, not far from our neighborhood. She told my mother she knew the singer, whose recitals she had attended many times. "Why are you interested in him?" the woman asked. My mother explained that she had met the singer in Odessa, where he promised to help locate her relatives. "He has retired and lives in Florida now," said the woman, "Maybe I can get his phone number." She then asked my mother about the relatives: who they were and where they had lived. My mother described the family. "I know them!" exclaimed the woman, "They left Newark long ago and now reside in other places." It turned out the caller used to live in Newark and had been neighbors with the Moskowitz household. Her own family was from the same part of Ukraine, possibly from a nearby town or from Chudnov itself, and they came to the US with the same immigration wave. The immigrants settled in the new country according to their original locales, and Newark became a common destination for Jews from the Ukrainian northwest, among whom Chudnov natives established a neighborhood of their own. They even buried their dead next to each other. Later on, after meeting her American relatives, my mother and I visited Jacob Moskowitz's grave in Newark. He died in 1931, still in his fifties (to the great chagrin of my grandmother, who received the sad news in the mail), and was buried in a Jewish cemetery now bordering the Garden State Parkway. For many moons after the Newark flight of the nineteen-sixties, the cemetery was sparsely attended, as the area became too dangerous to visit on foot; however, thirty years later, some more adventurous former city residents appeared on the burial grounds to pay their respect to the departed. A police cruiser provided by the local authorities around major Jewish holidays also helped the trend. My mother often mentioned to her relatives that she wanted to visit her grandfather's resting place, so one day, when her cousins ventured to make such a trip, they invited my mother and me to come along. We drove there on Sunday. The cemetery was relatively small. It was surrounded by a fence of poked stone and iron railings, with an arched entrance leading to an alley that divided the site. The place had a pungently nostalgic atmosphere of the old country, with stone porticos on both sides of the alley denoting interment sections after Ukrainian towns the resting hailed from. The inscription on one portico indicated the Chudnov section, and at the back of that plot stood Jacob's headstone, made of pink granite, with his photograph preserved under a plastic cover for over half a century…

The woman on the phone brought my mother up to date. All Jacob's younger children, who had come to America with him, were alive and well (his older sons had already died—they emigrated early, had little contact with their Chudnov sister, and seldom appeared in my mother's stories). Rose and Morris lived in New Jersey, while Sam lived in Florida. The caller kept in touch with them, especially Rose. "Let me break the news to your aunt," said the woman to my mother as they were about to end the call. An hour later, the phone rang again. It was Aunt Rose. My mother was still aflutter from the previous chat, so I went to another room to give more space to her emotions. She talked for a long time, then came to my room, teary-eyed, to tell me about the conversation. "My aunt is coming over this weekend," my mother said, "Her children will drive her from New Jersey. They will call you for directions…" It was already late in the evening, so Aunt Rose said that she would phone Sam and Morris tomorrow. The following day, Morris called, and later Sam, so my mother had her hands full, talking on the phone and preparing for the weekend.

The day was Sunday, I believe, when Aunt Rose and her children, with their spouses, descended on our Brooklyn apartment. My mother and her aunt, who knew each other only via old photographs, coalesced in an emotional embrace. After the introductions, my mother offered the guests tea and a cake she had baked earlier for the occasion. Our table was too small to seat the entire company, so everybody settled where they might (we had a sofa and an armchair by then) with teacups and plates… I was observing the visitors. Aunt Rose was a small, grey-haired woman, unpretentious and neat. She spoke English with a pronounced Yiddish accent. Her children and in-laws were what I perceived as typical Americans—confident, laid back, and speaking perfect English. It seemed peculiar that those people were related to me. They must have been similarly mystified, gazing at the hosts and the apartment's ascetic interior with amiable curiosity. Only my mother and her aunt were not a part of mutual reconnoitering—they seemed not puzzled at all and spent the afternoon together, talking buoyantly in Yiddish, with no trace of caution or reserve, as if they had known each other for a long time. Years later, reminiscing about that first encounter, Aunt Rose's daughter-in-law told me how surprised they were at the rapport between the aunt and the niece. "There you were, people from a different world," she said, "and all of a sudden, Rose is talking to your mother in a language we did not understand, looking completely at home…" And indeed, Rose felt at home, the one she had been born and spent the formative years of her life in. Another commonality between my mother and her aunt was their physical resemblance. That likeness was even more striking as no other Jacob's descendant (not even Rose's children) had a similar physique, which ought to be enough to prove the kinship.

6. Wedding Anniversary

I do not recall when Uncle Morris visited my mother's and my Brooklyn home for the first time—before his golden wedding anniversary or after it—but remember that visit well and our discussion of the upcoming presidential elections[6]. The anniversary happened soon after my mother connected with her American side, and her uncle wanted us at the celebration. He lived in southern New Jersey, near Philadelphia, but the party took place in the northern part of the state, closer to our home. I did not own a car at the time and had not driven in the United States or, for that matter, anywhere else, so Morris provided the transportation. On the way back, we got a lift from one of the party guests, and a similar arrangement could have been made to bring us there, but Morris wanted to send a limousine (which makes me believe he hadn't seen my mother yet). The driver of the limousine was a man in his fifties, animated and chatty. He told us he was a retired policeman and drove a limousine for extra income. The mention of the driver's former occupation surprised me since his joviality belied an image of a New York City police officer I had in my mind—a statuelike, taciturn figure in heavy boots and a high hat with all kinds of gear around the waist and a revolver menacingly sticking out of the holster. Such were the policemen I saw upon entering the US and later observed in the streets, subway, and government offices, projecting authority and readiness to safeguard the public. The revolver, I found especially impressive, as I had seldom seen a lawman with a gun before. In Vienna, one hardly encountered a policeman, with or without a weapon, and I did not recall conspicuously armed carabinieri. In the Soviet Union, some policemen walked with a pistol holster, but it was buttoned, and common wisdom stated that the holster contained lunch.

In the old country, I encountered a policeman brandishing a gun only once, and incredibly, I was the cause of the disturbance. It happened in my boarding school's middle period, fifth or sixth grade. I was heading home after an extended day, in the company of a classmate with whom I often traveled together, as we lived close to each other. Our route ran past a large apartment complex, toward a tram stop on the corner of an intersecting boulevard, several blocks from the school. The apartment complex adjoined the boarding school, but it was not where the blue-shade Kristallnacht would take place a few years later. That development was on the school's opposite side and had no demarcations, while the one we passed on the way home had a decorative fence that helped keep

---

[6] Carter-Reagan contest.

our students away... I remember that night well. It was already dark, and the dense fog from the sea enveloped the area, limiting the visibility to a yard or two. The air was dead still, and the street was completely empty, creating a phantasmagoric effect that put us slightly on edge. We were halfway toward the tram stop when the eerie silence was broken by a dog's bark coming from the complex's grounds. My companion barked back. The dog reacted with a barking sequence, and this time, I joined my friend in his response. The dog barked again. We then stopped and engaged in a barking match with an invisible dog in earnest. Shortly, the animal figured out the ruse and went silent, but my companion and I had already been on a roll, buoyed by comic relief from an unsettling background. We started screaming in prepubescent voices, "Murder," "Help," at our lungs' top. That continued for a minute, and we were about to resume our trip when we heard fast steps, and two men jumped out of the wall of fog illuminated by a streetlight in front of us. Both men were in uniform—one was a policeman, the other a military officer. The policeman had a gun in his hand. He heard our shrieks and rushed to the "rescue," mustering a military passerby as a backup. "What happened? Who screamed?" the policeman urgently addressed my friend and me, not realizing we were the source of the commotion. But the military man, who must have been a local resident, familiar with our school and its mischievous population, had already figured out what had happened. "They were the ones who yelled," he told the policeman, pointing at us, "Take them to the school. The class supervisor will punish them." The policeman thanked his helper and turned toward my friend and me. "Let's go," he said angrily, "And do not try to escape. See this?" and he waved the gun before our faces. We followed him back to the school building. But what punishment might one impose on a child for yelling in the street? After the policeman left, the class supervisor told my friend and me an old tale about a boy who cried wolf and let us go. He did not write a note, so my father never knew.

Of course, there were real crime fighters among the Soviet police who could be trusted with firearms, but the majority performed duties similar to those of auxiliary policemen in the United States. So timid a police presence was partly due to other layers of enforcement, including the KGB and military units of the Ministry of Internal Affairs, which handled more pressing matters, leaving the police to handle lesser felonies and administrative tasks. Accordingly, the policemen were poorly trained, often corrupt, and held in low regard by the public.

A typical Soviet police action I once observed from the window of our Odessa apartment. The window faced the street above the building's entrance, across the one-story elementary school I had attended in my first two grades. It was a summer Sunday afternoon, and the school's wall was being propped up by a drunk: a zombie-like, twenty-something fellow wrestling with the force of gravity. Meanwhile, a company of two women and two men perambulated the street on the school's side. The women walked first, and the men (the women's spouses, I presumed) followed. The couples were ordinary folk in their late thirties or early forties, dressed up and in a weekend mood. Perhaps they came from the park, where they had spent quality time, breathing fresh air, eating ice cream, and listening to a brass band. As the women passed the boozer, he said something into their backs, an insolent remark, no doubt, as one husband, a chunky balding fellow, angrily confronted the drunkard. But before the confrontation turned into a fight, the other husband pulled his companion aside. I could not hear what they talked about—possibly the "peacemaker" was asking his friend to ignore the insult ("the man had too much to drink, doesn't know what he is saying, it can happen to anybody") and not to ruin their weekend, to what the "warmonger" (as I will call the more aggressive stroller) was replying that the weekend had been ruined already, and the only way to salvage what remained of it was to punish the offender. During the discussion, the warmonger tried to reach the lout but was contained by the peacemaker. Finally, they must have agreed to give peace a chance. The warmonger stepped back while the peacemaker got in front of the drunkard and started reasoning with him, attempting perhaps to extract an apology promised to his friend. The drunkard listened blank-faced, nodding from time to time as if in complete agreement with the presented points, and then, all of a sudden, kicked the peacemaker in the groin. The peacemaker contorted in pain, clearing the way to the warmonger, who charged ahead like an attack dog let off the leash. He knocked the drunkard to the ground and started furiously stomping on the prostrate frame. Seconds later, the peacemaker recovered from the blow and joined his comrade in the dispensation of justice. A small crowd assembled on the scene—some witnessed the entire episode; others had just arrived. The peacemaker and warmonger finished their dance and wiped sweat, explaining to the latecomers what had happened. They waited for the police, someone had called from a street phone. The drunkard was lying on the sidewalk face up, without motion. He must have fallen asleep as he hit the pavement and slept through the beating without feeling a thing. The police arrived fast—two uniformed cops in a light pickup truck. They tried to awaken the drunk, but he just mooed and waved his hand as if brushing off a nuisance. Finally, the policemen ran out of patience. One grabbed the sot's feet, another gripped his ears(!); they lifted the drunk off the ground, threw him into the pickup's trunk, and sped away.

I recounted the Odessa incident to contrast it with another police action I observed from the window of our Brooklyn apartment. Like in Odessa, the apartment in Brooklyn was also on the third floor, and the windows faced the street above the building entrance, but here the similarity ended. What transpired outside looked like an episode from a law-enforcement TV series and revealed remarkable police expertise… One day, at two in the morning, I was awakened by screeching brakes, followed by a heavy thump. It sounded like a car crash, so I got up and looked outside. Our building was on the corner of a block, and from the bedroom window, I could see the intersection with a massive plane tree across the street. Crashed into the tree was a Chevrolet Impala. All the car's doors were open, and there was nobody inside. Immediately, from every direction, police cruisers began to arrive. They had been chasing the Impala and its occupants, who must have committed a serious crime. There ought to be at least four perpetrators (as many as the open car doors), and I first thought they had escaped through the backyards of single-family homes on the street's other side. Several police officers, including a woman, jumped out of the cruisers and started searching under the parked cars with flashlights. Suddenly, they gathered around a white van in front of our building, pulled out their revolvers, and, pointing them underneath the vehicle, yelled, "Show your hands," or something similar. A skinny black male in a white T-shirt crawled from under the van and sprawled facedown on the pavement in the crosshairs of police guns. One officer handcuffed the suspect, lifted him off the ground, and put him against the van. Another policeman frisked the arrested, then asked him about something, but received no answer and punched the suspect in the stomach, bending him in half. Meanwhile, the rest of the posse continued to shine their flashlights, looking for a crime weapon. They did not find anything and clustered in the middle of the street, talking on the radio and to each other. A SWAT vehicle arrived; several team members in SWAT uniforms got out holding rifles, but everything was under control, and they left. The pause continued for a few more minutes. Finally, the word must have come on the radio, as one of the officers separated from the group and went inside our building. He returned with a tenant who turned out to be the owner of the van the arrested had been hiding under. The police located the owner by a license plate. The owner opened his van, the police officer got behind the wheel, started the engine, and began to rock the vehicle until something fell out of the chassis onto the ground. It was the gun! The police then withdrew, leaving me in awe—not only did they know where to look for the suspect, they guessed what he had done with the weapon and how to retrieve it.

The Brooklyn police episode would have made a perfect conversation topic with our limo driver, who might shed more light on the NYPD's crime-fighting technique, but the action occurred a few years later, albeit at the same address where he picked us up. The subject of crime did arise, however, as it was a hot topic at the time, and our driver remarked that my mother's and my neighborhood was not among the safest. The driver told us he was of Italian descent and lived on Staten Island. "We don't have crime," he added, "We can walk our streets day or night without fear. And we need no police for that. We have the *Cosa Nostra*, or Mafia. Have you heard of them?" The former lawman's tacit approval of a criminal enterprise perplexed me, but then I realized that he viewed the notorious organization as a preserver of traditional values, which could provide better protection against street crime than any degree of police competence... With my mother and me, our limo driver was very friendly, asking curiously about the USSR (Soviet immigrants were a novelty at the time) and telling about his family and life on Staten Island all the way until we reached our destination.

The anniversary party was held at a restaurant (or a community center—I don't remember which one). Most of Jacob's offspring from New York and New Jersey attended the event with their families, and more came from farther away. My mother and I had already met Aunt Rose and her children, and the jury is still out whether we saw Uncle Morris before the festivities, but others were new to us. We got to know the children of Jacob's older sons, bringing the total of my mother's cousins to about a dozen. There were some, including from the deep South, who couldn't make it to the gathering and whom we eventually met under various circumstances. Sam was not in attendance—his wife was ill and could not fly from Florida—but there were many relatives of Morris' wife, as well as friends of the golden couple. The celebration assembled maybe a hundred attendees, most of whom traced their ancestry to a handful of emigres from greater Russia[7]. Some guests were flamboyant and upbeat, while others were deliberate and subdued; yet, they all projected a certain vigor that felt like tremors from a powerful blast of long ago. It seemed I had met those people before, at a wedding in Odessa or a New Year's party there, except they spoke a different language. But especially, I liked the company of my mother's aunt and

---

[7] Which at one time included Poland and Lithuania.

uncles: Rose, Morris, and later Sam. Their behavior conveyed simplicity and directness—perhaps an imprint of Chudnov and plain living in the Ukrainian countryside—that set them apart, as well as peaceful radiance, which I detected even in Baba Olya back in Yagodinka, and which was life's reward for carrying out its basic responsibilities. All in all, the anniversary was an exciting event, where my mother got to know most of her American relatives, Jacob's descendants. The piece of the puzzle had fallen into place.

Chapter 8

FULL CIRCLE

1. Associate in Arts

Connecting with her relatives aside, my mother's life in the United States was not much different from that of other Soviet immigrants of her generation, especially after she moved to a neighborhood where those immigrants flocked. Although apprehensive and suspicious at times, my mother was a sociable person who established acquaintances easily and had many friends. Some friends she knew from the Soviet Union, others she met on the way to America, or already there. She talked to her friends on the phone or met with them in places like Brighton Beach[1], not far from where she now lived. Their conversations included local gossip, news from the old country, and articles in Russian-language periodicals. When we first arrived in New York, the city (and the entire United States) had perhaps two Russian newspapers, which Soviet immigrants eagerly read. However, as the latter population increased, more Russian publications appeared, followed by radio and television programs, providing their audience with a sense of the old country. That came in handy for mature new Americans, with naturally reduced capacity for learning, yet hampered their grasp of the English language and the American way of life. The disincentive was particularly strong around Brighton Beach, where the ubiquity of spoken Russian rendered English largely redundant. Thus, many of my mother's associates spoke little English and had no interest in learning more, but she continued to improve her skills. Given that the bulk of her efforts occurred before the advent of Russian television in the US, she did not subscribe when it

---

[1] A Brooklyn neighborhood, home to the largest Russian-speaking community in the US.

became available, preferring American family shows. Television played a major role in my mother's bettering her English, and by the time of the Russian channel's birth, she could follow regular programs, becoming a soap opera fan. She looked forward to meeting her American relatives to talk about Luke, Laura, and other characters from those endless series, which she could not discuss with her immigrant friends. Her accented English was not perfect, but good enough to satisfy practical needs. A few years after coming to the United States, she was diagnosed with a chronic illness and remained under doctors' care for the rest of her life. Her physicians spoke neither Russian nor other languages my mother knew, so she first needed my help with translation, but later traveled to the city and handled most of her medical and other matters herself.

My mother's zest for study came to fruition when, already in her sixties, she enrolled at a college and earned an associate's degree. The enrollment was rather incidental. The country was in a recession, and the government decided to spend more money, directing some of the outlays to educational programs. The idea was to make it easier for graduates of those programs to find jobs, stimulating economic activity (albeit there was little evidence that the lack of such activity was caused by a shortage of qualified employees). Perhaps those courses served a useful purpose, after all, by enlightening those who, in better times, would have been too busy working to take advantage of the opportunity, yet seemed excessive for older adults with poor English and no prospects of a meaningful career. Still, it was that wasteful side of government tonic which brought my mother and her friends into the realm of American higher learning. The college that was to become their alma mater needed more conduits of public funds and reached out to the nearby immigrant community, renowned for valuing knowledge. I don't know who got the first word, but my mother learned about the opening from her friends and signed up. All her adult life, she regretted missing out on higher education. The war interrupted her enrollment at a dental school, and later, family, work, and poor living conditions had rendered similar attempts futile. Unlike in the United States, where one may attend college at any age, it was impossible to become a full-time college student after thirty in the Soviet Union, and the only other option was a correspondence or night school, for which my mother had little energy and time.

Career choices in the USSR were further constrained by the country's unbending societal order. Having full control over education and jobs, the Soviet government imposed strict rules that tied occupations to school degrees. Similar provisions exist in the United States (as well as in other places), but their scope is narrower and enforced unobtrusively via a licensing mechanism, absent in the Soviet Union of that time. Many such rules make perfect sense—one might prefer a physician to have gone to a medical school or a bridge designer to have an engineering diploma—however, the Soviet edicts went beyond those requirements, demanding, for example, that not only a plumber could not work as a physician, but a physician could not work as a plumber, as well. If a physician's interest in a plumber's occupation could be explained by the country's wage-scale imbalances, the government's objection to such a crossover was based on a claim that the state had paid for a doctor's schooling and was entitled to the money's worth. One might reason that the money belonged to the people, including students' parents, who had little say in financing their offspring's education (except maybe bribing an official), but nobody would argue with the regime.

In truth, I never met a doctor who wanted to become a plumber, but came across a former engineering student who had dropped out of college for the sole purpose of not getting a diploma so he could work as a machinist at a factory. That encounter took place at the engineering bureau, where I got a job right after military service. The job, my mother writes that she helped me with, was my second, but the engineering bureau did not materialize without her involvement, either. It happened that her sanatorium coworker's husband was a department head in that bureau, and he offered me a spot there. "I am going to make a good mechanical engineer out of him," he said to his wife, who passed it to my mother. I did not rejoice on hearing the news, especially the mechanical engineer's part, but there were no other prospects. So, I took the bureau offer—an easy decision, considering it was my first job with nothing to compare to.

The new workplace required a note of release from the postgraduate distribution, and I went to the university to obtain it. Such matters were handled by an administrative vice dean, a functionary rather than an academic position, and that vice dean fit his role very well. Despite graduating from the same university, he harbored deep mistrust of the intelligentsia and his urbane male students, who, he reckoned, had enrolled in the studies to avoid military service. "You all are hiding from the draft," I once heard the vice dean shouting at the group of students who confronted him with some demands (such an accusation seemed odd since the university did not offer any military classes and its male students had to serve in the army someday, but perhaps the vice dean viewed their enrollment as an initial phase of the avoidance scheme). Needless to say, little love was lost between the students and their vice dean, so seeing him was not an eagerly anticipated event on my part. He could not refuse me the release note, but could unleash bureaucratic formalities, causing me delays as well as the displeasure of meeting with him more than once. On the other hand, his adoration of the military could benefit my cause. He had not served in the army (because of some physical condition, I believe) and romanticized a soldier's life as a higher form of human existence, so my having trodden those elevated grounds might spare me the hassle. Just in case, I brought a commendation letter from my regiment commander (which he had given me upon discharge), but it turned out to be unnecessary—the vice dean produced a look as if acknowledging he had misjudged me in the past and signed the release note, which I promptly delivered to the bureau.

The bureau designed metal-cutting machines and was located in a remote, industrial part of the city, inside a plant that manufactured those machines. Despite using the plant's space and production facilities, the bureau was not part of the plant, receiving its directives straight from the ministry in Moscow. My next workplace, which engineered food-processing factories, also reported directly to Moscow, and so did Uncle Zinovy's firm, to name a couple. Perhaps the central bureaucrats chose Odessa as their planning site so they could travel to the Black Sea during the beach season; however, I rarely saw Moscow guests at my place of work any time of the year, and when cooperative effort was required, we were the ones traveling to the Soviet capital. Thus, Odessa's plenitude of drafting facilities was likely the result of other factors, such as the city's demographics, which boasted the highest density of Jews among major Soviet metropolises. Since its founding in the eighteenth century, Odessa attracted many Jews by the cosmopolitan character and vibrant economy of a major seaport, farther distance from oppressive monarchs, and the benevolent attitudes of the local governors. By the time of the October Revolution[2], Jews comprised one-third of the city's headcount, sharing it with smaller groups of Germans, Greeks, French, and Italians, as well as the dominant Russo-Ukrainian population. That human mix created a unique culture, with rich folklore sometimes alluding to the city's fishing industry. Over the years, that culture yielded a peculiar Russian dialect, spoken by ordinary folk, whose intonations and constructs appeared prominently in the "leak" complaint that Uncle Zachary once wrote to the building management.

After the Bolsheviks took over in Odessa in 1920, the city's sparkling ethnic mosaic started to fade. The Italians and French bailed out first, as I heard no mention of them thereafter, or met their descendants. Germans

---

[2] The Bolshevik coup of October 1917.

and Greeks remained in lesser quantities, and the number of Jews may have grown initially, as more moved to Odessa from the former Pale. Despite the hardship and turmoil of the immediate post-revolutionary years, the city's cultural life flourished, producing scores of writers, artists, and musicians, many of whom were of Jewish extraction. During World War II, more Jews survived the Nazi occupation in Odessa than in other parts of the Soviet Union, because the city was overseen by Hitler's Romanian allies, who were less hostile toward Jews and were easier to buy. Still, the majority of Jewish residents who remained in the city were executed or shipped to the death camps. After the Soviet victory in the war, more changes occurred in Odessa's ethnic makeup. The city's native Germans (what was left of them) were expelled to Central Asia, followed by the Greeks, Tartars, and other nationalities deemed to have been cozy with the occupiers. The city's population now comprised three major ethnic groups—Russians, Ukrainians, and Jews. The latest had partially replenished their ranks with returnees from the trenches and evacuation, yet multitudes had been killed, and many settled in new places, never to come back. The share of Jews in Odessa declined significantly; however, the city's distinct character endured. I recall colorful Odessa types, boxy trolley cars with manual doors, and fishermen selling the day's catch on street corners. My mother often fried fresh mackerel and flounder for dinner, which were abundant in Odessa in my early years but shortly disappeared, swept away by a new wave of industrialization.

Among my most memorable childhood experiences were visits with my father to his tailor. I was a preschooler then. My father had worn out his last suit and sold some of the remaining German trinkets to make himself a new costume. In the USSR of those days, buying a decent mass-produced suit was almost impossible, so people wore custom ones made of the material they purchased separately. It probably was cheaper, too, the complete opposite of today, when custom-made clothes are a luxury. My father's tailor was an old Jewish man who operated from a first-floor apartment where he lived. The living room of that apartment served as a tailor's shop and was accessible from the street through a narrow door in the building's shaved-off corner. I was mesmerized by that place, with its heavy drapery, wood-framed mirrors, big radio, old furniture, and a clutter of buttons, scissors, measuring tapes, and pieces of fabric. It felt like the magic shop from the like-titled story by H.G. Wells. Somehow, in my mind, that tailor shop became an embodiment of a wilting age of hardship-fostered idealism, when fish abundantly swam in the sea and there were more custom tailors than dentists. Even today, when I recall my father's tailor shop, the entire epoch suddenly breathes into my face.

Later on, I often tried to remember the location of that outfit. Its corner entrance was typical of the Odessa architecture, and while walking in the city, I sometimes encountered a similar layout, only to realize it was not where my father's tailor used to be. Like its counterpart from the H.G. Wells story, the tailor's shop disappeared, faded forever, together with an era of which it was an indelible part.

In the 1960s & 1970s, Odessa underwent rapid growth, accompanied by an influx of new residents, mostly Ukrainians from the countryside. That demographic shift had further reduced the share of Jews in the city; however, they remained a highly visible minority. By then, positions in the government and other pivots of the Soviet power structure were no longer accessible to Jews; however, skilled professions sheltered the latter in disproportionately large numbers. The occupations of physicians, teachers, scientists, and engineers exhibited a notable Jewish presence. The Soviet authorities did not view such a situation as desirable, though, and worked tirelessly to correct the imbalance. They could not reject qualified job applicants without violating the full-employment tenet of the planned economy, whose labor needs matched the output of training facilities, and so used college admission quotas to limit Jewish access to professions requiring a college degree. To make it "fair," the quota was applied to other nationalities as well, but only Jews felt its full impact. If Armenians or Estonians, for example, could also be rationed in Moscow colleges, they encountered no such constraints in their native republics, while Jews faced the allotted two or three percent wherever they went[3]. That included Odessa, with its Jewish population of over ten percent, so the quota system forced young Jews to seek higher education elsewhere, driving them away from their hometown. But even if the majority came back after graduation or transferred in the middle of their studies (as I did), the share of college graduates among Odessa's Jews should have been the same as among other nationalities, yet it was much higher. Of course, there were those who went to college before the war, when no nationality-based limits existed in the Soviet Union, and even later, it took some time for the restrictions to set in. My uncles never heard about quotas when they attended their polytechnic college in Odessa, Tsylia Ilyinichna obtained her medical degree without any official resistance, and other Jews in that age group experienced no discrimination while learning their trade. At the time of my career's launch, many of them

---

[3] Officially, Jews in the Soviet Union had a "homeland," the Jewish Soviet Autonomous Republic of Birobijan, located in uncultivated and often disputed territories of the Far East, but very few Jews lived there or planned to relocate.

were still active, adding to the ranks of Odessa's intelligentsia, although the quota generation wasn't doing badly, either. "We admit two percent of Jews every year, but twenty percent graduate," commented privately one of our university deans. Still, if local officials accepted such a state of affairs and even joked about it, the higher powers kept tightening the screws with deadly seriousness. They paid less heed to some professions and more to others. Case in point, it was difficult for a Jew to get into a medical school in the USSR, even though medicine had been a traditional Jewish occupation for centuries, and many physicians in the country were Jews. Things were better in the technical field, but the government tried to change that, too. Thankfully, the outcome of that undertaking never materialized—in the nineteen-seventies, Jews began to leave the Soviet Union, and twenty years later, the regime collapsed.

Whichever ultimate result of the quota system the Soviet rulers aimed for, they took advantage of the status quo, setting up shops in Odessa to utilize the city's educated and productive workforce. That was how, I believe, my engineering bureau came about, as well as other places that employed me in the old country. At least half of the bureau's engineers were Jews, including the majority of department heads. The situation was even "worse" at my next job, where Jewish presence exceeded every measure of official tolerance and was sustained only through the efforts of the company's chief—an aging, heavyset man with a square jaw and mane of white hair—whose powerful steadiness complemented the neurotic energy of his subordinates. Not that the Jewish factor played a role in my workplace choices. Jews in Odessa were largely acculturated even before the Russian Revolution, taking part in almost every aspect of the city's life, including organized crime. It did not spare them from persecution and pogroms, but the latter were rare and primarily targeted property.

My parents were acculturated, too, despite claiming Yiddish as their first tongue. My father was proud of his Jewish heritage; my mother was glad she had survived hers. My father talked about Jewish history and achievements, but also considered Judaism too stern a religion and often mused about the roots of antisemitism. As for my mother, the Jewish history bespoke mostly her Chudnov childhood. Neither of my parents disapproved of other nationalities or stated ethnic preferences my playmates had to satisfy, so it was only in high school that I discovered most of my close friends were Jews. Perhaps we felt more secure in such a company, having already developed sensitivity to anti-Jewish prejudice and knowing we would not encounter it in our midst, or maybe it was something else; still, I saw the above discovery as immaterial, especially after the boarding school where ethnic cohesion was weak. The extended time that we, the boarding school classmates, spent together neutralized antisemitic toxins, so the ancestral awareness could not take hold on those grounds alone. Still, Jewish undercurrents ran there, too, surfacing from time to time in surprising revelations, then and years later.

One case of a late disclosure involved my boarding school friend, a gymnastics champion and Mikhail Isayevich's frequent object of ire. Our paths diverged: I chose the technical field; he pursued sports. After graduating from a college that our coach (who coached a gymnastics team there) helped him get into, my friend joined his benefactor as an assistant, and when the coach emigrated to America a couple of years before me, he recommended his protégé as a replacement. Hence, at the age of thirty, my friend became a gymnastics coach at a major college, a prestigious and well-paid job. By then, we no longer stayed in touch but were always glad to run into each other and chat about old times. He was already married, had a child, and enjoyed a high standard of living in the USSR—a private apartment, a car, a good salary, and foreign travel—so it came as a surprise to me to learn from a mutual acquaintance that my gymnast friend had applied for an emigration visa to Israel. It was even more surprising, as I had never imagined that anybody in his family was Jewish. The news came a few days before my own departure, so I couldn't meet with him, but theorized that our coach, who had opened a gymnastics school in the United States, offered my friend a job there and arranged an invitation from non-existent relatives in Israel. But even if that theory were accurate, it did not preclude my friend from having a Jewish lineage on his wife's side or the side of his absentee father, whom I had never met and heard conflicting stories about. Either way, I was delighted I would have a close boyhood friend in America, but he did not reach his destination, falling victim to a murder in Odessa in a bizarre love triangle plot soon after I left.

Odessa's changes of the 1960s–1970s resulted in the virtual extinction of the old culture from everyday life. The unique jargon became confined to mostly theatrical productions, and the bubbly temperament of the city's dwellers gave way to expressions that were rather mundane. There remained societal pockets, however, where the old spirit ruled, and they were predominantly Jewish clusters, such as my engineering bureau. In the earlier times, my boarding school could also be seen as an example of Odessa culture—its brashness, energy, and cheerful opportunism—still, the Jewish gatherings embodied that culture's essence. A colorful display of characters, enthusiasm and mental agility of the people, originality of the ideas and a belief in their transformative force, all added to a climate where the vanishing tradition thrived in its pure, condensed form. It was the atmosphere that made my stint at the engineering bureau a satisfying experience despite the occupation's weak appeal. I worked there for less than a year, but remember the coworkers and events as if they betided yesterday. Things were even livelier at my next job, although it had its own chronicler—a massive, bald, bearded man who cruised the hallways with a big smile and a notebook, listening to conversations and recording spontaneous aphorisms of his colleagues—so in deference to him, I shall describe no more. Perhaps not everybody felt comfortable in such a setting, but all agreed that it was anything but dull.

I do not remember my job title at the bureau, but it had little to do with my duties, which initially were a series of unrelated tasks, almost errands. At first, I was deployed to assist one of the managers—a tall, portly fellow in a suit and tie, who looked like Malenkov[4] and always missed by a whisker direct eye contact with whomever he spoke to. The manager must have been installed in his position with a nod from political powers (as an aspiring functionary or an embarrassing relative), since he often bragged about having access to high circles and was disliked by everyone in the bureau. He sauntered around the building with an air of importance but was ignored by subordinates and superiors alike. As for the actual work, he did nothing, and my job was to assist him in that endeavor. "I sometimes come up with brilliant ideas," he told me once, "but forget them because I do not carry a notepad. Why don't you follow me and write them down?" He was not kidding. That suggestion attested to the ideas he might come up with, as well as to the man's buffoonery. Luckily, he neglected to ask me to write down the "writing-down" idea itself and must have forgotten about it, like all the others, as he never mentioned that request again.

After a month of wandering between assignments, I ended up in the lab under the supervision of its lead engineer—a short, forty-something fellow with a round head and receding hairline. "Supervision" was too strong a word to describe our relations, as my new boss did not want to supervise anybody. He asked me for favors, and I did them for him as a friend. I would characterize him as my mentor. He was very popular among coworkers, who appreciated his directness, sagacity, and sharp wit. At lunch and after work, people gathered in his office (a fenced area in the corner of the lab) to discuss perplexities of life, the latest news, or a new book, and to hear the host's brilliant quips and words of wisdom. Officially, he reported to the idea-forgetting manager but disliked the

---

[4] A Soviet leader; the first post-Stalin Soviet Premier.

latter intensely and kept him at arm's length. In his work, my mentor–boss often visited the plant and sometimes took me along. I enjoyed those trips—he showed me the workings of enormous machines the Soviet government was buying in Europe and Japan, and he showed me people. They were engineers and smiths who had worked with my boss on various projects or knew him socially. He would introduce me to a person, talk business or chat for a while, and later tell me a story about the new acquaintance, mostly entertaining and good-hearted. During one of those tours, we walked into a shop where, behind a metal-cutting machine, stood an oversized, bearded man in protective goggles, criss-crossed by spark jets shooting from under a chisel. "This is an interesting fellow; let's come say hello," suggested my guide, and we approached the machinist. The machinist stopped the machine, took off his goggles, and greeted the visitors warmly. I got the impression that he and my boss went back a long way—maybe attended the same school (they were the same age), or were neighbors. The chat started amicably. "This guy is among the most skilled workers anywhere," my mentor presented the machinist, "and he is almost an engineer." The machinist beamed, not realizing where the conversation was headed. "Explain to the man," my guide addressed the worker, pointing at me, "why you dropped out of college." The machinist's face showed some tension. "You know very well," he replied to his inquisitor, "that I got married and had to support a family." "But you had less than a year to graduate and were a good student," pressed my escort, "Don't tell me that your marriage could not wait." It was obvious that the machinist did not enjoy the topic. "I have a lot of work to do; perhaps we may continue another time," he said and put the goggles back on. "He will not admit," said my boss to me as we were leaving the shop, "he dropped out of college so he could work as a machinist. Workers at his skill level are paid by the number of items they produce, and he makes good money in this job. Two or three times what I make."

One might conclude from the above example that a college degree in the USSR was not very instrumental in providing its holders with a better lifestyle, but this was true primarily for men. For a Soviet woman, it was different. Few of them worked as machinists at a factory, served as career military, or managed warehouses—those were men's jobs. To attain better pay and a higher social status, a woman needed a college degree more than men did. Many college-educated women worked as schoolteachers and medical practitioners. Numerous family physicians in Odessa were women, and many internists, including those in the sanatorium, were women, too (specialists were usually men). Perhaps my mother chose to work for a medical establishment because she had aspired to be a doctor in the past, although I am unsure how satisfied she might have been if her aspirations were realized. I recall her discussions with my father about going to a nursing school when she was still a statistician. She never did it, but whatever the cause, I hardly picture my mother as a nurse. She was more of a managerial type and would likely have ended up as an administrator in some healthcare outfit if she had finished medical school. And although she held a prestigious post in the sanatorium, her self-esteem must have suffered among many women physicians. Hence, an opportunity to attend a college, even late in life, seemed to her like a second chance—a fulfillment of a dream. My mother did not need to worry about a career at that point, but she studied hard as if her life depended on it. She spent many hours reading textbooks, writing essays, preparing for exams, and, despite being one of the oldest students in her class, graduated at the top.

The graduation ceremony took place in the Avery Fisher Hall[5], which the college had rented for the occasion, and not for much money, as the times were lean. Wearing a black gown and a mortarboard, my mother received a diploma on the hall's stage. A small band played cheerful tunes. It was one of the happiest moments in her life. She wanted to pursue a bachelor's degree and had already started the semester when she was summoned to the registrar and informed that the state would no longer subsidize her tuition. My mother was disappointed and attributed the cancellation to the intrigues of her detractors, real and imaginary. She based the conspiracy claims on being the only one in her class who was bumped off the program, while her classmates, who had enrolled under similar circumstances, continued to study. However, in a couple of more weeks, those classmates were also kicked out. The cycle of profligate government spending ended, and another of austerity began.

---

[5] The main concert hall at the Lincoln Center in New York.

2. Baby Bird

A few years back, already after my mother's passing, I was walking down a Brooklyn street when I saw a baby bird sitting on the sidewalk under a train overpass. It probably fell out of the nest from a tree above. The bird was the size of a sparrow—gray, with a yellow beak, which she opened from time to time to produce a distress call. Normally, I do not meddle with wildlife (other than maybe squashing a bug), as I know more about unintended consequences than about animals, but at that moment, I recalled a childhood story about another strayed baby bird, rescued by her mother, and paused to see how such a story might play in real life. I also wondered what kind of bird the sidewalk stray was and hoped to get an answer by observing a grown specimen. Not to scare off the rescue, I positioned myself a few yards from the subject and waited... Several minutes passed, but no mother bird or other feathery relatives appeared on the scene. People walked by, paying no attention to the unfortunate chick like it did not exist. I was about to be on my way, too, when the nestling made a surprising move: it toddled over the distance between us and settled at my foot. "Smart bird," remarked my ninety-five-year-old neighbor, whom I told about the incident. Perhaps the bird mistook me for a tree, the only upright cylindrical object that did not move, yet, being prone to anthropomorphic impulses of humans toward animals and even things, I interpreted the bird's maneuver as a plea for help. Avoiding involvement was no longer possible; I reached down and picked the nestling up.

The bird did not resist, sitting quietly in my open hand as if she had entrusted her fate to me completely. I stood on the sidewalk, holding a warm, pulsating lump, for which I was now responsible, and did not know what to do. Suddenly, I recalled a Petco[6] store that had recently opened nearby. "Perhaps this is a rare bird, and the store may even thank me for donating my catch to their inventory, or at least they will give me some advice," I thought, and headed for the store. "You should not have brought it here," said the saleswoman to whom I showed the bird, shattering my hopes of becoming a Petco supplier. I explained the situation. The woman looked at my companion, whose kind she could not determine either, and softened a bit. "Wait," she said and vanished behind the showroom's wall. She returned, carrying a small cardboard box and a piece of paper with a few phone numbers written on it. "Call them," the woman said, "They may help you with your bird." The box

---

[6] A large pet-store chain.

was the right size, with handles and breathing holes. I put the nestling in the box and went home. Surprisingly, the bird did not like its new quarters—it kept scratching and squeaking throughout the trip, which luckily did not take long.

I came home and started calling. The first number on the Petco list was ASPCA. I called it, but got no answer. A visit to the ASPCA website convinced me they would not be of much help to my case. The second number was in Manhattan. The woman who answered the call informed me they dealt with exotic birds only, but there was another outfit on the same block that handled all types. She gave me their phone number. The number had an answering machine, so I left a message. Not expecting a callback soon, if ever, I went online to read up on baby birds. The first search yielded an explanation of what made my charge restive inside the box—the surface was too smooth for the nestling to grab; its claws were slipping, making the animal uncomfortable. I padded the box with a paper towel, and the protests stopped. The following twenty minutes passed in studying the avifauna, and then the phone rang. The woman on the other end was returning my call. I explained that I had found a baby bird and did not know what to do with it. The caller asked me to describe the find. "It is a starling," she said after I gave the description. "The nestling should be fed every three hours. It is not easy to care for." I sensed some hesitation in the woman's voice. She told me that her organization rehabilitated young and injured birds found on New York streets and brought in by the city's dwellers. After the birds recovered or grew up, they were released into the wild, around where they had been picked up. "Can I bring my bird, too?" I asked with rising hope. "Of course, you can," the woman replied joyously. She probably wanted to suggest it in the beginning, but was reluctant to impose on my sense of compassion. She then gave me her coordinates. I said I would be there in about an hour and began to pack.

The "Wild Bird Fund," which was the name of the bird-caring center, operated from inside a veterinary clinic on Manhattan's Upper West Side, not far from the familiar Hotel Lucerne. There was a direct subway line to that place, about an hour's ride from where I resided. I put the box with the bird in the bag and headed for the station. On the train, the nestling was calm, resting comfortably on a paper pad… The clinic was on the street corner, one block from the train stop. Next to the clinic's entrance stood a Wild Bird Fund sign, stating the organization's mission and its impending move to a dedicated location. The entrance door opened into a waiting room with two rows of chairs and a receptionist's desk. I asked for a woman with whom I had spoken on the phone. "Do you have an appointment?" inquired the receptionist. I replied that I did. The receptionist called an internal number to announce me. "She will be with you in a moment," said the receptionist, and gave me a form to fill out. I quickly wrote my name, described the "patient," where it had been found, and returned the form. There were a couple of pet owners in the room, plus two staff cats. The cats had learned to get along with other animals and showed no interest in my bag's contents. I sat next to a lady with a dog and waited.

In a short while, a dark-haired, slender woman came out to the front desk. "Are you Michael?" she addressed me. I got up. "So, what have you brought us?" the woman asked. I handed her the box with the bird. She carefully opened the top and looked inside. "Here is the little one," the woman said affectionately. She then told me to wait and went inside the clinic with the box. She returned minutes later, carrying the nestling in her hand so the bird's head stuck out of a gentle fist. In her other hand, the woman held a small, water-filled syringe, which she placed against the bird's mouth from time to time. "He is alright, just a little dehydrated," said the woman, "We have three more baby starlings and will put yours with them. They will be growing up together." "It was nice of you to travel all that distance to bring him here," she added. I did not mention that the nestling had practically begged me for help, and explained my effort tongue-in-cheek by a desire to shore up the anti-mosquito front. "Anyhow, we are grateful to you," the woman said, "*He* is grateful to you," and she pointed at the beaked head jutting out of her closed hand.

I walked out of the veterinary clinic with great relief—what would I do if I had not been able to billet my find? By then, I knew a starling was not a proper pet. The bird lived for twenty years, needed a lot of space, and was messy. Without special care (like that provided by the Wild Bird Fund), the nestling would have lost the ability to live in the wild within weeks. The only choice I might have had was to bring the bird back under the overpass in Brooklyn and leave it there, which, at that point, would have been like killing the animal with bare hands. Thus, as far as the gratitude was involved, among the three of us—the bird, the bird-caring center, and myself—I was the one who ought to be grateful the most, grateful to the Wild Bird Fund for taking the responsibility off my shoulders... In the excitement of the past few hours, I forgot to eat and was now hungry. Zabar's cafe was a few blocks away. I went there and ordered my usual sandwich with coffee. It never tasted so good.

3. Transit Strike

The baby bird episode occurred decades after my first encounter with the West, but still rang as a notable example of how a free society satisfied its people's needs. I never heard of a bird-caring body in the USSR, where an all-encompassing government would not have thought one up. And even if someone had suggested the idea, it would have been rejected because of "more important things than catering to birds." But here in New York, a handful of individuals, whom nobody appointed or told what to do, saw the need and acted upon it without asking anybody's permission. And whatever their stated goal was, the only needs they catered to were the needs of other humans. As a nonprofit entity, the Wild Bird Fund relied on charitable donations, yet nobody mentioned the financial side to me during my visit. They took the bird, and that was it. I made my contribution later.

The initiative it took to create a bird-caring center was everywhere in America, evidenced by the multitude of enterprises, big and small. In the beginning, the scope of the country's development astonished me. I was already impressed by the airplane we had flown from Italy on, and now observed awe-inspiring edifices, such as the Empire State Building and Verrazano Bridge, immersed in the unceasing activity of smaller scales. The history of civilizations' building grandiose structures dates back thousands of years and is illustrated by the Egyptian pyramids, the Colosseum, Moscow Metro, and other great monuments; however, the American creations stood out by the magnitude of their numbers, as well as the brevity of the time to put them all up. In only three hundred years, the people of the United States transformed their vast land, surpassing other nations in every aspect of industrial buildout, and did it with little involvement from the state. There were no five-year plans[7] in America, no government-set production goals, no attempts to subject all facets of life to central control. Those facets interacted freely, sometimes colliding but eventually striking the right balance. Untamed, the venture spirit permeated the entire society. It was in marked contrast to the old Soviet Union, where overwhelming governmental dictate resulted in a crude, malformed economy with living standards far below what the country's educated and capable population might have hoped for.

An impressive display of American organizational genius, I observed soon after coming to the United States. The occasion was the famous New York transit strike of 1980. I was several months into my first job

---

[7] A Soviet-style economic development scheme.

when we received a memorandum warning of a potential strike. The City negotiated with the transit union, the talks were not going well, and the union threatened a walkout... The mention of a transit strike touched in me a nostalgic chord of the Italian experience, but other New Yorkers were very concerned. The suspension of a service that moved millions of people in a single day would paralyze the city, causing much hardship to its residents. The Taylor Law[8] banned strikes by public employees; yet, the stoppage's dire consequences, the kind that had prompted the above law in the first place, led the union to believe the City would avoid the melee at any cost. Penalties for violations of the Taylor Law were mainly financial, judges often sympathetic to the strikers, and the first-term city mayor, Ed Koch, a former liberal congressman from Manhattan, was untested and likely viewed as wobbly under pressure[9]. Hence, the union leaders were certain their demands would be met.

The transit strike memo announced the creation of a crisis task force, or a committee, which, besides the city and the state officials, enlisted delegates from several New York corporations, including my employer. We were promised regular updates. Perhaps most committee members believed the strike would be averted; however, they had to act as if the stoppage were a certainty. Working in the public's favor was the coming school break, which would free a large fleet of yellow school buses. With those buses in mind, the task force outlined commuter routes connecting the outer boroughs to Manhattan, whilst employers compiled lists of employees who would be coming to work during the strike. My firm included me in its list, maybe because I lived near one of those routes. The designated workers received passes to the makeshift transit system, while the rest were told to stay home until the strike's end.

Despite two weeks of preparations and a few more memos, the strike came as a surprise, maybe because nobody believed it could actually happen. Surrounded by reporters and TV cameras, the mayor took a crowd of straphangers over the Brooklyn Bridge, opening a new chapter in the city's history. The bridge's Brooklyn side was now a yellow-bus terminal from where the commuters crossed the bridge on foot. My route

---

[8] The Public Employees Fair Employment Act of New York State.

[9] That perception could have something to do with the popular film *The Taking of Pelham 123*, where the character of New York City's mayor was undoubtedly inspired by Ed Koch. The movie was released in 1974, while Koch became mayor in 1978; however, he did run for the mayor's office in 1973 and was likely known to the film's creators as an unsuccessful candidate. In the movie, the mayor is portrayed as an inept, weak caricature of a person. Besides that mischaracterization, the film's plot dealing with the hijacking of a subway train made the movie oddly prophetic of the 1980 strike.

was different. I would board a yellow bus at the street corner two blocks away from where I lived, ride through Brooklyn and over the Verrazano Bridge to Staten Island, get off near the Staten Island Ferry, and walk a few hundred feet past April puddles and a line of city workers to the ferry's terminal. The riders then boarded a ferryboat and sailed over the mirror-like water surface, past smaller boats, little islands, the Statue of Liberty, and the Brooklyn Bridge, towards the cluster of stone giants looming over Manhattan's southern tip. My job was a couple of hundred yards from where the ferry docked. The entire trip took a long time, but it was far more enjoyable than a regular rush-hour subway ride, and cost me only twenty-five cents for ferry fare. The lunch I carried in my bag. The return route was the reverse. I enjoyed those rides—the scenery, the sense of adventure—and remember that transit strike as one of my most exciting experiences in the US.

The strike continued for eleven days—the city functioned without interruption. Every morning, a yellow bus would come to the same street corner and take me to Staten Island. The bus was almost empty at my stop, so I always secured a window seat, but there were enough seats for other riders who boarded along the way. Meanwhile, the City went to court, and the judge imposed a fine on the transit union, so that with every day of the strike, the union's bank account was getting noticeably smaller. Finally, an agreement was reached between the parties, and the strike came to an end. That moment was the turning point, from which New York City began its rise, and although one cannot dismiss the catalytic effect of adversity, it was the experience of reorienting millions of people in a matter of weeks that set an example for future changes.

4. Corporate Lounge

Handling the transit strike, building a skyscraper, or setting up a bird-caring center bespoke the talents and vision of the people involved, but also their eagerness to take charge. If, as the proverb suggests, a good start accounts for half of the success (and I never doubted the importance of starting, only its share of the outcome), America's advantage was aided by the country's subjects jumping into ventures like beach-goers into the water on a hot day. And if it were asked what spurred the energy and confidence behind that entrepreneurial drive, my answer would be, "Individual freedom." Obligatory courses in Marxist philosophy taught to us in Soviet schools defined freedom as an accepted necessity, a notion that favored the forbidding side of a due process line. But describing freedom in such a way amounts to declaring it a state of mind. In that sense, the Marxist definition was correct, yet disingenuous, as it ignored a vital issue—how much necessity people could accept without harming their psyche and ability to care for themselves.

A want for freedom is a basic instinct to explore, to progress through the stages of life, to fulfill every person's potential. It is what drives a little boy who has escaped his keeper's heed and, still unsteady on his feet, rushes with a happy smile into the big world. He will not get far, stopped by vigilant adults, but such attempts should not be punished harshly… At first, American self-confidence and optimism surprised me, as life appeared less certain in the United States than in my old country and even in Europe. In the Soviet Union, there were pronounced limits on how high a person could rise but also how low [s]he might fall, while in America, the bottom was nonexistent. The homeless on the streets and the rundown, crime-ridden neighborhoods were real and near, and so seemed the possibility of being consumed by such existence. Still, people seem not to be concerned. I was fascinated by the conduct of disgraced public officials shown on TV at an arraignment or sentencing. Imagining myself in their place (except for having been falsely accused), I would be nervous and depressed, yet the arraigned looked like they had won a jackpot, proclaiming cheerfully that they had done nothing wrong and would be vindicated. They tried to hide their doubts and fears, fighting to the very end. Perhaps there was a link between such audacity and the fact that Americans had fewer checks on their lives. I recall once visiting a pre-EU Holland, traditionally one of the freest and most tolerant places on Earth. My Norwich ferry arrived in Rotterdam at dawn, and I took a train to Amsterdam with other ferry riders, mostly English speakers. Soon after the train left the Rotterdam station, a conductor entered the railcar, checking tickets. "Good morning," the passengers greeted him in unison. "No, not 'good morning,'" replied the conductor in an instructive tone, as if talking to a kindergarten class, "Goedemorgen, goedemorgen," he repeated in Dutch. Surely, the conductor had the friendliest intentions, and his accent on the morning greeting's Dutch version reflected the quality of patriotism valued in every nation; however, I could hardly picture a similar scene in America, or at least in the parts where I lived. No stranger corrected me in a conversation there, including my early years in the country when such corrections would have been most welcome, and overall, a great deal was left to people's discretion, even when their behavior could be determined by law or other conventions. Amidst that doggedness and pragmatism, such deference to individual expression was heartwarming.

If you want to make an enemy, do someone a favor," goes a familiar saying, usually uttered in a tone of profound regret over the failings of human nature. Although a simplification, like most aphorisms, this one points to a specific trait but not a failing, as the adage implies. What it points to is a virtue and nothing other than the urge to be free. People often feel uncomfortable in the presence of a benefactor, as it reminds them of indebtedness, but that feeling seldom rises to enmity and is resolved by repaying the debt. There are other favors, though, which do breed resentment because they deprive the recipients of initiative. Such favors may look like entitlements or a godsend, but even if not perceived as charity, they limit individual choices, creating pent-up discontent. I once got curious about food riots in the US during the Great Depression, as I remembered no mention of them in books or movies. A subsequent Web search yielded no results. However, there was no lack of economic upheavals in other places, frequently directed against the very people who believed they had advanced the rioters' welfare. Hence, it appeared that the Great Depression riots were rare, and since Americans did not constitute an obedient lot, they likely carried less rage inside, having been scarcely subjected to the tyranny of spite and altruism. If nobody forced their decisions or promised them anything, whom would they blame and riot against?

From a historical perspective, individual freedom appears an unlikely enabler of political stability, as coercion has been a more popular tool for maintaining peace. The founding principles of the United States affirmed individual freedom as the cornerstone of American society, but what was to protect that society against the ravages of time and ambition? What was to prevent the entrepreneurial spirit that had created all that latitude and abundance from advancing corruption and deceit? That question popped up early in my American life when I was still at my first job. Our firm occupied a tall building in downtown Manhattan, with the second floor housing service and recreational facilities, such as a cafeteria and lounge. In those pre-downsizing times, firms like ours tried to comfort their employees at work, and the lounge was an example of that intent, furnished generously with armchairs and couches. I sometimes went there to concentrate and recharge my batteries, but mainly used the place to relax after meals during lunch breaks, as most other workers did. The lounge adjoined a glass wall above the building's entrance. Behind the glass opened a view of the elevated terrace below and the surrounding streets. That section of Manhattan was perhaps the city's windiest spot, notable for violent gusts blowing in every direction. The wind gusts were particularly hurtful when accompanied by rain or snow. The swirls of air lurked between the tall buildings and narrow streets, pouncing upon unwary pedestrians and ripping off their umbrellas. Twisted and torn umbrellas flew like birds, falling onto the ground and piling up there.

And so it was one of those windy, rainy days when I came down to the lounge and settled near the window, observing the street and people struggling with the angry nature. Suddenly, I heard a peal of loud laughter precipitated by a chorus of male voices on my right. The sound was coming from a group of men sitting on a couch ten feet away. They also watched the terrace below, bursting into guffaws every time a wind gust claimed another victim... Of course, the slapstick character of the sufferers' reaction did not escape me, but the humorous impulse was silenced by the realization of a human plight, as well as by the act's repetitiveness. However, my lounge neighbors seemed unaffected by the spectacle's somber side. They were very excited and ready to spend the rest of their lunchtime delighting in a free comedy show.

I had an uneasy feeling—a mix of disappointment and foreboding. I did not know anybody from the laughing crew and had never seen them before. They likely worked in the same building, but it was a vast place with numerous floors and departments. The spectators' glee was not malicious, not a schadenfreude type. Losing an umbrella or a hat posed no serious harm, and if, instead of being pounded by weather, the people outside were assaulted or mugged, the couch team would have called the police, I am sure, and even rushed downstairs to assist the attacked. Yet, as the laughing implied, such a response would have been a reaction to the affront of lawlessness rather than an act of compassion, and that made me uncomfortable. Something important was missing. There was no emotional connection between the people on the couch and those on the terrace, a connection not of conspiracy or tribalism but of a common beginning, which, like the force of gravity, is barely detectable among small masses yet holds multitudes of them together. Could it be that in breaking away from the old dominion, the new society downplayed its cultural roots—never renounced them, just didn't stress enough their importance? After all, even the contemporary notion of individual liberty can be traced to the ancient tenet of equality before God, and similar historical excursions might provide a deeper understanding of freedom and its limits. Perhaps when viewed in such a context, the new norms could make a more harmonious whole, adding vertebrae of sensibilities the couch's occupants seemingly lacked. The latter did not enjoy the show for much longer and soon left. Maybe they grew bored, or had to go back to work, or suddenly saw the situation in a different light.

5. People's Court

The transit strike propelled Ed Koch to the ranks of the country's most popular politicians, and later, he was re-elected twice. He was a good mayor, and his immediate multi-term successors—Rudolph Giuliani and Michael Bloomberg—were also pragmatic, capable administrators. Such continuity was partly due to a couple of events, which, albeit tragic on their own, helped perpetuate good governance of the city…

By the end of Koch's reign, the folly was on a rebound, which the election of the next mayor legibly confirmed, but then broke out the Crown Heights pogrom[10]. The riots continued for three days, and the new mayor did nothing to stop them, ensuring that his first term in office was also his last. He was defeated by Rudolph Giuliani, under whose lead the unthinkable happened: the city's crime rate plunged. Astounded New Yorkers rewarded their mayor with a second term. But people get accustomed to good things quickly, and soon after Giuliani's reelection, the nipping began. The purpose of the attacks was not to deny the mayor his third term—the same year Giuliani became mayor, the City Council passed a law limiting the mayoral span to two terms, so he could not run for reelection, anyhow—the issue was who might replace him, or which political philosophy the replacement would represent. If the incumbent were to leave on a high note, the replacement would likely continue along the old path, but if the departure were marred by a perception of failure, the opposition might have a better chance to chart the city's course. As Giuliani's last term was coming to an end, the criticism by his detractors intensified, which, together with personal issues and a couple of administrative scandals, resulted in a notable decline in the mayor's popularity. It looked like Giuliani's successor would be in the mold of his predecessor when terrorists flew planes into the World Trade Center. Amidst the shock and confusion that followed, Giuliani stepped up to the plate, and his popularity soared. He became almost a deity, whereat anointed Michael Bloomberg as an heir apparent. Under Bloomberg, the city recovered from the attack while the quality of life continued to improve. He was an effective manager who kept things running without much hullabaloo. In addition, his personal wealth and willingness to use it to finance his reelection made him a formidable candidate to beat. He even extracted an exemption from the City Council, allowing him to serve a third term… Together, Koch, Giuliani, and Bloomberg provided the city with competent and proactive leadership for thirty-two out of

---

[10] Crown Heights riot of 1991, directed mainly against the area's Hasidic population.

thirty-six consecutive years, a remarkably long stretch in a place like New York.

The three mayors had a similar vision for the city's future, but very different personalities. Koch was the most entertaining among the three and remained in the public eye long after the end of his political career. He wrote books, hosted a radio program, and, in the late nineteen-nineties, presided as a judge over the People's Court TV reality show. I found that show very instructive about the American legal system, plus it was good fun. Today, there are several such shows on every primary TV channel, but then, it was a novelty, and the cases were educational and droll. One case I remember particularly well. A store owner sued a computer contractor, claiming the job (a hard drive installation) had been improperly done. The defendant was a youngster in his twenties who eventually lost the case. During his testimony, he attempted to climb on the judge's good side and started to complain about the city's poor business climate, which he blamed on the current mayor, Giuliani (with whom Koch had a highly publicized feud at the time). "It was different when you were in charge, your honor," said the contractor to the judge, "You were a much better mayor." At the end of Koch's mayoralty, the defendant must have been in his early teens, which did not escape the judge's attention. "You remember how good a mayor I was?" asked Koch with a sardonic smile[11]. Meanwhile, the show host interviewed a street audience who watched the proceedings on a big TV screen outside the studios. "Is it all right to suck up to a judge like that?" the host asked the viewers, referring to the defendant's praise of the judge's mayoral past. To my surprise, the question puzzled the spectators. Some hesitated with an answer; others leaned toward the disapproval they felt was expected of them, and then came the turn of a young man who obviously had a strong opinion and was eager to share it with the world. "Of course, it is

---

[11] I once met Ed Koch on a Manhattan street. It happened in the early fall of 2012. I was walking up Broadway past the Ansonia building when I saw the former mayor limping through the crowd toward me. He was alone. Tall and still distinguished-looking, the great man moved with difficulty, leaning on a cane. His eyes glimmered painfully with anticipation, as if at a reception or a rally, yet passersby did not acknowledge him. The younger folk did not know who he was, while the older ones tried to respect his privacy. As I walked past him, our sights crossed. "Hello, Mayor," I said and kept going. I did not stop, despite an urge to do so, because of a similar privacy consideration; however, in that particular case, such concern was misplaced. If Koch wanted privacy, he wouldn't go to a busy street without an escort. He wanted to be recognized, surrounded by people, to feel the excitement of the city he loved, maybe for the last time. He would be pleased and even grateful if I had spoken to him... He died a few months later, portending the end of New York's renaissance, which he started thirty-five years earlier.

all right," exclaimed the young man as the microphone paused in front of his face, "This is America!"

Clearly, the young lad did not imply America was a land of sucking up to judges. What he was trying to convey was his version of America, where everybody did what they wanted as long as it was not against the law (or one could get away with it). Perhaps the young man's categorical pronouncement was partly a bravado before TV cameras or a rebellion against his family—he looked South-Asian to me, fully Americanized, born perhaps in the United States to immigrant parents who tried to instill in their son the old country's forbidding values—yet, regardless of the motives, his attitude reflected a schismatic trend that already became apparent then…

The laughing episode notwithstanding, my early years in the United States had yielded a satisfactory experience, as far as my relations with colleagues were concerned. At the time, the majority of workers in my field were suburban Americans who had found employment in a rapidly expanding sector of the otherwise unfriendly economy. Most did not have a matching education, but were smart enough to learn on the job. The rest were immigrants from Asia, England, South America, and other countries. My compatriots were few then. We all got along well. Each sort drew poise from a familiar homogeneity of home, emerging at a place of work ready to embrace human differences. The natives claimed to be of different ethnicities (Italian, Polish, Norwegian), too, yet showed little variance in that regard. They probably emphasized their origins to tell ethnic jokes, which they directed at each other from time to time. Those were innocent cracks, good-natured and often funny, yet would have been improper in the politically correct climate of today. But then, everybody laughed, and nobody got offended. On a more serious note, that ethnic pulse was likely driven by a desire for mutual awareness, whose lack explained the corporate lounge episode and the People's Court's young man. I am sure most of my indigenous colleagues did not view their homeland as an idea, but it was different for the newcomers, whose prior circumstance and loss of habitat had given them a better grasp of the adopted land's distinction. I enjoyed that motley company; however, it was not diversity itself that appealed to me, but that all those people, from various countries and cultures, had a common vision of their destiny. Amalgamation was taking hold, and then, the world of the People Court's young man stepped in.

6. Medical History

I do not intend to paint a bleak picture of the future. Life goes in cycles, and preservation corrects the faults. What is lost in one generation crops up in another, wrapped in a sense of discovery that sheds new light on the older truths. New waves arrive, and the old fade away, like people around us... As time passed, the energy and presence of Uncle Morris' anniversary crowd fizzled out. Stepped into the sunset my mother's aunt and uncles. My mother's illness was progressing, too. When we arrived in the United States, NYANA provided us with health insurance, like all the immigrants in its care. I do not remember what coverage it was, as I did not need medical attention during that period and was unaware of anybody who did. It ought to be something basic. During that time, the healthcare industry was less regulated, and insurance companies offered a wide range of individual and group plans. Some of those plans cost little; others were more expensive. The expensive plans paid more to their providers, so more doctors and hospitals accepted them, while cheaper policies were popular among foreign-born physicians, mainly immigrants from Asia, as well as Russian-speaking doctors who started to appear on New York's medical scene then.

For the purposes of sponsorship and entry, the atomic unit of the immigration flow was a family, so when I got a job and alighted from the NYANA roster, my mother was dismissed from there, too. But what was a family to NYANA did not necessarily constitute one to health insurers. I could not extend my workplace policy to include my mother, so she picked an individual health plan, the type that most immigrants chose in similar circumstances. The premiums were low, and so was the quality of care; still, the plan provided access to medical services, begetting some peace of mind. My mother's plan-assigned physician was an Indian immigrant who practiced in our neighborhood and spoke English with an accent. He was a knowledgeable professional, yet low reimbursement rates made him skeptical about patients' complaints. For about a year after coming to America, my mother had few such complaints, and then their number started to increase. Back in the Soviet Union, she frequently felt ill, suspecting severe gastrointestinal and other inner deformities. Working at a large medical establishment, she was friendly with many physicians and sought advice from the best of them. They responded with numerous tests, occasionally prescribing X-ray exams. In the USSR of that time, X-ray tests were used often and resulted in greater radiation exposure than current equipment. Perhaps my mother overdid those procedures, which contributed to her disorder.

My mother must have been ill already when she arrived in the United States, albeit in the early stage of a slowly progressing ailment, which, at that point, was not supposed to show symptoms. The main reason for her complaints had to be psychosomatic, stemming from the trauma of the war years and transition in the United States. As my mother's need for medical attention grew, her coverage's shortcomings became more apparent—she had fatigue and stomach pains, yet her primary physician was in no hurry to refer her to a specialist or a hospital. My mother felt abandoned, which further aggravated her physical state. She needed another opinion. Someone recommended a Russian-speaking doctor, and I called him to make an appointment. The doctor used to be a prominent surgeon in Moscow, from where he immigrated to the United States a few years before my mother and me. Soon after coming to America, he obtained a US medical license, but didn't go into surgery, opting for consulting work at a major New York City hospital and private practice in a small Manhattan office (which he shared with other physicians). He did not accept my mother's insurance, but even if he did, the plan would not have covered the visit without a referral, so I wrote him a check.

The Russian doctor was in his fifties, warm and caring—the qualities my mother could appreciate. He reminded me of the Brooklyn furniture store owner from whom we bought our first house fittings. The doctor examined my mother along the lines of his expertise but found nothing wrong. "You need a good internist who will investigate your complaints and make the right diagnosis," the doctor said. His daughter worked in the outpatient division of the same hospital as a nurse—she was familiar with the talent pool there and shared that knowledge with her father, who also knew what he had heard from his colleagues. According to him, there was a physician in his daughter's office, well-suited for the task. Besides being a brilliant internist, that physician specialized in gastroenterology, the field my mother thought dealt with her condition. "Let me put you in touch with my daughter," concluded the Russian doctor, "and she will arrange for that physician to see you."

The recommended internist did not accept my mother's insurance, but it was not an issue since office visits were among the least expensive parts of a prolonged treatment or comprehensive examination. More worrisome was that the hospital did not accept the said insurance, either, so if any procedures were to be done there, they would not be covered. Seeing the new physician was less urgent at the moment—my mother felt a little better—thus, I started looking for new insurance and found an individual policy that seemed to fit her needs. The insurance did not pay for office visits, but covered most other services, including hospital stays, and was accepted by most medical facilities and doctors in New York. The policy carried a preexisting conditions clause; however, at that point, my mother had not been diagnosed with any illness and was officially healthy. The premiums were one hundred eighteen dollars(!) per quarter. Today, such a plan (if it existed) might cost twenty times that amount—a staggering appreciation compared to an average price hike—but then, my modest income could easily accommodate the cost of that insurance. Thus, I filled out an application form, mailed it with the first premium check, and in a few weeks, my mother received an insurance card. She was ready for an appointment with the new doctor.

We went to the new physician's office together, as my mother needed a translator. It was one thing to speak with an Indian doctor from the old plan, who was expected to jump over language barriers, and another to communicate with someone in the upper crust of the American medical profession, who had likely dealt with very few immigrants. The Russian doctor's daughter was also there to assist with the examination. She was as friendly as her father and even looked like his female epitome. In contrast, the examiner himself was distant, pedantic, and, during the visit, did not smile once. He was in his forties, tall and thin, with an air of inwardness around him. The doctor began to ask my mother questions, making notes on a small piece of paper and ignoring her attempts to contribute to the diagnostic process. He made no arrangements to check her biological functions that she suspected were at fault, but prescribed a blood test and some other routine procedures. "He thinks I am making it up," my mother said to me when we got out of the building. She was a little disappointed—the doctor's abilities were not in doubt, but his congeniality was nowhere near what she desired. On my part, I felt she was in excellent hands, and the doctor would not miss a thing to come up with the correct conclusion.

A few days after the visit, the doctor's secretary called. She spoke to me as I handled most of my mother's communications at the beginning of the probe. The secretary said the doctor wanted to repeat the blood test. My mother went to the lab once more. The next day, the secretary called again. She told me that the analysis showed one abnormality, and before continuing with his investigation, the doctor wanted my mother to see a specialist about the results of that test. The secretary provided the specialist's name and office address, a few doors down the hall from their own. Once again, I accompanied my mother to the meeting. The specialist was a young man in his early thirties, of average height and build, with thinning black hair and sharp black eyes. My mother liked him right away. She was apprehensive of young physicians, whom she viewed as inexperienced, but here sensed the required knowledge; plus, the doctor was charming and friendly. He took another blood sample, although he was sure the previous results were correct. In his opinion, my mother had a chronic blood disorder. He did not elaborate—just said it was a rare condition that posed no immediate danger. It was necessary to do several more tests, some of which required brief hospitalization. "The doctor who referred you wants to do some testing of his own," the specialist told my mother, "so we will admit you for a couple of days and do everything together."

I wondered why the anomaly had not been recognized before. The test was rather basic; my mother must have done it under the previous insurance plan, and the results had to be abnormal then, too. Perhaps the oversight resulted from the old plan's constraints, but also from the condition's rareness. After her diagnosis was confirmed, the doctors' explanations were not enough to satisfy my mother's curiosity, and she asked me to find out more. I bought a home medical guide, but the book did not mention my mother's diagnosis. The Internet was unavailable at that time, so I went to the library to consult more exhaustive references, yet found nothing. Later on, my mother rated healthcare professionals she saw (including dentists) by their familiarity with her disorder. "This is a good doctor," she would say, "he has heard about my illness." Thus, the physician from my mother's old plan might not have treated a case like hers before and attributed the unusual result to a lab's mistake, something to check next time around, but not alarming enough to justify the expense of a repeat test. And it was rather fortunate because if my mother had been diagnosed under the old plan, she might not have received the best of care, and had she tried to switch insurance then, her condition would have been deemed preexisting.

7. Co-op

The socialization of medicine in the United States has masked, to some extent, the true cost of healthcare and its alarming rise. Today, we speak of insurance premiums and rarely mention the expense of underlying medical services; however, in a more innocent time of thirty years earlier, healthcare-cost inflation was widely discussed and vigorously addressed by insurers and hospitals. The hospital my mother was about to check into for her tests had also contributed to the cost-saving efforts and did so in a way that affected her sojourn. Not long before she walked its halls, the hospital created a special facility for those who, like her, needed a short inpatient stay to undergo a series of tests and procedures. The facility ("Co-op," as it was known) occupied one floor in the examination wing of the hospital's building. The Co-op looked nothing like a hospital ward, though. The hotel-like rooms had little medical equipment, and each room contained two regular beds: one for the patient and another for a family member or friend. The Co-op admission rules required each patient to bring a companion who would act as a helper. Thus, when my mother entered that facility, I checked in with her.

The Co-op was not large, maybe twenty rooms or so. We waited for a couple of weeks to get in. During their stay, Co-op patients had to be on the premises at all times, while helpers' duty was to sleep there, covering the staff's off-work hours. The helpers were also responsible for ushering patients to procedures and tests, but seldom did so, as the test facilities provided their own escorts. Hence, there was not much for helpers to do other than keep their wards company, and even that, mostly at night, as patients were pretty busy during the day... My mother's and my room was in the middle of the floor, next to a large hall where Co-op residents ate and socialized. We became friendly with another Co-op team: a patient husband and his helper wife. They were natives of Holland, living in Manhattan. The husband was a businessman, about fifty years of age, stocky, collected, with a large bald head. He had a chess set and needed a partner, so he and I played in the evenings. His wife was an attractive, young-looking, gregarious woman, a happy product of good nature and a good life. She stayed in the Co-op all day, spending much time with my mother when both women were free. Our new friends had grown-up children whose pictures they showed my mother and me. We also shared a table during meals—breakfast, lunch, and dinner. The hospital had a kitchen that served the beds, a cafeteria, and the Co-op. The food was colorful and tasty, and it was free to patients and helpers.

Looking back at my time in that Co-op, I can hardly believe I spent only three days there, and not even a full three days, as I kept stopping by at work—so many impressions they left me. "And this costs less than a hospital bed?" I asked myself in disbelief. Unlike semiprivate rooms in a hospital, Co-op rooms were essentially private since just one insurance policy covered both beds, and then, there were those meals (coming from a country where food was a major expense, I couldn't help but over-appreciate such an amenity). And despite all that "luxury," the cost of a Co-op room was relatively low: less than one-half of a hospital bed. However, the benefit I admired the most was not financial. Although the Co-op's patients looked normal (it was difficult to tell a patient from a helper), most were seriously ill, and such a setting helped ease their fears and buoy their spirits. The utilitarian goal of saving money engendered a humanitarian act... The tests confirmed my mother's diagnosis.

8. The House on the Hill

Like with the past threats in her life, my mother dealt with her illness proactively: she read medical references, studied prescribed medications, checked expiration dates, watched TV health shows, and sometimes saw other medical professionals with ever-narrowing specialization focus. Only now, the threat was from within, and time was not on her side. The disease was incurable, but some of its effects could be contained by medications. As a carrier of a rare disorder, my mother was welcomed by top physician-researchers and had access to the newest drugs, some still in the trial stage. The hematologist who diagnosed her illness remained my mother's primary physician throughout all those years, and he was the one who called me in the middle of the night when she died in the hospital twenty years later. His professional reputation was high in the beginning, and it only grew as time went by, yet in my mother's case, he mainly monitored her condition, fending off unnecessary treatments. The condition worsened in the last few years of her life when the illness took a more aggressive path, but before that, it developed slowly, leaving the possibility of an almost normal life. Not that my mother made the best of it. Things bothered her—street crime, noisy neighbors, and the ailment itself was at the top of the list. Shortly before her passing, I had a dream in which we walked together in a city and wandered into the remains of a destroyed building with no roof. It was late at night, and the scene was illuminated by the full moon and the stars. The wreckage looked like the one I used to visit as a child in Odessa, next to the clinic where my mother worked—the same one-story, fire-gutted structure, weed-covered ground, and charred remains of the outside walls—only the ruins in the dream were bigger, stretching far ahead of us. Ethereal calm permeated the setting. I suddenly felt content: we had found the place, spacious and peaceful. The absence of a roof was a drawback, but it seemed minor in the dream. My mother would be happy here.

One peculiar side of my mother's illness was a low cholesterol level in her changing blood formula. That oddity had likely helped her reach the average lifespan in the United States despite the affliction. Gaunt and ravaged by the illness, she still had little grey hair and retained the full mental acuity and sharpness of senses until her last days. In a way, it was unfortunate, as such lucidness made her fully aware of the disease's progress up to the latest stages. By then, her diagnosis was mentioned in every medical reference, while the advent of the Internet had made it easier to stay informed of new treatments. They were not miracle cures but mostly medications that claimed to prolong life, although not by much. My mother's doctor was skeptical about those promises; however, the most recent study alleged better results, and I wanted to discuss it with him during the next office visit. My mother was too weak to travel alone, so I drove her to the doctor's office. After the examination, I asked about the new treatment. Of course, the doctor knew about the study, but he had to talk to his colleagues who conducted it. "Call me in a few days," he said to me as my mother and I were leaving. I phoned as told. "I am going to prescribe this medication to your mother," said the doctor, "but I doubt it will have any effect other than cause her more discomfort. You should prepare for her departure." The illness had entered its final phase.

I did not tell my mother of the doctor's prognosis, nor did he mention it to her later. She didn't have to know. There were no preparations to be made. She led a simple existence, had few possessions, no public duties, and was almost as free of life's plaque as when she came to this world seventy-nine years earlier. She was weakened and traumatized by the illness, but not bedridden, and the promise of new treatment sustained a minute light of hope, so there was no point in extinguishing it. Neither was my mother unconcerned about what might happen after she was gone. She always felt a strong connection with the past, projecting it into the future. One of her concerns was a resting place. She wanted to be buried in the New Jersey cemetery where her aunt was interred. A few weeks after I spoke to her doctor, my mother asked me to take her to that cemetery. "We will choose a site and make the necessary arrangements," she said. I replied that it was too early to worry about those things, to which she answered that she had planned to reserve a plot for a while and might as well do it now. We decided to go that coming Sunday. The next day, my mother's doctor called. He received the latest lab results and wanted her to check into the hospital immediately. Thus, instead of a cemetery trip, I drove my mother to the hospital, and after that, her state precipitously went downhill. For her few remaining months, she was in and out of the hospital, yet in no condition to travel to New Jersey. I bought the plot and arranged the funeral over the phone the morning she died. The night before, an ambulance took her to the hospital, and I went along. Even at such a moment, my mother did not resign. Behind the curtain, she argued with the ER physicians and nurses who assisted her. "Why are you giving me this medication?" I heard her protest, "I do not need it. Call my doctor." Someone replied that they had been in contact with her doctor all the time and followed his instructions, but she did not believe it. She was still upset as her gurney was rolled out to the hall. "Michael," she cried in English when she saw me, "look what they did to us!" "She is feisty," said to me one of the physicians attending to her, "We have stabilized her and are taking her upstairs to a hospital room. You may go home and come back tomorrow." A few preceding sleepless nights must have reflected on my appearance... It was already late. I got home and went to my bed. When the phone rang at four in the morning, I knew right away what it was. My mother's doctor was on the line. He was calling from his home. The hospital called him, and he called me. My mother's heart stopped, and nothing more could be done. Passed into eternity the last live memory of the old house on the hill near a dusty road between the farmers' market and the river in the Ukrainian town of Chudnov.

KADDISH

The story of the Roman general Julius Caesar and the Egyptian queen Cleopatra inspired many works of art, literature, and music. There is a play by George Bernard Shaw, a movie with Rex Harrison and Elizabeth Taylor, and, case in point, Georg Friedrich Händel's opera *Giulio Cesare*. I am reluctant to bring up opera because of the genre's narrow appeal, and if the current theme were better illustrated by, say, hip-hop, I might have quoted that instead; however, the modern cultural phenomenon has shunned the subject. Not a big loss, as Händel did a great job, creating a masterpiece. The opera ends with a celebratory chorus, which seemed a little dull to me (compared to the amazing musical inventiveness of the entire score) until I came across a production where the directors took a different approach. In that performance, the final number was sung not by the opera choir but by the entire soloist cast. Good and bad, dead and alive, all the characters got together to deliver the final lines. A similar technique I once observed in a movie, where all characters, regardless of their scripted conditions, danced with each other in the last scene, albeit in that particular film, such an ending looked more like an apology for the viewers' wasted time. The effect in Händel's opera was different. The choral part that sounded too ceremonial before came suddenly alive when rendered by a band of personalities.

But what conveys a personality if not the detail? As I was putting these tomes together, my curiosity grew. I was eager to learn about the existence beyond the recorded episodes, to understand it in a broader context, even if that knowledge appeared in these pages only in a few footnotes or nowhere at all. And I wanted to know more about the people essential to the told story, especially those who preceded me. Not much was needed to sketch my compatriots. There were pictures of my grandparents, and even individuals I knew only by verbal description were easy to envisage for someone like myself, a product of the same environment. A ten-day trip to Chudnov placed me in the epicenter of the tragic past, as well as in close contact with its direct participants; plus, Baba Olya gave my mother Stepan's photograph. And with other domestic players who were not a part of my life, I could reconstruct their stories through imagination and random facts. It was different with foreigners, such as my mother's employers in Germany. I still feel I need to know more about them—their background and fate. Health issues notwithstanding, both could have lived beyond the immediate postwar years. Herr Hunke was a resourceful person who, upon the realization of Hitler's failure, likely dumped the uniform and vanished into the crowd. I can hardly picture him defending some part-destroyed building in Berlin or, for that matter, shooting at anybody. As for Frau Hunke, she survived the violence accompanying the Nazi regime's collapse, and if her husband made it, too, they might have found each other later and even opened another restaurant. Both sported resilience and a positive attitude, typical of their countrymen. Judging by their muted reaction to the apartment and the restaurant's bombing raid loss, Frau Hunke and her husband did not have to work for a living; yet, they rushed to start another business in the middle of uncertainty, as they could not remain idle for too long. And all those virtues were swept aside by an outbreak of madness and destruction. What had been built over years of diligence and perseverance was wrecked in an instant, perhaps as a reminder of a higher reason, which, on this side, tells only that everything must come to an end.

The events recounted in the preceding chapters span nearly a century across five countries, lining up numerous characters, each with their own stories, hopes, and failings. Few of them were pure evil, and I will not allude to those further, as they have been reserved a special place. The rest included the righteous, but the majority were regular folk who could be good or bad depending on circumstances and whose misdeeds, if any, have now fallen under history's statute of limitations. Most no longer inhabit this world, and some left it even before my time, but they are all our contemporaries in these pages, breathing life into the relics of the past. What purpose brought that medley of people under the roof of this narrative? I picture them having a reunion. The occurrence takes place near my mother's clinic in Odessa, in the building whose ruins I used to visit as a boy—only now, the structure is rebuilt. The tall windows are brightly lit, showing, behind the curtains, many silhouettes. There is a muffled drone of the conversations mixed with the clatter of moving plates. An invisible barrier prevents me from getting closer to look through the windows inside, but I know they are all there—my parents, uncles, my mother's Chudnov family, Uncle Zachary with Aunt Rose, Tsylia Ilyinichna, Aunt Yelena with Masha, and many others. And they know the answer.

ILLUSTRATIONS

Pictures #1 & #3. Courtesy of Dimitri Leshchenko.

Picture #6. Користувач: IgorTurzh, Ukrainian Wikipedia; desaturated; *https://uk.wikipedia.org/wiki/Файл:Зразок_старої_забудови_Чуднова.jpg*

Picture #7. Courtesy of Nadya Frid.

Picture #10. Courtesy of Elena Mirzoian.

Picture #13. By marcolan65, CC BY 3.0; fragment, desaturated; https://commons.wikimedia.org/w/index.php?curid=53028323

Other pictures in this section are owned by the author or in the public domain.

1. First home in Odessa.

2. Yefim (right) w. siblings: Aaron, Zinovy, and Fanya.

3. Sanatorium Lermontovsky.

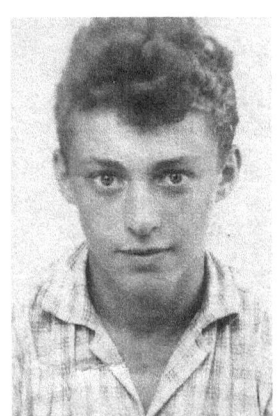
4. Misha at 16.

5. C. I. Gavril'chenko.

6. Office building in Chudnov (postwar photo).

7. T. I. Rosenblit.

8. Cape Fiolent; Balaklava, Crimea.

9. Zagorsk street; by Aristarkh Lentulov.

10. Aunt Fanya's residence in Kiev.

11. Odessa skyline. TI's apartment, 1979.

12. Old Vienna.

13. Monte Compatri

14. Hotel Lucerne in New York.

15. Eva with her aunt in Brooklyn.

16. College graduate.

17. Dusk near Zabar's.

End of Book 2

The image on the preceding page is attributed to: Alvesgaspar / CC BY-SA (https://creativecommons.org/licenses/by-sa/3.0); desaturated; https://commons.wikimedia.org/w/index.php?curid=3259348